FAYE LEVY'S
—*INTERNATIONAL*—
JEWISH
COOKBOOK

FAYE LEVY'S
—INTERNATIONAL—
JEWISH
COOKBOOK

VERMILION
LONDON

For my mother, Pauline Kahn Luria
And my mother-in-law, Rachel Levy

And to the memory of my father, Louis Kahn

First published in 1991 by Warner Books, New York

3 5 7 9 10 8 6 4 2

Editor: Barbara Croxford
Designer: Roger Daniels
Jacket illustration: Deborah Healy

First published in the United Kingdom in 1992 by Ebury Press

This paperback edition published by Vermilion
an imprint of Ebury Press
Random House, 20 Vauxhall Bridge Road, London SW1V 2SA

Random House Australia (Pty) Limited
20 Alfred Street, Milsons Point, Sydney
New South Wales 2061, Australia

Random House New Zealand Limited
18 Poland Road, Glenfield
Auckland 10, New Zealand

Random House South Africa (Pty) Limited
PO Box 337, Bergvlei, South Africa

Random House UK Limited Reg. No. 954009

A CIP catalogue record for this book
is available from the British Library

ISBN 0 09 177775 5

Typeset in Bembo by Textype Typesetters, Cambridge
Printed and bound in Great Britain by
Mackays of Chatham Plc, Kent

CONTENTS

ACKNOWLEDGEMENTS

I am grateful to Geula Resh and Yehiel Limor of At Magazine, Israel's most prestigious women's magazine, for inviting me to write the magazine's main cooking column four years ago.

Similarly, I appreciate the chance given to me by Jerusalem Post editors Matt Nesvisky, Haim Shapiro and Faye Bittker to write a biweekly cooking column for the Post's Weekend magazine.

One of the people who helped me most in my food writing career is Ruth Sirkis, the most prominent cooking expert in Israel.

I would like to thank the following magazine and newspaper editors: Zanne Zakroff of Gourmet magazine; Barbara Fairchild of Bon Appetit Magazine and Larry Levine of Western Chef Magazine. Russ Parsons of the Los Angeles Times Syndicate; Manuel Chait of the Jewish Bulletin; Charles Britton of Copley Los Angeles Newspapers; Maureen Clancy of the San Diego Union; Michael Bauer and Tom Sietsema of the San Francisco Chronicle; Helen Dollaghan of the Denver Post; Rosemary Black of the New York Daily News; Bob Kelleter and Phyllis Richman of the Washington Post; Carol Haddix of the Chicago Tribune; Evelyn Kramer and Gail Perrin of the Boston Globe; Iris Bailin of the Cleveland Plain Dealer; Barbara Gibbs Ostmann of the St. Louis Post-Dispatch; Susan Puckett of the Atlanta Journal and Constitution; Ginger Johnston and Barbara Durbin of the Portland Oregonian; Nanette Wiser of Copley News Service; Dale Curry of the New Orleans Times-Picayune; Mary Maushard of the Baltimore Evening Sun; Susan Wyland of the Detroit News; Muriel Stevens of the Las Vegas Sun; Kathy Lindsley of the Rochester Times-Union; Toni Cashnelli of the Cincinnati Enquirer; George Anderson of the Pittsburgh Post-Gazette; Donna Lee of the Providence Journal-Bulletin; Candy Sagon of the Dallas Times Herald.

Former food editors Ken Bookman of the Philadelphia Inquirer; Kit Snedaker of the Los Angeles Herald Examiner; Pucci Meyer of the New York Post; Taffy Jacaway of the Miami News; the late Pat Baldridge of the Baton Rouge Sunday Advocate; Winnifred Jardine of the Salt Lake City Deseret News; Ann Hoffman of the Norfolk Virginian-Pilot; the late Peggy Daum of the Milwaukee Journal; and Cynthia David, now at the Toronto Sun.

Thanks to Julia Child for giving me the idea for this book, in a letter she wrote to me seventeen years ago.

Most of all I wish to thank my husband Yakir, who helped me to research and write the book.

INTRODUCTION

During the seven years I spent in Israel, the melting pot of Jewish cooking, I was so impressed and intrigued by the extraordinary diversity of the Jewish culinary heritage that I decided to change careers and turn my hobby into my profession.

At the time I was a student of sociology and anthropology at the Hebrew University in Jerusalem and at Tel Aviv University. As soon as I graduated, I became the assistant to Israel's foremost culinary personality and cookbook author, Ruth Sirkis, and worked with her for two years.

It was fascinating to learn to prepare Jewish specialities beyond matzo ball soup, gefilte fish and blintzes. I discovered a rich and varied international cuisine of many wonderful dishes and exotic flavours. When I married Yakir, an Israeli-born Jew of Yemenite origin, I feasted at his mother's house on many superb dishes with Mediterranean flair – delectable stuffed vegetables, spicy meats, aromatic soups, tasty salads, a variety of cakes and breads, and both savoury and sweet pastries.

I felt that in a way Yakir and I symbolized the Israeli experience, which has contributed to the shaping of modern Jewish cuisine. We came from different worlds: I was born in the United States, my father's parents came to America from Russia, and my mother was born in Poland; Yakir was born and raised in Israel, and his parents were born in the Middle East (in the southern part of the Arabian Peninsula). All these areas were important Jewish centres with distinct styles of cooking.

Jewish cooking is what we both grew up with, although each of us was raised on totally different dishes. The major branches of Jewish cooking, the Ashkenazic, or eastern and central European, and the Sephardic, or Mediterranean and Middle Eastern, are well represented in our families. My mother, who spent most of her life in Washington, D.C., and has been a Jerusalem resident for over

7

twenty years, cooks traditional eastern European Jewish cuisine, the style most widely known in the United States. Yakir's mother lives near Tel Aviv and cooks in the Yemenite style, the delicious cuisine of the Jewish community of Yemen. My sister-in-law, who lives in Jerusalem, was born in India, where another popular style of Jewish cooking developed. Other in-laws are from Morocco and their aromatic Mediterranean cuisine is a favourite in Israel. We have enjoyed learning cooking from all of them, as well as from friends and neighbours from Romania, Tunisia, Iraq and other countries.

From Israel, I went to study cooking in Paris, the city with the largest Jewish population in western Europe. Yakir and I lived there for six years and while I studied French cuisine, we also learned first-hand about the culinary customs of European Jewry.

When I returned to the United States in 1982 and settled in Los Angeles, I became the Jewish cooking columnist of the *Los Angeles Herald Examiner* and the *Los Angeles Jewish Bulletin*. I also began to teach classes and to write articles on cooking for the Jewish holidays for newspapers throughout the country in which I presented the dishes that I learned abroad.

I have often been asked to define Jewish cuisine. I feel that describing Jewish cooking is quite similar to defining American cooking. Both America and the Jewish world comprise a great variety of ethnic groups. At an exhibition of the culture and cuisine of the Kurdish Jews, which we went to see in Israel's capital, the mayor of Jerusalem pointed out that 'the Jewish people have *always* been a nation of tribes'.

In each of the countries where Jews have lived, there has naturally been a resemblance between their cooking and the local cuisine, owing to cultural influences and available ingredients. Jewish cooks have adopted dishes like the Middle Eastern falafel, just as Americans adopted the Italian pizza. Jews have also popularized such specialities as eastern European rye bread with caraway seeds and Hungarian strudel in countries outside the area in which they were created, and these are today known to many people as part of Jewish cooking.

Traditional Jewish cooking is kosher, of course. Because of the requirements of keeping kosher and of following the Jewish holiday customs, the Jews also developed unique dishes of their own. For example, cold fish dishes and delicious, slow-baking stews and kugels were all created to fit in with the laws of the Sabbath.

Kosher cooking originated in the eastern Mediterranean area, at the convergence of the Middle Eastern and Mediterranean styles of cooking and dining. In this region the eating habits and tastes are often naturally in accord with the rules for keeping kosher. Pork is hardly used in the area; oil is the main cooking fat rather than butter or animal fat; and meat and poultry are rarely cooked with dairy products. Today, thousands of years later, thanks to the Jewish State, the Mediterranean birthplace of Judaic culture serves once again as an inspiration for Jewish cooking everywhere.

ASHKENAZIC AND SEPHARDIC JEWS – CULINARY PROFILES

From a cultural and culinary standpoint, the Jews are divided into two major groups: Ashkenazic and Sephardic. This is a simplification, however, since neither category is homogeneous.

The name Ashkenazic comes from the word *Ashkenaz*, a former Hebrew name for Germany, and refers to the Jews from eastern and central Europe. Sephardic comes from *Sepharad*, the Hebrew word for Spain, and stands for Jews from the Mediterranean area and the Middle East.

A large number of Sephardic Jews are indeed descendants of the Spanish Jews who were forced to leave Spain in 1492 and were dispersed throughout the Mediterranean region and eventually to other areas such as Holland and the New World. Many of the countries to which they moved already had non-Spanish Jewish residents, however, who had arrived during the Roman Empire and other periods. Some Jews were exiled to ancient Babylon (now Iraq) in the eighth century B.C.E. when the Assyrians conquered Israel, and from there many migrated to Iran. Historians are not sure where the Jews from Yemen, Ethiopia and India came from. They are also included in the Sephardic group, although their origins were not in Spain. In Hebrew the Sephardic Jews are also called *Edot Hamizrach*, or 'the communities of the East'.

Ashkenazic Jews are also made up of several groups, notably the German, Austrian, Hungarian, Polish and Russian Jews. Because Russia is so vast, some Jews from the southern and Asian parts of the Soviet Union have a cuisine totally unlike that of the western Russian style. The Jews from the Soviet areas of Georgia near the Turkish border, from the Caucasus area near the border with Iran, and from Bukhara near Afghanistan are Sephardic in a culinary sense.

The various branches of Jewish cooking are different from regional cuisines, such as those of France and Italy, owing to the movement of Jews from place to place throughout history, resulting in a mixture of Jews of different backgrounds in some countries. This was the case, for example, in Greece, Italy, France, Turkey and Syria. Thus different dishes and customs crept from a Jewish group's collective memory into each local cuisine and merged to varying degrees with the cooking of their Jewish and non-Jewish neighbours. This was true in ancient times and continues in the modern age.

Of course, Jews live in other parts of the world, too. Jews in North America are mainly Ashkenazic, although the first Jews to arrive were Sephardic. There are Sephardic and Ashkenazic Jews in South and Central America as well as in South Africa.

The fact that traditional Jewish cooking is kosher affects the choice of ingredients and how the dishes are combined in a menu, and is another way in which Jewish cooking is often different from that of their neighbours in any given country.

ASHKENAZIC COOKING

The principal culinary difference between the two major branches of Jewish cuisine lies in the use of flavourings. Ashkenazic cooks prefer simple seasonings and are more likely to use a small number of herbs and spices, while Sephardic cooks are more inclined to sprinkle foods with mixtures of spices or herbs and to add these in larger amounts.

Onions are important in all branches of Jewish cooking, but in Ashkenazic cooking they are frequently the main flavouring of a dish. Depending on the recipe, the onions might be raw, lightly sautéed or deeply browned.

A technique by which Ashkenazic cooks accent their dishes is to add thoroughly sautéed onions and paprika, and sometimes sautéed mushrooms as well. The mushrooms are usually button mushrooms, but for special occasions are wild mushrooms like cèpes or chanterelles that are normally associated with French cooking.

Popular fresh herbs are dill, parsley, and occasionally chives; nutmeg, allspice and bay leaves are also used. Garlic is well liked, although it is utilized with greater restraint than in Sephardic cooking. Gherkins are a favourite condiment and add zest to salads. Horseradish is served as a spicy accompaniment for most fish and meat.

The theme of sweet and sour runs through Ashkenazic cuisine, for cooking fish, meat and some vegetables. Sweet-and-sour sauces are made with sugar, honey or raisins as the sweetener, and with vinegar, lemon juice or sour salt as the sour agent.

Well-made Ashkenazic food can be delicate but is not bland. In fact, the Hungarian branch can be surprisingly spicy, because of the sweet and hot paprika and the peppers that enter their soups and stews. Cooks of Polish and Russian origin, however, mostly prefer subtly flavoured foods over spicy ones and might season a dish only with salt, pepper and paprika so that the taste of the main ingredient is emphasized rather than that of the spices. Still, even dishes with fruit or sweet seasonings are balanced with the sharpness of black pepper. Traditional cooks used chicken or goose fat for sautéing for meat meals and butter for dairy meals, but most modern cooks have replaced the poultry fats with vegetable oil and margarine.

Chicken and meat often are roasted or braised or stewed with winter vegetables – carrots, turnips, potatoes and onions. Veal, goose and duck are reserved for special occasions. Freshwater fish are preferred, since they are familiar from central Europe. Smoked and cured fish, such as lox, smoked white fish and pickled herring, are choice items for brunch, light meals and appetizers. Spreads made with creamy cheeses are also favourites.

Ashkenazic Jews are fond of egg noodles – fine noodles for clear soups, short noodles called farfel for bean soups, bow ties and any other shape of noodles served as a side dish with sautéed onions and mushrooms. Potatoes appear often on the menu and are the basis of creamy salads, crisp pancakes and hearty kugels. Asparagus, carrots, beetroots, cauliflower and cabbage are popular, and so is sauerkraut. Fruit is used extensively, not just for dessert but in first-course soups and to complement main courses.

Ashkenazic Jews are renowned in America for their baking, which is done mostly in the Hungarian or Austrian style. The light tortes, rich strudels, luscious cheesecakes, buttery yeast cakes, marble cakes, honey cakes, bread puddings and delicious blintzes all have their counterparts in eastern Europe. Cakes and desserts are flavoured with walnuts, fruit, poppy seeds and wine. Challah, bagels, rye bread and pumpernickel are the best-loved breads.

Poland and Russia Jews from Poland and Russia opt for simple seasonings – mainly onion, garlic in small amounts, bay leaves to flavour soups, and sometimes sweet-and-sour tomato sauces. Pearl barley and kasha (buckwheat groats) are frequently served grains. Combinations of vegetables cooked with fruit, such as potatoes with prunes, are favourite side dishes for holidays. Soured cream enriches and accompanies dairy dishes.

11

Alsace and Germany The Jews of Alsace in eastern France share their compatriots' love for sweet and savoury flans, foie gras and wine. They use the French bouquet garni of thyme, bay leaves and parsley as a flavouring for soups and stews, in which they also simmer a whole onion studded with cloves, in the French manner. They add fresh herbs like tarragon and chives to sauces, and nutmeg to meat dishes and stuffings. Jews from Germany like similar flavourings. Prunes and raisins are frequent partners for meat or poultry, and dumplings are classic accompaniments for meats and additions to soups.

Hungary, Austria and Romania Hungarian Jewish cooks are famous for their beef goulash prepared with paprika and caraway seeds, served with noodles or dumplings, and both they and Austrian Jews bake wonderful tortes, pastries and other desserts. Hungarian and Romanian Jews prepare some spicy dishes with peppers and aubergines, which may have been influenced by the Sephardic tradition of their neighbours farther south in Bulgaria and Turkey.

SEPHARDIC COOKING

Generous use of herbs and spices makes this style of cuisine aromatic and, in some cases, quite hot. Olive oil, garlic and lemon are prominent seasonings throughout most of the Sephardic world.

In some Sephardic Jewish communities, fresh herbs are the dominant flavourings, whereas in others, especially those from North Africa and the Middle East, the emphasis is on pungent spices, a heritage from the days when the spice caravans passed through much of the area. Dill is popular among some Sephardic Jews, especially those from Greece and Turkey, but is seldom found in the saucepans of those from the Maghreb countries of Morocco, Algeria, Tunisia and Libya. On the other hand, cumin, dried ginger and fresh coriander are preferred by Jews from North Africa and the eastern Mediterranean, but rarely enter the kitchens of those from the countries north of the Mediterranean. A touch of cinnamon perfumes the casseroles of Sephardic Jews from Greece, Turkey, Lebanon, Iraq and North Africa.

Lamb is a choice meat among most Sephardic Jews and rice is a favourite accompaniment. Saltwater fish are the preferred type. Pita is the best-loved bread, especially among Jews from the Middle East. Olives are used extensively as appetizers and garnishes.

Vegetables are prepared in a great variety of ways, and a lavish spread of vegetable salads is a typical way to begin a festive Sephardic meal. Mediterranean vegetables such as aubergine, courgettes, artichokes, tomatoes, peppers, broad beans and okra appear frequently on the tables of Sephardic Jews. Vegetables are often served with tomato sauce and, for special occasions, are stuffed and braised.

Desserts are based on nuts (especially almonds, pistachios and pine nuts), sugar, eggs and filo dough rather than dairy products, but desserts in general are less central to Sephardic than to Ashkenazic cooking. Orange flower water, cinnamon and dates are beloved Sephardic dessert flavourings.

North Africa North African cooks make liberal use of garlic and herbs, especially fresh coriander and Italian parsley, followed by mint. Hot pepper in the form of cayenne powder or fresh and dried chillies is well liked, and is often paired with garlic in spicy stews and tomato sauces. A great variety of spices flavour meats, fish and vegetables, and many dishes contain a blend of several spices. Couscous is the favourite side dish.

Moroccan cooking is the most varied and refined of the cuisines of the Jews of North Africa. It is sometimes hot and sometimes delicate, but always aromatic. Saffron is especially popular, as are copious amounts of fresh herbs and garlic. Lemon juice and salt-preserved lemons impart a tang to some dishes. Meat main courses might be flavoured with cumin, fresh coriander and hot and sweet paprika, or with fruit and a mixture of 'sweet spices' – ginger, cinnamon, nutmeg, mace and allspice.

The Jews of Algeria and Tunisia prefer a seasoning trio of cumin, hot pepper and garlic for main courses. Libyan Jews have a reputation for hot food. They are fond of chillies, which they often ally with garlic and sometimes also with cumin or turmeric.

Southern Europe and Turkey Lemon juice is used generously in the Greek and Turkish Jewish kitchen. Unlike many other Sephardic Jews, Greek Jews cook with white and red dry wine. A hint of honey or sugar adds a sweet touch to some meat and fish dishes as well as tomato sauces, and sometimes is balanced with lemon juice.

Jews from Greece and Turkey regularly use dill, parsley, mint and spring onions to flavour cheese and meat dishes, and also like rosemary and oregano. Cinnamon and coriander seeds occasionally flavour meat stews. Walnuts and almonds sometimes enrich sauces

13

for fish and meat. Turkish cooking can be quite peppery, with generous amounts of cayenne added to some dishes.

Feta and parmesan cheeses enhance dairy dishes. Yogurt is a frequent accompaniment to pastries and vegetable dishes, both here and among Jews from the Middle East. Filo dough is used in dessert pastries, with fillings of nuts and dried fruit. Jews from Bulgaria, which borders Greece and Turkey, share many culinary characteristics.

The cooking of the Jews of Georgia, an area of the Soviet Union near Turkey, bears a certain resemblance to that of the Turkish Jews. Aubergine and other Mediterranean vegetables are favourites, as are dishes flavoured with plenty of garlic and sauces made with walnuts, and pastries with spicy meat fillings.

The Jews of Italy cook in the general Sephardic fashion but, like their compatriots, prepare many pasta dishes and use the seasonings popular in Italian cooking, such as rosemary, sage, basil, garlic, olive oil and fresh tomato sauce.

Middle East and India The aromatic cuisine of the Jews from Syria and Lebanon relies mainly on the tastes of lemon, olive oil, fresh coriander, mint and garlic. The emphasis is on fresh flavourings rather than on spices. Tahini (sesame sauce) plays an important part in the kitchens of Jews from the eastern Mediterranean countries and is loved in Egypt as well.

The cooking of the Jews from Egypt resembles that of Jews of Syria and Lebanon more than those from the rest of North Africa. The food is flavourful but not fiery. Cooks have a fondness for lemon juice, garlic and allspice. They use cumin or turmeric in discreet amounts but do not usually combine them in the same dish. For seasoning meat or poultry, turmeric is often paired with lemon juice, or cumin with garlic. Cardamom and fresh and dried coriander are other well-liked spices.

The cooking of the Yemenite Jews is simple, direct and hearty. The most popular seasoning is a mixture of cumin, turmeric and black pepper and is sprinkled liberally into soups, meat, fish and vegetable dishes. Garlic is used abundantly, and sometimes dishes are flavoured with fresh coriander. Chillies might be added to the food but generally appear on the table as chilli-garlic chutney, for each person to add to taste. Cardamom sometimes seasons meat, and also appears in a spice blend with ginger, cinnamon and cloves to flavour coffee. From a culinary standpoint, the Jews of Ethiopia have quite a lot in common with the Jews of Yemen.

Jews from Iraq and from Kurdistan, an area that is now part of Iran, Iraq and Turkey, use fresh herbs and greens in lavish quantities, both wild ones and common ones like dill, Italian parsley, fresh coriander, celery leaves and spinach. Garlic, chilli, cumin and a spice mixture resembling curry powder also add zest to main courses, which are accompanied by wheat berries, bulgar wheat or rice.

Plenty of fresh herbs go into the pots of Iranian Jews – dill, mint, coriander, celery leaves, parsley and spring onions, often several in the same dish. These flavour soups, as well as meat stews with dried beans. Spices used include saffron, cumin, turmeric, coriander seeds, cardamom and hot red pepper, but are generally added in discreet amounts. Prunes, dates and quinces are occasionally cooked with poultry and meat, and fruit sometimes garnishes rice.

The Jews of India are divided into three groups: those of Bombay, also known as Bene Israel; those of Cochin; and those whose families originated in Iraq and arrived in India during the last century. As with the general cooking of India, spices are very important to all the groups. A single dish might include cumin, cinnamon, cloves, nut-meg, turmeric, cardamom, bay leaves and coriander seed, as well as garlic, chillies, ginger and fresh coriander. Of course, there are also dishes with just a few flavourings. The cooking of the Indian Jews from Iraq is influenced by both Indian and Iraqi cuisines. A popular seasoning combination for their soups and main courses is cumin, garlic and fresh dill.

In this book I present recipes for the kinds of dishes that are being cooked today in Jewish households throughout the world, from Jerusalem to Paris to Los Angeles. They include traditional Ashke-nazic favourites as well as Sephardic specialities, that together make up a cuisine that is colourful, fresh and delicious.

Bon appétit, or as we say in Hebrew, *'Bétéavon'*!

FAYE LEVY

PART 1

Holiday Menus and Recipes

PASSOVER
The Springtime Holiday

 Of all the Jewish holidays, Passover is the one most associated with good eating. Paradoxically, on Passover there are extra regulations beyond the usual rules of keeping kosher. It seems that Jewish cooks set out to prove that, in spite of these additional restraints, for Passover they can produce the most delicious cuisine of the year.

Passover, or *Pesach* in Hebrew, is a celebration of the ancient Hebrews' deliverance from slavery in Egypt. The holiday is observed for eight days (seven days in Israel) and takes place in the spring. The food customs of Passover exist to commemorate this historic event in a concrete way, to encourage everyone to identify with the joyous experience of his or her ancestors' liberation.

A Passover Primer

On the Passover table matzo is served instead of bread, as a reminder of the Hebrews' hurried escape. The Torah, or Jewish bible, relates that in their haste to leave Egypt about 3000 years ago, the Hebrews did not have time to let their bread, which was most likely a form of sour dough bread, rise. The resulting flat bread became the first matzos.

From this arose the prohibition against eating leavened bread during the week of Passover, and against using wheat flour, because it can leaven, or ferment, naturally upon contact with liquid. (This is the sour dough principle, that a mixture of flour and water left to sit catches wild yeast from the air.)

Matzo itself is made from wheat flour but the regulations surrounding its baking ensure that the dough will be mixed as quickly as possible and baked immediately, to prevent it from fermenting. Cakes, biscuits and dumplings for Passover are made from either potato flour or matzo meal, made from ground matzos, or a more finely ground version called matzo cake meal. (See Note on page 34.)

Things are not quite so simple, however. Because the Jews were scattered throughout much of the world, different communities developed varying interpretations of the Passover laws over time. Therefore, most Ashkenazic Jews (from eastern and central Europe) will not eat corn, rice or beans (which are known collectively as *kitniyot*) during Passover, since these can ferment. Many Sephardic communities do eat these foods during the holiday, however. This leads to interesting labelling of kosher products in those areas where members of both communities live, such as Israel and France. Some products will be labelled Kosher for *Pesach* for Those Who Eat *Kitniyot*, which basically means 'Kosher for Passover for Bean Eaters'.

In Orthodox homes, Passover involves plenty of preparation. When I was growing up, a few days before the holiday my parents went down to the storage room to bring up both sets of Passover dishes, pans and silverware – those for dairy meals and those for meat, which replaced the usual dairy and meat dishes of the rest of the year. Eating on these special plates, that appeared on the table during just one week of the year, added to the feeling of festivity.

The Seder

The Seder, or ceremonial Passover dinner, takes place throughout the world on the first and second nights of the holiday, but in Israel on the first night only. On a special decorative Seder plate, which is divided into sections, are displayed small portions of the foods for the ritual. Each section is labelled with a word, usually in Hebrew, denoting where to place each food. These symbolic foods recall the Jews' lives as slaves, escape to freedom, and establishment as a community in the land of Israel. 'Bitter herbs', usually grated fresh horseradish on Ashkenazic Seder plates and bitter lettuce on Sephardic ones, symbolize the bitterness of life during the period of slavery. A roasted lamb shank or chicken neck is a reminder of the sacrifices at the Temple in Jerusalem. A hard-boiled egg also appears on the plate to commemorate the offerings brought to the Temple on holidays. To celebrate spring, a stick of celery or a sprig of parsley also has its place on the Seder plate.

The best-loved of the Seder foods is undoubtedly haroset, a spread or condiment made of apples, sometimes dried fruits, nuts and cinnamon. Its reddish brown colour recalls the mortar and bricks the Hebrew slaves were forced to make in Egypt. The tasting of haroset is part of the Seder ceremony before dinner, but it remains on the table so everyone can enjoy it throughout the meal. Some families make enough haroset for the entire week of Passover, and serve it as a sweet and satisfying snack with matzo.

After tasting the ritual foods and drinking wine in the order explained in the Haggadah, the special book of procedures and prayers of the Seder, the dinner itself begins.

Passover Menus

On many tables, a fish dish is a frequent choice for a Passover appetizer, often followed by chicken soup. Roast chicken is a popular main course among most Jews, and Ashkenazic cooks often like to add a matzo-based stuffing. Roast lamb is another frequent choice on the Sephardic holiday menu.

Passover cakes and biscuits are often flavoured with nuts, which give them an appealing richness, yet at the same time they are light because they do not contain flour. It is amazing how well this age-old culinary custom fits the food trends of today!

Sweet red wine is practically synonymous with Passover wine, but today dry Passover wines are gaining in popularity. At a Seder that my husband and I attended in Paris, we enjoyed a kosher-for-Passover dry red Bordeaux. I find it best to provide both sweet and dry wine to satisfy everyone's taste. For the blessings before dinner, most people are used to sweet wine and tend to prefer it.

Other ideal Passover dishes:

Artichokes with Lemon Dressing (page 171)

Ashkenazic Chicken Soup with Fresh Dill and Light Matzo Balls (made without baking powder) (page 99)

Spicy Roast Chicken with Matzo-Onion Stuffing (page 234)

Potato Kugel with Asparagus and Broccoli (page 256)

Sweet Carrot Kugel (page 257)

Moist Coconut Macaroons (page 321)

Nut and Chocolate-Studded Meringues (page 322)

Following are some menu suggestions and descriptions of Passover Seders that I have particularly enjoyed.

PASSOVER IN PARIS

During the six years my husband and I spent in France, we were glad to have the chance to attend Parisian Passover Seders and to explore French Jewish cuisine. Most of the Jews in France are either of North African or eastern European origin, and the taste of both groups is reflected in the holiday fare. Although much of the Passover menu is dictated by tradition and some dishes are standard throughout the world, the French influence is also evident.

One time we went to a Seder given at a Parisian synagogue, where the menu was especially intriguing. It featured time-honoured Jewish dishes alongside classic French ones, and was the inspiration for our menu here.

For a first course, we were offered a choice of either *saumon en gelée, sauce verte* (French salmon in aspic with herb sauce), or gefilte fish (Ashkenazic light fish dumplings). Next were delicate leek fritters in the Sephardic Jewish tradition. Serving roast lamb is a Passover custom dating from biblical times; ours was flavoured with garlic and onions Mediterranean style, and was accompanied by roasted potatoes and a courgette casserole.

Since the Passover Seder is one of the most festive dinners of the year, we were served two desserts: one was a light matzo-raisin kugel from Alsace, and the second was a luscious French chocolate hazelnut gâteau, made with a small amount of potato flour.

PARISIAN PASSOVER MENU

Triple-Nut Haroset

Cold Salmon Steaks with Herb Sauce, or Gefilte Fish

Roast Lamb with Garlic, Onions and Potatoes

Courgette Casserole with Dill

Alsatian Almond-Raisin Matzo Kugel

Chocolate-Hazelnut Gâteau

TRIPLE-NUT HAROSET

Toasted hazelnuts combine with walnuts, almonds, apples, cinnamon and wine to give his haroset, prepared in the Ashkenazic manner, an intriguing flavour.

MAKES 8 SERVINGS

40 g (1½ oz) walnuts
40 g (1½ oz) almonds
40 g (1½ oz) hazelnuts
30–45 ml (2–3 tbsp) sugar
1 medium or large apple,
  peeled, halved and
  cored
150 g (5 oz) stoned dates,
  chopped

3.75 ml (¾ tsp) ground
  cinnamon
30–60 ml (2–4 tbsp) red
  wine
30–45 ml (2–3 tbsp) strained
  fresh orange juice (optional)
pinch of black pepper
  (optional)
matzos, for serving

Grind walnuts, almonds and hazelnuts with 30 ml (2 tbsp) sugar in a food processor until fairly fine, leaving a few small chunks. Transfer to a bowl. Coarsely grate apple, then add to nut mixture. Stir in dates, cinnamon and 30 ml (2 tbsp) wine. Add orange juice or more wine if desired. Taste, and add pepper and more sugar if desired.

Spoon into a serving bowl. Serve at room temperature or cold, accompanied by matzos.

COLD SALMON STEAKS WITH HERB SAUCE

This tasty French dish makes an elegant first course for the Seder or can be served as a refreshing summer main course for four, accompanied by sliced tomatoes and cucumbers.

MAKES 8 SERVINGS

8 small salmon steaks, about
  2.5 cm (1 inch) thick,
  about 900 g (2 lb)
15 ml (1 tbsp) finely chopped
  shallot, about 1 medium
  shallot

120 ml (4 fl oz) dry white
  wine
2 sprigs fresh thyme or 2.5 ml
  (½ tsp) dried
1 bay leaf
salt and freshly ground pepper

HERB SAUCE

20 spinach leaves, stalks
  removed, leaves rinsed well
15 g (½ oz) watercress leaves
10 g (⅓ oz) small parsley
  sprigs
30 ml (2 tbsp) tarragon leaves
  (optional)

250 ml (8 fl oz) mayonnaise
salt and pepper
30–45 ml (2–3 tbsp) warm
  water (optional)
lettuce leaves, for serving

Preheat oven to 220°C (425°F) mark 7. Remove any scales from fish steaks. Generously grease a 2.3-litre (4-pint) oval gratin dish or other heavy shallow baking dish with soft margarine. Cut an oval piece of nonstick paper to size of dish and grease paper. Sprinkle base of dish with chopped shallot. Arrange fish pieces in dish in one layer. Pour wine over them and add thyme and bay leaf. Sprinkle fish lightly with salt and pepper. Set greased paper directly on fish.

Bake fish for 12 minutes. To check if done, insert a fine skewer into thickest part of fish for about 5 seconds, then touch skewer to underside of your wrist; it should be hot to touch. If fish is not quite done, bake for another 2 minutes and test again.

Remove fish carefully to plate with 2 fish slices. Cool to room temperature.

To make sauce, plunge spinach and watercress into a medium saucepan with boiling water. Return to the boil and drain. Rinse under cold water and drain thoroughly. Squeeze to remove excess liquid.

Purée the spinach, watercress, parsley and tarragon in a food processor until smooth. If necessary, add 30–45 ml (2–3 tbsp) mayonnaise to help make a smoother purée. Add remaining mayonnaise and process until smooth. Taste, then add salt and pepper if needed. If sauce is very thick, beat in warm water 15 ml(1 tbsp) at a time until it is just thin enough to be poured. (Sauce can be kept, covered, for 1 day in refrigerator.)

Serve cold, or at cool room temperature.

Remove skin from fish by scraping with paring knife and pulling it with your fingers. Serve salmon steaks on lettuce leaves, accompanying each serving with a spoonful of sauce. Serve any remaining sauce separately.

GEFILTE FISH

Gefilte fish means 'filled fish', and in some old-fashioned versions of the recipe the minced fish mixture is actually stuffed into fish slices. Now most people shape the 'filling' into ovals or balls and omit the fish slices. Traditionally the dish is made from a mixture of equal quantities of three freshwater fish – carp, pike and white fish – but today cooks vary the fish according to what is available where they live. I use mostly white fish with a little halibut, since the result is very delicate in flavour and has an appealing white colour.

Gefilte fish is generally served on a bed of lettuce, with each piece garnished with a carrot slice. Sharp horseradish is the accompaniment de rigueur in most homes, but the family of a friend of mine from Mexico City serves gefilte fish with spicy chilli sauce!

MAKES 18 TO 20 PIECES; 9 OR 10 SERVINGS

1 × 1.4 kg (3 lb) white fish (including bones and head), filleted	10 ml (2 tsp) salt
	2.5 ml (½ tsp) ground pepper
	30 ml (2 tbsp) matzo meal
350 g (12 oz) halibut fillets	2 large carrots, peeled and sliced
2 large eggs, size 1 or 2	
2 medium onions, finely chopped	bottled horseradish prepared with beetroots, for serving

FISH STOCK

1.4 kg (3 lb) additional fish bones and head (optional)	3 sprigs parsley
	5 ml (1 tsp) salt
2 medium onions, sliced	1.4 litres (2½ pints) water

Place white fish fillets on a board, skin side down. Slip blade of a flexible knife between flesh and skin and use it to remove skin of fish, sliding knife away from you with one hand and pulling off skin with other. Run your fingers carefully over fish fillets and remove any small bones remaining in flesh. Set fillets aside.

Rinse bones and heads of fish under cold water for at least 5 minutes. Combine all ingredients for stock in a large, deep saucepan. Bring to the boil and skim off foam as it accumulates. Cover and simmer for 30 minutes. Strain and return to the pan. Taste for seasoning.

Work white fish and halibut fillets in 2 batches in a food processor until very fine. Return half the fish to food processor and add 1 egg, half the chopped onions, 5 ml (1 tsp) salt and 1.25 ml (¼ tsp) pepper. Process well, then transfer to a large bowl. Repeat with remaining fish, egg, onions, salt and pepper. Transfer to bowl and mix with first batch. Stir in matzo meal.

Add carrots to strained stock and bring to a simmer. With moistened hands, shape fish mixture into ovals or balls, using about 40 g (1½ oz) mixture for each. Carefully drop fish balls into simmering stock. Add enough hot water to barely cover them, if necessary, pouring it carefully into stock near edge of pan. Return to a simmer, cover and simmer over low heat for about 1 hour. Leave to cool in stock. Refrigerate fish and carrots in stock for at least 4 hours before serving. (Can be kept for 3 days in refrigerator.)

To serve, garnish each fish ball with a carrot slice. Pass horseradish separately.

ROAST LAMB WITH GARLIC, ONIONS AND POTATOES

To facilitate the preparation of this succulent dish, a favourite of Jews in southern France, ask the butcher to trim the fat and skin from the lamb, and then to bone, roll and tie it. Courgettes with Tomatoes and Dill (page 263) also makes a good accompaniment.

MAKES 8 SERVINGS

8 garlic cloves	8 medium potatoes
2.5 kg (5½ lb) shoulder of lamb, boned and tied in a rolled roast (about 1.6 kg (3½ lb) after boning), bones reserved if possible	2 medium onions, sliced
	150 ml (¼ pint) water
	1 large tomato, peeled, seeded and chopped
salt and pepper	10 g (⅓ oz) fresh parsley, chopped

Preheat oven to 190°C (375°F) mark 5. Cut 12 very thin lengthways slivers from garlic; chop remaining garlic. Pierce lamb with point of a sharp knife. With aid of knife, hold a slit open and insert a garlic sliver. Repeat with remaining garlic slivers, spacing them fairly evenly. Sprinkle lamb with salt and pepper. Put lamb bones in centre of a large roasting tin and set roast on top of them; or set it on a rack.

Peel and quarter potatoes and put in tin around meat.

Sprinkle potatoes with remaining chopped garlic, salt and pepper. Add sliced onions and water to tin.

Cover and bake for 1 hour. Uncover and stir potatoes gently. Bake for 30 minutes. Add tomato to pan juices and stir. Roast lamb until it is very tender and an instant-read or meat thermometer registers 65°C (150°F) for medium or 70°C (160°F) for well done, about 1 hour and 10–15 minutes; during roasting, baste lamb and potatoes occasionally, turn potatoes once or twice, and add a few spoonfuls water to tin if it becomes dry.

Leave meat to rest on a board for 10–15 minutes before carving. Meanwhile, spoon pan juices over potatoes and keep them warm in low oven. If bones are meaty, cut meat from bones. Remove strings from meat. Carve lamb into 1-cm (½ -inch) slices, using a very sharp large knife. With a small knife, remove excess fat from slices.

Sprinkle potatoes and lamb with parsley and serve hot. Season pan juices to taste with salt and pepper; serve separately.

COURGETTE CASSEROLE WITH DILL

A Sephardic-style kugel, or baked vegetable casserole, this makes a nice accompaniment for roast lamb or chicken.

MAKES ABOUT 8 SERVINGS

900 g (2 lb) courgettes	*10 g (⅓ oz) fresh dill,*
1 large onion	*snipped*
5 large eggs,	*generous 25 g (1 oz) matzo*
size 1 or 2	*meal*
10 g (⅓ oz) fresh parsley,	*60 ml (4 tbsp) olive oil*
chopped	*salt and pepper*

Preheat oven to 190°C (375°F) mark 5. Grate courgettes and onion on large holes of grater. Put both in a strainer and squeeze firmly to remove excess liquid. Transfer courgette and onion to a bowl. Add eggs, parsley, dill, matzo meal and 15 ml (1 tbsp) oil. Season quite generously with salt and pepper so mixture will not be bland. Mix well.

Heat 30 ml (2 tbsp) of the oil in a shallow 20-cm (8-inch) square baking dish in oven for 3–4 minutes. Add courgette mixture to hot dish. Sprinkle with remaining oil. Bake for 50 minutes–1 hour or until set. Leave to stand for about 5 minutes before serving. Serve hot.

ALSATIAN ALMOND-RAISIN MATZO KUGEL

The province of Alsace in eastern France has long been the home of a large Ashkenazic Jewish community and also happens to be one of the best regions of France for desserts, such as this unusually light matzo kugel, with crunchy chopped almonds, raisins and a cinnamon-brandy glaze.

MAKES ABOUT 8 SERVINGS

6 matzos	5 large eggs, size 1 or 2,
75 g (3 oz) raisins	separated
90 g (3½ oz) whole	pinch of salt
almonds	6.25 ml (1¼ tsp) ground
100 g (4 oz) sugar	cinnamon

GLAZE	
50 g (2 oz) sugar	2.5 ml (½ tsp) ground
30 ml (2 tbsp) brandy, plus	cinnamon
5 ml (1 tsp) if needed	

Preheat oven to 190°C (375°F) mark 5. Grease a 23-cm (9-inch) square baking dish with margarine. Break matzos in small pieces and put in a bowl. Cover with hot water and leave to stand for 2 minutes. Put in a strainer and squeeze out as much water as possible. Put in a large bowl. Cover raisins with hot water. Leave to stand for 5 minutes and drain.

Work almonds in a food processor with 30 ml (2 tbsp) sugar until fine. Add to bowl of matzo, then stir in egg yolks, salt, cinnamon, raisins and 60 ml (4 tbsp) sugar.

Beat egg whites until just stiff. Add remaining 30 ml (2 tbsp) sugar and beat at high speed for another ½ minute or until glossy. Gently fold egg whites, in 4 portions, into matzo mixture.

Spoon mixture into greased dish. Bake for about 25 minutes or until firm.

Meanwhile prepare glaze: combine sugar, 30 ml (2 tbsp) brandy and cinnamon in small bowl and stir until well blended. If mixture is too thick to pour, add an additional 5 ml (1 tsp) brandy.

When kugel is done, remove from oven and spoon glaze evenly over top. Brush glaze gently over cake. Cut in squares and serve hot or warm.

CHOCOLATE-HAZELNUT GATEAU

This cake is very rich, moist and delicious without icing. For a meatless dinner, you can substitute butter for the margarine and serve the cake with whipped cream (see Variation). Potato flour is often used in Passover cakes like this one and produces a tender, slightly crumbly texture.

MAKES 8 SERVINGS

115 g (4½ oz) hazelnuts	4 large eggs, size 1 or 2,
100 g (4 oz) sugar	separated, at room
150 g (5 oz) plain chocolate,	temperature
chopped	5 ml (1 tsp) vanilla essence
30 ml (2 tbsp) water	30 ml (2 tbsp) potato flour
100 g (4 oz) unsalted non-	
dairy margarine, cut into	
8 pieces, at room	
temperature	

Preheat oven to 180°C (350°F) mark 4. Toast hazelnuts in a shallow baking tin in oven for about 8 minutes or until skins begin to split. Transfer to a strainer. While nuts are hot, remove most of skins by rubbing nuts energetically with a tea towel against strainer. Cool nuts.

28

Reduce oven temperature to 160°C (325°F) mark 3. Lightly grease a 20-cm (8-inch) spring clip tin with 6-cm (2½-inch) sides, line its base with nonstick paper or foil, and grease paper or foil.

Grind hazelnuts with 30 ml (2 tbsp) sugar in a food processor until as fine as possible. Transfer to a bowl.

Place chocolate and water in a large bowl and put over a pan of hot water over low heat to melt. Stir until smooth. Add margarine and stir until blended. Remove from pan of water.

Whisk egg yolks to blend. Gradually add yolks to chocolate mixture, whisking vigorously. Stir in 50 g (2 oz) sugar, followed by vanilla, nuts and potato flour. Mix well.

Whisk egg whites in a large bowl until soft peaks form. Gradually beat in remaining 30 ml (2 tbsp) sugar and whisk at high speed until whites are stiff and shiny but not dry. Gently fold whites into chocolate mixture in 3 batches. Fold lightly but quickly, just until mixture is blended.

Transfer mixture to prepared tin and spread evenly. Bake for about 1 hour or until a fine skewer inserted in centre of cake comes out clean.

Cool in tin on a wire rack for about 10 minutes. Run a thin-bladed flexible knife or palette knife carefully around side of cake. Invert cake onto wire rack, gently release spring and remove side and base of tin. Carefully remove paper and cool cake completely. Invert cake onto another wire rack, then onto a serving plate so that smooth side of cake faces up. (Cake can be kept, wrapped, for up to 2 days at room temperature or in refrigerator.) Serve it at room temperature.

VARIATION

Whipped Cream and Decoration

For a dairy meal serve with whipped cream.

250 ml (8 fl oz) double cream	*grated plain chocolate, for*
10 ml (2 tsp) sugar	*sprinkling*
5 ml (1 tsp) vanilla essence	

Whip cream with sugar and vanilla in chilled bowl until stiff. Spread over top and sides of cake and sprinkle lightly with grated chocolate; or serve whipped cream separately. Chill cake at least 1 hour before serving.

PASSOVER IN JERUSALEM

Passover has always been my favourite holiday. But I liked it more than ever during the years I lived in Israel as a college student. Back in my old home in Washington, D.C., Passover used to be a time for a family get-together and good traditional Ashkenazic food. In Israel there was the excitement of discovering the holiday specialities of my many new Sephardic in-laws. To me their food was fascinating.

One memorable Passover I celebrated was at my mother's new home in Jerusalem. We decided to prepare the Seder together with several of my new in-laws. Each person promised to cook a favourite dish. This would make it easier for everyone and would give us all the chance to taste each other's food.

First my mother and I went to the bustling Mahaneh Yehudah market to buy produce for the dinner, including the ritual foods for the Seder – celery, horseradish and apples and nuts for haroset. This was the busiest time of the year, as everyone was getting ready for the Jewish festival with the greatest focus on cooking. Women were discussing their Passover menus while trying to keep their children from handling the fruit. There was a certain feeling of anticipation and, even though our shopping took longer than usual, it was fun.

On the morning of the Seder we began cooking. My sister-in-law, of Moroccan origin, prepared a colourful, exuberant first course – a salad of peppers and chillies sautéed with tomatoes and garlic, often referred to in Israel simply as 'Moroccan salad'. Another sister-in-law made a delicious Israeli aubergine salad enriched with the local olive oil. A diced vegetable salad was the responsibility of my Israeli-born brother-in-law, since he has the patience to cut the vegetables in very tiny cubes, and everyone in the family agrees that his version of this refreshing Mediterranean salad is the best.

For the main course, we decided on turkey, and my mother-in-law, who is from Yemen, made a wonderful, aromatic matzo-mush-room stuffing seasoned with garlic and fresh coriander. Her sister brought an unusual treat – round homemade matzos.

To serve with the turkey, my mother, who was born in Poland, baked an eastern European potato and vegetable kugel, a delicate casserole of potatoes, carrots, squash or pumpkin and sautéed onions.

For dessert, my mother and I prepared an Austrian-style almond cake and topped it with a fluffy orange icimg. The cake gained its body from a generous amount of almonds and a little matzo meal, and was light textured and intensely flavoured with almonds.

JERUSALEM PASSOVER MENU

Haroset with Dates and Pine Nuts

Zesty Pepper-Tomato Salad

Roasted Aubergine Salad with Olive Oil and Garlic

Israeli Vegetable Salad

Roast Turkey with Matzo-Mushroom Stuffing

Potato and Vegetable Kugel

Passover Almond Cake with Orange Icing

HAROSET WITH DATES AND PINE NUTS

Dates are a frequent addition to haroset in Israel, especially among Jews from North Africa, Iran and Italy, and date juice flavours a version of haroset from India. In certain Sephardic recipes for haroset there are no apples; instead, a larger proportion of dried fruits is used, for a concentrated fruit taste. Sometimes the haroset is very thick and is rolled into balls or small log shapes. A Moroccan style of presenting haroset is to spread the mixture on plates and garnish it with toasted pine nuts, as in this recipe.

MAKES 8 SERVINGS

50 g (2 oz) pecans or walnuts	2.5 ml (½ tsp) ground ginger
45–60 ml (3–4 tbsp) sugar	65 g (2½ oz) almonds,
2 medium apples, peeled and	chopped
cored	12 stoned dates, chopped
30–45 ml (2–3 tbsp) lemon	25 g (1 oz) pine nuts
juice	matzos, for serving
5 ml (1 tsp) ground cinnamon	

Grind pecans or walnuts with 45 ml (3 tbsp) sugar in a food processor until fine. Grate apples and add 30 ml (2 tbsp) lemon juice. Stir in ground nuts, cinnamon, ginger, almonds and dates. Taste and add more sugar or lemon juice if liked.

To serve, spread on a flat dish and sprinkle decoratively with pine nuts. Serve as a spread with matzos.

ZESTY PEPPER-TOMATO SALAD

This spicy salad, regarded by Jews of Morocco, Algeria and Turkey as their own, is one of my favourite appetizers. It is made of sautéed peppers that are then simmered gently with tomatoes, garlic and chillies. It is great for Passover but also for Rosh Hashanah, when tomatoes and peppers are at the peak of their season. Cooking mellows the flavours, so that the garlic and chillies add sparkle but do not overwhelm the dish.

MAKES 6 TO 8 SERVINGS

75–90 ml (5–6 tbsp) olive oil
2 large green peppers, diced in 1-cm (½-inch) pieces
2 large red peppers, diced in 1-cm (½-inch) pieces
1.4 kg (3 lb) ripe tomatoes, peeled, seeded and diced; or 3 × 794-g (28-oz) cans plum tomatoes, drained and diced

salt to taste
4 jalapeño chillies, finely diced
12 medium garlic cloves, chopped

Heat 60 ml (4 tbsp) of the oil in a large frying pan over medium-low heat. Add peppers and sauté until softened, about 15 minutes. Remove with slotted spoon.

Add tomatoes to oil, sprinkle with salt and cook over medium-low heat for about 15 minutes or until thickened. Add sautéed peppers, chillies and garlic and cook over low heat for about 10 minutes or until peppers are tender and mixture is thick. Remove from heat and stir in remaining 15–30 ml (1–2 tbsp) oil. Taste and adjust seasoning. Serve at room temperature.

ROASTED AUBERGINE SALAD WITH OLIVE OIL AND GARLIC

Variations on this delectable appetizer, which is also known as 'aubergine caviar', are prepared throughout the eastern Mediterranean, from a Greek version flavoured with oregano to a Lebanese with yogurt and mint to an Egyptian with tahini (sesame paste). In Israel this is called salad but it is really more like a spread.

Instead of being baked, the aubergine can be barbecued so it acquires a smokey flavour. Serve it with matzos during Passover, and with bread or pita during the rest of the year.

MAKES 8 TO 10 SERVINGS

4 medium aubergines, about 2 kg (4½ lb) total	5–10 ml (1–2 tsp) strained fresh lemon juice (optional)
2–3 medium garlic cloves, finely chopped	30–45 ml (2–3 tbsp) chopped fresh coriander (optional)
45–60 ml (3–4 tbsp) extra-virgin olive oil	salt and freshly ground pepper fresh parsley sprigs

Preheat oven to 200°C (400°F) mark 6. Pierce each aubergine a few times with a fork to prevent it from bursting. Bake whole aubergines on a large baking sheet lined with foil for 30 minutes. Turn aubergines over and bake them for 30–40 minutes or until very tender when pricked with a fork. Leave aubergines until cool enough to handle. Holding stalk end, peel off skin of each aubergine. Drain aubergines in a colander for 1 hour.

Cut off aubergine tops. Chop the flesh, using a knife, until it is a chunky purée. In a large bowl combine aubergine purée, garlic, oil, lemon juice, coriander and salt and pepper to taste; mix well – salad should be highly seasoned. Refrigerate for at least 30 minutes before serving. (Salad can be kept, covered, for up to 3 days in refrigerator.)

Spoon salad into a shallow bowl and garnish with parsley sprigs.

NOTE: If you like, make this a smooth purée. Purée the aubergine with the garlic in a food processor until smooth. With machine running, pour in olive oil, then add lemon juice. Stir in remaining ingredients.

ISRAELI VEGETABLE SALAD

In Israel this salad of diced raw vegetables is a must at all kinds of meals, from the most festive party to the simplest supper. Cubes of tomato and cucumber are the basic ingredients but frequent additions are diced peppers, shredded green or red cabbage, diced radishes or a small amount of diced celery or chopped red or ordinary onion. For a pretty presentation, cut the vegetables in dice no larger than 1 cm (½ inch) and serve the salad in a glass bowl.

MAKES 8 SERVINGS

8 medium tomatoes, cut into small dice
1 cucumber, cut into small dice
2 medium red or green peppers, cut into small dice
45 ml (3 tbsp) chopped fresh parsley
45 ml (3 tbsp) chopped fresh coriander (optional)

45 ml (3 tbsp) chopped spring onions (optional)
30–45 ml (2–3 tbsp) extra-virgin olive oil or vegetable oil
10–15 ml (2–3 tsp) strained fresh lemon juice
salt and freshly ground pepper

Mix the diced tomatoes, cucumber, peppers, parsley, coriander and spring onions. Add oil, lemon juice and salt and pepper to taste. Serve at cool room temperature.

NOTE

If matzo meal is not available, you can make it from matzos. Break a matzo into a few pieces and grind it to a fine powder in a food processor, then sift it. One average matzo makes about 45 ml (3 tbsp) matzo meal.

If matzo cake meal is not available, matzo meal can be used, but the result will not be quite as light.

ROAST TURKEY WITH MATZO-MUSHROOM STUFFING

This turkey is a good choice for entertaining, whether for Passover or Thanksgiving! For Rosh Hashanah, I like turkey with a fruity rice stuffing, as in the chicken recipe on page 91. Potato and Vegetable Kugel makes a delicious accompaniment.

MAKES 6 TO 8 SERVINGS

Matzo-Mushroom Stuffing
4.5-5.5 kg (10–12 lb) fresh
  or frozen turkey, thawed
salt and freshly ground pepper
100 g (4 oz) non-dairy
  margarine, softened
750 ml (1¼ pints) chicken
  soup or stock

*120 ml (4 fl oz) dry white
  wine
20 ml (4 tsp) potato flour,
  dissolved in 45 ml (3 tbsp)
  dry white wine
30 ml (2 tbsp) chopped fresh
  coriander or parsley*

Prepare stuffing. Preheat oven to 220°C (425°F) mark 7 and remove top rack. Sprinkle turkey inside and out with salt and pepper. Spoon some stuffing into neck cavity. Fold neck skin under body and fasten with a skewer. Pack body cavity loosely with stuffing and cover opening with a crumpled piece of foil. Truss turkey if desired with a trussing string and needle or close it with skewers. Spoon remaining stuffing into an oiled 1-litre (1¾ -pint) baking dish.

Spread turkey with 50 g (2 oz) of the margarine and set it, breast side up, on a rack in a large roasting tin. Roast for 30 minutes, basting twice. Melt remaining 50 g (2 oz) margarine in a medium saucepan and put 20-cm (8-inch) double piece of muslin in saucepan of margarine.

Reduce oven temperature to 180°C (350°F) mark 4. Cover turkey breast with soaked muslin, then roast turkey for 1½ hours, basting with pan juices and any remaining margarine every 15 minutes. If tin becomes dry, add 60 ml (4 tbsp) chicken soup or stock.

Put dish of extra stuffing in oven and baste with a little of turkey juices. Cover with foil; bake for about 45 minutes. Meanwhile, continue roasting turkey, basting occasionally, until juices run clear when leg is pricked or meat thermometer inserted into thickest part of thigh registers 82°C (180°F), for about 20–45 minutes. Transfer turkey carefully to serving plate or large board. Discard strings, skewers and muslin. Baste once with pan juices, and cover turkey.

Skim excess fat from juices in tin. Add wine and 120 ml (4 fl oz) soup or stock and bring to the boil, stirring and scraping to dissolve any brown bits in tin. Strain into a saucepan. Add remaining soup and bring to the boil over medium heat. Whisk in potato flour mixture then return to the boil, whisking, and simmer until thick enough to lightly coat a spoon. Add coriander or parsley. Taste and adjust seasoning.

Carve turkey and arrange on serving platter. Spoon stuffing onto platter or into a serving dish. Reheat sauce briefly, then pour into a sauceboat and serve with turkey.

MATZO-MUSHROOM STUFFING

Although this stuffing is designed for Passover, it makes a great partner for poultry all year round. In addition to the mushrooms, the stuffing owes its good taste to onions, garlic and a generous amount of fresh coriander.

---

8 matzos	4 large garlic cloves, finely
350 ml (12 fl oz) hot chicken	chopped
soup or stock	3 large eggs, size 1 or 2,
75 ml (5 tbsp) olive oil	beaten
2 large onions, chopped	15 g (½ oz) fresh coriander
salt and pepper	or parsley, chopped
225 g (8 oz) small button	
mushrooms, quartered	

Crumble matzos into a large bowl and pour hot soup or stock over them.

Heat 60 ml (4 tbsp) of the oil in a large frying pan and add onions and a pinch of salt and pepper. Sauté over medium heat, stirring often, for about 7 minutes or until onions begin to turn golden. Add remaining oil, then add mushrooms and sauté for 5 minutes or until tender. Remove from heat and stir in garlic. Add mushroom mixture to matzo mixture and leave to cool. Stir in eggs and coriander or parsley and taste for seasoning.

POTATO AND VEGETABLE KUGEL

For better colour and a more interesting flavour, my mother often adds grated carrots and squash as well as sautéed onions to the familiar grated potato kugel.

MAKES 6 TO 8 SERVINGS

30 ml (2 tbsp) plus 5 ml (1 tsp) vegetable oil	5 ml (1 tsp) salt
1 large onion, chopped	1.25 ml (¼ tsp) ground pepper
450 g (1 lb) yellow squash	15 g (½ oz) fresh parsley, chopped
2 large carrots, peeled	
2 large potatoes	5 ml (1 tsp) paprika
3 large eggs, size 1 or 2	25 g (1 oz) matzo meal

Preheat oven to 180°C (350°F) mark 4. Heat 30 ml (2 tbsp) oil in a frying pan, add onion and sauté over medium-low heat until softened, about 10 minutes.

Coarsely grate squash and carrots. Transfer to a large bowl and add sautéed onion. Peel and coarsely grate potatoes, put in large strainer and squeeze out excess liquid; add to bowl of vegetables. Add eggs, salt, pepper, parsley, paprika and matzo meal.

Generously grease a 20-cm (8-inch) square tin or a 1.5-litre (2¾-pint) baking dish. Heat briefly in oven, then add vegetable mixture. Sprinkle with 5 ml (1 tsp) oil, then shake a little paprika on top. Bake for about 1 hour or until brown and set.

PASSOVER ALMOND CAKE WITH ORANGE ICING

As is typical in Passover baking, a generous quantity of ground almonds is used to give this cake flavour, richness and body. The cake is wonderful on its own, but the luscious fresh citrus icing and the sprinkling of toasted sliced almonds make for a festive look. Serve the cake with fresh strawberries or orange segments.

MAKES 8 TO 10 SERVINGS

about 225 g (8 oz) whole unblanched almonds	*225 g (8 oz) granulated sugar*
25 g (1 oz) matzo meal	*4 large eggs, size 1 or 2, separated*

ORANGE ICING

175 g (6 oz) unsalted non-dairy margarine, softened slightly	*45 ml (3 tbsp) strained fresh orange juice*
65 g (2½ oz) caster sugar	*30 ml (2 tbsp) toasted slivered almonds, for decoration (optional)*
15 ml (1 tbsp) finely grated orange rind	

Preheat oven to 180°C (350°F) mark 4. Grease a 23-cm (9-inch) spring clip tin with margarine and flour tin with a little matzo meal.

Work almonds with matzo meal and 50 g (2 oz) granulated sugar in food processor until fine. Beat egg yolks with 100 g (4 oz) sugar at high speed of mixer until light and fluffy. Set aside.

In clean bowl, whisk egg whites to soft peaks. Gradually beat in remaining sugar, beating until stiff and shiny.

Alternately in 3 batches, fold whites and almond mixture into yolk mixture. Transfer to tin and bake for about 35 minutes or until a fine skewer inserted in centre of cake comes out dry. Cool slightly, then run a palette knife gently around cake and remove sides of tin. Cool on a wire rack. Cake will sink slightly.

For icing, cream margarine and sugar until smooth. Add grated orange rind, then gradually add juice and beat until smooth and fluffy. Spread icing on sides and top of cake. Sprinkle top with toasted slivered almonds. (Cake can be kept, covered, for 2 days in refrigerator but remove 1 hour before serving.) Serve at room temperature.

PASSOVER IN CALIFORNIA

Many of the Passover dishes most familiar in the United States come from eastern and central Europe and are based on ingredients that were available there. Since in America we are lucky to be blessed with an extraordinary variety of fresh vegetables and fruits, we now use them in our traditional dishes to add a touch of elegance, colour and lightness for a festive Seder menu.

In addition, we like to cook some of the specialities of the Mediterranean and Middle Eastern Jews to add new flavours to our Passover menus. These dishes are perfectly suited to southern California, since the climate and produce are similar.

In this spirit, the familiar matzo ball soup is transformed into a chicken soup with asparagus and almond matzo balls. Roast lamb, a favourite for the Seder menu, comes with a fresh spinach stuffing and is served with Sephardic cauliflower in an aromatic tomato sauce. Haroset, the apple and nut spread served with matzo, is prepared in the Moroccan style – flavoured with the tang of citrus juice and garnished with pine puts. A pecan and cocoa torte, using the New World's pecans as the basis for a rich European-style cake, makes a grande finale for the Passover feast.

ECLECTIC PASSOVER MENU

Haroset with Dates and Pine Nuts (page 31)

**Chicken Soup with Asparagus
and Almond Kneidlach**

**Roast Shoulder of Lamb
with Spinach Stuffing**

Cauliflower in Tomato Sauce

Green Salad

**Pecan-Cocoa Torte with
Chocolate-Cinnamon Frosting**

CHICKEN SOUP WITH ASPARAGUS AND ALMOND KNEIDLACH

Passover is the holiday of spring, so asparagus is a natural, fresh addition to the customary chicken soup. Ground almonds and a surprise blanched almond in the centre of each kneidel (matzo ball) add a festive note.

MAKES 8 SERVINGS

900 g (2 lb) chicken wings	2 celery sticks, including leafy
2 litres (3½ pints) cold	tops
water	5 parsley sprigs
1 large onion, peeled	salt and pepper
1 large carrot, peeled	16 asparagus spears

ALMOND MATZO BALLS

2 large eggs, size 1 or 2	2.5 ml (½ tsp) salt
15 ml (1 tbsp) vegetable oil	pinch of ground ginger
50 g (2 oz) matzo meal	30 ml (2 tbsp) water
30 ml (2 tbsp) finely chopped	12–15 blanched almonds,
blanched almonds	cut in half lengthways

To make chicken soup, combine chicken wings, water, onion, carrot, celery, parsley and salt in a large saucepan and bring to the boil. Skim thoroughly. Partly cover and simmer for 1½–2 hours, skimming occasionally. Skim off excess fat. (Chicken soup can be kept for 3 days in refrigerator; skim fat again and reheat before serving.) Add pepper and taste for seasoning.

Peel asparagus and cut off white bases. Cut stalks in 2.5-cm (1-inch) pieces and leave tips whole.

To make matzo balls, lightly beat eggs with oil in a medium mixing bowl. Add matzo meal, chopped almonds, salt and ginger and stir until well blended. Stir in water. Leave mixture to stand for 20 minutes so matzo meal absorbs liquid.

Bring about 1.7 litres (3 pints) salted water to the boil in a large saucepan. With wet hands, take about 5 ml (1 tsp) of matzo ball mixture and roll it between your palms into a ball; mixture will be soft. Set balls on a plate. Push half a blanched almond into centre of each, letting one end of almond show. With a spatula, carefully slide balls

40

into boiling water. Cover and simmer over low heat for about 30 minutes or until firm. Keep them warm and covered until ready to serve. (Matzo balls can be made 2 days ahead and kept covered, in their cooking liquid, in refrigerator; reheat gently in cooking liquid or in soup before serving.)

Discard onion, carrot, celery and parsley from soup. Shortly before serving, add asparagus to soup and simmer for about 7 minutes or until tender. To serve, ladle soup into bowls and add a few asparagus pieces to each. With a slotted spoon, add 2 or 3 matzo balls, with their almonds showing. Serve hot.

ROAST SHOULDER OF LAMB WITH SPINACH STUFFING

Lamb is the meat of choice for Passover in many Sephardic communities. Here it is spread with an Italian-style garlic-flavoured spinach matzo stuffing, then rolled and roasted.

MAKES 8 TO 10 SERVINGS

SPINACH AND MATZO STUFFING

4 matzos	4 garlic cloves, finely chopped
250 ml (8 fl oz) hot chicken soup or stock	1.4 kg (3 lb) fresh spinach, or 2 × 275-g (10-oz) packets frozen leaf spinach
60 ml (4 tbsp) vegetable oil	3 large eggs, size 1 or 2
2 medium onions, finely chopped	freshly grated nutmeg to taste
salt and pepper	

2.5–2.7-kg (5½–6-lb) shoulder of lamb, boned, with a pocket cut for stuffing (about 2 kg (4½ lb) after boning)	1 garlic clove, halved salt and pepper

---

Preheat oven to 230°C (450°F) mark 8. To make stuffing, crumble matzos into small pieces in a bowl and pour soup or stock over them. Mix well. Leave to stand for about 15 minutes. Heat oil in a large frying pan and add onions, salt and pepper. Sauté over medium heat, stirring often, for about 10 minutes or until softened. Add garlic and cook for ½ minute.

If using fresh spinach, remove stalks and rinse leaves well. Cook spinach, uncovered, in a very large saucepan of boiling salted water over high heat until tender, about 3 minutes; or cook frozen spinach for 2 minutes. Rinse with cold water and squeeze by hand until dry. Chop with knife or in food processor.

Add onion mixture, spinach and eggs to matzo mixture and season to taste with salt, pepper and nutmeg. Mixture should be generously seasoned so it will stand up to flavour of lamb.

Fill pocket in lamb shoulder with stuffing, packing it in firmly; you will need about half the stuffing. Close pocket with skewers or sew it closed with trussing needle and kitchen string. Set lamb in a medium roasting tin. Rub lamb vigorously with cut garlic clove and sprinkle it with salt and pepper. Roast for 15 minutes to sear lamb, then reduce oven temperature to 180°C (350°F) mark 4 and continue roasting until very tender, about 1¾–2 hours longer or until a meat thermometer inserted in meat registers 68–71°C (155–160°F).

Meanwhile, spoon the remaining stuffing into a greased deep 1-litre (1¾-pint) baking dish; bake alongside lamb for about 30 minutes or until firm.

Leave meat to rest on a chopping board for 15 minutes. Carve into 1–2-cm (½–¾-inch) slices, using a very sharp large knife. With a small knife, remove any excess fat from each slice. Use a broad spatula to transfer slices to each plate. Serve extra stuffing separately.

CAULIFLOWER IN TOMATO SAUCE

Sephardic Jews prepare many vegetables in tomato sauce and in general prefer them cooked until very tender rather than crunchy. When this dish is prepared the old-fashioned way, the cauliflower is dipped in batter and fried before being simmered in tomato sauce, but this is a lighter version, more in keeping with today's style.

MAKES 4 TO 6 SERVINGS

30 ml (2 tbsp) olive or
   vegetable oil
½ medium onion, chopped
2 large garlic cloves, finely
   chopped
1.1 kg (2½ lb) ripe tomatoes,
   peeled, seeded and chopped;
   or 2 × 794-g (28-oz) cans
   plum tomatoes, drained and
   chopped

15 ml (1 tbsp) tomato purée
120 ml (4 fl oz) water
1 bay leaf
2.5 ml (½ tsp) dried oregano
salt and pepper to taste
1 large cauliflower, divided
   into medium florets
15 ml (1 tbsp) chopped fresh
   parsley (optional)

Heat oil in a large saucepan over medium heat. Add onion and sauté, stirring occasionally, for about 5 minutes or until it begins to brown. Add garlic, tomatoes, tomato purée, water, bay leaf, oregano, salt and pepper. Cook over medium heat, stirring often, for about 30 minutes or until tomatoes are soft and mixture is thick and smooth. Discard bay leaf. Taste and adjust seasoning. (Sauce can be kept, covered, for 2 days in refrigerator. Reheat before continuing.)

Cook cauliflower uncovered in a large pan of boiling salted water over high heat for about 3–4 minutes or until nearly tender. Drain, rinse with cold water and drain thoroughly.

Add cauliflower to tomato sauce, cover and simmer, gently turning florets occasionally, for about 5 minutes or until very tender. Taste and adjust seasoning. Serve hot or at room temperature. Sprinkle with parsley when serving.

PECAN-COCOA TORTE WITH CHOCOLATE-CINNAMON FROSTING

For an impressive Passover dessert, this cake is often my choice. The luscious cinnamon frosting is wonderfully rich and chocolatey but not overly sweet.

MAKES 12 SERVINGS

350 g (12 oz) pecans
350 g (12 oz) granulated
  sugar
75 ml (5 tbsp) matzo cake
  meal or sifted matzo meal

30 ml (2 tbsp) cocoa powder
5 ml (1 tsp) ground cinnamon
6 large eggs, size 1 or 2,
  separated, at room
  temperature

CHOCOLATE-CINNAMON FROSTING
150 g (5 oz) plain chocolate,
  chopped
225 g (8 oz) unsalted non-
  dairy margarine, at room
  temperature
100 g (4 oz) caster sugar
15 ml (1 tbsp) cocoa powder

2.5 ml (½ tsp) ground
  cinnamon
2 large eggs, size 1 or 2, at
  room temperature
8–10 pecan halves, for
  decoration

Preheat oven to 180°C (350°F) mark 4. Using margarine, grease two 23-cm (9-inch) round cake tins about 4 cm (1½ inches) deep. Line base of each with nonstick paper or foil and grease paper or foil. Use a little matzo cake meal to flour sides of tins and lined bases, tapping to remove excess.

In a food processor, work pecans with 100 g (4 oz) granulated sugar in 2 batches to a fine powder. Transfer to a bowl. Sift cake meal with cocoa and cinnamon. Add to pecan mixture and stir until blended.

Beat egg yolks with 100 g (4 oz) sugar in a large bowl for about 5 minutes or until mixture is pale yellow and very thick.

Beat egg whites in another large bowl until soft peaks form. Gradually add remaining sugar and whisk at high speed for about ½ minute or until whites are very stiff and shiny but not dry. Sprinkle one-third of pecan mixture over yolks and fold gently until nearly

44

blended. Spoon one-third of whites on top and fold gently. Repeat until all pecan mixture and whites are added. Fold just until blended and no white streaks remain.

Pour into prepared tins and quickly spread evenly. Bake for about 30 minutes or until a fine skewer inserted in centre of cakes comes out clean. Without releasing cakes, set a wire rack on each tin, turn over and leave upside down for 10 minutes, with tin still on each cake. Turn back over. Run a palette knife around sides of each cake. Turn out onto wire racks, carefully peel off paper and leave to cool completely.

To make frosting, melt chocolate in a small saucepan set above hot water over low heat. Leave to cool. Cream margarine in a large bowl until very soft and smooth. Add sugar, cocoa and cinnamon and beat until smooth. Beat in eggs one by one at high speed, then beat in melted chocolate.

Spread about one-third of the frosting on one cake layer. Set second cake on top. (Carefully trim top layer if necessary, using a serrated knife, so cake is even.) Spread frosting on sides and top of cake and smooth with a palette knife. Garnish top with a circle of pecan halves near edge of cake. Refrigerate for at least 1 hour before serving. (Frosted cake can be kept for 2 days in refrigerator.)

DAIRY PASSOVER MENU

For the first night of Passover, the Seder is usually planned around a main course of roast meat or poultry. The second night is often more casual. When I was growing up, my mother always prepared a *milchig* dinner, featuring dairy foods, for the second Seder. To us, as children, this dinner was even more fun than the Seder of the first night because we were allowed to spread butter on our matzos.

On this night we could enjoy our favourite treats: Passover cheese kugel topped with soured cream, Passover pancakes and fried matzo with eggs. Sometimes my mother even made special Passover rolls that could double as cream puffs. For dessert, we could look forward to a rich chocolate-nut cake coated with real whipped cream. It was a true feast that we would remember for the rest of the year.

DAIRY PASSOVER MENU

Savoury Mushrooms with Thyme and Olive Oil

**Orange-Scented Haroset with
Wine**

Gefilte Fish (page 24)

**Passover Cheese Pancakes,
or
Fried Matzo with Eggs**

**Steamed Broccoli
or
Other Green Vegetable**

Passover 'Rolls'

Lemon-Scented Cheese Kugel with Raisins

**Ashkenazic Walnut Torte with
Chocolate Glaze,
or
Chocolate Hazelnut Gâteau with Whipped Cream
(page 28)**

SAVOURY MUSHROOMS WITH THYME AND OLIVE OIL

A mushroom first course or side dish like this one, flavoured with the Moroccan seasoning combination of garlic, cumin, paprika and thyme, can be found in many Israeli homes and is the mushroom dish we cook most often. We use olive oil on its own for cooking the mushrooms for a meal that includes meat, or a mixture of olive oil and butter for a fish dinner. The cooking time is relatively long so the mushrooms absorb the seasonings well.

MAKES 4 SERVINGS

60 ml (4 tbsp) olive oil or 50 g (2 oz) butter	5 ml (1 tsp) dried thyme, crumbled
1 medium onion, chopped	2.5 ml (½ tsp) paprika
450 g (1 lb) fairly small button mushrooms, quartered	5 ml (1 tsp) ground cumin
	cayenne pepper to taste
salt and freshly ground pepper	15 ml (1 tbsp) chopped fresh parsley

Heat oil in a large frying pan over medium heat. Add onion and sauté for about 7 minutes or until tender. Add mushrooms, salt, pepper, thyme, paprika and cumin. Sauté, stirring often, for 15–20 minutes or until mushrooms are well coated with spices and any liquid that accumulated in pan has evaporated; reduce heat towards the end of cooking time if necessary. Add cayenne; taste and adjust seasoning. (Mushrooms can be kept, covered, for 2 days in refrigerator. Reheat over medium heat.) Add parsley and serve.

FRIED MATZO WITH EGGS

O riginally a Passover dish, known in Yiddish as *matzo brei*, this simple preparation has become a favourite of many Ashkenazim throughout the year. There are various ways to cook the matzo and egg mixture – as an omelette, scrambled eggs or small pancakes. It makes a good breakfast, brunch or light supper dish. Serve it alone or accompanied by apple sauce, sugar or jam.

MAKES 4 SERVINGS

4 matzos	2.5 ml (½ tsp) salt
4 large eggs, size 1 or 2	40–50 g (1½–2 oz) butter

Soak matzos in cold water for about 10 minutes and drain. Break them into bite-size squares or larger. Beat eggs with salt and pour over matzos. Stir until matzos are coated.

Melt butter in a heavy frying pan and add batter. Cook the mixture as you like, frying it until done to your taste: either add all the mixture and brown it on both sides, like a flat omelette; fry by spoonfuls, like small pancakes; or fry, stirring, like scrambled eggs.

ORANGE-SCENTED HAROSET WITH WINE

T his is a fresh-tasting haroset, made of apples and nuts and flavoured with orange juice and rind. Other fresh fruit can be added as well. Iranian Jews sometimes add bananas and pears to their haroset, and season it with saffron and pepper as well as wine.

MAKES 8 SERVINGS

50 g (2 oz) hazelnuts	45 ml (3 tbsp) sweet red wine
50 g (2 oz) walnuts	30 ml (2 tbsp) strained fresh
50 g (2 oz) sugar	orange juice
2 large apples, peeled, halved	grated rind of ½ orange
and cored	matzos, for serving

Grind hazelnuts and walnuts with sugar in a food processor until fairly fine, leaving a few small chunks. Transfer to a bowl. Chop apples in food processor until fine, then add to nut mixture. Stir in wine, orange juice and grated rind.

Spoon into a bowl. Serve at room temperature or cold, accompanied by matzos.

PASSOVER CHEESE PANCAKES

S erve these with a mixture of cinnamon and sugar or with a bowl of soured cream. Alternatively, serve them as an appetizer with a topping of sautéed vegetables, especially mushrooms or leeks.

MAKES 4 TO 6 SERVINGS

225 g (8 oz) cottage cheese	*pinch of black pepper*
4 large eggs, size 1 or 2,	*(optional)*
beaten	*50 g (2 oz) butter and 60 ml*
50 g (2 oz) matzo meal	*(4 tbsp) vegetable oil, for*
25 g (1 oz) butter, melted	*frying*
pinch of salt	

Mix cottage cheese with eggs, matzo meal, melted butter, and salt and pepper to taste.

Heat 25 g (1 oz) butter and 30 ml (2 tbsp) oil in a large heavy frying pan. Add about 15 ml (1 tbsp) batter for each pancake and fry over medium heat until lightly browned on each side, about 2 minutes per side. Use 2 slotted spatulas to turn them carefully. Remove with a slotted spoon when done and continue frying remaining batter, adding more butter and oil as pan becomes dry; reduce heat if fat begins to brown. Serve hot.

PASSOVER 'ROLLS'

These rolls are a traditional recipe among Ashkenazic Jews, and are sold in Paris by Jewish bakeries in the 'European Jewish' section of the city on and around rue des Rosiers. The rolls are actually made of cream puff dough, or *pâte à choux*, with matzo meal used instead of flour. Like cream puffs, they are hollow in the centre. They can also be split, filled and served as appetizer or dessert cream puffs.

MAKES ABOUT 20 ROLLS

250 ml (8 fl oz) water	*5 ml (1 tsp) salt*
100 g (4 oz) unsalted	*175 g (6 oz) matzo meal*
margarine or butter	*5 large eggs, size 1 or 2*

Preheat oven to 200°C (400°F) mark 6. Grease 2 baking sheets. Heat water, margarine and salt in a medium saucepan over medium–low heat until margarine melts. Raise heat and bring to the boil. Remove from heat and add matzo meal all at once. Mix well. Return pan to low heat and cook, stirring, for 1 minute. Remove from heat and cool for about 5 minutes.

Beat in 1 egg. When mixture is completely smooth, beat in a second egg. Continue adding eggs one by one, beating thoroughly after each addition.

Drop batter by heaped spoonfuls (measuring about 30 ml (2 tbsp) each) onto baking sheets, allowing about 4 cm (1½ inches) between them. Bake for about 40 minutes or until golden brown and firm.

LEMON-SCENTED CHEESE KUGEL WITH RAISINS

During Passover, matzos replace the usual noodles in kugel. For a meatless Passover menu, this slightly sweet baked pudding enriched with cottage cheese and studded with nuts and raisins can play the role of either main course or dessert.

MAKES 6 SERVINGS

4 matzos	75 g (3 oz) raisins
450 g (1 lb) cottage cheese	50 g (2 oz) broken or coarsely
3 large eggs, size 1 or 2	chopped walnuts
2.5 ml (½ tsp) salt	75 g (3 oz) unsalted butter,
65 g (2½ oz) sugar	melted
15 ml (1 tbsp) lemon juice	soured cream, for serving
grated rind of ½ lemon	

Preheat oven to 160°C (325°F) mark 3. Soak whole matzos in cold water to cover until slightly softened but not mushy, about 1½ minutes. Drain thoroughly. Mix cottage cheese, eggs, salt, sugar, lemon juice, lemon rind, raisins and walnuts.

Pour about 45 ml (3 tbsp) melted butter into a 20-cm (8-inch) square baking dish or 1.7-litre (3-pint) cake tin. Set 1 whole matzo in tin, filling in any spaces with pieces from another matzo. Spread half the cheese mixture in tin. Cover with another layer of matzos. Spread remaining cheese mixture in tin. Top with a layer of matzos. Sprinkle remaining melted butter on top. Bake for about 1 hour or until set and top is browned.

Serve hot or lukewarm. Cut in squares and serve with soured cream.

ASHKENAZIC WALNUT TORTE WITH CHOCOLATE GLAZE

Ground nuts and matzo meal instead of flour give body to this rich Hungarian-style sponge cake. Matzo meal is made from ground matzos; matzo cake meal is more finely ground.

After baking, the cake is cooled upside down in the tin so it won't sink. The cake should be baked in an angel cake tin that has small 'feet' to enable the air to circulate under the cake while it cools. If your ring tin does not have feet, you can cool the cake on a rack. The pan is not greased or the cake would fall out. For the same reason, nonstick pans should not be used.

MAKES ABOUT 10 SERVINGS

200 g (7 oz) walnuts	7 large eggs, separated
25 g (1 oz) matzo cake meal	grated rind ½ orange
or matzo meal	15 ml (1 tbsp) orange juice
250 g (9 oz) sugar	tiny pinch of salt

CHOCOLATE GLAZE (OPTIONAL)

75 g (3 oz) plain or bitter	45 ml (3 tbsp) sugar
chocolate	8–10 walnut halves, for
45 ml (3 tbsp) water	decoration
40 g (1½ oz) unsalted	
margarine	

Preheat the oven to 180°C (350°F) mark 4. Have ready a 25-cm (10-inch) angel cake tin with 10.5-cm (4⅛-inch) sides and a removable base. Do not grease tin.

In a food processor, finely grind the walnuts with matzo cake meal and 45 ml (3 tbsp) sugar, using on/off motion. Transfer to a bowl.

In a large bowl, beat yolks until blended. Gradually beat in 150 g (5 oz) sugar. Beat at high speed for about 5 minutes or until yolk mixture is very thick and light in colour. Beat in orange rind, then gradually beat in orange juice.

In another large bowl whip egg whites with a pinch of salt until soft peaks form. Gradually beat in remaining 75 ml (5 tbsp) sugar. Whip at high speed for about ½ minute until glossy. Fold one-third of the nut mixture into yolks, followed by one-third of whites. Continue with remaining mixtures, adding last batch of whites before nuts are completely blended in. Fold lightly and quickly.

Transfer mixture immediately to tin and smooth top. Bake in centre of oven for about 1 hour and 5 minutes or until a fine skewer inserted into cake comes out dry. (Cake rises more at sides than in centre but will look fine when it's turned out.) Turn cake upside down in tin and leave for about 2 hours or until completely cool.

To remove cake from tin, run a thin bladed knife around sides of cake. Push up base and remove sides of tin. Slide knife around tube, then very carefully under cake. Turn cake over onto a large serving plate. (Cake can be kept, covered, for 2 days in refrigerator).

To make glaze, combine all ingredients except nuts in a small heavy saucepan and heat over low heat, stirring until smooth. Spoon slowly over cake and allow glaze to drip down sides. Decorate with walnut halves. Refrigerate briefly so glaze sets.

A SEPHARDIC SEDER

For the majority of Jews in America, who are of Ashkenazic, or eastern and central European, origin, Passover menus begin with gefilte fish, followed by chicken soup with matzo balls and roast chicken as a main course. This had been my own experience when I was growing up, and I always looked forward to the holiday dinners. But Passover menus became even more exciting for me when I moved to Israel and discovered the flavourful Sephardic, or Mediterranean Jewish, cuisine.

Sephardic Seders also feature fish as an appetizer, but it is likely to be baked with olive oil, garlic and saffron. Chicken soup appears, too, but it is embellished with spring vegetables.

Lamb, a Mediterranean favourite, is a popular choice for the main course on the Sephardic holiday menu, but braised beef, chicken or even both, might be offered instead. In keeping with the Mediterranean tradition, a colourful assortment of salads – of both cooked and uncooked vegetables – adorns the Seder table. Dessert is usually fresh fruit, fruit salad or a light cake.

The following menu is for a Seder in the Sephardic tradition, and includes Moroccan and Yemenite Jewish specialities. To make cooking easier, virtually the entire meal can be prepared ahead.

A SEPHARDIC SEDER MENU

Date–Almond–Walnut Haroset

Baked Fish with Saffron and Red Peppers

Spring Vegetable Soup with Fresh Herbs

Mediterranean Vegetable Salad

Carrot and Asparagus Salad

Yemenite Beef and Chicken Casserole,
or
Yemenite Braised Lamb with Cumin and Garlic

Moroccan Potato Casserole

Passover Almond Cake with Strawberry Sauce

BAKED FISH WITH SAFFRON AND RED PEPPERS

Moroccan Jews make this dish with whole fish, but fillets make it easier to prepare and to eat. Serve it hot or at room temperature.

MAKES 8 SERVINGS

90 ml (6 tbsp) extra-virgin olive oil	*900 g (2 lb) halibut, cod or sea bass steaks or fillets,*
1 large red pepper, diced in 1-cm (½-inch) pieces	*about 1–2-cm (½–¾-inch) thick, cut into 8 pieces*
5 large garlic cloves, chopped	*2.5 ml (½ tsp) dried thyme,*
1.25 ml (¼ tsp) saffron threads	*crumbled*
cayenne pepper to taste	*salt and freshly ground pepper*
	20 ml (4 tsp) chopped parsley

Preheat oven to 200°C (400°F) mark 6. Heat 60 ml (4 tbsp) olive oil in a large ovenproof frying pan. Add pepper and cook over low heat for 10 minutes or until tender. Add garlic, saffron and cayenne and cook for ½ minute.

Divide mixture between 2 frying pans if necessary, so that fish will form a single layer; heat second frying pan for a few seconds. Set fish on pepper mixture, folding under any thin 'tails'; turn fish to coat with seasoning mixture. Sprinkle fish with remaining 30 ml (2 tbsp) oil, then with thyme, salt and pepper. Cover with foil and bake for 15 minutes or until fish can just be flaked. Check seasoning.

Serve fish hot or lukewarm. Sprinkle with parsley, then spoon some of the cooking juices with peppers over each piece.

DATE-ALMOND-WALNUT HAROSET

Sephardic versions of haroset have an intense fruit flavour, as in this recipe, which contains a generous amount of dates. While Ashkenazic haroset has a large proportion of apples, Sephardic versions may or may not contain them.

MAKES 8 TO 12 SERVINGS

225 g (8 oz) stoned dates
50 g (2 oz) almonds
50 g (2 oz) walnuts
about 60 ml (4 tbsp) sweet red
   wine (traditional Passover
   wine)
3.75 ml (¾ tsp) ground ginger

2.5 ml (½ tsp) ground
   cinnamon
pinch of freshly ground black
   pepper
2 pinches ground cloves
1 medium apple

Halve dates and remove any remaining stones or stone fragments. Finely chop almonds and walnuts in food processor and remove. Add dates, 60 ml (4 tbsp) wine and spices to processor and grind until fairly smooth. Mix with nuts. Grate apple coarsely and stir in. Add more wine, teaspoons at a time, if necessary to make a mixture that is spreadable but still thick.

MEDITERRANEAN VEGETABLE SALAD

Versions of this salad are enjoyed in Israel all year round, but for Passover it includes spring onions and small radishes.

MAKES 8 SERVINGS

4 large spring onions, chopped
8 small radishes, diced in
   about 0.5 cm (¼ inch)
   pieces
12 plum tomatoes, diced
1 cucumber, peeled and diced
   in 1-cm (⅜-inch) pieces
15 g (½ oz) parsley, chopped

salt and pepper
cayenne pepper to taste
40 ml (8 tsp) extra-virgin
   olive oil
20 ml (4 tsp) fresh lemon
   juice
spring onion fan (optional)

Mix vegetables and parsley in a bowl. Sprinkle with salt, pepper and cayenne and mix well. Sprinkle with olive oil, mix, then sprinkle with lemon juice and mix again. Taste and adjust seasoning.

To make a spring onion fan, cut off all but 7.5 cm (3 inches) of the white part of a spring onion. Make several parallel, lengthways cuts outward from the centre of the white part, beginning 2.5 cm (1 inch) up from the bottom. Put in ice water in refrigerator for about an hour. Ends will curl. Use to garnish salad.

SPRING VEGETABLE SOUP WITH FRESH HERBS

Northh African Jews prepare this light soup for Passover with fresh broad beans. If your family doesn't eat beans for the holiday, substitute the courgettes.

MAKES 8 SERVINGS

1.4 litres (2½ pints)
chicken stock
450 ml (¾ pint) water
1 large onion, diced
2 garlic cloves, chopped
2 celery stalks, thinly sliced
salt and freshly ground pepper
2 large leeks, about 450 g
(1 lb), split and cleaned
700 g (1½ lb) fresh broad
beans, shelled; or
1 × 275-g (10-oz) packet
frozen broad beans; or
2 courgettes, diced

4 fresh artichokes or 16 pieces
frozen artichoke hearts
1 lemon (if using fresh
artichokes)
15 g (½ oz) fresh mint,
chopped
15 g (½ oz) fresh parsley,
chopped
15 g (½ oz) fresh coriander,
chopped
cayenne pepper to taste
matzos, as accompaniment

Combine stock, water, onion, garlic, celery, salt and pepper in saucepan. Bring to the boil. Cover and cook over low heat for 20 minutes. Slice the white, light green and 5 cm (2 inches) of dark green parts of leeks and add to soup. Add beans or courgettes and frozen artichoke pieces, if using, and return to the boil. Cover and cook over low heat for 30 minutes or until vegetables are tender.

If using fresh artichokes, prepare artichoke hearts and cook them separately (see page 344). Quarter them and add to soup.

Add mint, parsley, coriander and cayenne to soup. Taste and adjust seasoning. Serve with matzos.

CARROT AND ASPARAGUS SALAD

Moroccan and Tunisian Jewish cooks prepare a great variety of salads of cooked vegetables. This dish is usually made with carrots alone, or sometimes with carrots and artichokes.

MAKES 8 SERVINGS

900 g (2 lb) medium carrots (about 10), peeled
salt
700 g (1½ lb) medium asparagus, peeled and cut into 5-cm (2-inch) pieces
90 ml (6 tbsp) vegetable oil
2 medium onions, halved and thinly sliced

2.5 ml (½ tsp) red chilli flakes
2.5 ml (½ tsp) caraway seeds
2.5 ml (½ tsp) paprika
2.5 ml (½ tsp) ground cumin
60 ml (4 tbsp) strained fresh lemon juice
cayenne pepper to taste

Cut carrots in 5-cm (2-inch) lengths and quarter the pieces. Halve any pieces that are wider than the others. In a saucepan, cover carrots with water and add a pinch of salt. Bring to the boil and simmer over medium heat for 15 minutes or until just tender. Remove with slotted spoon. Add asparagus to cooking liquid and boil uncovered for 3–4 minutes or until just tender. Remove asparagus, reserving cooking liquid. Rinse asparagus with cold water; drain well.

Heat oil in a large frying pan over medium heat. Stir in onions and fry for 10 minutes or until tender. Add 120 ml (4 fl oz) vegetable cooking liquid, chilli flakes, caraway seeds, paprika, cumin and a pinch of salt. Bring to the boil, stirring. Reduce heat to low.

Add carrots. Simmer, uncovered, for 5 minutes or until sauce is reduced and coats carrots thoroughly. Add asparagus and mix gently. Serve hot, warm or cold. Add lemon juice just before serving. Taste and add more salt and cayenne if necessary; salad should be fairly spicy.

YEMENITE BEEF AND CHICKEN CASSEROLE

My Israeli mother-in-law prepares this aromatic 'meat in one dish' of chicken and beef when several relatives arrive for lunch or dinner, since this way each person has his or her choice of beef or chicken. And the resulting cooking juices, flavoured with garlic and cumin, are heavenly. At home we refer to this dish as 'Yemenite *daube*' because it is prepared by a method similar to that of the traditional southern French *daube* – the meat is simply put in the casserole without preliminary sautéing, and browns slowly.

MAKES 8 SERVINGS

---

30 ml (2 tbsp) vegetable oil
  or chicken fat
2 medium onions, chopped
8 medium garlic cloves,
  chopped
45 ml (3 tbsp) ground cumin
7.5 ml (1½ tsp) turmeric
15 ml (1 tbsp) tomato purée
250 ml (8 fl oz) water
900 g (2 lb) braising or
  stewing steak, excess fat
  removed, cut in 2.5–4-cm
  (1–1½-inch) cubes

1.4 kg (3 lb) chicken pieces
8 medium potatoes, about
  900 g (2 lb), peeled
15 g (½ oz) fresh parsley,
  coarsely chopped
salt and freshly ground black
  pepper
350 g (12 oz) ripe tomatoes,
  chopped, or 1 × 397-g
  (14-oz) can plum tomatoes,
  drained and chopped

Position shelf in lower third of oven and preheat to 150°C (300°F) mark 2. Heat oil in a large, deep, heavy flameproof casserole over medium-low heat, add onions and sauté until golden, about 12 minutes. Remove from heat. Stir in garlic, cumin, turmeric, tomato purée and 120 ml (4 fl oz) water.

Add beef, chicken, potatoes, parsley, salt and pepper, and tomatoes to casserole and mix well; meat and chicken should be well coated with spices. Cover tightly and bake for about 3 hours or until beef is very tender; check occasionally and add remaining water, if necessary, so there is just a little sauce but meat does not get dry. Taste sauce and adjust seasoning. (Casserole can be kept overnight in refrigerator and reheated, covered, in low oven or over low heat.)

YEMENITE BRAISED LAMB WITH CUMIN AND GARLIC

This type of aromatic braised meat is a favourite of my in-laws from Yemen. I find it convenient to cook the lamb one day ahead so the flavours can blend and the chilled sauce can be more thoroughly skimmed of fat.

MAKES 8 SERVINGS

30 ml (2 tbsp) vegetable oil
2 medium onions, chopped
6 large garlic cloves, chopped
20 ml (4 tsp) cumin, freshly
  ground if possible
5 ml (1 tsp) turmeric
15 ml (1 tbsp) tomato purée
350 g (12 oz) ripe tomatoes,
  chopped, or 1 × 397-g
  (14-oz) can plum tomatoes,
  drained and chopped

8 middle or best end neck lamb
  chops, about 1.8 kg
  (4 lb) total, excess fat
  trimmed
salt and freshly ground black
  pepper
120 ml (4 fl oz) water
90 ml (6 tbsp) chopped fresh
  coriander or parsley

Position shelf in lower third of oven and preheat to 180°C (350°F) mark 4. Heat oil in a large, heavy flameproof casserole over medium-low heat, add onions and sauté until golden, about 20 minutes. Remove from heat and stir in garlic, cumin, turmeric, tomato purée and tomatoes. Remove and reserve two-thirds.

Sprinkle lamb with salt and pepper on both sides. Put pieces in casserole in layers, scattering some of seasoning mixture over each and rubbing seasoning mixture into meat. Add any remaining seasoning mixture to casserole. Pour water into pan.

Cover tightly and cook for 45 minutes. Turn meat over, baste it and continue cooking for about 1 hour more or until meat is tender when pierced with a knife; check occasionally and add water if necessary so pan does not become dry. Remove meat from pan, then skim fat from sauce. If sauce is too thin, boil it for 3–4 minutes to reduce slightly. Taste sauce and adjust seasoning. (Meat can be kept overnight in refrigerator; skim the sauce of fat, then reheat meat in sauce, covered, in low oven or over low heat.)

Add 60 ml (4 tbsp) coriander or parsley to sauce. Serve hot, with some of sauce spooned over each meat piece. Sprinkle with herbs.

MOROCCAN POTATO CASSEROLE

If your family does not serve peas for Passover, substitute the combination of celery and courgette. Sometimes diced cooked chicken or other meat is added to this casserole to turn it into a festive main course lunch during Passover week.

MAKES 4–6 SERVINGS;
8 SERVINGS AS PART OF LARGE MENU

---

900 g (2 lb) potatoes, scrubbed

1 medium carrot, peeled and halved crossways

150 g (5 oz) fresh shelled or frozen peas or 50 g (2 oz) celery and 50 g (2 oz) courgette, diced

60 ml (4 tbsp) vegetable oil

2 large onions, 450 g (1 lb), chopped

6 large eggs, size 1 or 2

1.25 ml (¼ tsp) turmeric

5 ml (1 tsp) salt

2.5 ml (½ tsp) ground black pepper

15 g (½ oz) fresh parsley, chopped

Preheat oven to 180°C (350°F) mark 4. Put potatoes and carrot in saucepan, cover with water and add a pinch of salt. Bring to the boil and cook for about 20 minutes or until carrot is tender. Remove with a slotted spoon. Cook potatoes for 10 minutes more or until tender, then remove. Add peas or celery and courgette mixture to liquid; boil frozen peas for 1 minute, fresh peas or courgette for 2–5 minutes, or until just tender. Rinse peas or courgette mixture with cold water and drain. Dice carrot.

Heat 45 ml (3 tbsp) oil in a large frying pan over medium heat, add onions and sauté until they begin to brown, about 20 minutes.

Peel potatoes and finely mash with potato masher. Add eggs to potatoes one by one, beating well after adding each. Stir in turmeric, salt, pepper, parsley and onions with their oil. Taste and adjust seasoning. Fold in carrot and peas.

Heat remaining 15 ml (1 tbsp) oil in a 1.7-litre (3-pint) casserole in oven for 2 minutes or until hot. Remove with oven gloves and swirl casserole carefully so oil coats sides. Carefully add potato mixture; do not mix in oil from sides of pan. Cook for 50 minutes or until a knife inserted in centre comes out dry. Serve hot or cold.

PASSOVER ALMOND CAKE WITH STRAWBERRY SAUCE

The traditional light cakes made for Passover, such as this Italian Jewish almond cake, are often flavoured with nuts, which given them an appealing richness, and contain a little matzo meal as a substitute for flour. For a modern presentation, the cake is accompanied by strawberries tossed with strawberry sauce and sprinkled with mint.

MAKES 8 SERVINGS

240 g (8½ oz) whole
  unblanched almonds
25 g (1 oz) matzo cake meal
  or matzo meal
225 g (8 oz) sugar
4 large eggs, size 1 or 2,
  separated
6.25 ml (1¼ tsp) grated
  lemon rind

salt
double recipe of Strawberry
  Sauce (page 73)
275 g (10 oz) fresh
  strawberries, sliced
20 ml (4 tsp) very thin strips
  fresh mint (optional)
mint sprigs, for decoration
  (optional)

Preheat oven to 180°C (350°F) mark 4. Grease a 23-cm (9-inch) spring clip tin with margarine.

Grind almonds with matzo meal and 50 g (2 oz) sugar in food processor until fine. Beat egg yolks with 100 g (4 oz) sugar at high speed of mixer until light and fluffy. Beat in lemon rind just until blended. Set aside.

In a clean bowl whisk egg whites with a pinch of salt to soft peaks. Gradually beat in remaining sugar, beating until stiff and shiny.

In 3 batches alternately fold whites and almond mixture into yolk mixture. Transfer to tin and bake for about 35 minutes or until a fine skewer inserted in centre of cake comes out dry. Cool slightly, then run a palette knife gently around cake and remove sides of spring clip tin. Cool on a wire rack. Cake will sink slightly. (Cake can be kept, covered, for 1 day at room temperature or in refrigerator.) Serve at cool room temperature.

Make double recipe of strawberry sauce, using caster sugar instead. Mix 120 ml (4 fl oz) sauce with the sliced berries.

To serve, cut cake in wedges and put on dessert plates. Spoon a few sliced berries on one side of cake and sprinkle with mint strips. Spoon sauce on other side of cake. Decorate with mint sprigs.

A FESTIVE PASSOVER SABBATH MENU

Since Passover lasts for eight days, there are plenty of meals to prepare besides the Seder menus of the first two nights. The Sabbath dinner menu is especially festive, although with fewer items than the Seder menu, and each family has its favourite dishes. For the following menu, the first and main courses are North African, the dessert is European style, and the almond macaroons are Passover favourites of Jews of all origins.

A FESTIVE PASSOVER SABBATH MENU

Spicy Potato Salad

Israeli Vegetable Salad (page 34)

Spring Lamb Stew with Many Vegetables (Msouki)

Strawberry Cream Puffs for Passover,
or
Chocolate Mousse for Passover

Citrus-Scented Almond Macaroons

SPICY POTATO SALAD

If you think potato salads need a large quantity of rich dressing to be good, try this tasty appetizer from the Tunisian repertoire. The intriguing combination of caraway, cumin and coriander in a light, tangy dressing make this aromatic potato salad one of the best.

MAKES 5 OR 6 SERVINGS

900 g (2 lb) red-skinned potatoes, scrubbed but not peeled	*2.5 ml (½ tsp) paprika*
	15 ml (1 tbsp) water
	30 ml (2 tbsp) olive oil
salt to taste	*1.25 ml (¼ tsp) caraway seeds*
45 ml (3 tbsp) fresh lemon juice	*15 ml (1 tbsp) chopped fresh coriander*
10 ml (2 tsp) ground cumin	
2.5 ml (½ tsp) Tabasco sauce	

Put potatoes in large saucepan, cover with water by about 1 cm (½ inch) and add salt. Bring to boil, cover and simmer over low heat for about 25 minutes, or until a knife can pierce centre of the largest potato easily and potato falls from knife when lifted.

Meanwhile prepare dressing. In a bowl large enough to contain potatoes, whisk lemon juice with cumin, a pinch of salt, Tabasco sauce, paprika and water. Add olive oil and caraway seeds and whisk again.

Drain potatoes and leave just until cool enough to handle. Peel them and cut in 2.5-cm (1-inch) dice. Add potatoes to bowl and mix gently but thoroughly with dressing. Leave to cool. Serve cold or at room temperature. Just before serving, sprinkle with coriander.

SPRING LAMB STEW WITH MANY VEGETABLES (MSOUKI)

We enjoyed this Passover stew, a speciality of Jews from Algeria and Tunisia, at restaurants in the North African Jewish section of Paris near rue Montmartre. It is a slightly spicy, colourful stew made with a great variety of vegetables and either lamb or beef, and it is thickened with crumbled matzo. In Paris they use a special round 'Tunisian' matzo that is decorated with a lacy pattern and is thicker than the familiar square matzos; these pretty matzos are also served on the side. Some people serve the stew for the Seder, while others prefer it for dinners during Passover week.

Like many traditional dishes, msouki comes in many forms – it can be a soup, a stew or a plate of vegetables topped by a piece of braised meat. Usually it has many vegetables, but some cooks prefer to add only artichokes, spring onions, spinach and broad beans. North African Jews do not avoid beans for Passover, but Ashkenazim who wish to omit them will still find this stew to have an interesting medley of textures and tastes.

MAKES 6 SERVINGS

---

900 g (2 lb) shoulder of lamb, excess fat removed
salt and freshly ground pepper
5 ml (1 tsp) paprika
45 ml (3 tbsp) olive oil
450 ml (¾ pint) water
15 ml (1 tbsp) tomato purée
2 medium onions, halved and sliced
6 medium garlic cloves, chopped
2 medium carrots, diced
1 celery stalk, diced
700 g (1½ lb) fresh spinach, or 1 × 275-g (10-oz) packet frozen spinach, thawed and squeezed
700 g (1½ lb) fresh broad beans, shelled; or 1 × 275-g (10-oz) pack frozen broad beans

1 leek, split, cleaned and sliced
4 fresh artichoke hearts (see page 344 for preparation), or 1 × 250-g (9-oz) pack frozen artichoke hearts
1 lemon (if using fresh artichokes)
2 medium courgettes, diced
15 g (½ oz) fresh parsley, chopped
15 g (½ oz) fresh coriander, chopped
15 g (½ oz) fresh mint, chopped
cayenne pepper to taste or 5 ml (1 tsp) Tabasco sauce
2 matzos, broken into about 2.5-cm (1-inch) pieces

Cut lamb into 2.5-cm (1-inch) pieces. Sprinkle lightly with salt, pepper and paprika.

Combine oil, water and tomato purée in a large enamel casserole and whisk to blend. Add onions, garlic, carrots, celery, salt and pepper and mix well. Set seasoned lamb pieces on top. Bring to the boil, cover and cook over low heat, stirring from time to time, for 30 minutes. Add spinach, broad beans, leek, frozen artichoke pieces if using, and courgettes and return to the boil. Cover and cook for 30 minutes or until meat is tender.

Taste stew and adjust seasoning. Reserve 15 ml (1 tbsp) parsley and 15 ml (1 tbsp) coriander for garnish. Add fresh artichokes if using, mint, remaining parsley and coriander, and cayenne to stew and cook for 3 minutes. Taste and adjust seasoning. Put matzo pieces on top, stir gently, cover and leave to stand for 1–2 minutes to soften. Sprinkle with reserved herbs and serve.

CHOCOLATE MOUSSE FOR PASSOVER

When a Hebrew edition of my book, *Chocolate Sensations*, was published in Israel, every recipe that was suitable for Passover was marked with an asterisk. Until then I had not realized that so many of my favourite chocolate desserts are perfect for Passover.

This chocolate mousse does not contain cream, so it is a great finale for kosher dinners featuring meat. Serve this mousse on its own or accompanied by almond macaroons or Passover meringues.

MAKES 4 SERVINGS

200 g (7 oz) plain or bitter chocolate, chopped	15 g (½ oz) unsalted non-dairy margarine
60 ml (4 tbsp) sweet red Passover wine, orange juice or water	4 large eggs, size 1 or 2, separated
	15 ml (1 tbsp) sugar

In a medium bowl melt chocolate with wine above a saucepan of hot water over low heat. Remove from pan of water and stir until smooth. Stir in margarine, then add egg yolks, one by one, stirring vigorously after each addition.

Beat egg whites until stiff. Beat in sugar and continue beating for about 30 seconds or until whites are very shiny. Quickly fold a quarter of the whites into chocolate mixture. Gently fold in remaining whites. Pour into 4 dessert dishes, ramekins or stemmed glasses. Cover and chill for at least 2 hours or until set. (Mousse can be kept, covered, for 2 days in refrigerator.

STRAWBERRY CREAM PUFFS FOR PASSOVER

Made from Passover rolls, these elegant puffs are filled with strawberries in a white wine custard and served with Strawberry Sauce. They contain no dairy products and are perfect for a meat or poultry dinner. For dairy meals, you can instead prepare Passover profiteroles by filling the puffs with vanilla ice cream and serving them with warm Chocolate Sauce (page 325).

MAKES 10 SERVINGS

WHITE WINE PASTRY CREAM

175 ml (6 fl oz) dry white wine	30 ml (2 tbsp) potato flour
60 ml (4 tbsp) water	25 g (1 oz) unsalted non-dairy margarine
3 large egg yolks, size 1 or 2	5 ml (1 tsp) vanilla essence
75 ml (5 tbsp) sugar	

225 g (8 oz) strawberries, halved and sliced	10 Passover 'Rolls' (page 50)
20 ml (4 tsp) sugar	Strawberry Sauce (page 73, optional)

In a small, heavy saucepan bring wine and water to the boil; remove from heat.

Whisk egg yolks and sugar in a bowl until smooth. Gently stir in potato flour, using a whisk. Gradually add hot wine mixture, whisking quickly, then return mixture to saucepan. Cook over medium-low heat, whisking constantly, until mixture comes just to the boil, then reduce heat to low and, whisking constantly, cook for 1 minute. Remove from heat and whisk in margarine, then vanilla. Transfer to a bowl and cool to room temperature, stirring often to prevent a skin from forming. Refrigerate for at least 1 hour or up to 2 days.

Sprinkle strawberries with sugar and toss well. Leave to stand for a few minutes. Whisk pastry cream until smooth and fold in berries.

Fill puffs just before serving. Cut 'rolls' nearly in half and spoon berry mixture inside. Serve with Strawberry Sauce, if desired.

CITRUS-SCENTED ALMOND MACAROONS

Jewish pastry shops in Paris display almond macaroons all year round, but as Passover treats they are the most popular. Be sure to use fresh almonds.

MAKES ABOUT 20 MACAROONS

190 g (6½ oz) whole blanched almonds	5 ml (1 tsp) grated orange rind
225 g (8 oz) sugar	5 ml (1 tsp) grated lemon rind
2 large egg whites, size 1 or 2	
5 ml (1 tsp) orange juice	

Position shelf in upper third of oven and preheat to 180°C (350°F) mark 4. Line a baking sheet with non-stick paper or greaseproof paper; grease paper lightly with margarine.

Grind almonds with 60 ml (4 tbsp) sugar in food processor by processing continuously until mixture forms fine, even crumbs. Add egg whites, orange juice and orange and lemon rinds and process until smooth, about 20 seconds. Add remaining sugar in 2 additions and process for about 10 seconds after each or until smooth.

With moistened hands, roll about 15 ml (1 tbsp) of the mixture between your palms into a smooth ball. Put on prepared baking sheet. Continue with remaining mixture, spacing them about 2.5 cm (1 inch) apart.

Press to flatten each macaroon slightly so it is about 1 cm (½ inch) high. Brush entire surface of each macaroon with water. Bake until very lightly but evenly browned, 18–20 minutes; centres should still be soft. Remove from oven.

Lift one end of paper and pour about 30 ml (2 tbsp) water under it, onto baking sheet; the water will boil on contact with hot baking sheet. Lift other end of paper and pour about 30 ml (2 tbsp) water under it. When water stops boiling, remove macaroons carefully from paper. Transfer to a wire rack to cool. (Macaroons can be kept for 1 week in airtight containers.)

SHAVUOT
The Cheesecake Holiday

 The Jewish festival of Shavuot, which is celebrated in May or June, has many names. Because it comes seven weeks after Passover, in Hebrew it is called *Shavuot*, or 'weeks'. In English it is Pentecost, which comes from a Greek word meaning 'fifty days'. Often it is referred to as the Festival of the Torah, because it commemorates Moses' receiving the Ten Commandments and the Torah, or Judaic scriptures. Still another name is Feast of the First Fruits, which was observed in ancient Israel because this was the joyful time of the harvest of grain and early fruits.

One more nickname should be added: the holiday of cheesecake. It is a custom, although not a law, to prepare dairy delicacies for Shavuot. Some say this is because the Hebrews abstained from eating meat the day before they received the Torah. Another explanation is based on economics: a large amount of cheese is produced because cows, goats and sheep give more milk in the spring. No matter what the reason, this holiday is a good excuse to enjoy cheesecake one day, and cheese blintzes the next, since the festivities last for two days.

In Israel Shavuot is celebrated for only one day, but that one day can become a real feast! In addition to cheesecake, blintzes and noodle and soured cream kugels prepared by Jews of eastern European origin, there are the bourekas preferred by some of the Sephardic communities. These rich, savoury pastries often made with filo dough are known under various names in Greece, Turkey and much of the Middle East. They can contain many fillings, but for Shavuot a zesty cheese mixture is a favourite.

One of the greatest pleasures of festivals is the traditional dishes that go with them. Many of the foods of Shavuot have become so popular that they can be bought all year round. But they are even more delicious and enjoyed much more when prepared at home, among family or friends.

Other ideal Shavuot dishes:

Savoury Cheese Knishes (page 161)

Creamy Noodle Kugel with Almonds (page 330)

Meringue-Topped Cheesecake (page 311)

A SHAVUOT PARTY

Although cheese dishes are a tradition for Shavuot, you would probably not serve several of them at dinner because it would be too rich.
For a get-together with quite a few guests, you might like to prepare
a selection of dairy specialities, and those who wish can try small portions of each. This menu features mainly Ashkenazic dishes (blintzes
and cheesecake), but the filo turnovers are Sephardic. Today in Israel
all these dishes are well-loved by most people, and it's not at all
unusual to find them together at the same party.

For a dinner for a small number of people, use the same menu but
choose either the blintzes or the cheesecake, and prepare a simple
baked or grilled fish such as Grilled Salmon with Moroccan Seasonings (page 219) for a main course.

A SHAVOUT PARTY MENU

Cheese Filo Turnovers (Cheese Bourekas)

Israeli Vegetable Salad (page 34)

Cheese-Walnut Challah

Classic Cheese Blintzes with Strawberry Sauce

Salad of Seasonal Fruits

Creamy Cheesecake,
or
Cheesecake with Pine Nuts and Orange

CHEESE FILO TURNOVERS (CHEESE BOUREKAS)

In Israel these turnovers are known as *bourekas* and are considered a speciality of Sephardic Jews, especially those from Turkey and Syria. They have become as popular as pizza and can be found at many cafés throughout the year. Restaurant chefs often make them with filo dough but home cooks sometimes substitute purchased puff pastry, since in Israel it is easier to find.

Cheese-filled bourekas can be triangular, ring-shaped or half-moons. For the filling I like to mix a flavourful cheese such as kashkaval, parmesan or feta with a mild cheese such as cottage cheese. These pastries are great for entertaining, and few parties in Israel are complete without some form of this savoury appetizer.

MAKES ABOUT 32 TURNOVERS; 10 TO 12 SERVINGS

---

450 g (1 lb) filo dough
(about 20 sheets)
225 g (8 oz) butter or
margarine, melted

about 10 ml (2 tsp) sesame
seeds, for sprinkling

CHEESE FILLING
50 g (2 oz) low-fat cottage
cheese
2 large eggs, size 1 or 2,
beaten lightly
275 g (10 oz) cheese, grated,
such as Swiss, kashkaval or
Cheddar

2 spring onions, finely
chopped
salt (optional) and pepper to
taste

If filo sheets are frozen, thaw them in refrigerator for 8 hours or overnight. Remove sheets from refrigerator 2 hours before using and leave them in their packet.

Put cottage cheese in a strainer and press gently to remove excess liquid; do not push cheese through strainer. Leave cheese in strainer for 10 minutes and press gently again. Mix cottage cheese with eggs, grated cheese and spring onions until smooth. Add pepper; taste before adding any salt.

Remove filo sheets from packet and unroll them on a dry tea

towel. Using a sharp knife, cut stack in half lengthways to form 2 stacks of sheets of about 40 × 18 cm (16 × 7 inches) each. Cover filo immediately with a piece of greaseproof paper, then with a damp tea towel. Work with only one sheet at a time and always keep remaining sheets covered with paper and tea towel so they don't dry out.

Remove a filo sheet from pile. Brush it lightly with melted butter and fold it in half lengthways so its dimensions are about 40 × 8.5 cm (16 × 3½ inches). Dab it lightly with butter. Place about 7.5 ml (1½ tsp) cheese filling at one end of strip. Fold end of strip diagonally over filling to form a triangle and dab it lightly with butter. Continue folding it over and over, keeping it in a triangular shape after each fold, until end of strip is reached. Set triangular pastry on a buttered baking sheet. Brush it lightly with butter. Shape more pastries with remaining filo sheets and filling. (Pastries can be shaped 1 day ahead and refrigerated on baking sheets or on plates. Cover them tightly with cling film.)

Preheat oven to 180°C (350°F) mark 4. Brush pastries again lightly with melted butter and sprinkle with sesame seeds. Bake for 20–25 minutes or until golden brown. Serve warm (not hot) or at room temperature.

CHEESE-WALNUT CHALLAH

Cheese-flavoured challah is not a traditional recipe, but challah is delicious prepared in this manner and is especially appropriate to make for Shavuot, the holiday of dairy specialities. The cheese is kneaded into the dough, which is then sprinkled with walnuts, rolled up like a Swiss roll, and baked in a loaf tin.

MAKES 1 MEDIUM LOAF

Challah dough (page 289), made with 5 ml (1 tsp) sugar	*about 75 g (3 oz) walnut pieces, coarsely chopped*
about 150 g (5 oz) Swiss cheese, grated	*1 large egg, size 1 or 2, beaten with a pinch of salt, for glaze*

When making dough, sprinkle 5 ml (1 tsp) sugar over yeast mixture. Prepare dough by any method and leave to rise twice.

Grease a 23 × 13-cm (9 × 5-inch) loaf tin. After dough has risen

71

for second time, sprinkle about half the cheese over a 13-cm (5-inch) square area on work surface. Put dough on top and pat it out over cheese. Sprinkle remaining cheese over dough. Knead in lightly.

Pat dough out into a 23-cm (9-inch) square. Sprinkle evenly with walnuts and press them into dough. Roll up tightly in a cylinder. Put in prepared loaf tin. Cover with a warm, slightly damp cloth and leave to rise until nearly doubled in size, about 1 hour. Preheat oven to 190°C (375°F) mark 5.

Brush risen loaf gently with beaten egg. Bake until top and bottom of bread are firm and bread sounds hollow when tapped on bottom, about 45 minutes.

Run a thin-bladed flexible knife carefully around bread. Turn out of tin and cool on a wire rack.

CLASSIC CHEESE BLINTZES WITH STRAWBERRY SAUCE

Blintzes can be served as a main course, a dessert or a breakfast treat. For dessert, use the larger quantity of sugar in the filling and add 60–75 ml (4–5 tbsp) raisins if desired. The fresh Strawberry Sauce is a relatively modern partner for the blintzes, but you can instead serve the customary accompaniments of fruit preserves or jam, or a mixture of 15 ml (1 tbsp) sugar and 2.5 ml (½ tsp) cinnamon. For a main course, omit the sweet accompaniments and serve the blintzes only with soured cream or natural yogurt. A mixture of cheeses is best for filling blintzes.

MAKES 12 TO 14 BLINTZES;
4 TO 6 MAIN-COURSE SERVINGS

Basic Blintzes, 23 cm
  (9 inches) in diameter (page 207)

FILLING

*about 425 g (15 oz) curd
  cheese, drained*
*45 ml (3 tbsp) cream cheese,
  softened*
*75 ml (5 tbsp) rich cottage
  cheese or cottage cheese*

2 large egg yolks, size 1 or 2
*45–60 ml (3–4 tbsp) sugar or
  to taste*
*1.25–2.5 ml (¼–½ tsp)
  ground cinnamon or to taste*

40–50 g (1½–2 oz) butter   Strawberry Sauce (see below,
  for frying or baking blintzes   optional)
soured cream or natural
  yogurt, for serving

Prepare blintzes, stack them, and keep them warm, covered with a tea towel.

Mash cheeses. Beat them with egg yolks, sugar and cinnamon until mixture is smooth and thoroughly blended.

Spoon 37.5–45 ml (2½–3 tbsp) filling onto brown side of each blintz near one edge. Fold over edges of blintz to right and left of filling so that each covers about half the filling; roll up, beginning at edge with filling. (Blintzes can be filled 1 day ahead and refrigerated, covered.)

Blintzes can be baked or fried. To bake them, preheat oven to 220°C (425°F) mark 7. Arrange blintzes in one layer in a shallow buttered baking dish. Dot each blintze with 2 small pieces of butter. Bake for about 15 minutes, or until heated and lightly browned.

To fry blintzes, heat butter in a frying pan. Add blintzes open end down. Fry over low heat for 3–5 minutes on each side; be careful not to let them burn.

Serve blintzes hot, with soured cream and Strawberry Sauce.

STRAWBERRY SAUCE

This bright red, fresh-tasting sauce is great with blintzes or cheesecake. If you wish to make it for Passover, sweeten the berries with 15–30 ml (1–2 tbsp) caster instead of icing sugar.

MAKES 4 TO 6 SERVINGS

275 g (10 oz) fresh or frozen   few drops fresh lemon juice
  strawberries, thawed   (optional)
45 ml (3 tbsp) icing sugar,
  sifted, or more to taste

Purée the strawberries in a food processor or blender until very smooth. Whisk in icing sugar, taste and add more sugar if desired. Add lemon juice. Refrigerate until ready to use. (Sauce can be kept, covered, for 2 days in refrigerator.)

CREAMY CHEESECAKE

This is my favourite cheesecake. I love its pure flavour of sweetened cheese enhanced only with a hint of lemon and vanilla, as well as its creamy texture, which is lighter than most cream cheese cakes. For my taste, the soured cream topping is all the embellishment it needs. If you prefer a colourful dessert, serve it with Strawberry Sauce (page 73) or with fresh strawberries.

MAKES 8 TO 10 SERVINGS

PECAN AND CRUMB CRUST

150 g (5 oz) digestive biscuits   *45 ml (3 tbsp) sugar*
25 g (1 oz) pecan halves   *75 g (3 oz) unsalted butter, melted*

CHEESE FILLING

450 g (1 lb) cream cheese, cut into pieces and softened   *grated rind of 1 large lemon*
120 ml (4 fl oz) soured cream   *1 vanilla pod, split lengthways,*
175 g (6 oz) sugar   *or 5 ml (1 tsp) vanilla*
3 large eggs, size 1 or 2   *essence*

SOURED CREAM TOPPING

350 ml (12 fl oz) soured cream   *45 ml (3 tbsp) sugar*
      5 ml (1 tsp) vanilla essence

Prepare the crust. Preheat oven to 180°C (350°F) mark 4. Process digestive biscuits in a food processor to fine crumbs, or put them in a bag and crush them with a rolling pin. Chop pecan halves, then mix with crumbs and add sugar. Add melted butter and mix well. Lightly butter a 23-cm (9-inch) spring clip tin. Press pecan mixture in an even layer on bottom and about 2.5 cm (1 inch) up sides of tin. Bake for 10 minutes, then leave to cool completely.

For the filling, beat cream cheese with soured cream at low speed until very smooth. Gradually beat in sugar, then beat in eggs, one by one. Beat in lemon rind. If using a vanilla pod, scrape its seeds with the point of a knife into cheese mixture; or stir in vanilla essence. Carefully pour filling into cooled crust and bake for about 45 minutes or until firm in centre. Remove from oven and cool for 15 minutes. Raise oven temperature to 220°C (425°F) mark 7.

For the topping, mix soured cream, sugar and vanilla. Carefully spread topping on cake in an even layer, without letting it drip over crust. Return cake to oven and bake for 7 minutes.

Remove cake from oven and cool to room temperature. Refrigerate for at least 2 hours before serving. (Cake can be kept 3 days in refrigerator.) Remove sides of tin just before serving.

CHEESECAKE WITH PINE NUTS AND ORANGE

Pine nuts lend an exotic note to the delightful, light-textured streusel topping of this cheesecake and provide an intriguing contrast to the smooth, rich, orange-scented cheese filling. I got the idea for this cake from a course given by WIZO, the Women's International Zionist Organization, in Tel Aviv. During the years I lived in Israel I looked forward eagerly to these classes, which took place on a regular basis in many communities. I found them especially exciting because of the chance to exchange culinary tips with other women.

MAKES 10 SERVINGS

ORANGE-SCENTED PASTRY
275 g (10 oz) plain flour
100 g (4 oz) sugar
pinch of salt
225 g (8 oz) cold unsalted
  butter, cut into small pieces

10 ml (2 tsp) grated orange
  rind
1 large egg, size 1 or 2,
  beaten

CHEESE FILLING
450 g (1 lb) cottage cheese
450 g (1 lb) cream cheese,
  softened
175 g (6 oz) sugar
2 large eggs, size 1 or 2

2 large egg yolks, size 1 or 2
120 ml (4 fl oz) double cream
25 ml (5 tsp) grated orange
  rind

40 g (1½ oz) pine nuts

Lightly butter a 23-cm (9-inch) spring clip tin. For the pastry, combine flour, sugar and salt in food processor. Process briefly to blend, then scatter butter pieces over mixture. Mix using on/off turns until mixture resembles coarse breadcrumbs. Sprinkle with grated rind and pour egg evenly over mixture in processor. Process with on/off turns, scraping down occasionally, until dough forms sticky crumbs; do not allow them to come together in a ball.

Sprinkle two-thirds of crumbs evenly in tin. Put rest of crumbs in a bowl in freezer. With floured hands press crumbs in tin together and pat them 5 cm (2 inches) up side of tin. Chill tin in freezer while preparing filling. Preheat oven to 180°C (350°F) mark 4.

For cheese filling, push cottage cheese through a strainer. Beat cream cheese with sugar until smooth. Add eggs, one by one, and beat after each addition, then beat in yolks. Stir in cottage cheese, cream and orange rind.

Pour filling into lined tin. Crumble remaining pastry crumb mixture between your fingers and sprinkle on top of filling. Sprinkle pine nuts over crumbs and pat very gently so topping adheres to filling.

Set spring clip tin on a baking sheet. Bake for 1¼ hours or until set. If topping is not brown enough, grill for about 30 seconds, checking every few seconds, until golden brown. Cool completely. Refrigerate for at least 2 hours before serving. (Cake can be kept for 3 days in refrigerator.) Serve cold.

ROSH HASHANAH
The Jewish New Year

The timing of the Jewish holidays is determined by the traditional Jewish calendar, which is lunar. For this reason the holidays occur on different dates of the common (solar) calendar each year, although they are always in the same season. The first month of the Jewish calendar, Tishrei, is in September or October, and the first two days of this month are the Jewish New Year, Rosh Hashanah.

In modern days many of the time-honoured culinary traditions gain new value. Food customs for the Jewish New Year are a good example. They somehow are in accord with the latest nutritional guidelines.

Rosh Hashanah menus often begin with fish, an ancient symbol of fertility and abundance. In some families, the fish is served with its head on, to stand for 'the head of the year', the literal meaning of the words *Rosh Hashanah*. Today fish is the appetizer of choice for an additional reason – its lean flesh is considered one of the most healthy of foods.

The date of Rosh Hashanah coincides with the beginning of the agricultural year, according to ancient tradition in the Middle East. As tokens of the wish for a plentiful harvest, vegetables and fruits play an important role on the Jewish New Year table. Part of the ritual of the holiday teaches appreciation of the season's bounty, since it involves saying a blessing over a fruit that is tasted for the first time in the year. A first sampling of the new produce is a custom in all ethnic groups, and many people precede dinner with a taste of pomegranate, dates and figs. Among Jews from Iraq, pomegranate juice is a favourite holiday drink. Today, of course, an abundance of produce on the menu also signifies a concern for healthy eating.

The best-known food custom of Rosh Hashanah seems to have been developed with children in mind. On this holiday, one is

supposed to eat sweet foods! The wish for a sweet year is taken literally in menu planning, and seems to have inspired the tone of the
dinner. Honey appears in many dishes. In biblical times honey was
the sweetener. It also represented richness and good living, as in the
Bible's many romantic references to Israel as 'the land of milk and
honey'. Today honey-sweetened desserts are considered among the
most nutritious of sweets.

Jews throughout the world begin the holiday meal with the traditional apples dipped in honey (and, in some North African families,
dipped in toasted sesame seeds as well). Fruit appears in unexpected
places – cinnamon-scented quince are featured as an appetizer in
Moroccan dinners, and fruits and vegetables are cooked together in a
special Ashkenazic stew called *tzimmes*, which includes carrots,
prunes and sometimes sweet potatoes. Tzimmes can be a vegetable
side dish or can include beef and become a colourful main course.

Sweet vegetables, especially carrots, winter squash or pumpkin,
and sweet potatoes, are favourites on Rosh Hashanah menus. Their
sweetness is often accentuated in the kitchen. For example, carrots
are glazed with honey in Romanian and Hungarian Jewish cuisine,
while winter squash or pumpkin is cooked with sugar and cinnamon
in certain Sephardic communities. Other Sephardim prepare these
vegetables as savoury pancakes.

The Prophet Nehemiah is said to have introduced to the ancient
Israelites the Persian custom of eating something sweet to celebrate
the new year. So important is this tradition that it also works in the
other direction: many people avoid sour ingredients such as vinegar.

Many foods served at the traditional Jewish New Year feast have a
special meaning. Carrots, besides being sweet, stand for prosperity
because carrot slices resemble gold coins. They provide a lively decoration for the Ashkenazic gefilte fish, which is popular at many holiday meals. Sephardim serve a spinach omelette to illustrate a 'green'
year with plenty of produce, and accompany the main dish with rice,
a symbol of abundance.

Challah, or Jewish egg bread, is made differently for Rosh
Hashanah. Raisins and sometimes honey are added, so that the challah is slightly sweeter than usual. Its shape is round to represent a full
year – either smooth and dome shaped or plaited to form a crown.

Other ideal Rosh Hashanah dishes:

Zesty Pepper-Tomato Salad (page 32)

Couscous with Lamb and Seven Vegetables (page 249)

Beef Stew with Winter Squash and Raisins (page 101)

Honey-Glazed Carrots (page 121)

Courgettes with Tomatoes and Dill (page 263)

Noodle Kugel with Colourful Vegetables (page 104)

Honey-Glazed Biscuits with Walnuts (Tayglach) (page 316)

AN ASHKENAZIC ROSH HASHANAH

For a traditional holiday menu that requires practically no last-minute work, start with apple wedges and slices of challah, and provide small bowls of honey for dipping. Serve gefilte fish as a first course, as well as a green bean salad garnished with pecans, and follow these with beef tzimmes with sweet potatoes and carrots for the main course. Finish with a cinnamon-scented honey cake or an apple cake with honey frosting for dessert, and have a sweet New Year!

ASHKENAZIC MENU FOR ROSH HASHANAH

Apples and Honey

Round Holiday Challah with Raisins

**Gefilte Fish (page 24),
or Chicken Soup with Kreplach**

Green Bean Salad with Pecans

Beef and Sweet Potato Tzimmes

**Light Honey Cake with Cinnamon and Walnuts,
or Apple Cake with Honey Frosting**

ROUND HOLIDAY CHALLAH WITH RAISINS

Plaited challahs are most often made for Sabbath, while round challahs, often sweetened with honey, are the custom for Rosh Hashanah. They can be purchased at Jewish bakeries, but are also fun to make at home. Sometimes they contain raisins, as in this loaf. If some raisins start to come out of the dough when you are shaping these loaves, pinch the dough around them; otherwise the exposed raisins will burn in the oven.

This recipe gives two alternatives for shaping the challah: as a round dome or as a round plait.

MAKES 2 SMALL LOAVES: 1 ROUND AND 1 PLAIT, OR 2 OF EITHER ONE

450 g (1 lb) plain flour
120 ml (4 fl oz) plus 45 ml (3 tbsp) lukewarm water
25 ml (5 tsp) dried yeast
2.5 ml (½ tsp) sugar
45 ml (3 tbsp) honey
75 ml (5 tbsp) vegetable oil
2 large eggs, size 1 or 2
10 ml (2 tsp) salt

75 g (3 oz) raisins, rinsed, drained and dried on paper towels
1 large egg, size 1 or 2, beaten with a pinch of salt, for glaze
10 ml (2 tsp) sesame seeds (optional)

Sift 425 g (15 oz) flour into a large bowl. Make a large well in the centre and pour in 120 ml (4 fl oz) lukewarm water. Sprinkle yeast on top and add sugar. Leave for 10 minutes until yeast is foamy. Whisk honey with remaining 45 ml (3 tbsp) water. Add honey mixture, oil, eggs and salt to the well. Mix in flour, first with a spoon and then by hand, until ingredients come together to a dough.

Knead dough vigorously on a work surface, gradually adding remaining 60 ml (4 tbsp) flour, until dough is very smooth, fairly stiff, and no longer sticky, about 12 minutes. Transfer to a clean oiled bowl, cover with a damp cloth and leave to rise in a warm place for 1–1¼ hours or until nearly doubled in volume.

Remove dough again to a lightly floured surface and knead lightly. Return to bowl, cover and leave to rise for 30–45 minutes or until nearly doubled again.

Pat dough to approximately a 23-cm (9-inch) square on a work surface. Sprinkle evenly with raisins. Roll up tightly from one end to other, as in making a Swiss roll; lightly flour surface if dough begins to stick.

Cut roll of dough in 2 equal parts. To form a smooth round loaf, roll one part backwards and forwards on a working surface, pressing with your palms, to form a smooth rope about 60 cm (2 feet) long. Twist dough around one end in a spiral; pull other end upwards over spiral and press it on centre of loaf. Press whole loaf firmly with your hands to adhere end to top and to give loaf an even dome shape. Repeat for second loaf, or follow next paragraph.

To form a plaited round loaf, divide remaining dough in 3 equal parts. Roll each backwards and forwards on a work surface, pressing with your palms, to form a smooth rope about 30 cm (12 inches) long and tapered slightly at ends. Put ropes side by side, with one set of ends close to you. Join ends far from you; cover end of rope on your right side with end of centre rope, then end of left rope. Press to join. To plait, bring outer ropes alternately over centre one; plait tightly, pinch ends to join ropes. Bring ends of plait together, curving plait into a circle and pinch ends together.

Oil 2 baking sheets. Set loaves carefully on them. Cover with a damp cloth and leave to rise for about 45 minutes or until nearly doubled in volume.

Preheat oven to 180°C (350°F) mark 4. Brush each challah with beaten egg. Sprinkle plaited loaf with sesame seeds. Bake for about 20 minutes or until beginning to brown. Reduce oven temperature to 160°C (325°F) mark 3 and bake for about 25 more minutes or until bottom of bread sounds hollow when tapped. Cool on a wire rack.

CHICKEN SOUP WITH KREPLACH

Of Russian and Polish origin, kreplach are most often served in soup. Owing to their shape, they are sometimes called 'Jewish tortellini', although I have seen them shaped as half-moons, triangles or squares. Making kreplach used to be a lot of work, but today with the help of a food processor, the dough can be made in a few minutes.

Cooked chicken or meat mixed with sautéed onions is the favourite filling, but others include cheese and potato, chicken liver, potato and fried onion, and kasha (buckwheat). There are even sweet kreplach, with fillings of berries or stoned cherries stewed with sugar or honey, thickened lightly with cornflour, and served with soured cream or fruit.

The most popular way to enjoy chicken or meat kreplach is in clear chicken soup. Some members of my family prefer their kreplach cooked directly in the soup, since this gives them more flavour, while others like them cooked in water so the starch does not cloud the soup. Kreplach are also good served in other ways: drizzled with oil or melted margarine and heated briefly in the oven, tossed with herb-flavoured tomato sauce, or added to a pan of fried onions and sautéed lightly.

MAKES ABOUT 50 KREPLACH; 10 SERVINGS

NOODLE DOUGH

3 large eggs, size 1 or 2
3.75 ml (¾ tsp) salt

215 g (7½ oz) plain flour

CHICKEN FILLING

30 ml (2 tbsp) vegetable oil, non-dairy margarine or chicken fat
1 medium onion, finely chopped
225 g (8 oz) boneless, skinless chicken thighs or breasts

salt and pepper to taste
1 large egg, size 1 or 2, beaten
30 ml (2 tbsp) chopped fresh parsley

Chicken Soup, for serving (page 345)

Make the dough: in a food processor combine eggs, salt and 175 g (6 oz) flour. Process until dough begins to form a ball. Add remaining flour 15 ml (1 tbsp) at a time and process for a few seconds after each addition. Process for 30 seconds so dough forms ball; if dough is not very smooth, knead for a few seconds by hand on a lightly floured surface. Place dough on a plate, cover with an overturned bowl and leave for 30 minutes at room temperature. (Dough can be refrigerated, covered, for 1 day.)

Make the filling: heat oil in a small frying pan, add onion and sauté until soft and just beginning to brown, about 10 minutes. Add chicken and sprinkle with salt and pepper. Cover and cook over low heat for about 7 minutes. Turn over, cover and cook for about 5 more minutes or until just tender. Be careful not to let onion burn. Remove chicken and leave to cool. Cut chicken into pieces and grind in food processor until fine. Add egg and purée again until fine. Transfer to a mixing bowl. Mix in sautéed onion and parsley. Taste for seasoning; mixture should be highly seasoned. Leave to cool.

Set rollers of a pasta machine to widest setting. Cut dough in 2 or 3 pieces. Work with 1 piece at a time and keep others covered. Flour the piece of dough, pat to flatten it slightly and put it through rollers. Fold in 2 or 3 pieces and put it through again, still at widest setting. Put it through 6 or 7 times, or until very smooth.

Set rollers at next setting. Lightly flour the dough and put it through without folding. Continue putting dough through machine, once at each setting, until you reach the next-to-finest setting; if dough isn't smooth after putting it through a certain setting, put it through again.

Place 2.5-ml (½-tsp) mounds of filling about 4 cm (1½ inches) apart on sheet of dough, then cut dough in approximately 6-cm (2½-inch) squares. Brush 2 adjacent sides of each square lightly with water; fold dough over filling into a triangle, pressing moistened sides to unmoistened sides; and press edges firmly to seal. (If desired, join 2 edges to form a ring shape.) If necessary dampen edges with a little water so they are easier to join. Lay each triangle on a floured sheet of greaseproof paper as it is completed. Repeat rolling and shaping with remaining dough and filling, using 1 piece of dough at a time. (Kreplach can be made ahead to this point, put in one layer on a floured paper or tray, covered, and kept 1 day in refrigerator.)

To cook kreplach, add half of them to a large pan of boiling, salted water. Bring to the boil, reduce heat so water simmers, cover and cook over low heat for 15 minutes. Remove kreplach with a slotted spoon and drain in a colander. Repeat with second batch. (Cooked kreplach can be kept for 2 days in refrigerator. They can also be frozen.)

To serve, simmer kreplach in hot chicken soup or meat soup to heat through for 10–15 minutes. Serve in soup, with a few carrot slices and parsley.

GREEN BEAN SALAD
WITH PECANS

This simple salad makes a beautiful platter and can be served buffet style as a first course or side dish. The dressing has no lemon juice or vinegar, since some communities avoid sour ingredients for Rosh Hashanah; besides, acid ingredients turn the colour of the green beans from bright green to grey. For other occasions, add 30 ml (2 tbsp) lemon juice to the dressing if you wish, and spoon it over the beans at the last moment.

MAKES 8 SERVINGS

50 g (2 oz) pecans	salt and pepper
120 ml (4 fl oz) vegetable or olive oil	4 hard-boiled large eggs, size 1 or 2
30–45 ml (2–3 tbsp) finely chopped spring onions	1.4 kg (3 lb) green beans, ends removed

Preheat oven to 180°C (350°F) mark 4. Toast pecans in a baking dish in oven, shaking pan occasionally, until nuts are aromatic and very lightly browned, about 5 minutes. Transfer to a plate and cool. Chop fine but not to a powder.

Mix oil with spring onions, salt and pepper to taste. Halve hard-boiled eggs and remove yolks. Chop whites and yolks separately.

Boil beans in a large pan of boiling salted water until crisp-tender, about 5 minutes. Rinse under cold water until cool and drain thoroughly. Gently pat dry.

Transfer beans to a large round platter, with all beans pointing to centre. Spoon oil mixture evenly over beans.

Sprinkle nuts over centre, covering partly where ends of beans meet. Sprinkle chopped egg yolks in a circle around nuts. Then sprinkle chopped egg whites in a circle around yolks. Allow ends of green beans to show. Serve at room temperature.

BEEF AND SWEET POTATO TZIMMES

Tzimmes is a dish from eastern Europe that usually includes sweet vegetables, dried fruit or a mixture of both. Sometimes it is simply a sweetened vegetable stew – for example, of carrots simmered with honey. Or it can be a more elaborate casserole including beef, sweet potatoes, carrots and prunes as in this main-course version, which is similar to the tzimmes I grew up with.

MAKES 4 TO 6 SERVINGS

15 ml (1 tbsp) vegetable oil or chicken fat	2 large potatoes
	2 yams or sweet potatoes
900 g (2 lb) chuck or stewing steak, cut into 4-cm (1½-inch) cubes	75–100 g (3–4 oz) honey
	2.5 ml (½ tsp) ground cinnamon
2 large onions, chopped	pinch of pepper
5 large carrots, peeled and cut into 2.5-cm (1-inch) chunks	225 g (8 oz) stoned prunes
2.5 ml (½ tsp) salt	15 ml (1 tbsp) plain flour (optional)
750 ml–1 litre (1¼–1¾ pints) water	15 ml (1 tbsp) chopped fresh parsley (optional)

Heat oil in a heavy casserole over medium heat. Add meat and brown well on all sides; if necessary brown meat in batches to avoid crowding. Remove meat from pan and add onions and sauté until browned. Return meat to pan and add carrots, salt and enough water to just cover. Bring to boil, skimming occasionally, then cover and simmer over low heat, skimming once or twice, for 1 hour.

Peel both types of potatoes and cut in large dice. After meat and carrots have cooked for 1 hour, add potatoes, sweet potatoes, honey, cinnamon and pepper to pan and mix gently. Push vegetables into liquid and bring to the boil. Partly cover and simmer for 30 minutes. Meanwhile, soak prunes in enough hot water to cover for about 30 minutes.

Gently stir stew once. Remove prunes from their liquid, reserving liquid if later thickening the stew, and add prunes to pan. Uncover and simmer for 30 minutes longer or until meat is very tender. Shake pan occasionally to prevent sticking but avoid stirring.

The stew should be moist but not soupy. If allowed to stand for 1 hour or more before being served, it will absorb enough of the excess liquid. If too much liquid remains, cook uncovered in a 180°C (350°F) mark 4 oven for 15–30 minutes. Alternatively, stir flour with 30 ml (2 tbsp) prune liquid in a bowl, gradually stir in about 250 ml (8 fl oz) of meat cooking liquid and return mixture to pan; simmer for about 5 minutes. (Stew can be made 1 day ahead and reheated gently in a covered pan over low heat or in a 150°C (300°F) mark 2 oven.) Serve from a deep serving dish. Sprinkle with parsley if desired.

LIGHT HONEY CAKE WITH CINNAMON AND WALNUTS

Honey cake usually contains more than one flavouring and in fact the Alsatian version is called *pain d'épices*, or 'spice bread'. This honey cake has less oil and sugar than many versions and therefore fewer calories, but the coffee, cinnamon and nuts, as well as the honey, give it plenty of flavour.

MAKES 8 TO 10 SERVINGS

7.5 ml (1½ tsp) instant coffee granules	1.25 ml (¼ tsp) ground ginger
	small pinch of ground cloves
90 ml (6 tbsp) hot water	2 large eggs, size 1 or 2
175 g (6 oz) plain flour	100 g (4 oz) sugar
5 ml (1 tsp) baking powder	175 g (6 oz) honey
2.5 ml (½ tsp) bicarbonate of soda	75 ml (5 tbsp) vegetable oil
	50 g (2 oz) walnuts, coarsely chopped
2.5 ml (½ tsp) ground cinnamon	

Preheat oven to 160°C (325°F) mark 3. Lightly grease a 20 × 10-cm (8 × 4-inch) loaf tin, line it with non-stick paper or greaseproof paper, and grease the paper.

In a cup, dissolve the instant coffee in the hot water. Leave to cool. Sift flour with baking powder, bicarbonate of soda, cinnamon, ginger and cloves.

Beat eggs lightly. Add sugar and honey and beat until mixture is very smooth and light in colour. Gradually add oil and beat until blended. Stir in flour mixture alternately in 2 batches with coffee. Stir in walnuts.

Pour mixture into prepared tin and bake for 50–55 minutes or until a fine skewer inserted in cake comes out clean. Cool in tin for about 15 minutes. Turn out onto wire rack and carefully peel off paper. Wrap in foil when completely cool. (If tightly wrapped, cake keeps for 1 week at room temperature.) Serve in thin slices.

APPLE CAKE WITH HONEY FROSTING

I developed this recipe with the Rosh Hashanah apple and honey theme in mind. The easy-to-make cake is moist and delicious on its own, but the honey frosting turns it into a lavish holiday dessert. The cake and frosting can be made with butter for meatless meals.

MAKES 12 SERVINGS

1 kg (2¼ lb) sweet apples, such as Golden Delicious, peeled, halved, cored and finely diced	3 large eggs, size 1 or 2
	350 g (12 oz) plain flour
	12.5 ml (2½ tsp) baking powder
275 g (10 oz) sugar	10 ml (2 tsp) finely grated orange rind
250 g (9 oz) unsalted non-dairy margarine or butter, softened	100 g (4 oz) walnuts, coarsely chopped
75 g (3 oz) honey	

HONEY FROSTING (OPTIONAL)

2 large eggs, size 1 or 2, at room temperature	50 g (2 oz) walnuts, coarsely chopped, for decoration
175 g (6 oz) honey	
225 g (8 oz) unsalted non-dairy margarine or butter, slightly softened but still cool	

Preheat oven to 180°C (350°F) mark 4. Lightly grease a 33 × 23-cm (13 × 9-inch) cake tin with 5-cm (2-inch) sides. Line base and sides of tin with a sheet of foil and grease foil.

87

Thoroughly mix apples and 100 g (4 oz) sugar. Leave to stand while preparing cake mixture.

Beat margarine until smooth. Add remaining 175 g (6 oz) sugar and beat until fluffy. Beat in honey, then add eggs one by one, beating well after each addition. Sift flour with baking powder and stir into egg mixture. Stir in orange rind. Add apple mixture, which will be syrupy, and nuts.

Spread mixture in prepared cake tin and smooth top. Bake for 45 minutes or until cake tests done with a fine skewer. Cool in tin on a wire rack for about 20 minutes or until just warm. Turn out onto a rack. Cool to room temperature.

To make frosting, beat eggs in a large bowl until smooth and fluffy. Bring honey to the boil in a small saucepan, then gradually pour honey onto eggs, whisking constantly. Whisk at high speed of mixer until completely cool and thick, about 5 minutes.

Cream margarine in a large bowl until smooth and fluffy. Beat in honey mixture gradually until thoroughly mixed.

Spread frosting over top and sides of cake. Sprinkle top with chopped walnuts. Refrigerate for about 2 hours before serving. Serve cool or at room temperature.

A NOTE ABOUT YOM KIPPUR

Ten days after Rosh Hashanah is the most solemn holiday of the Jewish calendar, Yom Kippur. This is a day of fasting, but there are food customs for before and after the fast. The dinner prior to the fast takes place in the evening before Yom Kippur day. It is a copious dinner that is less seasoned than usual, so that people won't become too thirsty during the fast. Generally chicken is the main course. Often it is a whole poached chicken that also produces a rich chicken soup. Some Ashkenazic families serve the soup with kreplach.

Following the fast, a fairly light meal is usually prepared. What to serve depends on family traditions. Some families have a dairy supper, such as bagels with lox and cream cheese, or other foods that require little preparation. When I was growing up, a favourite treat in our family for breaking the fast was a slice of Soured Cream Coffee Cake with Walnuts (page 305).

AN ECLECTIC MEAL FOR ROSH HASHANAH

This menu for the Jewish New Year is composed of dishes from a variety of Jewish groups and fits the spirit of a traditional and healthy Rosh Hashanah dinner. Italian-style fish in a tomato and garlic sauce is a zesty Sephardic speciality and will come as a surprise to those who are used to thinking that gefilte fish is the only Jewish way of preparing fish. Roast chicken stuffed with rice and fruit is a favourite in both Israel and America, and is accompanied here by Sephardic pumpkin pancakes. The honey cake comes to us from eastern Europe, while the sweet and spicy quince compote with cinnamon is a North African Jewish treat for beginning the holiday as an appetizer or for a dessert.

ECLECTIC ROSH HASHANAH MENU

Apples and Honey

Round Holiday Challah with Raisins (page 80)

Italian-Style Fish in Tomato-Garlic Sauce

Roast Chicken with Rice and Fruit Stuffing

Sephardic Pumpkin Pancakes

Hazelnut Honey Cake (Lekach),
or
Chocolate-Almond
Cake with Chocolate-Honey Frosting

Quince Compote with Cinnamon

ITALIAN-STYLE FISH IN TOMATO-GARLIC SAUCE

For a delicious cold fish appetizer of pure, fresh flavours, try this speciality of the Jews of Italy. The fish is cooked directly in an easy-to-make, quick-cooking tomato sauce, for which a food processor comes in very handy. I usually chop the parsley first in the processor, then the garlic, and finally the onion. Then I wipe the processor bowl and purée the tomatoes. The fish is also very good served hot as a main course, accompanied by rice or pasta.

MAKES 4 SERVINGS

60 ml (4 tbsp) olive oil
40 g (1½ oz) onion, finely
  chopped
3 medium garlic cloves, finely
  chopped
700 g (1½ lb) ripe tomatoes,
  peeled, seeded and puréed;
  or 1 × 794-g (28-oz) and
  1 × 397-g (14-oz) can plum
  tomatoes, drained and
  puréed

2.5 ml (½ tsp) dried leaf
  oregano
salt and pepper
700–800 g (1½–1¾ lb) fish
  fillets, such as halibut,
  about 2.5 cm (1 inch) thick
45 ml (3 tbsp) chopped fresh
  parsley, preferably flat-leaf

In a large sauté pan or frying pan, heat 45 ml (3 tbsp) oil with onion and sauté over medium-low heat for 5–6 minutes or until onion begins to turn golden. Add garlic and sauté for 30 seconds. Add tomatoes, oregano, salt and pepper and cook over medium-high heat, stirring often, for about 8–10 minutes or until thick. (Sauce can be kept, covered, for 1 day in refrigerator. Reheat in sauté pan before continuing.)

Add fish in one layer to hot sauce and sprinkle with 15 ml (1 tbsp) oil, salt and pepper. Cover and cook over medium-low heat, spooning sauce over fish from time to time, for about 10 minutes or until thickest part of fish has changed colour inside when checked with a sharp knife. Taste sauce and adjust seasoning. Stir parsley gently into sauce. Serve fish hot or cold.

ROAST CHICKEN WITH RICE AND FRUIT STUFFING

The light fruity stuffing fits the Rosh Hashanah theme and provides a delicate hint of sweetness. It's also delicious with turkey or goose; double it for a 4.5–5.5-kg (10–12-lb) turkey or multiply it by 1½ for an 3.6–4-kg (8–9-lb) goose.

MAKES 4 SERVINGS

50 g (2 oz) pecan halves (optional)	salt and pepper
60 ml (4 tbsp) vegetable oil	1 small apple
1 small onion, finely chopped	75 g (3 oz) raisins
50 g (2 oz) celery, chopped	1.25 ml (¼ tsp) ground cinnamon
200 g (7 oz) long-grain rice	5 ml (1 tsp) finely grated orange rind
350 ml (12 fl oz) hot chicken soup or water	1.6–1.8-kg (3½–4-lb) roasting chicken
120 ml (4 fl oz) orange juice	

Preheat oven to 200°C (400°F) mark 6. If using pecans, toast lightly in oven for 5 minutes. Cool and cut in half lengthways.

Heat 45 ml (3 tbsp) oil in a deep frying pan or sauté pan, add onion and celery, and cook over low heat for about 5 minutes or until tender. Add rice and sauté over medium heat for about 2 minutes. Add hot soup, orange juice, salt and pepper and bring to the boil. Cover and cook over low heat for 10 minutes. Meanwhile, peel, halve and core apple and cut it into small dice. Add raisins and apple to rice and stir very lightly with a fork. Cover and cook for 5 more minutes or until rice is nearly tender. Stir in cinnamon, orange rind and pecans and taste for seasoning. Leave to cool.

Sprinkle chicken with salt and pepper on all sides. Spoon enough stuffing into chicken to fill it, packing it lightly; reserve extra stuffing at room temperature. Set chicken in a roasting tin and roast for about 1 hour; when a skewer or trussing needle is inserted into thickest part of leg, juices should come out clear. If juices are pink, roast for a few more minutes. Leave to stand for 5–10 minutes before serving.

Heat remaining 15 ml (1 tbsp) oil in a frying or sauté pan and add remaining stuffing. Cook for 3 minutes over low heat until very hot.

Serve chicken and its stuffing on a platter, and remaining rice mixture in a side dish or next to chicken.

SEPHARDIC PUMPKIN PANCAKES

These delicately flavoured pancakes, made with pumpkin, make a colourful addition to festive menus and are ideal for Rosh Hashanah, Succot or Hanukkah.

MAKES 22 TO 24 SMALL PANCAKES; 4 TO 6 SERVINGS

800–900 g (1¾–2 lb) *pumpkin*	*1.25 ml (¼ tsp) sugar*
	1.25 ml (¼ tsp) salt
50 g (2 oz) plus 15 ml *(1 tbsp) plain flour*	*pepper to taste*
	about 75 ml (5 tbsp) vegetable
2 large eggs, size 1 or 2	*oil, for frying*

Cut pumpkin into 6 or 8 pieces. Add to a large saucepan with enough boiling salted water to cover it. Bring to the boil, cover and simmer over low heat for 15 minutes or until tender. Drain thoroughly and cut off peel. Cut in pieces and mash with a fork. Press gently in a strainer to remove excess liquid. Transfer to a bowl.

In a medium bowl mix flour, eggs, sugar, salt and pepper to a very thick batter. Add to mashed pumpkin and mix very well. Taste for seasoning.

Heat 60 ml (4 tbsp) oil in a heavy frying pan over medium heat. Fry pumpkin mixture in tablespoons, flattening each after adding it, for about 2 minutes or until golden brown on each side. Turn carefully using 2 slotted spatulas. Transfer to paper towels to drain. Continue making pancakes, adding more oil to pan if necessary. Serve hot or at room temperature.

HAZELNUT HONEY CAKE (LEKACH)

Known in Yiddish as *lekach*, honey cake is very easy to prepare and is the traditional treat served by Jews of eastern European extraction on the first night of Rosh Hashanah and during Succot two weeks later. This version is moist, delicately enhanced with fresh lemon rind and sweet spices, and studded with nuts. Another great advantage of honey cake is its keeping qualities; if wrapped in foil, it will stay fresh-tasting for two weeks. In fact, it is best to make this cake one or two days ahead so its flavour matures.

MAKES 9 TO 12 SERVINGS

250 g (9 oz) plain flour	175 g (6 oz) dark brown
11.25 ml (2¼ tsp) baking	sugar
powder	350 g (12 oz) honey
3.75 ml (¾ tsp) bicarbonate of	175 ml (6 fl oz) vegetable oil
soda	7.5 ml (1½ tsp) grated lemon
3.75 ml (¾ tsp) ground	rind
cinnamon	120 ml (4 fl oz) unsweetened
2.5 ml (½ tsp) ground ginger	apple purée
pinch of cloves	75 g (3 oz) hazelnuts,
3 large eggs, size 1 or 2	chopped

Preheat oven to 180°C (350°F) mark 4. Lightly grease a 23-cm (9-inch) square tin, line it with non-stick paper or greaseproof paper, and grease the paper. Sift the flour with the baking powder, bicarbonate of soda, cinnamon, ginger and cloves.

Beat the eggs lightly. Add the brown sugar and honey and beat until the mixture is smooth and lightened in colour. Gradually add the oil and beat until blended. Beat in the lemon rind. On low speed, beat in the flour mixture alternately in 2 batches with the apple purée. Stir in the nuts.

Pour the mixture into the prepared tin. Bake for about 55 minutes or until your finger does not leave an indentation when you press lightly on top of cake, and a fine skewer inserted in the centre comes out clean. Cool in the tin for about 15 minutes.

Turn cake out onto wire rack and carefully peel off the paper. Cover tightly when completely cool. (If tightly wrapped, cake keeps for 2 weeks at room temperature.) Cut into squares or bars.

CHOCOLATE-ALMOND CAKE WITH CHOCOLATE-HONEY FROSTING

Although honey symbolizes a sweet new year, for some people honey and chocolate say this even better! The frosting is flavoured with honey, which marries very well with the taste of chocolate.

MAKES 12 SERVINGS

about 200 g (7 oz) almonds
175 g (6 oz) plain chocolate
175 g (6 oz) sugar
25 g (1 oz) plain flour
2.5 ml (½ tsp) baking
   powder
175 g (6 oz) unsalted non-
   dairy margarine or butter

6 large eggs, size 1 or 2,
   separated, at room
   temperature
1.25 ml (¼ tsp) cream of
   tartar

CHOCOLATE-HONEY FROSTING

120 ml (4 fl oz) non-dairy
   creamer or double cream
175 g (6 oz) plain chocolate,
   finely chopped
75 g (3 oz) unsalted non-
   dairy margarine or butter,
   slightly softened

50 ml (3 tbsp plus 1 tsp)
   honey
about 25 g (1 oz) blanched
   almonds, chopped, for
   decoration

Preheat oven to 180°C (350°F) mark 4. Toast almonds in shallow baking dish in oven for 7 minutes. Transfer to plate and cool completely.

Melt chocolate in a double saucepan above hot water over low heat. Stir until smooth, then remove from pan of water and leave to cool.

Lightly grease a 23-cm (9-inch) spring clip tin with 7.5-cm (3-inch) sides. Line base of tin with non-stick paper or foil and grease paper or foil. Flour side of tin and lined base, tapping to remove excess.

In a food processor, grind 75 g (3 oz) almonds with 30 ml (2 tbsp) sugar as finely as possible.

Transfer to a large bowl. Repeat with remaining almonds and 30 ml (2 tbsp) sugar and add to first batch. Sift flour and baking powder onto almond mixture and mix thoroughly.

Cream margarine and 90 ml (6 tbsp) sugar. Beat in egg yolks, one by one. Stir in melted chocolate.

Whisk egg whites with cream of tartar in a large bowl until soft peaks form. Gradually beat in remaining 30 ml (2 tbsp) sugar and whisk at high speed until whites are stiff but not dry. Sprinkle about one-third of almond mixture over chocolate mixture and fold in gently, followed by about one-third of whites. Repeat with remaining almond mixture and whites in 2 batches. Fold lightly but quickly just until mixture is blended.

Transfer mixture to prepared tin and spread evenly. Bake for about 45 minutes or until a fine skewer inserted in centre of cake comes out clean. Cool in tin on a wire rack for 10 minutes. Cake will settle slightly in centre during cooling.

Run a thin-bladed flexible knife or palette knife carefully around cake. Invert cake onto rack, release spring, and remove sides and base of tin. Carefully peel off paper. Invert cake onto another rack so its smooth side is against rack; leave to cool completely. (Cake can be wrapped and kept for 2 days in refrigerator.) Turn cake back over so smooth side is up. Transfer to a serving plate.

For frosting, bring cream to the boil in a small, heavy saucepan. Remove from heat and immediately add chopped chocolate. Using a small whisk, stir quickly until chocolate is completely melted and mixture is smooth. Transfer to a bowl and cool to room temperature. Whip mixture at high speed for about 3 minutes.

Cream margarine until very soft and smooth. Add chocolate mixture in 3 batches, beating constantly until frosting is smooth. Gradually beat in honey.

Spread frosting on top and side of cake. Using spatula, swirl frosting at top, from edge inward, forming small curves. Spoon remaining frosting into piping bag fitted with small star tube. Pipe a ring of rosettes of frosting about halfway between edge and centre of cake. Fill centre of ring with chopped almonds. Press gently so they adhere to frosting. Chill for at least 1 hour before serving. When frosting is firm, cake can be wrapped. (Cake can be kept, covered, for 3 days in refrigerator.)

QUINCE COMPOTE WITH CINNAMON

This is a prized Rosh Hashanah dish among Jews of different ori-gins – Moroccan, Greek and Turkish, for example. Along with apple slices and bowls of honey, pomegranate seeds and other fruits, it is placed on the table before the actual dinner begins. This sweet compote also makes a tasty dessert.

MAKES 4 SERVINGS

3 large quince, about 800 g (1¾ lb) total	*60 ml (4 tbsp) strained fresh lemon juice (optional)*
225 g (8 oz) sugar	*10 ml (2 tsp) ground cinnamon*

Peel quince, cut them in eighths, and cut out core and seed section from each piece. Put into a heavy saucepan, add water just to cover and bring to the boil. Cook, uncovered, over medium heat, carefully turning slices from time to time, for about 50 minutes or until they are tender and much of the water is evaporated and slices are about half-covered. (Cooking time varies with size of quinces and their degree of ripeness.)

Add sugar, lemon juice and cinnamon. Swirl pan and baste quince with the liquid to dissolve the sugar. Cook over medium heat for 5 minutes, then over low heat for 30 minutes, basting from time to time. When quince are ready, they should be very tender, have turned a pink hue, and appear shiny and glazed; syrup should taste concentrated. Spoon them into serving dishes with their syrup. Serve cold.

SUCCOT
The Harvest Holiday

 Succot is a festival to show appreciation for the harvest, and is celebrated in early autumn (for eight days in Israel and nine days outside Israel). Meals are served in a *succah*, a hut with a roof of leafy branches, to commemorate the temporary shelters in which the Hebrews lived when they fled from Egypt. (Although the escape from Egypt is the theme of Passover, this major event in Jewish history is recalled in the customs of other festivals as well.) From the roof of branches, fruit are suspended on pieces of string, as a natural decoration.

The agricultural theme is echoed in the holiday foods – Succot is the time to serve plenty of fruits and vegetables. In Israel stuffed vegetables are frequently prepared for the holiday. Popular choices are stuffed cabbage leaves, aubergines, courgettes and peppers. As on Rosh Hashanah, tzimmes, a stew with vegetables and fruits, is a favourite item on the menu of Jews of eastern European origin.

Even the holiday ritual involves produce. A special 'ceremonial' fruit for Succot is the citron, called an *etrog* in Hebrew and an *esrog* in Yiddish. It plays a part in special Succot prayers. The fruit is rare and expensive and is usually not used for cooking. In Israel, however, the fruit is sometimes made into preserves. My in-laws have an *etrog* tree in their garden and use the fruit to prepare a wonderful marmalade.

Other ideal Succot dishes:

Zesty Pepper-Tomato Salad (page 32)

Mushroom-Barley Chicken Soup (page 196)

Sephardic Pumpkin Pancakes (page 92)

Courgettes with Tomatoes and Dill (page 263)

Stuffed Aubergine with Meat, Pine Nuts and Almonds (page 258)

Okra with Tomatoes and Coriander (page 267)

Beef and Sweet Potato Tzimmes (page 85)

Veal with Olives, Tomatoes and Fresh Herbs (page 248)

Spiced Apple Blintzes (page 326)

Cinnamon-Scented Apple Noodle Kugel (page 151)

AN ASHKENAZIC SUCCOT

Succot menus are quite individual, with each family selecting its own favourites. The dishes should be easy to carry to the succah, which is located outside the house – a fragile soufflé would definitely not be chosen! The most festive dinners are served during the first and last days of Succot, and on the Sabbath that may fall in the middle of the holiday.

Ashkenazic cooks make lavish use of both vegetables and fruits throughout the meal. Stuffed vegetables, such as stuffed cabbage, might also be featured or casseroles of vegetables and fruit.

ASHKENAZIC SUCCOT MENU

**Ashkenazic Chicken Soup with Fresh Dill
and Light Matzo Balls**

Beetroot Salad with Apples

**Beef Stew with Winter Squash and Raisins,
or
Roast Duck with Prunes and Red Wine**

Noodle Kugel with Colourful Vegetables

**Pear Strudel, or
My Mother's Chocolate Apple Cake**

ASHKENAZIC CHICKEN SOUP WITH FRESH DILL AND LIGHT MATZO BALLS

Matzo balls, also known as kneidlach, are the subject of an ongoing controversy in many families, including ours. Some people like them light and airy, while others prefer them more substantial. A friend of mine calls them 'floaters' versus 'sinkers'. My mother taught me that light matzo balls require a very soft mixture and gentle shaping. If it is firm enough so the balls can be formed in a neat, perfectly round shape, they will not be fluffy.

MAKES 8 SERVINGS

900 g (2 lb) chicken wings or
    drumsticks
2 litres (3½ pints) cold water
1 large onion, peeled
1 large carrot, peeled
1 small parsnip, peeled
    (optional)

2 celery stalks, including leafy
    tops
5 parsley sprigs
3 dill sprigs
salt and pepper
15 ml (1 tbsp) snipped fresh
    dill

MATZO BALLS
2 large eggs, size 1 or 2
30 ml (2 tbsp) vegetable oil
50 g (2 oz) matzo meal
2.5 ml (½ tsp) salt

2.5 ml (½ tsp) baking powder
15–30 ml (1–2 tbsp) water or
    chicken soup

about 1.7 litres (3 pints)
    salted water, for simmering

Combine chicken wings, water, onion, carrot, parsnip, celery, parsley and dill sprigs, and pinch of salt in a large saucepan and bring to the boil. Partly cover and simmer for 2 hours, skimming occasionally. Skim off excess fat. (Chicken soup can be kept for 3 days in refrigerator or can be frozen; reheat before serving.)

Make matzo balls: in a medium bowl, lightly beat eggs with oil. Add matzo meal, salt and baking powder and stir until smooth. Stir in water, then stand for 20 minutes so matzo meal absorbs liquid.

Bring salted water to the boil. With wet hands, roll about 5 ml

(1 tsp) of matzo ball mixture between your palms into a ball; mixture will be very soft. Set balls on a plate. With a spatula, carefully slide balls into boiling water. Cover and simmer over low heat for about 30 minutes or until firm. Cover and keep warm until ready to serve. (Matzo balls can be kept for 2 days in their cooking liquid in a covered container in refrigerator; reheat gently in cooking liquid or in soup.)

To serve soup, remove chicken wings, onion, celery, parsnip and parsley and dill sprigs. Take meat off bones and add to soup; or reserve for other uses. Add pepper to soup, stir in snipped dill and taste soup for seasoning. Slice carrot and add a few slices to each bowl. With a slotted spoon, add a few matzo balls. Serve hot.

BEETROOT SALAD WITH APPLES

I learned to prepare this salad of eastern European inspiration at a cooking course I took at the Institute for Nutrition and Home Economics in Tel Aviv. With students of so many different ethnic origins, we enjoyed learning each other's favourite recipes.

The delicately sweet, bright pink salad is good with fresh pumpernickel bread. For meatless dinners, 30 ml (2 tbsp) soured cream can replace half the mayonnaise.

MAKES 3 OR 4 SERVINGS

7 medium beetroots, 4 cm (1½ inch) diameter, about 350 g (12 oz), (not including greens), trimmed	20 ml (4 tsp) prepared mustard
2 sharp apples, such as Granny Smith	60 ml (4 tbsp) mayonnaise
	5 ml (1 tsp) sugar
	salt and freshly ground pepper
	lettuce leaves (optional)

In a medium saucepan cover beetroots with water and cook, covered, for about 45 minutes – 1 hour or until tender when pierced with a sharp knife. Rinse and peel. Slice beetroots, then cut them into 2.5-cm (1-inch) sticks about 0.5 cm (¼ inch) thick. Coarsely grate the apples and mix with beetroots. Stir together remaining ingredients. Add to beetroot mixture and mix. Taste and adjust seasoning. Serve cold, on a bed of lettuce leaves.

BEEF STEW WITH WINTER SQUASH AND RAISINS

Some say that a fondness for sweet-and-sour dishes accounts for the Jewish taste for Chinese food. This version of the sweet Ashkenazic stew known as tzimmes has a touch of soy sauce and cinnamon, which impart a nice flavour and result in a dish that borrows from both styles of cooking. The Noodle Kugel with Colourful Vegetables in this menu makes a pleasing accompaniment for the beef and its rich sauce, as do plain noodles, rice or couscous.

MAKES 8 SERVINGS

45 ml (3 tbsp) vegetable oil	600 ml (1 pint) water
1.6–1.8 kg (3½–4 lb) chuck steak, cut into 3.5–4-cm (1¼–1½-inch) pieces, trimmed of fat and patted dry	30 ml (2 tbsp) soy sauce
	1 cinnamon stick, about 5 cm (2 inches) long; or a pinch of ground cinnamon
2 large onions, chopped	pinch of freshly ground pepper
30 ml (2 tbsp) plain flour	1.4 kg (3 lb) orange-coloured winter squash or pumpkin
350 ml (12 fl oz) dry white wine	45 ml (3 tbsp) mild honey
	75 g (3 oz) raisins

Heat oil in a large heavy casserole over medium-high heat. Add beef in batches and brown on all sides. Using slotted spatula, transfer it to a plate. Add onions to casserole and sauté over medium-low heat until softened, for about 7 minutes. Return meat to pan, reserving any juices on a plate, and sprinkle meat with flour. Toss lightly to coat meat with flour. Cook over low heat, stirring often, for 5 minutes.

Stir in wine, water, juices from plate and soy sauce, add cinnamon stick and pepper, then bring to the boil, stirring often. Cover and cook over low heat, stirring and turning beef cubes occasionally, until beef is very tender, about 2½–2¾ hours; when a cube is pierced and lifted with thin-bladed sharp knife, it should fall from knife. Discard cinnamon stick.

Meanwhile, scrape off any stringy parts from centre of squash with spoon. Cut squash into large pieces, cut off peel and cut squash into 2.5-cm (1-inch) cubes. When meat is tender, stir in honey. Add squash and raisins, and push squash down into liquid. Cover and

101

simmer for 10 minutes. Turn squash pieces over, cover and simmer until squash is tender, about 15 minutes more.

Sauce should be thick enough to lightly coat a spoon; if it is too thin, uncover and simmer over low heat, stirring occasionally very gently, until lightly thickened, about 10–15 minutes. Taste and adjust seasoning. Serve stew from deep serving dish.

ROAST DUCK WITH PRUNES AND RED WINE

Duck with prunes is popular among Jews from central Europe and France, since the sweetness of the fruit is a pleasing balance for the duck's richness. This duck also makes an elegant main course for Rosh Hashanah, accompanied by rice or potatoes and by sugar-snap peas or shelled peas.

MAKES 6 SERVINGS

16 stoned prunes, about 175 g (6 oz)	*salt and freshly ground pepper*
175 ml (6 fl oz) dry or lightly sweetened red wine	*350 ml (12 fl oz) chicken stock or soup*
175 ml (6 fl oz) water	*5 ml (1 tsp) potato flour or cornflour dissolved in 10 ml (2 tsp) water*
2 ducks, each about 2–2.3 kg (4½–5 lb), thawed if frozen, patted dry	

Combine prunes, wine and water in small deep bowl or cup and cover. Soak prunes for 2 hours.

Preheat oven to 230°C (450°F) mark 8. Remove fat from inside ducks near tail and under neck skin. For easier carving, remove wishbone from each duck: set duck on its back and lift neck skin; the first bone above neck is V-shape wishbone. Outline it carefully with a thin-bladed knife and pull wishbone out.

Sprinkle duck inside and out with salt and pepper. Using skewer, pierce skin all over, especially where fat is thickest, at intervals of about 1 cm (½ inch); do not pierce meat.

Set ducks on their side on rack in a heavy roasting tin. Roast for 10 minutes, then turn ducks onto other side and roast for 10 minutes more. Remove fat from tin. Set ducks on their breasts and roast for 10 minutes. Turn ducks on their backs and roast for 10 minutes more.

Reduce oven temperature to 200°C (400°F) mark 6 and roast duck, discarding fat occasionally, for about 40 minutes. To check whether duck is done, prick thigh meat in plumpest part; if juices that escape are still red, duck is not done; if they are clear, duck is well done. If browner skin is desired, transfer duck to a grill pan and grill about 13 cm (5 inches) from heat source until skin is deep brown.

Transfer ducks to a platter, draining juices from inside duck into roasting tin. Cover loosely and keep warm. (Ducks can be kept warm for 30 minutes in oven with heat turned off and door slightly ajar.)

When ducks are nearly done, transfer prunes with their soaking liquid to a saucepan. Add more water, if necessary, to barely cover them and bring to a simmer. Cover and cook over low heat until prunes are just tender, about 10 minutes. Pour liquid into bowl and set prunes aside.

Pour off fat from roasting tin but leave darker duck juices. Reheat juices in a pan over medium-high heat, then add 120 ml (4 fl oz) stock and bring to the boil, stirring and scraping up any browned bits and moving pan backwards and forwards over burner to heat evenly. Strain into medium saucepan. Add prune liquid and remaining stock. Boil until sauce is reduced to about 300 ml (½ pint), about 5 minutes. Remove from heat. Skim excess fat from sauce.

Bring sauce to a simmer over medium heat. Whisk potato flour mixture to blend, then gradually whisk into simmering sauce. Return to the boil, whisking, and cook over low heat for 1 minute. Add salt and pepper to taste. Add prunes, cover and leave to stand for 2 minutes.

Spoon prunes around ducks and spoon a little sauce over prunes. Serve remaining sauce separately.

NOODLE KUGEL WITH COLOURFUL VEGETABLES

Serve this savoury noodle kugel flavoured with carrots, courgettes and sautéed mushrooms as an accompaniment for meat, chicken or fish.

MAKES 8 TO 10 SERVINGS

450 g (1 lb) wide egg noodles
135 ml (9 tbsp) vegetable oil
2 large onions, finely chopped
350 g (12 oz) small
  mushrooms, sliced
salt and freshly ground pepper
  to taste
5 ml (1 tsp) dried thyme
5 ml (1 tsp) paprika

5 large eggs, size 1 or 2,
  beaten
2 large carrots, coarsely grated
2 small courgettes, coarsely
  grated
15 g (½ oz) fresh parsley or
  coriander, chopped
cayenne pepper to taste

Preheat oven to 180°C (350°F) mark 4. Cook noodles, uncovered, in a large pan of boiling salted water over high heat, stirring occasionally, for about 4 minutes or until nearly tender but firmer than usual, since they will be baked. Drain, rinse with cold water, then drain again. Transfer to a large bowl.

Heat 90 ml (6 tbsp) oil in a large frying pan over medium-low heat. Add onions and sauté for about 15 minutes or until very tender. Add 30 ml (2 tbsp) oil and heat again. Add mushrooms, salt, pepper, thyme and paprika and sauté for about 15 minutes or until mushrooms are tender and onions are browned. If mixture is watery, increase heat and cook for about 5 minutes or until excess liquid evaporates.

Add mushroom mixture, eggs, carrots, courgettes and parsley to noodles and mix well. Add cayenne. Taste and adjust seasoning. Oil a 3.5–4-litre (6–7-pint) baking dish or two 1.7–2-litre (3–3½-pint) baking dishes and add noodle mixture. Sprinkle with remaining 15 ml (1 tbsp) oil.

Bake for 45–55 minutes or until set; kugel will bake faster in shallow dishes than in deep ones. Serve hot, from baking dish.

PEAR STRUDEL

Whether in Paris, New York or Los Angeles, if you were look-
ing for strudel, your best bet would be to go to a Jewish pastry shop. This eastern European speciality was adopted by Jewish
cooks and showcased in Jewish bakeries and delicatessens throughout
the West. For home cooks, strudel used to be a lot of work, but now
it's easy to make using bought filo dough, which is sometimes
labelled 'strudel dough'. For dairy meals, prepare the strudel with
butter and serve with whipped cream or vanilla ice cream.

MAKES 6 SERVINGS

PEAR FILLING

50 g (2 oz) dried pears or
  sultanas, finely chopped
50 g (2 oz) pecans, chopped
2 large ripe pears, 350–400 g
  (12–14 oz) total, peeled,
  cored and thinly sliced

50 g (2 oz) sugar
10 ml (2 tsp) strained fresh
  lemon juice
5 ml (1 tsp) grated lemon rind
5 ml (1 tsp) ground cinnamon
30 ml (2 tbsp) apricot jam

4 strudel or filo sheets, thawed
  if frozen
75 g (3 oz) unsalted non-
  dairy margarine or butter,
  melted

60 ml (4 tbsp) dry biscuit
  crumbs or breadcrumbs
icing sugar, for serving

Thoroughly mix dried pears with pecans in a large bowl. Add
remaining filling ingredients and mix well.

Preheat oven to 190°C (375°F) mark 5. Lightly grease a baking
sheet. Lay 1 filo sheet on a large sheet of greaseproof paper. Brush
with melted margarine and sprinkle with 15 ml (1 tbsp) crumbs. Top
with a second sheet of filo. Brush with butter and sprinkle with
15 ml (1 tbsp) crumbs. Keep remaining filo sheets covered.

Put half the filling near one long end of top sheet, arranging it in a
log shape and leaving a 2.5-cm (1-inch) border. Starting with that
end, carefully roll up dough as for a Swiss roll, using the paper to
help support dough. End the roll with the seam on the bottom.
Transfer roll to baking sheet and brush top with margarine. Repeat
with remaining filling and remaining dough. Bake for 25 minutes or
until golden. Serve warm, sprinkled with icing sugar.

MY MOTHER'S CHOCOLATE APPLE CAKE

My mother often bakes this cake for Sabbath, and it has served as many a birthday cake as well. Apple purée gives it moistness, and it is rich, dark and delicious, although it is enriched with oil rather than butter, has a low proportion of eggs and contains no dairy products. The chocolate icing and decoration of chopped nuts are optional, but they do give the cake a festive note. This is one of the quickest and easiest cake recipes I know.

MAKES 8 TO 10 SERVINGS

120 ml (4 fl oz) vegetable oil
225 g (8 oz) sugar
1 large egg, size 1 or 2
175 g (6 oz) plain flour
scant 40 g (1½ oz) cocoa
    powder

7.5 ml (1½ tsp) ground
    cinnamon
5 ml (1 tsp) bicarbonate of
    soda
225 g (8 oz) unsweetened
    apple purée

EASY CHOCOLATE ICING (OPTIONAL)
75 g (3 oz) plain chocolate
25 g (1 oz) unsalted non-
    dairy margarine, cut in 4
    pieces, softened

25 g (1 oz) pecans or
    walnuts, diced

Preheat oven to 180°C (350°F) mark 4. Grease and flour a 20- or 23-cm (8- or 9-inch) square baking tin. Beat oil, sugar and egg until pale in colour and fluffy. Sift flour with cocoa, cinnamon and bicarbonate of soda. Stir flour mixture alternately with apple purée into egg mixture and mix well. Bake in greased tin for 25-35 minutes, depending on tin size, or until a fine skewer inserted in cake comes out clean. Turn out onto a wire rack or leave in the tin; cool completely.

Melt chocolate for icing in a medium saucepan set above hot water over low heat. Remove from heat and stir in margarine. Cool for about 2 minutes or until thick enough to spread. Spread over top of cake and sprinkle with nuts. Refrigerate for about 1 hour or until set. (Cake can be kept, covered, for 3 days in refrigerator.) Serve at room temperature.

A SEPHARDIC SUCCOT

A selection of stuffed vegetables is the star on the Succot menu of most Sephardic Jews. Many cooks prepare a large batch of a single stuffing and use it to fill a few different vegetables. In addition to or as alternatives to the recipes here, stuffed peppers or stuffed aubergine might be featured (recipes are in 'Vegetables'). Instead of the first course, many families serve a variety of salads, such as aubergine salad, potato salad, hummus and carrot salad, together with pita bread.

SEPHARDIC SUCCOT MENU

Sautéed Aubergine in Spicy Tomato Sauce,
or
Moroccan Sea Bass with Red Peppers

Aromatic Stuffed Onions

Stuffed Courgettes with Lamb, Almonds and Raisins

Middle Eastern Stuffed Cabbage Leaves

Fresh Fruit, or Pine Nut–Almond Filo Fingers

SAUTEED AUBERGINE IN SPICY TOMATO SAUCE

Aubergine appears in a great variety of recipes in Israel, ranging from salads to fritters to stews to sautés. Jews in the Middle East like their vegetables well seasoned and very tender, as in this Yemenite aubergine recipe. If you like, the sautéed aubergine slices can be simmered in the tomato sauce instead of baked in it. The dish can be served with rice for a vegetarian meal, or as a vegetable accompaniment for chicken or meat.

As with many aubergine dishes, courgette can also be prepared this way. But I don't think that I'd go so far as my friend Haim Shapiro, the restaurant critic of the *Jerusalem Post*, who feels that anything made with aubergine can be made – even better – with courgette.

MAKES 4 SERVINGS

1 large aubergine, about 550 g (1¼ lb)
salt

90 ml (6 tbsp) olive or vegetable oil, for sautéing

SPICY TOMATO SAUCE

45 ml (3 tbsp) olive or vegetable oil

1 medium onion, finely chopped

7.5 ml (1½ tsp) ground cumin

3.75 ml (¾ tsp) paprika

1.25 ml (¼ tsp) turmeric

1 kg (1¾ lb) ripe tomatoes, peeled, seeded and chopped; or 2 × 794-g (28-oz) cans plum tomatoes, drained and chopped

salt and freshly ground pepper

pinch of cayenne pepper

10 ml (2 tsp) tomato purée (optional)

3 medium garlic cloves, finely chopped

Cut peel from aubergine with a knife and discard ends. Cut aubergine into 1-cm (⅜-inch) crossways slices. Sprinkle lightly but evenly with salt on both sides and put in a colander. Place bowl with a weight on top, pressing against slices, and leave to drain for 1 hour, turning slices over after 30 minutes. Pat dry with paper towels.

Heat oil for sauce in large saucepan. Add onion and sauté over medium-low heat for about 7 minutes or until soft and light brown. Add cumin, paprika and turmeric and cook, stirring, for 30 seconds. Add tomatoes, salt, pepper and cayenne and stir well. Bring to the boil over medium-high heat. Cook over low heat, uncovered, stirring occasionally, for about 30 minutes or until tomatoes are very soft. Sauce will be chunky. Add tomato purée and taste for seasoning. Stir in garlic. (Sauce can be kept, covered, for 2 days in refrigerator.)

Preheat oven to 180°C (350°F) mark 4. Heat 45 ml (3 tbsp) oil in a large heavy frying pan. Quickly add enough aubergine slices to make one layer. Sauté over medium heat for about 2 minutes on each side; remove to plate. Add 45 ml (3 tbsp) oil to frying pan, heat oil and sauté second batch of aubergine in same way.

Lightly oil a shallow 1.1-litre (2-pint) baking dish. Arrange alternate layers of aubergine and sauce, ending with sauce. Bake for 30 minutes or until aubergine is very tender, basting occasionally. Serve hot or at room temperature.

MOROCCAN SEA BASS WITH RED PEPPERS

From Moroccan Jews comes this flavourful fish dish, dotted with bright red sautéed peppers, coriander leaves and sautéed garlic. It is simple to make and is delicious hot or cold, as a first course for Sabbath or a main course on other occasions.

MAKES 4 OR 5 FIRST-COURSE SERVINGS OR 2 OR 3 MAIN-COURSE SERVINGS

60 ml (4 tbsp) vegetable oil
2 red peppers, diced
20 medium garlic cloves,
  finely chopped
90 ml (6 tbsp) finely chopped
  fresh coriander
700 g (1½ lb) small sea bass
  steaks, about 2.5 cm
  (1 inch) thick, or 550 g
  (1¼ lb) sea bass fillets

salt and pepper
5 ml (1 tsp) paprika
450 ml (¾ pint) water

In a sauté pan large enough to hold fish in one layer, heat oil and add peppers. Sauté lightly over medium heat for 2 minutes. Add garlic and coriander and cook over low heat, stirring, for 1 minute. Add fish and sprinkle with salt, pepper and paprika. Add water and bring to a simmer, basting fish occasionally. Cover and cook over very low heat for about 8 minutes or until fish is just tender; when a thin skewer is inserted into centre of fish, it should come out hot to the touch.

Transfer fish to a deep serving dish, using a slotted spoon. Remove skin from fish.

Boil liquid with peppers, stirring occasionally, until only about 120 ml (4 fl oz) liquid remains. Taste for seasoning and pour it over fish. Serve hot or cold.

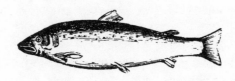

AROMATIC STUFFED ONIONS

I learned the technique for preparing stuffed onions from Suzanne Elmaleh of Jerusalem, who cooks in the traditional style of the Jews of Lebanon. For a special touch, she adds a few spoonfuls of pomegranate juice to the cooking liquid when the onions are nearly done, for an intriguing hint of sweetness. The juice can be found in specialist food shops and some supermarkets. If you prefer a sharp note, add 30 ml (2 tbsp) lemon juice instead.

MAKES ABOUT 6 SERVINGS

90 g (3½ oz) long-grain white rice	2.5 ml (½ tsp) pepper
250 ml (8 fl oz) boiling water	15 ml (1 tbsp) vegetable oil
3 large onions, about 900 g (2 lb) total, peeled	100 g (4 oz) lean minced beef
pinch of ground cinnamon	250 ml (8 fl oz) water
1.25 ml (¼ tsp) ground allspice	45 ml (3 tbsp) pomegranate juice (optional)
2.5 ml (½ tsp) salt	Basic Tomato Sauce (page 345, optional)

In a bowl combine rice and boiling water. Leave to stand until mixture is cool.

Slit each onion once halfway to centre cutting from top to bottom. Put onions in a large pan of boiling salted water and boil for about 20 minutes or until it is easy to separate them in layers. Drain and leave until cool enough to handle. Separate carefully in layers.

Drain rice thoroughly. Mix with cinnamon, allspice, salt, pepper and oil. Taste for seasoning. Add beef. Knead to mix well. Put about 5 ml (1 tsp) stuffing at one end of an onion piece and roll it up tightly, following shape of onion. Cut any large onion pieces in half, to make 2 stuffed onion pieces.

Put onions in a sauté pan, arranging them in a tight layer seam side down. Add enough water to barely cover them. Sprinkle with salt and bring to a simmer. Cover and cook over low heat for about 1 hour or until onions are very tender, adding a little water from time to time if pan gets dry; watch them, as onions burn easily. If desired, add pomegranate juice and cook for 5 more minutes.

If not adding pomegranate juice, serve onions with tomato sauce.

STUFFED COURGETTES WITH LAMB, ALMONDS AND RAISINS

There are several ways to stuff courgettes. You can simply halve them, remove the centre and fill and bake them, as here. Or you can turn them into little tubes and simmer them as in the variation. To hollow out the courgette for stuffing in this manner, buy a special tool for this purpose or use an apple corer or vegetable peeler. Jews from the Middle East use very small courgettes for this dish.

MAKES 4 TO 6 SERVINGS

LAMB AND RICE STUFFING

90 g (3½ oz) long-grain white rice, rinsed and drained	*1 medium onion, finely chopped*
750 ml (1¼ pints) boiling water	*225 g (8 oz) lean minced lamb*
30 ml (2 tbsp) plus 5 ml (1 tsp) vegetable oil	*30 ml (2 tbsp) chopped fresh parsley*
45 ml (3 tbsp) slivered almonds	*45 ml (3 tbsp) raisins*

about 1 kg (2–2½ lb) small courgettes	*salt and pepper*
15 ml (1 tbsp) tomato purée	*4 medium garlic cloves, coarsely chopped*
60 ml (4 tbsp) water	*30 ml (2 tbsp) vegetable oil*

Add rice to boiling salted water in a medium saucepan and boil for 10 minutes. Rinse with cold running water and drain well.

Heat 5 ml (1 tsp) oil in a small frying pan over medium-low heat. Add almonds and sauté lightly for about 5 minutes. Transfer to a plate and leave to cool.

Heat 30 ml (2 tbsp) oil in a frying pan, add onion and sauté over medium-low heat until softened for about 5 minutes. Leave to cool. Mix all stuffing ingredients and taste for seasoning..

Preheat oven to 220°C (425°F) mark 7. Cut courgettes in half lengthways. Use a spoon to scoop out centres. Rinse courgette shells and pat them dry, then put into a baking dish large enough to fit them in 1 layer. Fill each with stuffing.

Mix tomato purée with water and a pinch of salt and pepper. Spoon mixture over courgettes then add enough water to dish to cover by one-third. Add garlic and spoon oil over courgettes. Cover and bake for 15 minutes. Reduce oven temperature to 180°C (350°F) mark 4 and bake for 15 more minutes. Uncover and bake, basting occasionally, for 15 minutes or until courgettes are tender.

MIDDLE EASTERN STUFFED CABBAGE LEAVES

Stuffed cabbage is typical of the cuisine of Jews of many origins, and is a traditional dish for Succot. This aromatic version of stuffed cabbage is based on my mother-in-law's recipe and includes the favourite Middle Eastern spices of cumin and turmeric. In the Polish sweet-and-sour stuffed cabbage, the stuffing is seasoned with salt and pepper only and the sauce is cooked with raisins, a little sugar and vinegar or lemon juice.

MAKES 6 SERVINGS

1.4 kg (3 lb) green cabbage, cored

STUFFING

90 g (3½ oz) long-grain white rice
750 ml (1¼ pints) water
salt
30 ml (2 tbsp) olive oil
1 medium onion, finely chopped

2.5 ml (½ tsp) ground cumin
1.25 ml (¼ tsp) turmeric
225 g (8 oz) lean minced beef
30 ml (2 tbsp) finely chopped fresh parsley
freshly ground pepper

SAUCE

45 ml (3 tbsp) olive oil
1 medium onion, finely chopped
2 medium garlic cloves, finely chopped
2.5 ml (½ tsp) ground cumin
1.25 ml (¼ tsp) turmeric

750 ml (1¼ pints) chicken soup or stock, beef stock or Yemenite Beef Soup (page 197)
15 ml (1 tbsp) tomato purée
salt and freshly ground pepper

112

Carefully remove 15 large outer cabbage leaves by cutting them from core end of cabbage. In a pan of boiling salted water, boil leaves for 5 minutes. Transfer them carefully to a colander and rinse gently with cold water. Pat dry with a tea towel. Coarsely chop remaining cabbage, add to boiling water and boil for 2 minutes. Drain, rinse with cold water and drain well.

Sprinkle rice into a medium saucepan with boiling salted water and boil it, stirring occasionally, for 10 minutes. Drain rice, rinse with cold water and drain well. In a frying pan, heat oil, add onion and cook over medium-low heat for 7 minutes, or until softened. Add cumin and turmeric and cook, stirring, for 1 minute. Transfer mixture to a large bowl and leave to cool. Stir in rice, beef, parsley and salt and pepper to taste. Knead by hand to blend ingredients thoroughly.

Heat oil for sauce in a large casserole, add onion and cook over low heat, stirring, for 5 minutes or until softened. Stir in garlic and cook for 1 minute. Add cumin and turmeric and cook for another minute. Remove from heat.

Trim thick ribs of each cabbage leaf slightly so leaf can be easily bent. Put 30 ml (2 tbsp) of stuffing near stalk end of each leaf and fold stalk end over it. Fold sides over stuffing to enclose it. Beginning at stalk end, roll up leaf to a neat package. If any leaves are torn, place a piece of another leaf over hole and make cabbage rolls from these, too. Arrange cabbage rolls tightly, with seam end down, side by side in casserole. Chop any remaining leaves and add them to casserole.

Add most of stock to casserole. Mix tomato purée with remaining stock until smooth, then add to casserole, with salt and pepper to taste. Bring to a simmer, cover and simmer over low heat for 1¼ hours. Taste cooking liquid for seasoning. To serve, spoon chopped cabbage into shallow bowls, with cabbage rolls on top. Spoon cooking liquid over cabbage rolls.

PINE NUT-ALMOND FILO FINGERS

Unlike some Middle Eastern filo pastries, these are not drenched in syrup, but rather are crisp, light, delicate and not very sweet. I learned to make them from Suzanne Elmaleh, who lives in Jerusalem.

The filling is quickly made by chopping nuts in the food processor. Many versions of this pastry call for ground nuts, but I prefer them the way Mrs Elmaleh taught me, with small but distinct pieces so the filling has a more interesting texture. Fresh, good quality nuts are essential to the fine taste of these pastries.

MAKES ABOUT 30 PASTRIES

225 g (8 oz) packet filo sheets	icing sugar, for sprinkling
100 g (4 oz) unsalted non-dairy margarine, melted	

NUT FILLING

75 g (3 oz) almonds	5 ml (1 tsp) ground cinnamon
75 g (3 oz) walnuts	30 ml (2 tbsp) icing sugar
25 g (1 oz) pine nuts	(optional)

If filo sheets are frozen, thaw them in refrigerator for 8 hours or overnight. Remove filo sheets from refrigerator 2 hours before using and leave them in their packet.

In food processor, chop almonds and walnuts together, leaving some pieces; do not grind finely. Transfer to a bowl and stir in pine nuts, cinnamon and icing sugar.

Line 2 baking sheets with non-stick paper or grease them. Remove filo sheets from their packet and unroll them on a dry tea towel. Using a sharp knife, cut stack in half lengthways then in half crossways. Cover filo dough immediately with a piece of greaseproof paper, then with a damp tea towel. Work with only one sheet at a time and always keep remaining sheets covered with paper and tea towel, so they don't dry out.

Remove one pastry square from pile. Brush it lightly with melted margarine. Put about 10 ml (2 tsp) filling at one end of a filo square so it extends all along the edge. Fold the 2 ends of dough in slightly over filling, then roll up tightly to form a thin finger. Transfer to baking sheet. Make more filo fingers with remaining dough and filling. (Pastries can be shaped 1 day ahead and refrigerated, tightly covered with cling film, on baking sheets or on plates; or frozen.)

Preheat oven to 180°C (350°F) mark 4. Bake pastries for 15–20 minutes or until very light golden. Cool on a wire rack. (Pastries can be kept in airtight container in freezer, or 1 day at room temperature.) Before serving, sprinkle generously with icing sugar.

HANUKKAH
The Festival of Lights and Latkes

 The feast of Hanukkah has different meanings for different people. To the religious scholar, it is a commemoration of a historic event – the rekindling of the eternal light in the Temple in Jerusalem. To a Jewish child in the United States, it means Hanukkah parties, potato pancakes and presents. To his cousin in Israel, it is the time to enjoy fluffy doughnuts filled with red jam.

The miracle of the oil, the central theme of Hanukkah, lies behind the holiday's traditions. A little over 2000 years ago, the Jews defeated the Syrians, who had tried to force them to give up their culture and to worship Greek gods. The Jews drove the foreign army out of Jerusalem, cleansed the Temple, and relit the light in the Temple with pure oil. Legend says that only enough ritually clean oil for one day could be found, but it miraculously lasted for eight days, until more could be prepared. For this reason, Hanukkah is celebrated for eight days and is known as the Festival of Lights. The lights are only a symbol; the real celebration is of religious freedom.

The most important Hanukkah custom is the lighting of colourful candles. These are placed in a menorah, a candelabrum with eight branches of equal size, one for each night of Hanukkah, and one prominent branch that holds the candle used to light the others. On the first night one candle is lit and each succeeding night another is added so that on the last night all eight are alight.

Traditional foods also symbolize the miracle of the oil. Potato pancakes have become a Hanukkah speciality not because of the potato, which did not exist in Israel at the time of the Temple, but because of the oil.

Potato pancakes, called *latkes* in Yiddish and *levivot* in Hebrew, appear to have come to us from Russia. There, the Jews make latkes from a great variety of other ingredients, from cheese to buckwheat flour to noodles. A latke usually is a shallow-fried pancake but it sometimes can be a deep-fried fritter.

Besides potatoes, latkes can be made from other vegetables. Creative Jewish cooks have extended the repertoire and now many prepare pancakes from courgettes, corn, cauliflower, spinach and even mixtures of several vegetables. Our courgette cakes with garlic are of Sephardic origin, while the dill-flavoured vegetable pancakes are eastern European. Cumin, one of the favourite spices in Israel, adds a special taste to the corn cakes.

Vegetable pancakes can be served the same way as potato pancakes. They are delicious as appetizers, as vegetarian main courses, or as partners for roasts or braised poultry or meat; of course, any toppings with dairy products would be omitted.

The Israeli doughnuts, or soofganiyot, originated in central Europe and are prepared in a broad area stretching from Romania through Hungary, Austria and Germany to Alsace in France. They have become so widespread in Israel because many of the pastry chefs there are Austrian and Hungarian Jews. Indeed, the common Hebrew word for pastry shop is *konditoria*, from the German *konditorei*. Soofganiyot are lighter than ordinary ring doughnuts and do not have holes. Two types are prepared in Israel, the 'classic' type made with yeast and a quick version made with baking powder. At Hanukkah, the yeast version is sold fresh by all the bakeries.

The remaining dishes served for the holiday are usually family favourites of the season and vary from one country to another. Brisket or roast chicken, goose or duck appear on the tables of many homes, either on the first night of Hanukkah or on the Saturday that falls during the holiday week. Apples are popular, both in desserts and as apple purée to accompany the latkes.

Hanukkah is a time for parties and fun. The children play special Hanukkah games and often receive gifts or coins made of chocolate. Family and friends get together for relaxed dinners or buffet-style parties. Hanukkah food suits this atmosphere. Crisp latkes and light doughnuts disappear quickly when served at a casual get-together of family or friends and add warmth to the cold winter days.

Other ideal Hanukkah dishes:

Spinach Pancakes (page 270)

Easy Cauliflower Latkes (page 269)

Potato and Walnut Fritters (page 266)

Sephardic Pumpkin Pancakes (page 92)

Potato and Vegetable Kugel (page 37)

Yemenite Tomato Dip (page 163)

Savoury Pastries with Buckwheat Filling (Kasha Knishes)
(page 164)

Roast Goose with Apples (page 243)

HANUKKAH DINNER

The following menu is composed of dishes that are quick and easy to prepare and are ideal for serving as a Hanukkah buffet dinner or party.

HANUKKAH DINNER MENU

Chopped Liver and Aubergine Pâté

Israeli Vegetable Salad (page 34)

**Aromatic Poussins with Raisins, or Brisket,
American-Jewish Style**

Honey-Glazed Carrots

Celery and Potato Pancakes with Dill

**Apple Cake with Pecans and Cinnamon,
or
Hanukkah Doughnuts (Soofganiyot),
or
Quick Hanukkah Pastry Puffs**

CHOPPED LIVER AND AUBERGINE PATE

Aubergine gives this version of chopped chicken liver a lighter texture. Jaklyn Cohen of Holon, Israel, who was born in Iraq, taught me this speciality of hers.

MAKES 8 TO 10 SERVINGS

1 medium aubergine, 450–550 g (1–1¼ lb)	2 medium onions, chopped
	salt and freshly ground pepper
135 ml (9 tbsp) vegetable oil	4 hard-boiled large eggs,
450 g (1 lb) chicken livers	size 1 or 2

GARNISH

2 hard-boiled large eggs, quartered, size 1 or 2	fresh bread or crackers, for serving
fresh parsley sprigs	

Peel aubergine, halve it lengthways and cut into thin slices. Heat 30 ml (2 tbsp) oil in a large frying pan, add about third of the slices and sauté over medium-high heat for about 1 minute on each side or until they begin to brown. Cover and cook over low heat for about 5 minutes or until very tender. Remove and repeat with remaining aubergine in 2 batches, adding 30 ml (2 tbsp) oil to pan each time.

Preheat grill with rack about 7.5 cm (3 inches) from heat. Rinse livers and pat dry on paper towels; cut off any green spots. Put livers on foil in grill and sprinkle with salt. Grill for 3 minutes or until top is light brown. Turn livers over, sprinkle second side with salt, and grill for 3 – 4 more minutes or until cooked through and colour is no longer pink; cut to check. Discard juices. Cool livers and halve.

Heat 45 ml (3 tbsp) oil in a large frying pan. Add onions and sauté over medium-low heat for about 15 minutes, or until very tender and light brown. Add livers, salt and pepper and sauté over medium heat, tossing and stirring constantly, for 2 minutes.

Work half the onions, liver, aubergine and eggs in a food processor until fairly fine but not completely puréed. Remove and repeat with remaining ingredients. Season to taste with salt and pepper. Refrigerate for 1 hour before serving, or up to 3 days.

To serve, spoon into a bowl and garnish. Serve cold or at room temperature, accompanied by fresh bread or crackers.

AROMATIC POUSSINS WITH RAISINS

This dish is based on a recipe I learned from my friend and culinary mentor, Ruth Sirkis, a famous cookery writer in Israel. It is typical of the new cuisine that is developing in the Jewish state, featuring a combination of Western techniques, Israeli fruit and Middle Eastern spices. The poussins are fragrant from the spices but are not hot. Serve them for Hanukkah with potato latkes, and for other occasions with rice.

Makes 4 Servings

2 poussins, 550–700 g
  (1¼–1½ lb) each, thawed
  if frozen
7.5 ml (1½ tsp) ground cumin
5 ml (1 tsp) paprika
2.5 ml (½ tsp) salt
pinch of cayenne pepper
1 medium onion, thinly sliced
1 small carrot, thinly sliced
1 celery stalk, thinly sliced
250 ml (8 fl oz) fresh orange
  juice

250 ml (8 fl oz) dry white
  wine
30 ml (2 tbsp) vegetable oil
40–50 g (1½–2 oz) raisins
2 oranges, divided into neat
  segments, with juice
  reserved
30 ml (2 tbsp) water
10 ml (2 tsp) potato flour
  or cornflour

Cut each poussin into 4 pieces by first cutting off leg and thigh pieces at thigh joint, then breast and wing pieces. Cut off backs and reserve for soup. Mix cumin, paprika, salt and cayenne pepper and rub mixture thoroughly into poussin pieces. Put them in a large bowl and add onion, carrot, celery, orange juice and wine. Cover and refrigerate for at least 2 hours or overnight.

Preheat oven to 200°C (400°F) mark 6. Pat poussin pieces dry, reserving their marinade. Heat oil in a large heavy frying pan, add pieces in batches and sauté over medium-high heat until brown on each side. Transfer them to a shallow baking dish.

Discard fat from frying pan, add marinade with vegetables and bring to the boil, stirring. Pour mixture over poussin pieces, cover and bake for 30 minutes. Uncover and bake for 10–15 more minutes or until tender. Remove poussin pieces and strain cooking juices into a pan. Return poussin to baking dish, cover and keep warm.

Add raisins and juice from orange segments to poussin cooking juices and boil until raisins are tender and sauce is concentrated and well flavoured. Whisk water into potato flour to form a smooth mixture. Add to simmering sauce, stirring, and bring just back to the boil. Taste for seasoning. Add orange segments, heat over low heat a few seconds, then pour sauce with raisins and oranges over poussin pieces.

BRISKET,
AMERICAN-JEWISH STYLE

In America brisket has come to symbolize Jewish cooking, perhaps because Jewish cooks have developed tasty recipes for using this cut of meat to best advantage. Brisket is sometimes cubed and used in tzimmes with fruit and vegetables (page 85), or cooked as hamin (page 156). But the image that comes to mind most often is of brisket that is roasted slowly as one succulent piece, either pot-roasted on top of the cooker or baked in a covered tin in the oven, as here.

American cooks often flavour the brisket with ketchup, which adds a tangy note, as in this version that I learned to prepare from my aunt, Sylvia Saks. She prefers to serve the brisket with tasty Garlic-Scented Roast Potatoes (page 266), but if you wish to cook everything in the same tin, you can instead roast some potatoes around the brisket.

If you are preparing brisket for Hanukkah, for which it is a favourite, accompany it with potato pancakes.

MAKES 5 OR 6 SERVINGS

4 large garlic cloves, crushed	1.4 kg (3 lb) piece boneless
3.75 ml (¾ tsp) pepper	brisket, excess fat trimmed
5 ml (1 tsp) paprika	225 g (8 oz) tomato ketchup
5 ml (1 tsp) salt	120 ml (4 fl oz) water
5 ml (1 tsp) vegetable oil	900 g (2 lb) large baking
2 medium onions, sliced	potatoes (optional)

Mix garlic, spices, salt and oil to a paste and rub into meat. Leave to stand for about 30 minutes. Preheat oven to 200°C (400°F) mark 6.

Put onions in a small roasting tin and top with brisket, fat side up.

120

Cover with foil and roast for 15 minutes. Reduce oven temperature to 160°C (325°F) mark 3. Pour ketchup over brisket and spread lightly. Add water to tin, pouring it around, not over, meat. Cover and bake for 1½ hours, occasionally adding a few spoonfuls water to tin if it becomes dry.

Peel and quarter potatoes. Add them to tin around meat. Baste meat and potatoes with pan juices and sprinkle potatoes lightly with salt. Cover and roast for 45 minutes; turn potatoes over and roast for 45 minutes longer or until brisket and potatoes are very tender when pierced with a fork.

Remove meat to board, ketchup side up. Remove onions with slotted spoon. Put 50 g (2 oz) onions in a medium saucepan and add roasting juices from meat. Boil for about 5 minutes or until well flavoured and slightly thickened. Taste this sauce and adjust seasoning. If desired, heat remaining onions in a separate small saucepan to serve on the side.

With a thin-bladed sharp knife, carve meat in thin slices crossways. Serve sauce and onions separately.

HONEY-GLAZED CARROTS

A popular Rosh Hashanah vegetable dish in the Romanian and Hungarian kitchen, glazed carrots are also a favourite among the Jews in France. A hint of grated lemon adds a fresh touch to balance the delicate sweetness of the dish.

MAKES 4 SERVINGS

450 g (1 lb) carrots, peeled and sliced	15 ml (1 tbsp) honey
	30 ml (2 tbsp) vegetable oil
250 ml (8 fl oz) water	2.5 ml (½ tsp) grated
pinch of salt	lemon rind
15 ml (1 tbsp) sugar	

Combine carrots, water and salt in a medium saucepan. Bring to the boil and simmer, uncovered, for 10 minutes. Add sugar, honey and oil and continue cooking over medium-low heat, stirring occasionally, until carrots are very tender and liquid is absorbed, about 15 minutes. Watch so mixture does not burn. Add grated lemon rind and remove from heat. Serve hot or at room temperature.

CELERY AND POTATO PANCAKES WITH DILL

Celery adds a pleasing flavour to the usual potato pancakes, and these make a nice change for Hanukkah. They are good with Roast Duck with Prunes and Red Wine (page 102).

MAKES 14 OR 15 PANCAKES; 3 OR 4 SERVINGS

4 medium celery stalks, about 225 g (8 oz) total, trimmed
30 ml (2 tbsp) plain flour
2.5 ml (½ tsp) baking powder
550 g (1¼ lb) baking potatoes
1 large egg, size 1 or 2
2.5 ml (½ tsp) salt

1.25 ml (¼ tsp) ground white pepper
30 ml (2 tbsp) finely chopped fresh dill
about 120 ml (4 fl oz) vegetable oil, for frying

Peel celery with vegetable peeler to remove strings and cut into 4×0.3×0.3-cm (1½×⅛×⅛-inch) matchsticks. Mix flour with baking powder. Peel potatoes and grate them, using grating/shredding disc of food processor or large holes of hand grater. (Work quickly so they won't discolour.) Transfer potatoes and celery to colander. Squeeze mixture by handfuls to remove as much liquid as possible.

Beat egg with salt and pepper and stir in dill. Add to potato mixture and mix well. Add flour mixture and mix well. Do not let batter stand or it will discolour.

Heat oil in 25–30-cm (10–12-inch) heavy frying pan over medium heat. For each pancake, drop about 30 ml (2 tbsp) of potato mixture into frying pan. Flatten pancake with back of spoon, pressing ingredients together, so it is 6–7.5 cm (2½–3 inches) in diameter. Shape 2 more pancakes. Fry over medium heat until golden brown on bottom, about 4 minutes. Turn carefully using 2 slotted spatulas. Fry until second side is golden brown, about 4 minutes. Drain on paper towels.

Keep pancakes warm if necessary in 200°C (400°F) mark 6 oven while frying rest of mixture. Stir mixture before frying each new batch. If oil becomes too hot, reduce heat slightly. Add more oil to pan if needed and heat it before making more pancakes. (Pancakes can be kept 4 hours at room temperature and reheated on baking sheet in 200°C (400°F) mark 6 oven, but won't be as crisp as when freshly fried.) Serve pancakes hot.

APPLE CAKE WITH PECANS AND CINNAMON

When I worked at the Tel Aviv University library, exchanging recipes with my co-workers was my preferred coffee-break pastime. This recipe is based on the cake that my librarian friend baked often for *Shabbat*. Diced apples flavour the mixture and sliced apples are arranged on top in an attractive pattern and glazed with sugar and cinnamon. Use sharp or medium-sharp eating apples.

MAKES 16 TO 20 SERVINGS

10 ml (2 tsp) ground
  cinnamon
225 g (8 oz) sugar
700 g (1½ lb) apples, peeled,
  halved, cored and diced
200 g (7 oz) unsalted non-
  dairy margarine or butter

2 large eggs, size 1 or 2
225 g (8oz) plain flour
7.5 ml (1½ tsp) baking
  powder
100 g (4 oz) pecans, coarsely
  chopped

TOPPING

2 large apples, about 450 g
  (1 lb)
30 ml (2 tbsp) unsalted
  non-dairy margarine or
  butter, melted

105 ml (7 tbsp) sugar
10 ml (2 tsp) ground
  cinnamon

Preheat oven to 200°C (400°F) mark 6. Mix cinnamon and 100 g (4 oz) sugar in a large bowl. Add apples and mix.

In another bowl beat margarine until smooth. Add remaining 125 g (4 oz) sugar and beat until fluffy. Add eggs one by one, beating well after each addition. Sift flour with baking powder and stir into egg mixture. Stir in apple mixture and pecans. Spread in a greased 33×23-cm (13×9-inch) baking tin with 5-cm (2-inch) sides. Smooth top.

Peel, halve and core apples and cut them into thin slices. Lay slices in overlapping rows to cover cake completely. Brush slices with melted margarine. Mix sugar and cinnamon and sprinkle evenly over top. Bake for 1 hour or until apples are very tender. Cool in tin on a rack. (Cake can be kept, covered, for 3 to 4 days in refrigerator.)

To serve, cut cake into squares. Serve at room temperature.

HANUKKAH DOUGHNUTS (SOOFGANIYOT)

Fluffy doughnuts without holes similar to these are known by many names; I've seen them as Bismarck Jam Doughnuts, *krapfen*, and in France as *boules de Berlin* (Berlin balls). Probably Austrian bakers brought them to Israel, and now they rival potato pancakes in popularity as Hanukkah food. Other common flavourings for these doughnuts, besides the brandy used in this recipe, are vanilla, grated lemon rind, cinnamon and nutmeg.

Before frying the doughnuts, read 'Hints on Deep-Frying'.

MAKES 14 LARGE DOUGHNUTS
(NOT INCLUDING THE SCRAPS)

175 ml (6 fl oz) lukewarm water

15 g (½ tsp) dried yeast

50 g (2 oz) granulated sugar

450 g (1 lb) plain flour, plus 30 ml (2 tbsp) more if necessary

2 large eggs, size 1 or 2

2 large egg yolks, size 1 or 2

90 g (3½ oz) unsalted non-dairy margarine or butter, at room temperature

30 ml (2 tbsp) brandy

10 ml (2 tsp) salt

at least 1 litre (2 pints) vegetable oil, for deep-frying

about 75 g (3 oz) apricot or strawberry jam

sifted icing sugar, for sprinkling

Pour 120 ml (4 fl oz) lukewarm water into a small bowl. Sprinkle yeast on top and add 5 ml (1 tsp) sugar. Leave to stand 10 minutes.

Spoon flour into mixer bowl or another large bowl. Make a well in centre and add remaining sugar, eggs, yolks, margarine, brandy, remaining water and salt. Mix with mixer dough hook or wooden spoon until ingredients are blended. Add yeast mixture and mix with dough hook at low speed or with spoon until ingredients come together to a dough. Beat at medium speed, scraping down dough occasionally, for 5 minutes; or knead by hand for 5 minutes. If dough is very sticky, add 30 ml (2 tbsp) flour. Knead for 5–10 minutes more until very smooth.

Put dough in a clean, oiled bowl and turn to coat with oil. Cover with a damp cloth and leave to rise in a warm place for 1–1½ hours or until doubled in volume.

On a floured surface roll out half the dough until 0.5 cm (¼ inch) thick, flouring dough occasionally. Using a 6–7.5-cm (2½–3-inch) cutter, cut dough in rounds. Put 2.5 ml (½ tsp) apricot or strawberry jam on centre of half the rounds. Brush rim of round lightly with water, then set a plain round on top. With floured fingers, press dough firmly all around to seal it. Transfer this 'sandwich' immediately to floured tray. If it has stretched out to an oval, plump it gently back into a round shape. Continue with remaining dough. Cover pastries with a slightly damp cloth and leave to rise in a warm place for about 30 minutes.

Knead the scraps of dough, put them in an oiled bowl, cover with a damp cloth and leave to stand for about 30 minutes.

Heat oil to 180°C (350°F); if a deep-fat thermometer is not available, heat oil until it bubbles gently around a small piece of dough added to it. Add 4 doughnuts or enough to fill pan without crowding. Fry doughnuts for about 3 minutes on each side or until golden brown. Drain on paper towels. Pat tops gently with paper towels to absorb excess oil.

Make more doughnuts with scraps if you like; they won't be as light but will still be good.

Serve warm or at room temperature, sprinkled with icing sugar. Don't serve these immediately because the jam is boiling hot.

HINTS ON DEEP-FRYING

It's important to follow a few simple rules so that deep-frying is a pleasant and safe experience.

- Don't fill the pan more than half full of oil.
- Hold ingredients near the surface of the oil and slide them in gently. Don't hold ingredients high above oil and drop them in because they'll splash the hot oil.
- When food is added to the oil, it bubbles vigorously. Don't crowd the pan because the oil can bubble up to the top and even overflow.
- Regulate the heat if necessary to keep the oil at the right temperature.
- Give your full attention to the frying; don't leave in the middle to do something else.

QUICK HANUKKAH PASTRY PUFFS

These are made by home cooks in Israel as quick substitutes for the yeast-leavened doughnuts. They are ready in minutes and taste good, but are not as light as the yeast version.

MAKES 8 OR 9 LARGE OR 16 TO 20 SMALL PASTRIES; 4 TO 6 SERVINGS

---

150 g (5 oz) plain flour
6.25 ml (1¼ tsp) baking powder
2 large eggs, size 1 or 2
45 ml (3 tbsp) granulated sugar
60 ml (4 tbsp) vegetable oil

60 ml (4 tbsp) water or milk
1.25 ml (¼ tsp) salt
5 ml (1 tsp) vanilla essence
at least 1 litre (2 pints) oil, for deep-frying
sifted icing sugar, for sprinkling

Sift flour with baking powder. Combine eggs, sugar, oil, water or milk, salt and vanilla in a bowl and whisk until smooth. Add flour mixture and mix to a smooth, thick batter.

Heat oil to 180°C (350°F), if a deep-fat thermometer is not available, heat oil until it bubbles gently around a small piece of dough added to it. Slide mixture gently into oil by rounded 15 ml (1 tbsp) spoons for large ones, or by 5 ml (1 tsp) spoons for small; if mixture doesn't easily come off spoon, dip another spoon in the oil and use to push it off. Do not drop dough into oil from high above or it might make hot oil splatter. Fry for 2–3 minutes on each side or until golden brown. Drain on paper towels. Pat tops gently with paper towels to absorb excess oil.

Serve hot or warm, sprinkled with icing sugar.

A LATKE PARTY

A selection of several types of pancakes of different colours makes great Hanukkah party fare, especially when presented with a choice of toppings, like the mint- and garlic-scented yogurt or the dill soured cream in our recipes here. The addition of an Israeli-style salad of diced tomatoes, peppers and cucumber and a chocolate-almond layer cake turns the menu into a lovely vegetarian Hanukkah feast.

LATKE PARTY MENU

My Mother's Potato Pancakes (Potato Latkes)

Apple Compote

**Courgette Pancakes with Garlic and
Yogurt Mint Topping,
or
Corn Cakes with Cumin**

Vegetable Pancakes with Dill Soured Cream

Bright Red Cabbage Salad

**Orange-Pecan Torte,
or
Chocolate-Almond Cake
with Chocolate-Honey Frosting (page 94)**

MY MOTHER'S POTATO PANCAKES (POTATO LATKES)

The eight-day festival of Hanukkah is celebrated with parties, candles, games and gifts but most of all, potato pancakes. The pancakes have become the symbol of the holiday and are a must for any Hanukkah party.

These crisp, lacy pancakes are easy to prepare with the aid of a food processor for grating the vegetables. The usual flavouring is grated onion, but some cooks add grated carrots or courgettes to the potato mixture as well. For a sweet note, others stir in a grated apple and sometimes a pinch of cinnamon, or a little sugar and lemon juice.

Potato pancakes are sprinkled with sugar or accompanied by apple purée when served on their own. They can also be served with meat or chicken, and in this case the sugar and apple purée are usually omitted. If they are part of a meatless meal, they can be topped with a dollop of soured cream or yogurt.

MAKES ABOUT 15 PANCAKES; 4 OR 5 SERVINGS

*4 large potatoes, about 550 g
(1¼ lb), peeled
1 medium onion, about 225 g
(8 oz)
15 ml (1 tbsp) chopped fresh
parsley (optional)
1 large egg, size 1 or 2
5 ml (1 tsp) salt*

*1.25 ml (¼ tsp) white pepper
30 ml (2 tbsp) plain flour
2.5 ml (½ tsp) baking powder
about 120 ml (4 fl oz)
vegetable oil, for frying
apple purée, Apple Compote
(opposite), soured cream
or sugar, for serving*

Grate potatoes and onion, using grating disc of a food processor or large holes of a grater. Transfer to a colander; squeeze mixture to press out as much liquid as possible. In a large bowl mix potatoes, parsley, egg, salt, pepper, flour and baking powder.

Heat oil in a deep, heavy 25–30-cm (10–12-inch) frying pan. For each pancake, drop about 30 ml (2 tbsp) of potato mixture into pan. Flatten with back of a spoon so each cake is about 6–7.5 cm (2½–3 inches) in diameter. Fry over medium heat for about 4–5 minutes on each side, or until golden brown and crisp. Turn carefully with 2 spatulas so oil doesn't splatter. Cook until crisp on other side, then drain on paper towels. Stir potato mixture before frying each new batch. If all the oil is absorbed, add a little more to pan. Serve hot, accompanied by apple purée, compote, soured cream or sugar.

NOTE: Potato pancakes can be prepared ahead and refrigerated or frozen on a baking sheet; when frozen, they can be transferred to a bag. They can be reheated (after being slightly defrosted if they were frozen) on a baking sheet in a 230°C (450°F) mark 8 oven for a few minutes.

APPLE COMPOTE

Instead of canned apple sauce, this freshly made accompaniment for potato pancakes can be served as a chunky topping, or can be puréed in a food processor to turn it into a flavourful apple purée. When the apples are left in pieces, the compote can be served as a dessert on its own; it's especially good served hot, with ice cream.

MAKES ABOUT 8 TO 10 SERVINGS

900 g (2 lb) Golden Delicious apples	5 ml (1 tsp) lemon juice
40 g (1½ oz) butter or margarine	1.25–2.5 ml (¼ –½ tsp) ground cinnamon (optional)
	30–45 ml (2–3 tbsp) sugar

Peel and halve the apples. Core them and cut into thin wedges or slices.

Melt butter in a large frying pan or sauté pan over medium-high heat. Add apples and sauté, turning pieces over from time to time, for about 2 minutes or until they are coated with butter. Add lemon juice and cinnamon, cover and cook over low heat for 5 minutes, or until liquid begins to come out of apples. Uncover and continue cooking over low heat, gently stirring occasionally, for 15–20 minutes or until apples are tender and begin to fall apart.

Add 30 ml (2 tbsp) sugar and sauté over medium-high heat, turning apple wedges over, for about 2 minutes or just until sugar dissolves. Remove from heat. Taste and add more sugar if necessary; heat, tossing apples gently, until sugar dissolves. (Apple compote can be kept, covered, for 2 days in a refrigerator.) Serve it warm or at room temperature, to accompany potato pancakes.

COURGETTE PANCAKES WITH GARLIC AND YOGURT MINT TOPPING

In these pancakes the delicate green colour of the courgette shows through the golden brown crust. The Sephardic-style yogurt and mint topping is a refreshing complement to the light pancakes and is also good with plain sautéed courgettes or aubergine or with cooked green beans.

MAKES 12 SMALL CAKES; 4 APPETIZER OR SIDE-DISH SERVINGS

GARLIC AND YOGURT MINT TOPPING

120 ml (4 fl oz) natural yogurt

7.5 ml (1½ tsp) chopped fresh mint

½ small garlic clove, finely chopped

salt and freshly ground pepper

COURGETTE PANCAKES

about 3 courgettes, total about 350 g (12 oz), coarsely grated

15 ml (1 tbsp) chopped garlic

salt and freshly ground pepper

1 large egg, size 1 or 2, lightly beaten

45 ml (3 tbsp) plain flour

60 ml (4 tbsp) vegetable oil, for frying

mint sprigs, for garnish

Mix yogurt with mint and garlic. Season to taste with salt and pepper. Set aside at room temperature.

Combine courgette, garlic, salt and pepper. Add beaten egg and stir in lightly. Stir in flour. Heat oil in a deep, heavy, large frying pan. For each pancake, drop heaped tablespoons courgette mixture into pan. Flatten slightly with back of a spoon and fry over medium heat for about 2–3 minutes on each side, or until golden brown. Turn very carefully so oil doesn't splatter. Drain on paper towels. Stir mixture before frying each new batch. If all the oil is absorbed, add a little more to pan. Serve hot, with topping. Garnish with mint sprigs.

CORN CAKES WITH CUMIN

A combination of whole and puréed sweetcorn kernels gives these cakes a great corn flavour. Serve them for Hanukkah instead of or in addition to potato pancakes. Cumin is a common seasoning in Jewish dishes from the Middle East and goes very well with corn.

MAKES 12 SMALL CAKES;
4 APPETIZER OR SIDE-DISH SERVINGS

325 g (11 oz) fresh or frozen sweetcorn kernels, cooked, drained and cooled	1 large egg, size 1 or 2
	30 ml (2 tbsp) plain flour
	60 ml (4 tbsp) vegetable oil, for frying
salt and pepper	
5 ml (1 tsp) ground cumin	

TOPPING (OPTIONAL)

120 ml (4 fl oz) soured cream or natural yogurt, at room temperature	15 ml (1 tbsp) chopped fresh coriander or parsley
	50 g (2 oz) ripe tomato, finely diced

Purée 75 g (3 oz) cooked sweetcorn; a few chunks may remain. Mix puréed corn with salt, pepper, cumin and egg. Stir in flour, then sweetcorn kernels.

Heat oil in a deep, heavy, large frying pan. For each pancake, drop heaped tablespoons corn mixture into pan. Flatten slightly with back of a spoon and fry over medium heat for about 2–3 minutes on each side, or until golden brown. Turn carefully with 2 spatulas so oil doesn't splatter. Drain on paper towels. Stir mixture before frying each new batch. If all the oil is absorbed, add a little more to pan. Serve hot.

If desired, top each pancake with 7.5–15 ml (½–1 tbsp) soured cream or yogurt, then sprinkle with coriander and diced tomato. Serve remaining soured cream or yogurt separately.

VEGETABLE PANCAKES WITH DILL SOURED CREAM

Green peas peak out of these golden brown eastern European-style pancakes, which also contain sautéed mushrooms, onion and carrot.

MAKES 14 SMALL PANCAKES; 4 OR 5 APPETIZER OR SIDE-DISH SERVINGS

DILL SOURED CREAM

250 ml (8 fl oz) soured cream or natural yogurt

15 ml (1 tbsp) snipped fresh dill

VEGETABLE PANCAKES

100 g (4 oz) small mushrooms

120 ml (4 fl oz) vegetable oil

1 medium onion, finely chopped

25 g (1 oz) celery, chopped

1 large carrot, coarsely grated

75 g (3 oz) cooked fresh or frozen peas

2 large eggs, size 1 or 2, lightly beaten

salt and pepper

15 ml (1 tbsp) snipped fresh dill

30–45 ml (2–3 tbsp) matzo meal

Mix soured cream or yogurt and dill. Season to taste with salt and pepper. Set aside at room temperature.

Separate mushroom stalks from caps; halve both caps and stalks lengthways and cut into thin slices. Heat 60 ml (4 tbsp) oil in a large frying pan over medium-low heat. Add onion and sauté for 5 minutes. Add mushrooms and celery and sauté for 8–10 minutes.

Leave to cool, then transfer to a bowl. Stir in grated carrot. Add cooked peas, eggs, salt and pepper, dill and 30 ml (2 tbsp) matzo meal. Mix well; if watery, add another 15 ml (1 tbsp) meal.

Heat remaining 60 ml (4 tbsp) oil in a deep, heavy, large frying pan. For each pancake, drop good 15 ml (1 tbsp) vegetable mixture into pan. Flatten slightly with back of a spoon and fry over medium heat for about 2–3 minutes on each side, or until golden brown. Turn very carefully using 2 spatulas. Drain on paper towels. Stir mixture before frying each new batch. If all the oil is absorbed, add a little more to pan. Serve hot, accompanied by dill soured cream.

BRIGHT RED CABBAGE SALAD

In Israel I was always intrigued by the vibrant colour of the red cabbage salad often served in Middle Eastern-style restaurants. Eventually I learned their secret – pouring a small amount of boiling vinegar over the shredded vegetable. This salad is especially good with sausages, cold meats and roast poultry and meats.

MAKES 6 TO 8 SERVINGS

½ small red cabbage, about 400 g (14 oz)	salt and freshly ground pepper
105 ml (7 tbsp) white wine vinegar	175 ml (6 fl oz) vegetable oil
15 ml (1 tbsp) prepared mustard	40 g (1½ oz) spring onions, chopped
	100 g (4 oz) toasted walnut halves or pieces (optional)

Cut cabbage half in two and cut out core. Shred cabbage in a food processor or cut into very thin strips with a large knife. Put cabbage in a large bowl.

In a small saucepan bring 60 ml (4 tbsp) vinegar to the boil. Pour it over cabbage and toss quickly until mixed well.

In a medium bowl, whisk mustard with remaining 45 ml (3 tbsp) vinegar, salt and pepper. Whisk in oil. Add dressing gradually to cabbage, tossing. Taste and adjust seasoning. (Salad can be kept for 2 days in refrigerator.)

A short time before serving, add chopped spring onions to salad. Serve sprinkled with toasted walnuts.

ORANGE PECAN TORTE

Moistening a cake with orange juice after it is baked rather than the classic sugar syrup is a trick I learned in Israel. The juice gives the cake a fresh orange flavour. Each slice of this luscious torte has whipped cream on three sides because the cake is baked in an angel cake tin.

MAKES ABOUT 10 SERVINGS

133

90 g (3½ oz) pecans
30 ml (2 tbsp) plus 10 ml
  (2 tsp) breadcrumbs
175 g (6 oz) sugar
4 large eggs, size 1 or 2,
  separated, at room
  temperature

5 ml (1 tsp) grated orange
  rind
1.25 ml (¼ tsp) cream of
  tartar

60 ml (4 tbsp) strained fresh
  orange juice
250 ml (8 fl oz) double cream

10 ml (2 tsp) sugar
6–8 pecan halves

Preheat oven to 160°C (325°F) mark 3. Butter an 18-cm (7¼-inch) angel cake tin with 7.5-cm (3-inch) sides. Line base with non-stick paper or foil (with hole cut in centre for tube) and butter paper or foil. Flour sides of tin and lined base, shaking out excess.

In a food processor grind pecans with breadcrumbs and 50 g (2 oz) sugar to a fine powder. Transfer mixture to a bowl.

Beat egg yolks in large bowl of mixer until blended. Add 75 ml (5 tbsp) sugar and beat until pale yellow and thick, about 5 minutes. Beat in orange rind.

Beat egg whites with cream of tartar in another large bowl with clean beater until stiff. Gradually add remaining sugar and whip at high speed until whites are stiff but not dry, about ½ minute. Sprinkle one-third of pecan mixture over yolks and fold gently. Spoon one-third of whites on top and fold gently. Repeat until pecan mixture and whites are folded in. Fold as lightly but as quickly as possible.

Spoon mixture carefully into tin and smooth top. Bake for 30–35 minutes or until a fine skewer inserted in comes out clean. Without loosening cake, cool in tin upside down on a rack for 30 minutes.

Run a thin-bladed flexible knife around sides of cake, then around tube. Turn out onto wire rack set above tray. Using a fine skewer, poke 12 holes at equal distances in cake from top nearly to bottom. Slowly pour in orange juice; cake should absorb it. Slide cake carefully onto serving plate. Refrigerate for at least 1 hour or up to 2 days.

Whip cream with sugar in chilled bowl until stiff. Spread whipped cream all over cake including inside edge. Decorate with pecan halves. Refrigerate for at least 1 hour before serving. (Cake can be iced 8 hours ahead.)

PURIM
The Hamantaschen Holiday

 Purim is a joyous festival celebrated in late February or early March. Most people practice a custom of *mishloah manot*, which literally means 'sending of portions' but which could be described as a Jewish 'biscuit exchange'. Friends, relatives and neighbours send each other boxes of sweets – favourite biscuits, slices of cake and most of all the filled three-cornered biscuits called *hamantaschen*, Yiddish for 'Haman's pockets'.

In Hebrew these traditional Purim treats are called *Oznei Haman* or 'Haman's ears', and are meant to recall the story of Esther, in which the Jewish Queen of Persia helped foil the evil intentions of the wicked Prince Haman, who wanted to destroy the Jews. This story is read on Purim in the synagogue, and every time Haman's name comes up, the children in the congregation make lots of noise with special noisemakers they bring for the occasion.

The first time I made hamantaschen, I found it surprising to be instructed to cut the dough in a circle in order to obtain a triangle. I assumed the intriguing triangular shape of hamantaschen was unique to Jewish cooking, and so I was astonished to discover in France a cheese-filled pastry of the same shape known as *talmouses*, which the French claim date from the Middle Ages.

Hamantaschen make a wonderful treat with coffee, tea or milk. The time-honoured filling for these pastries is of poppy seeds, but other fillings are made as well, from a variety of dried fruit. The filling can be enclosed in a tender soured cream dough, a crisp dough, or a rich yeast dough. Since hamantaschen keep well, they are perfect as gifts of homemade goodies to friends. In addition to hamantaschen with several fillings, Purim boxes often include Chocolate Coconut Rum Balls, Strawberry Pecan Squares and, in general, cakes that can be easily cut into bite-size portions.

Other ideal Purim dishes:

Cinnamon-Nut-Raisin Crescents (Rugelach) (page 312)

Citrus-Scented Almond Macaroons (page 67)

Chocolate-Coconut Rum Balls (page 318)

Strawberry Pecan Squares (page 320)

A BOX OF SWEETS FOR PURIM

Hamantaschen with Poppy Seed-Raisin Filling

Date-Filled Hamantaschen

Hamantaschen with Fig Filling

Hamantaschen with Prune Filling

Soft Coconut-Chocolate Chip Cookies

HAMANTASCHEN WITH POPPY SEED-RAISIN FILLING

Hamantaschen are triangular filled biscuits traditional for Purim. The best-loved filling is made from poppy seeds. You can use a spice grinder for a delicate textured ground seed filling, or you can leave the seeds whole for a more crunchy filling. Both ways are good – which you choose is a matter of personal taste.

Some people simply mix the poppy seeds with the other ingredients, but I much prefer the creamier texture and enhanced flavour achieved by cooking the seeds with milk and honey, a method that is prevalent in Israel.

MAKES ABOUT 32 HAMANTASCHEN

100 g (4 oz) poppy seeds
120 ml (4 fl oz) milk
65 g (2½ oz) sugar
30 ml (2 tbsp) honey
75 g (3 oz) raisins
40 g (1½ oz) butter or
  margarine

5 ml (1 tsp) grated lemon rind
Soured Cream Dough
  (page 138) or One, Two,
  Three Biscuit Dough (recipe
  follows)

If you like, grind poppy seeds in a spice grinder. In a small saucepan combine poppy seeds, milk, sugar and honey and bring to a simmer. Cook over low heat, stirring often, for about 15–20 minutes or until thick. Add raisins and butter and stir over low heat until butter melts. Remove from heat. Stir in grated lemon rind. Chill well before using.

Use a quarter of dough at a time. Roll it out on a lightly floured surface until about 0.3 cm (⅛ inch) thick. Using a 7.5-cm (3-inch) biscuit cutter, cut dough into circles. Brush edges lightly with water. Put 5 ml (1 tsp) filling in centre of each circle. Pull up edges of circle in 3 arcs that meet in centre above filling. Close them firmly and pinch edges to seal. Put on greased baking sheet and refrigerate. Refrigerate scraps.

Roll remaining dough and scraps and shape more hamantaschen. Refrigerate for at least 30 minutes before baking to firm dough. (Unbaked, they can be kept overnight in refrigerator.) Preheat oven to 190°C (375°F) mark 5. Bake hamantaschen for about 14 minutes or until they are light golden at edges. Cool on a wire rack. (They can be kept for about 4 days in an airtight container.)

NOTE: Close hamantaschen well and do not be tempted to use extra filling, or it will come out during baking. If using One, Two, Three Biscuit Dough, some dough will be left over; use it to make biscuits.

ONE, TWO, THREE BISCUIT DOUGH

I learned to make this biscuit dough at a cooking course I took in Tel Aviv, run by the Israeli Nutrition and Home Economics Institute. The dough is known as 'One, Two, Three' for two reasons: (1) preparing it is 'as easy as one-two-three', especially in the version I now make, in the food processor; and (2) its basic proportions are

100 grams sugar, 200 grams butter and 300 grams flour. This Austro-Hungarian pastry is well liked in Israel for hamantaschen and biscuits; they come out crisp, sweet and delicious.

MAKES ABOUT 1 KG (2¼ LB) DOUGH; ENOUGH FOR 48 HAMANTASCHEN (INCLUDING SCRAPS)

---

1 large egg, size 1 or 2	290 g (10½ oz) cold unsalted
1 large egg yolk, size 1 or 2	butter or margarine, cut in
425 g (15 oz) plain flour	small pieces
175 g (6 oz) icing sugar	12.5 ml (2½ tsp) grated
7.5 ml (1½ tsp) baking	orange rind
powder	15–30 ml (1–2 tbsp) orange
1.25 ml (¼ tsp) salt	juice (optional)

Beat egg with yolk to blend. Combine flour, icing sugar, baking powder and salt in a food processor fitted with a metal blade. Process briefly to blend. Scatter butter pieces over mixture. Mix using on/off motion until mixture resembles coarse breadcrumbs. Sprinkle with grated rind and pour egg mixture evenly over mixture in processor. Process with on/off motion, scraping down occasionally, until dough just begins to come together in a ball. If crumbs are dry, sprinkle with 15 ml (1 tbsp) orange juice and process briefly; repeat if crumbs are still dry.

Transfer dough to a work surface. Knead lightly to blend. With a spatula, transfer dough to a sheet of cling film. Wrap it and push it together. Shape dough in a flat round. Refrigerate for at least 3 hours or up to 3 days.

NOTE: If you like, use some of dough to make hamantaschen, and the rest to make Ashkenazic Poppy Seed Biscuits (page 319).

SOURED CREAM DOUGH

This dough is very tender and delicate in flavour. It is only lightly sweetened and is less crisp than One, Two, Three Dough but is easier to work with and can be used for any of the hamantaschen fillings in this chapter.

MAKES ABOUT 700 G (1½ LB) DOUGH; ENOUGH FOR 32 HAMANTASCHEN

1 large egg, size 1 or 2	1.25 ml (¼ tsp) salt
30–45 ml (2–3 tbsp) soured cream	200 g (7 oz) cold unsalted butter or margarine, cut into small pieces
275 g (10 oz) plain flour	
50 g (2 oz) icing sugar	7.5 ml (1½ tsp) grated lemon rind
5 ml (1 tsp) baking powder	

Beat egg with 30 ml (2 tbsp) soured cream. Combine flour, icing sugar, baking powder and salt in a food processor. Process briefly to blend. Scatter butter pieces over mixture. Mix using on/off motion, until mixture resembles coarse breadcrumbs. Sprinkle with grated lemon rind and pour egg mixture evenly over mixture in processor. Process with on/off motion, scraping down occasionally, until dough just begins to come together in a ball. If mixture is dry, add remaining 15 ml (1 tbsp) soured cream, putting it in teaspoons over mixture, and process briefly again.

Transfer dough to a work surface. Knead lightly to blend. With a spatula, transfer dough to a sheet of cling film, wrap it and push it together. Shape dough into a flat round. Refrigerate for at least 2 hours or up to 3 days.

NOTE: If you wish to make dough by hand instead of in food processor, follow method in variation of French Sweet Pastry (page 310).

DATE-FILLED HAMANTASCHEN

Cocoa enriches this smooth, easy filling and tempers the natural sweetness of the dates. In Israel dates are sold ground so they can be used in hamantaschen or to fill other biscuits, but whole dates can be puréed in no time in the food processor.

MAKES ABOUT 32 HAMANTASCHEN

350 g (12 oz) stoned dates	One, Two Three Biscuit Dough or Soured Cream Dough (opposite)
45 ml (3 tbsp) cocoa powder	
45 ml (3 tbsp) tangy jam, such as plum jam	

Grind dates in food processor. Add cocoa and jam and process to blend.

Follow shaping and baking instructions for Hamantaschen with Prune Filling (opposite).

NOTE: If using One, Two, Three Biscuit Dough, some dough will be left over for making biscuits. Or if you wish to use all the dough to make hamantaschen, prepare the filling with the following quantities: 450 g (1 lb) dates, 25 g (1 oz) cocoa powder, 75 g (3 oz) jam.

HAMANTASCHEN WITH FIG FILLING

The intriguing filling of dark figs gives a delicious Middle Eastern accent to these originally European pastries.

MAKES ABOUT 32 HAMANTASCHEN

---

100 g (4 oz) small dried figs, stalks removed, halved
75 g (3 oz) raisins
25 g (1 oz) pecans, chopped
75 g (3 oz) plum jam

25 g (1 oz) desiccated coconut
One, Two, Three Biscuit Dough or Soured Cream Dough (page 138)

Combine figs and raisins in bowl of food processor. Chop them together, then transfer to a mixing bowl and stir in nuts, jam and coconut.

Follow shaping and baking instructions for Hamantaschen with Prune Filling (oppposite).

NOTE: If using One, Two, Three Biscuit Dough, some dough will be left over for making biscuits. Or if you wish to use all the dough to make these hamantaschen, prepare the filling with the following quantities: 175 g (6 oz) figs, 115 g (4½ oz) raisins, 40 g (1½ oz) pecans, 100 g (4 oz) plum jam, and 25 g (1 oz) desiccated coconut.

HAMANTASCHEN WITH PRUNE FILLING

When I was a girl, I enjoyed helping my mother shape these haman-taschen, and they have been my favourite version ever since. The prune filling is very simple to prepare. A touch of grated orange rind gives it a fresh note. These hamantaschen are small and dainty, in contrast to the large ones often found in bakeries.

MAKES ABOUT 32 HAMANTASCHEN

225 g (8 oz) stoned prunes	10 ml (2 tsp) grated orange
25 g (1 oz) walnuts	rind
90 ml (6 tbsp) plum or	One, Two, Three Biscuit
strawberry jam	Dough or Soured Cream
75 g (3 oz) raisins (optional)	Dough (page 138)

Cover prunes with cold water and soak for 8 hours or overnight; or cover them with boiling water and soak for 15 minutes.

Grind walnuts to a fine powder. Drain prunes and chop finely or purée in food processor. Mix prune purée with walnuts, jam, raisins and orange rind.

Use one quarter of dough at a time. Roll it out on a lightly floured surface until about 0.3 cm (⅛ inch) thick. Using a 7.5-cm (3-inch) biscuit cutter, cut in circles. Brush edges lightly with water, then put 5 ml (1 tsp) filling in centre of each. Pull up edges of circle in 3 arcs that meet in centre above filling. Close them firmly and pinch edges to seal. Put on greased baking sheet and refrigerate. Refrigerate scraps.

Roll remaining dough and scraps and shape more hamantaschen. Refrigerate for at least 1 hour to firm dough. (They can be kept overnight in refrigerator.)

Preheat oven to 190°C (375°F) mark 5. Bake hamantaschen for about 14 minutes or until they are light golden at edges.

NOTE: If using One, Two Three Biscuit Dough, some dough will be left over for making biscuits. If you wish to use all the dough to make these hamantaschen, prepare the prune filling with the following quantities: 350 g (12 oz) prunes, 40 g (1½ oz) walnuts, 135 ml (9 tbsp) jam, 100 g (4 oz) raisins, and 15 ml (1 tbsp) grated orange rind.

SOFT COCONUT-CHOCOLATE CHIP COOKIES

For the yearly Purim biscuit exchange, American Jewish cooks like to offer American-style cookies, like these moist, rich chocolate chip cookies, alongside the hamantaschen. The cookies are enriched with soured cream and highlighted with a touch of lemon.

MAKES ABOUT 42 COOKIES

150 g (5 oz) plain flour
6.25 ml (1¼ tsp) baking powder
1.25 ml (¼ tsp) bicarbonate of soda
1.25 ml (¼ tsp) salt
100 g (4 oz) unsalted butter, at room temperature
175 g (6 oz) sugar

1 large egg, size 1 or 2
10 ml (2 tsp) grated lemon rind
60 ml (4 tbsp) soured cream
175 g (6 oz) desiccated coconut
250 g (9 oz) plain chocolate chips

Preheat oven to 180°C (350°F) mark 4. Butter 3 baking sheets. Sift flour, baking powder, bicarbonate of soda and salt into a medium bowl.

Cream butter in a mixer bowl, add sugar and beat until smooth and fluffy. Add egg and beat until smooth. Add lemon rind and beat until blended. Stir in half the flour mixture until blended. Stir in half the soured cream. Repeat with remaining flour mixture and soured cream. Stir in coconut and chocolate chips.

Push mixture from a 5 ml spoon (1 tsp) with a second 5 ml spoon (1 tsp) onto prepared sheets, using about 15 ml (1 tbsp) mixture for each cookie, mounding them high and spacing them about 5 cm (2 inches) apart.

Bake for about 12 minutes or until light brown at edges and nearly set but still soft to touch in centre. Using a palette knife, carefully transfer cookies to wire racks. Cool completely. Cool baking sheets and butter them. Make more cookies with remaining mixture. (Cookies can be kept for up to 1 week in an airtight container at room temperature; or they can be frozen. They lose their softness after 3 days but still taste good.)

SABBATH
The Weekly Feast

 The Sabbath, or *Shabbos* in Yiddish or *Shabbat* in Hebrew, is the time when Jewish families enjoy the best meal of the week. The finest china, the prettiest tablecloth and the most delicious food is reserved for this day of rest. Special white *Shabbat* candles add to the atmosphere of festivity.

All the members of the family, and often of the extended family as well, get together for the main meal. Actually there are two *Shabbat* dinners: the first on Friday night after sundown, when the Sabbath begins, and the second on Saturday around noon.

The rhythm of much of the week revolves around preparing for and celebrating *Shabbat*. On Wednesday thoughts turn to planning the menu for the two main *Sabbath* meals. Cooks who bake their own bread prepare the dough on Thursday, and some might bake cakes, too. The markets in Israel are most crowded on Thursday, when everyone is buying fresh produce, fish and meat for *Shabbat*. Friday is another busy market day, as there are plenty of last-minute shoppers.

Jews all over the world have created special dishes for the holiday. The food is different from that of the rest of the week also because during the Sabbath itself cooking is not permitted. In observant households everything is cooked ahead, making Friday quite a hectic day. The food is either kept warm or reheated, depending on the custom of the family. Even if the food is reheated, the stove is not turned on during Sabbath, but rather a hot plate or the oven is left on.

These rules have led to the development of such tasty dishes as hamin, a rich stew of meat and beans that is prepared in different versions by both Ashkenazic and Sephardic Jews, and of a variety of appetizers that are suitable for being served cold.

Roast chicken and other poultry are also favourite Jewish choices for main courses for the holiday. Often they are served with roasted potatoes, or might include a stuffing based on bread, rice or, in the case of Moroccan Jews, couscous. Vegetables are most likely to be served as salads, or as side dishes of the type that taste good when very tender, such as Honey-Glazed Carrots (page 121) or Sautéed Aubergine in Spicy Tomato Sauce (page 93). A festive presentation of vegetables for *Shabbat* is to bake them as a kugel.

A beautiful challah or fresh homemade bread is one of the highlights of the Sabbath table. Baking breads, cakes and biscuits for *Shabbat* is an important activity in many families, including ours. When I lived in Israel, my favourite weekly radio programme was called 'A Cake for *Shabbat*'. It remained one of the most popular radio shows in Israel for many years.

The Sabbath dinner generally includes several courses. When I was growing up, the menu usually began with either chopped liver or gefilte fish as well as simple tomato and lettuce salad, and was followed by chicken soup with fluffy matzo balls. For the main course we had roast chicken, noodle kugel and cooked carrots or other seasonal vegetables. Dessert was often a chocolate cake, such as My Mother's Chocolate Apple Cake (page 106) or Chocolate-Nut Chiffon Cake. This is still my mother's weekly Sabbath menu, and sometimes is mine as well.

My mother-in-law's *Shabbat* menu features a garlic-pepper chutney, an aubergine salad with olive oil or a fenugreek dip, and an Israeli diced vegetable salad. The main course might be hamin, cumin-flavoured chicken in the pot, or a savoury chicken and meat casserole served with rice and a seasonal cooked vegetable. For dessert, there is luscious fresh seasonal fruit – it might be guavas, mangos or a variety of citrus fruit.

Other ideal Sabbath dishes:

Piquant Cooked Carrot Salad (page 187)

Yemenite Chicken Soup (page 197)

Chicken Soup with Rice, Tomatoes and Coriander (page 195)

Chicken Soup with Kreplach (page 81) or with Egg Noodles

Iranian Meatball Soup for Shabbat (page 199)

Sweet and Sour Salmon (page 218)

Fish with Light Lemon and Dill Sauce (page 225)

Moroccan Sea Bass with Peppers and Tomatoes (page 227)

Braised Cod with Chick Peas and Olive Oil (page 221)

Roast Chicken with Noodle-Mushroom-Walnut Stuffing
(page 232)

Couscous with Lamb and Seven Vegetables (page 249)

Roast Lamb with Garlic, Onions and Potatoes (page 25)

Veal with Olives, Tomatoes and Fresh Herbs (page 248)

Cauliflower Kugel with Mushrooms (page 255)

Potato and Vegetable Kugel (page 37)

Potato Kugel with Asparagus and Broccoli (page 256)

Noodle Kugel with Onions and Mushrooms (page 277)

Challah (Egg Bread) (page 289)

Shabbat Breakfast Bread (Kubaneh) (page 293)

HOLIDAY MENUS AND RECIPES

Shabbat Pastry Rolls (Jihnun) (page 303)

Browned Eggs (page 216)

Soured Cream Coffee Cake with Walnuts (page 305)

Chocolate-Orange Marble Cake (page 306)

Pear Strudel (page 105)

Raspberry Almond Tart (page 308)

Crisp Almond Slices (Mandelbrot) (page 314)

Dried Fruit Compote with Wine (page 323)

ASHKENAZIC SHABBAT MENU
Chopped Liver, or Gefilte Fish (page 24)

Challah (purchased or homemade, page 289)

Tomato and Lettuce Salad

**Ashkenazic Chicken Soup with Fresh Dill and
Light Matzo Balls (page 99)**

Roast Chicken with Pecan and Herb Stuffing

**Jerusalem Noodle Kugel,
or
Cinnamon-Scented Apple Noodle Kugel**

**Honey-Glazed Carrots (page 121),
or
Other Seasonal Vegetables**

**Chocolate-Nut Chiffon Cake,
or
My Mother's Chocolate Apple Cake (page 106)**

CHOPPED LIVER

This may be the favourite Jewish appetizer, and perhaps the best known as well. The proportions of grilled liver, sautéed onions and hard-boiled eggs vary considerably, according to each family's preference. Traditional recipes call for chicken fat for sautéing the onion, but my mother has always made it with oil; either way, it tastes wonderfully rich.

Chopped liver is often served in a scoop or spoonful on a bed of lettuce, with a garnish of tomato slices, radishes, parsley sprigs, chopped onion, olives, cucumber slices, gherkins or pickled peppers and chillies. It should be accompanied by or spread on challah, rye bread, crackers or matzo. At my brother's wedding in Jerusalem, the caterer served it as a filling for swan-shaped cream puffs!

MAKES 4 TO 6 APPETIZER SERVINGS

350–450 g (12 oz–1 lb) chicken livers	*1–2 hard-boiled large eggs, size 1 or 2, coarsely grated or chopped*
salt	
45 ml (3 tbsp) vegetable oil or chicken fat	*freshly ground pepper*
2 medium onions, chopped	*lettuce leaves and tomato slices, for serving*

Preheat grill with rack about 7.5 cm (3 inches) from flame. Rinse livers and pat dry on paper towels; cut off any green spots. Put livers on foil under grill and sprinkle with salt. Grill for 3 minutes or until top is light brown. Turn livers over, sprinkle second side with salt, then grill for 3–4 more minutes or until cooked through and colour is no longer pink; cut to check. Discard juices from foil. Cool livers slightly.

Heat oil or fat in a large heavy frying pan over medium-low heat. Add onions and sauté, stirring occasionally, for 15 minutes or until tender and beginning to turn golden.

Chop the liver in a food processor. Add onions and chop with on/off pulses until blended in. Transfer to bowl and lightly mix in eggs. Season well with salt and pepper. (Chopped liver can be kept, covered, for 2 days in refrigerator.) Serve cold, in scoops on lettuce leaves. Garnish with tomato slices.

NOTE: If using rendered chicken fat in a jar, stir to blend before using if it is in 2 layers.

ROAST CHICKEN WITH PECAN AND HERB STUFFING

Like most Ashkenazic Jews, my mother frequently serves roast chicken for the Sabbath meal. She often prepares a bread stuffing like this one, enhanced with chopped nuts, sautéed onions and celery. Occasionally she adds a grated carrot and grated courgette for a tasty variation, and sometimes a diced red pepper and chopped mushrooms as well.

Since a chicken cannot hold as much stuffing as everyone wishes to eat, this recipe includes extra stuffing for baking in a separate dish.

MAKES 4 SERVINGS

PECAN AND HERB STUFFING

50 g (2 oz) pecans
about 100–150 g (4–5 oz) day-old or stale challah or French or Italian white bread
50 g (2 oz) non-dairy margarine or vegetable oil
1 medium onion, finely chopped
50 g (2 oz) celery, chopped
1 bay leaf
salt and freshly ground pepper
1 medium courgette, coarsely grated (optional)
1 medium carrot, coarsely grated (optional)
2.5 ml (½ tsp) dried thyme, crumbled
5 ml (1 tsp) finely chopped fresh sage, or 2.5 ml (½ tsp) dried, crumbled
scant 15 g (½ oz) fresh parsley, chopped
1 large egg, size 1 or 2, beaten (optional)
30–60 ml (2–4 tbsp) chicken soup or stock
15–25 g (½–1 oz) non-dairy margarine, for baking

1.6–1.8-kg (3½–4-lb) chicken
1.25 ml (¼ tsp) salt
1.25 ml (¼ tsp) pepper
2.5 ml (½ tsp) paprika
10 ml (2 tsp) vegetable oil
60–120 ml (4–8 tbsp) chicken soup or stock, for basting

Preheat oven to 180°C (350°F) mark 4. Toast nuts on a small baking sheet until lightly browned, about 5 minutes. Cool nuts and coarsely chop.

Reduce oven temperature to 140°C (275°F) mark 1. Cut bread in 1-cm (½-inch) cubes. Put bread cubes on 1 large or 2 small baking

148

sheets. Bake until crisp and dry, stirring frequently, for about 20 minutes. Cool and transfer to a large bowl.

Heat 45 ml (3 tbsp) margarine in a medium frying pan over medium heat. Add onion, celery, bay leaf, and a pinch of salt and pepper. Cook, stirring occasionally, until onion is softened, about 10 minutes. Add remaining margarine, courgette, carrot, thyme and sage and stir until blended. Remove from heat; discard bay leaf.

Add onion mixture, parsley, egg and nuts to bread and toss lightly until blended. Gradually add soup or stock, tossing lightly. Mixture may appear dry, but will become much moister from juices in bird. Taste and adjust seasoning. (Stuffing can be refrigerated for up to 1 day in covered container. Do not stuff bird in advance.)

Preheat oven to 190°C (375°F) mark 5. Discard excess fat from chicken. Mix salt, pepper, paprika and oil. Rub chicken all over with mixture. Spoon stuffing lightly into chicken. Fold skin over stuffing; truss or skewer closed, if desired. Set chicken in a roasting tin.

Add a little more soup or stock, if necessary, to extra stuffing so that most of bread is very lightly moistened. Grease a baking dish of same or slightly larger volume than amount of remaining mixture and spoon stuffing into it. Dot with margarine and cover dish.

Roast chicken for 45 minutes. Put extra dish of stuffing in oven and roast both together for about 45 minutes more, basting chicken occasionally with pan juices if desired, and basting stuffing occasionally with a few spoonfuls soup or stock. To check whether chicken is done, insert a skewer into thickest part of drumstick; it should be tender and juices that run from chicken should be clear. If juices are pink, roast chicken for a few more minutes and check it again. Also insert a skewer into stuffing inside chicken; it should come out hot.

Transfer chicken to a carving board or serving platter and remove any trussing strings. Carve chicken and serve hot, with stuffing.

NOTE: To bake all of stuffing separately, preheat oven to 160°C (325°F) mark 3. Grease a 1.4-litre (2–2½-pint) casserole and spoon stuffing into it. Dot stuffing with margarine and cover casserole. Bake for 1 hour, basting twice with 60 ml (4 tbsp) soup. Uncover for last 10 minutes for crisper top.

To save time, omit toasting the bread cubes; stuffing will be softer.

JERUSALEM NOODLE KUGEL

Although kugel is an Ashkenazic speciality, Jerusalemites of all origins prepare this rather peppery version of the dish. It is flavoured with caramelized sugar but is not sweet because the caramel is cooked until it is very dark. The secret to avoiding chunks of caramel is to cook the sugar mixture without stirring and to add it to the still-warm pasta. The traditional way to prepare this kugel of fine noodles is to bake it all night in a very low oven, so that it turns a deep brown throughout. For serving, it is turned out and cut in slices like a cake.

At Jerusalem synagogues this kugel often appears on the table for the light meal that is served after the morning services on *Shabbat*.

MAKES 8 TO 10 SERVINGS

350 g (12 oz) fine egg noodles	*2 large eggs, size 1 or 2*
	5 ml (1 tsp) salt
120 ml (4 fl oz) vegetable oil	*5 ml (1 tsp) ground pepper*
50 g (2 oz) sugar	*few pinches of cayenne pepper*

Cook noodles in a large pan of boiling salted water for about 5 minutes or until barely tender. Drain well, return to pan and toss briefly with 60 ml (4 tbsp) oil. Keep warm on cooker, uncovered.

Pour remaining 60 ml (4 tbsp) oil into heavy saucepan, then add sugar. Heat over low heat without stirring, but shaking pan gently from time to time. Cook until sugar turns dark brown; this can take between 15–25 minutes. Gradually add mixture to noodles, mixing well with tongs.

Beat eggs with salt, pepper and cayenne. Add to noodles and mix well. Taste and adjust seasoning; mixture should be quite peppery. Transfer to a greased round 1.5–1.8-litre (2³/₄–3¹/₄-pint) casserole. Cover with foil and with a lid. (Kugel can be kept for a few hours in refrigerator at this point.)

Preheat oven to lowest setting. Bake kugel overnight, or for about 14 hours. Run a knife around edge and turn out onto a round serving plate. Serve hot. (To reheat leftovers, you can slice them, wrap in foil and heat in oven at about 180°C (350°F) mark 4.

NOTE: For a quicker version, bake kugel uncovered at 180°C (350°F) mark 4 for 1 hour. It will not be as deep brown.

CINNAMON-SCENTED APPLE NOODLE KUGEL

Meltingly tender apples form a layer in the centre of this nut- and raisin-studded baked noodle pudding. I like to sauté the apples to give them a rich taste and delicate texture instead of adding them raw, as in most apple-noodle kugels. Serve this as a slightly sweet accompaniment for meat or chicken, or for a supper or brunch dish with yogurt or soured cream. In the unlikely event you have leftovers, they can be cut into portions, wrapped in foil and reheated in the oven.

MAKES 8 SERVINGS

400 g (14 oz) medium egg noodles	50 g (2 oz) pecans, walnuts or almonds, coarsely chopped
3 Golden Delicious apples, about 700 g (1½ lb) total	50 g (2 oz) raisins
75 g (3 oz) non-dairy margarine	5 ml (1 tsp) grated lemon rind
	pinch of salt
90 ml (6 tbsp) sugar	4 large eggs, size 1 or 2, separated
5 ml (1 tsp) ground cinnamon	5 ml (1 tsp) vanilla essence

Preheat oven to 180°C (350°F) mark 4. Grease a 33×23-cm (13×9-inch) baking dish with 5-cm (2-inch) sides. Cook noodles in a large pan of boiling salted water until barely tender, for about 5 minutes. Drain, rinse with cold water and drain well again. Transfer to a large bowl. Separate noodles with your fingers.

Peel apples, halve, core and slice them. Heat 25 g (1 oz) margarine in a large frying pan over medium heat. Add half the apples and sauté over medium heat for 5 minutes, turning once. Remove with a slotted spoon, add rest of apples to pan and sauté them also. Return all apples to pan, sprinkle with 30 ml (2 tbsp) sugar and 2.5 ml (½ tsp) cinnamon, then sauté for another minute, tossing apples to coat well. Transfer to a bowl. Add remaining margarine to pan and melt it over low heat. Add 45 ml (3 tbsp) melted margarine to noodles and mix well. Stir in nuts, raisins, lemon rind and salt.

Whisk egg whites until soft peaks form. Beat in remaining 60 ml (4 tbsp) sugar and whisk at high speed until whites are stiff but not dry. Stir egg yolks and vanilla into noodles. Stir in one quarter of the whipped egg whites, then fold in remaining egg whites carefully.

Add half the noodle mixture to the greased baking dish. Top with sautéed apples in an even layer and sprinkle with any margarine remaining in bowl. Top with remaining noodle mixture and spread gently to cover apples. Sprinkle with remaining 2.5 ml (½ tsp) cinnamon, then with remaining melted margarine. Cover dish and bake for 30 minutes. Uncover and bake for 15–20 minutes or until set. Serve hot.

CHOCOLATE-NUT CHIFFON CAKE

Chiffon cakes like this one are frequently made by Jewish cooks for the Sabbath dinner because they taste rich but do not contain dairy products. And chocolate is a useful ingredient for kosher desserts, since there is no problem in using it for meat meals as long as it's not milk chocolate or white chocolate, which contain milk powder. A generous proportion of chocolate makes this chiffon cake especially rich. For meatless meals it's even richer with the chocolate cream frosting.

MAKES 14 TO 16 SERVINGS

75 g (3 oz) plain chocolate, chopped
50 g (2 oz) bitter chocolate, chopped
100 g (4 oz) pecans
350 g (12 oz) sugar
225 g (8 oz) sifted cake flour
5 ml (1 tsp) salt

15 ml (1 tbsp) baking powder
6 large egg yolks, size 1 or 2
120 ml (4 fl oz) vegetable oil
175 ml (6 fl oz) cold water
8 large egg whites, size 1 or 2, at room temperature
2.5 ml (½ tsp) cream of tartar

FROSTING (OPTIONAL)
175 g (6 oz) plain chocolate, chopped
45 ml (3 tbsp) water
2 large egg yolks, size 1 or 2
300 ml (½ pint) double cream, well chilled

30 ml (2 tbsp) sugar
10–12 pecan halves, for decoration

Preheat oven to 160°C (325°F) mark 3. Have ready a 26-cm (10-inch) angel cake tin with 10-cm (4-inch) sides and removable tube, do not butter tin.

Melt chocolates for cake in a medium bowl set above hot water over low heat. Stir until smooth, then remove from pan of water and leave to cool.

Grind pecans in food processor with 50 g (2 oz) sugar, then transfer to a bowl. Sift the flour, salt and baking powder into a large bowl, add 175 g (6 oz) sugar and stir until blended. In another bowl combine egg yolks, oil and water and beat until smooth.

Make a large well in the bowl of dry ingredients and pour in yolk mixture. Gently stir dry ingredients into yolk mixture, using a wooden spoon. Add chocolate and stir just until there are no lumps.

Whisk egg whites with cream of tartar in a large bowl until soft peaks form. Gradually beat in remaining 100 g (4 oz) sugar and whisk at high speed until whites are stiff but not dry. Fold about one quarter of the whites into chocolate mixture until nearly incorporated. Gently fold chocolate mixture into remaining whites. Sprinkle ground pecans over mixture and fold in lightly but quickly, just until mixture is blended. Pour mixture into tin. Bake for about 1 hour 10 minutes or until a fine skewer inserted in cake comes out clean.

Turn tin upside down and cool cake in tin on a wire rack for 1½ hours. Run a palette knife gently around cake. Push up centre to remove sides of tin, then run a thin-bladed knife around tube. Run palette knife carefully under cake to free it from base and turn out carefully onto a serving plate. (Cake can be kept, wrapped, for 2 days at room temperature.)

Place chocolate and water for frosting in a medium bowl and set it above a pan of hot water over low heat. Whisk until smooth, then remove from pan of water. Whisk egg yolks, one by one, into chocolate mixture. Set bowl of chocolate mixture back above pan of hot water over low heat and cook, whisking, for 1 minute. Remove from pan of water and leave to stand for about 15 minutes or until cool but not set; mixture will be very thick.

Whip cream with sugar in a large chilled bowl until soft peaks form. Stir about 120 ml (4 fl oz) cream into chocolate mixture. Return mixture to bowl of cream and fold gently until blended.

Brush any loose crumbs off top of cake. Spread frosting evenly and generously all over cake, including inner surface. Decorate with pecans. Refrigerate for at least 1 hour before serving. (Frosted cake can be kept, covered, for 3 days in a refrigerator.)

Yemenite Shabbat Menu

Chilli-Garlic Chutney (Zehug)

Pita Bread (purchased or homemade, page 296)

Fried Cauliflower with Cumin and Turmeric

Israeli Vegetable Salad (page 34)

**Aromatic Beef and White Bean Casserole (Hamin), or
Yemenite Beef and Chicken Casserole (page 58)**

Easy Rice Pilaf (if not serving bean casserole)

Fresh Fruit

CHILLI-GARLIC CHUTNEY (ZEHUG)

The Yemenite condiment known as *zehug* is a fiery chilli paste, made basically of equal parts of uncooked fresh chillies and garlic, and is a well-known feature of Yemenite cuisine. It tastes somewhat like certain hot fresh Indian chutneys. Zehug is made in two basic variations: green zehug from green chillies and red zehug from red chillies. Like chutney, it appears on the table from the beginning of the meal, for spreading on bread. It can also be used as a hot seasoning for sauces.

Zehug is popular among Israelis of many origins, and in Israel is readily available, but many people prefer the taste of homemade.

Makes about 4 to 6 Servings

5 medium jalapeño chillies, about 50 g (2 oz) total	*15 g (½ oz) fresh coriander*
	2.5 ml (½ tsp) salt
50 g (2 oz) medium garlic cloves, peeled	*freshly ground black pepper to taste*
30–45 ml (2–3 tbsp) water, if needed	*15 ml (1 tbsp) cumin, preferably freshly ground*

154

Wear gloves when handling chillies. Remove stalks from chillies; remove seeds and core, if desired (so chutney will be less hot). Put garlic and chillies in food processor and purée until finely chopped and well blended. If necessary, add 30–45 ml (2–3 tbsp) water, just enough to enable food processor to chop mixture. Add coriander and process until blended. Add salt, pepper and cumin. Keep in a jar in refrigerator. (It keeps for about 1 week.)

FRIED CAULIFLOWER WITH CUMIN AND TURMERIC

This is one of the most delicious cauliflower recipes I know. The spiced batter imparts a wonderful aroma and taste to the vegetable, as well as a lovely golden colour.

MAKES 4 SERVINGS

900 g (2 lb) cauliflower	50 g (2 oz) plain flour
2.5 ml (½ tsp) salt	2 large eggs, size 1 or 2
pinch of black pepper	30 ml (2 tbsp) water
1.25 ml (¼ tsp) turmeric	1.1 litres (2 pints) vegetable
5 ml (1 tsp) ground cumin	oil, for frying

Divide cauliflower into fairly large florets with stalks attached. Cook cauliflower, uncovered, in a large pan of boiling salted water for 3 minutes, but do not cook completely. Drain and rinse to cool.

Mix salt, pepper, turmeric, cumin and flour in a medium bowl. Sprinkle cauliflower florets lightly with spice mixture. Add eggs and water to remaining spice mixture and stir with whisk until blended to a smooth, thick batter. Dip a floret in batter – it should coat floret lightly; if it sticks to floret in a thick layer, stir in 5 ml (1 tsp) water.

Heat oil in a deep, heavy saucepan to 180–185°C (350–360°F), or until it bubbles vigorously around a batter-coated floret. Holding floret by its stalk, dip flower and part of base in batter and add gently to oil. Dip 5 or 6 more florets. Fry for about 2–3 minutes or until golden brown. Drain on paper towels. Serve as soon as possible.

NOTE: If you prefer to shallow-fry, cook for 5 minutes per side.

AROMATIC BEEF AND WHITE BEAN CASSEROLE (HAMIN)

French books on Jewish cooking refer to hamin as 'Jewish cassoulet'. Both share the technique of slow, gentle cooking of meat and beans, so the meat gives the beans a rich taste. This stew exists in many versions among Jews.

The ingredients vary widely. Some cooks use haricot beans or kidney beans, while others use chick peas; some add kasha, barley or wheat berries. The meat can be beef, lamb or chicken. Most cooks flavour the casserole with onions and some add potatoes to the pot. The seasonings might include any number of spices.

This stew traditionally cooks for about eighteen hours; it is put in the oven just before sundown on Friday and is served on Saturday for an early lunch. There is no need to soak the beans beforehand.

MAKES 6 SERVINGS

900 g (2 lb) chuck steak, trimmed and cut into 5-cm (2-inch) pieces

275 g (10 oz) haricot beans, picked over and rinsed

4 medium boiling potatoes, about 550 g (1¼ lb) total, peeled and halved

100 g (4 oz) wheat berries (available at health food shops), rinsed

1 large onion, sliced

4 medium garlic cloves, chopped

10 ml (2 tsp) salt

2.5 ml (½ tsp) pepper

25 ml (5 tsp) ground cumin

20 ml (4 tsp) turmeric

1.5 litres (2¾ pints) water

6 large eggs in shells, size 1 or 2, rinsed

Preheat oven to lowest setting. In a large heavy casserole combine meat, beans, potatoes, wheat berries, onion and garlic. Sprinkle with salt, pepper, cumin and turmeric and mix thoroughly. Add water and bring to the boil, stirring occasionally. Remove from heat. Set eggs gently on top and push them slightly into liquid.

Cover tightly and bake mixture, without stirring, for 10–11 hours, or until most of the liquid is absorbed by the beans. Serve stew from casserole, or carefully spoon it into a heated serving dish. Shell and halve the eggs and set them on top for garnish.

NOTE: For a faster method, bake beef mixture in a preheated 120°C (250°F) mark ½ oven for 5 hours, then simmer, uncovered, over low heat without stirring for 1 more hour, or until enough liquid evaporates so mixture is moist but no longer soupy.

EASY RICE PILAF

On the menus of Sephardic Jews, rice pilaf appears often as an accompaniment for meats, poultry and vegetables. Many cooks sauté the onion until golden, in contrast to the way pilaf is prepared in classic French cooking, with onions that are softened but remain white. Next, the rice is sautéed with the onion, to help keep the grains separate. Rice cooked with water will be lighter in colour but less flavourful than rice cooked with chicken stock. For a slightly spicy rice, use Yemenite Chicken Soup (page 197) for the cooking liquid.

MAKES 4 TO 6 SERVINGS

30 ml (2 tbsp) vegetable or olive oil	750 ml (1¼ pints) hot chicken soup, stock or boiling water
1 medium onion, finely chopped	pinch of pepper
290 g (10½ oz) long-grain white rice	2.5 ml (½ tsp) salt (optional)

Heat oil in a sauté pan or large frying pan. Add onion and cook over low heat, stirring occasionally, for about 10 minutes or until golden. Add rice and sauté, stirring, for about 2 minutes or until grains turn milky white.

Add soup, stock or water and pepper. Add salt if using unsalted or lightly salted soup, stock or water. Bring to the boil, then stir once with a fork and cover. Cook over low heat, without stirring, for 18–20 minutes or until rice is tender and liquid is absorbed. Remove from heat and leave to stand, covered, for 10 minutes. Taste and adjust seasoning. (Rice will keep hot for about 45 minutes. It can be prepared 2 days ahead and kept, covered, in refrigerator. To reheat, heat 15 ml (1 tbsp) oil in a large frying pan, add rice and heat over low heat, stirring gently with a fork.) Fluff it with a fork just before serving. Serve hot.

PART II

Every Day Jewish Dishes

APPETIZERS

Festive Jewish meals, whether Ashkenazic or Sephardic, generally begin with several appetizers. One is most likely to be a spread or dip, such as chopped chicken liver, avocado spread, the chick pea spread called *hummus*, or the sesame dip known as *tehina* or tahini sauce. All are accompanied, of course, by good fresh bread and frequently by piquant treats such as olives and pickled vegetables. Fiery Chilli-Garlic Chutney (page 154) and a hot tomato dip, as well as a tangy dip made from fenugreek seeds, are served on the tables of Yemenite Jews.

For special occasions like weddings there will often be a pastry appetizer, such as Russian piroshki, eastern European knishes or Sephardic bourekas.

Perhaps the most famous Israeli appetizer is falafel or chick pea croquettes. Falafel is most commonly served in a pita, with tahini and Israeli salad, as a quick meal or satisfying snack. In recent years falafel restaurants have expanded on the theme and serve falafel with a selection of sauces each person can add, which include tomato sauce, chilli sauce, fenugreek sauce, and a sort of curry sauce, as well as an assortment of pickles and fried aubergine slices. Falafel balls also make a delicious hors d'oeuvre or cocktail snack, served with tahini sauce for dipping.

Fish is a popular appetizer as well. It might be smoked or pickled fish or lox purchased from a delicatessen, served on its own or made into salads; or a home-cooked fresh fish.

In Israel an assortment of appetizers might be the basis of a light meal or party menu. They might be accompanied by cut vegetables and perhaps some cheeses or sliced cold meats. The breads are chosen according to the type of appetizer – pita is the natural choice for serving with hummus, tahini sauce or marinated aubergine slices, while challah or rye bread is a favourite with chopped liver.

SAVOURY CHEESE KNISHES

Appetizer pastries known as knishes symbolize the Ashkenazic kitchen almost as much as gefilte fish. Besides cheese, fillings vary from buckwheat groats to chopped meat to liver to potatoes.

Knishes do have a reputation for being heavy, perhaps because some bought ones are made quite large. These knishes, although rich and satisfying, are fairly small. They make delightful appetizers and are much easier to prepare than most other knishes.

MAKES 16 TO 18 PASTRIES

SOURED CREAM DOUGH

175 g (6 oz) plain flour	*100 g (4 oz) unsalted butter*
5 ml (1 tsp) baking powder	*or margarine*
2.5 ml (½ tsp) salt	*75 ml (5 tbsp) soured cream*

FOUR-CHEESE FILLING

100 g (4 oz) curd cheese,	*50 g (2 oz) feta cheese, finely*
drained	*crumbled*
30 ml (2 tbsp) cream cheese,	*1 large egg, size 1 or 2*
softened	*pepper to taste*
75 g (3 oz) Swiss cheese,	
grated	

In a food processor combine flour, baking powder, salt and butter and process with on/off switch until mixture resembles coarse bread-crumbs. Spoon soured cream fairly evenly over mixture. Process with on/off switch until dough just holds together and forms sticky crumbs, adding 5 ml (1 tsp) water if necessary. Knead lightly. Wrap dough and flatten to a square. Refrigerate for 2 hours.

Mix all ingredients for filling with fork. Season with pepper.

Lightly grease a baking sheet. Divide dough into 2 pieces. Roll one to a 20×23-cm (8×10-inch) rectangle, slightly under 0.3 cm (⅛ inch) thick. Spread with half the filling, leaving a 1-cm (½-inch) border. Beginning at a long side, roll up tightly like a Swiss roll. Cut in slices 2.5 cm (1 inch) thick. Put them on baking sheet with cut side (the less open side) facing down. Refrigerate slices. Repeat with remaining dough and filling. Refrigerate 30 minutes or overnight.

Preheat oven to 200°C (400°F) mark 6. Bake knishes for 15–18 minutes or until lightly browned. Serve hot or warm.

SEPHARDIC SPINACH-STUFFED FILO TURNOVERS (SPINACH BOUREKAS)

Spinach rivals cheese as the filling of choice for the savoury Sephardic pastry known as bourekas. Some cooks simply use strips of raw spinach leaves, but I like to cook the spinach first.

MAKES ABOUT 32 TURNOVERS; 10 TO 12 SERVINGS

450 g (1 lb) filo sheets (about 20 sheets)
225 g (8 oz) butter or margarine, melted

about 10 ml (2 tsp) sesame seeds, for sprinkling

SPINACH FILLING
900 g (2 lb) fresh spinach, stalks discarded, leaves rinsed well; or 1 × 450-g (16-oz) packet frozen leaf spinach
45 ml (3 tbsp) olive oil
1 medium onion, finely chopped

2 large eggs, size 1 or 2
100 g (4 oz) Swiss cheese, grated
salt and pepper to taste
freshly grated nutmeg to taste

If filo sheets are frozen, thaw them in refrigerator for 8 hours or overnight. Remove sheets from refrigerator 2 hours before using and leave them in their packet.

Place spinach leaves in a large frying pan with water clinging to them or put frozen spinach in frying pan with amount of water specified on packet. Cover and cook over medium-high heat, stirring occasionally, for about 4 minutes or until wilted. Drain, rinse and squeeze to remove as much liquid as possible. Chop spinach finely with a knife. Heat oil in a frying pan, add onion and cook over low heat, stirring, for about 10 minutes or until tender. Remove from heat, transfer to a bowl and leave to cool slightly. Mix with spinach, eggs and cheese and season to taste with salt, pepper and nutmeg; filling should be highly seasoned.

Remove filo sheets from their packet and spread them out on a dry tea towel. Using a sharp knife, cut stack in half lengthways, to form 2 stacks of sheets of about 40×18 cm (16×7 inches). Cover filo immediately with a piece of greaseproof paper, then with a damp tea towel. Work with only 1 sheet at a time and always keep remaining sheets covered with paper and towel, so they don't dry out.

Remove 1 pastry sheet from pile. Brush it lightly with melted butter and fold it in half lengthways, so its dimensions are about 40 × 9 cm (16 × 3½ inches). Dab it lightly with butter. Place about 7.5 ml (1½ tsp) spinach at one end of strip. Fold end of strip diagonally over filling to form a triangle, and dab it lightly with butter. Continue folding it over and over, keeping it in a triangular shape after each fold, until end of strip is reached. Set pastry on a lightly buttered baking sheet. Brush it lightly with melted butter. Continue making pastries with remaining filo sheets and filling. (Pastries can be shaped 1 day ahead and refrigerated on a baking sheet or on plates. Cover them tightly with cling film.)

Preheat oven to 180°C (350°F) mark 4. Brush pastries again with melted butter and sprinkle with sesame seeds. Bake for 20–25 minutes or until golden brown. Serve warm or at room temperature.

YEMENITE TOMATO DIP

Yemenite women often make this dip by adding cut-up tomatoes to the food processor after making Zehug (page 154). Otherwise, an amount of Zehug to taste is stirred into fresh tomato purée. There is no need to peel the tomatoes, since the peel is ground up finely in the food processor.

Serve as a dip or appetizer with pita or other bread, or for Sabbath breakfast, with Browned Eggs (page 216) and rich breads or pastries like Shabbat Breakfast Bread (page 293) or Shabbat Pastry Rolls (page 303). It can also play the role of chutney or ketchup, and has the advantage over the latter in being fresh and free of preservatives and sugar.

MAKES 150 ML (¼ PINT); ABOUT 4 SERVINGS

100 g (4 oz) ripe tomatoes	salt to taste
10–15 ml (2–3 tsp) Chilli-Garlic Chutney (page 154), or to taste	

Purée the tomatoes in a food processor. Stir in chutney and salt to taste. Serve cold.

SAVOURY PASTRIES WITH BUCKWHEAT FILLING (KASHA KNISHES)

Roasted buckwheat kernels, also known as kasha, are a frequently used ingredient in the Russian Jewish community. Besides playing the role of a filling for knishes, kasha can be served on its own as a side dish for chicken or meat; simply omit the second egg and the almonds in the recipe below. Another time-honoured Ashkenazic recipe for serving the kasha, after flavouring it with sautéed onions, is to toss it with cooked bow tie pasta. Kasha is heated with an egg to keep it fluffy.

MAKES ABOUT 40 SMALL KNISHES

PASTRY

175 g (6 oz) unsalted margarine or butter, well chilled
275 g (10 oz) plain flour
3.75 ml (¾ tsp) salt

75–105 ml (5–7 tbsp) iced water
1 large egg, size 1 or 2, beaten with pinch of salt, for glaze

KASHA FILLING

2 large eggs, size 1 or 2
salt and pepper
50 g (2 oz) kasha (buckwheat groats or kernels)
250 ml (8 fl oz) boiling water
45 ml (3 tbsp) vegetable oil

1 medium onion, chopped
100 g (4 oz) mushrooms, chopped
salt and pepper
30 ml (2 tbsp) chopped almonds

Cut margarine into small pieces. Combine flour and salt in food processor and blend briefly. Add margarine and process with on-off switch until mixture resembles small crumbs. With blades turning, add iced water gradually, until dough begins to clump together. Wrap dough, press together to form a ball and flatten to a round. Refrigerate dough for at least 1 hour or up to 2 days before using it.

Beat 1 egg for filling with a pinch of salt. Combine kasha with

164

beaten egg in a wide bowl and stir with a fork until grains are thoroughly coated. Add to a heavy frying pan and warm it over medium heat for about 3 minutes, stirring to keep grains separate. Add boiling water and stir. Cover and cook over low heat for 15 minutes or until all water is absorbed. Stir with a fork to fluff.

Heat oil in a frying pan, add onion and sauté over medium-low heat until soft and beginning to brown. Add mushrooms, sprinkle with salt and pepper and sauté over medium-high heat for 2 minutes. Stir into kasha with a fork and add chopped almonds. Transfer to a bowl. Cool slightly. Beat second egg and stir into mixture. Taste for seasoning; mixture should be generously seasoned with salt and pepper. Cool completely.

Roll out half the dough on a lightly floured surface until as thin as possible, at most 0.3 cm (⅛ inch) thick. Using a 7.5-cm (3-inch) cutter, cut dough into circles. Put about 7.5 ml (1½ tsp) filling in centre of each. Moisten edges about halfway around circle and fold in half, bringing unmoistened side over to moistened side. Pinch edges together to seal. Put pastries on a greased baking sheet. Continue making knishes from remaining dough and from scraps left from cutting. Chill knishes for 30 minutes or up to overnight.

Preheat oven to 190°C (375°F) mark 5. Brush knishes with beaten egg. Make 2 or 3 slits in pastry with a small sharp knife so steam can escape, then bake knishes for 20–25 minutes or until light brown. Knishes can be baked ahead and reheated in a low oven. Serve warm.

FALAFEL
(CHICK PEA CROQUETTES)

With its humble ingredients of chick peas, garlic and spices, it might be surprising that falafel has become the number one snack in Israel. It is for Israel what the hamburger is for America – fast, inexpensive and adored as a snack or quick meal. And it is available everywhere, from restaurants to markets to central bus stations. There is even a song in Hebrew about 'falafel, the national dish'.

Actually, falafel is loved throughout the Middle East. The chick pea version in Israel is similar to that made in Lebanon, while in Egypt falafel is made of broad beans. Falafel is rising in popularity, partly because it is vegetarian and thus in tune with today's food preferences.

I learned to make falafel from my mother-in-law, Rachel Levy, who prepared falafel at her restaurant near Tel Aviv every day. She served them the way they are preferred in Israel: in a pita with tahini sauce and Israeli salad of diced cucumber and tomato and shredded green or red cabbage. For those who wanted, she added a pickled chilli or chilli sauce, which she made by mixing Zehug (page 154) with a little water.

Professionals use a gadget known as a falafel maker for shaping the balls evenly, but they are easy to shape by hand, too. Note that the chick peas are soaked but are not boiled – the frying cooks them enough.

MAKES 47 FALAFEL BALLS; ABOUT 8 TO 10 SERVINGS

350 g(12 oz) dried chick peas	30 ml (2 tbsp) ground
2 medium heads garlic	coriander
(22–24 medium cloves),	30 ml (2 tbsp) ground cumin
peeled	12.5 ml (2½ tsp) salt
1 medium onion	10 ml (2 tsp) ground black
scant 15 g (½ oz) small	pepper
parsley sprigs (optional)	45 ml (3 tbsp) plain flour
30 ml (2 tbsp) small sprigs	5 ml (1 tsp) baking powder
fresh coriander (optional)	1.4 litres (2½ pints) vegetable
1 slice stale white bread,	oil, for frying
crusts removed	

FOR SANDWICH
pita
Israeli Vegetable Salad (page   Tahini Sauce (page 177)
 34)   chilli sauce

Soak chick peas overnight or for 12 hours in water to generously cover; drain in colander and rinse.

Finely chop garlic in food processor; remove. Finely chop onion in processor; remove. Dry processor. Finely chop parsley and coriander; remove. Sprinkle bread with about 15 ml (1 tbsp) water, then squeeze dry. Grind chick peas and bread in processor in batches. Add onion, garlic, parsley, fresh coriander, ground coriander, cumin, salt, pepper, flour and baking powder.

Knead thoroughly with hands to mix very well. (Mixture can be kept in refrigerator for 2 days.)

To shape falafel, squeeze 15 ml (1 tbsp) mixture to compact it, then press into a ball. Roll lightly between your palms to give it a smooth round shape.

Heat oil to about 180°C (350°F). Add about one-quarter to one-third of the falafel balls. Slide them into hot oil near surface; do not drop them into oil from high or the oil will splash. Fry for about 2 minutes until falafel balls are deep golden brown and coating is crisp. Drain briefly on paper towels. Serve hot.

To serve falafel in sandwiches, use either a half or whole pita for each serving. If using a whole pita, cut off a thin strip near one edge to make a pocket. Put in a few falafel balls, top with salad and spoon in a little Tahini Sauce. Serve more Tahini Sauce and chilli sauce.

AVOCADO AND EGG SALAD

It was during my college years in Israel that I tasted avocado for the first time. In this avocado-rich country many people prepare the fruit by simply mashing its pulp with salt and pepper and perhaps a squeeze of lemon juice and spreading it on bread.

In this variation of the basic spread, the avocado is mixed with grated hard-boiled egg.

The proportions of avocado and egg can change as you like; if you add more eggs, you will have a new version of egg salad. Egg salad is a favourite at Jewish delicatessens, either in the familiar form in which the grated eggs are mixed with mayonnaise, or as eggs and onions, for which the eggs are combined with sautéed onions.

MAKES 2 SERVINGS

1 large or 2 small ripe avocados	1–2 hard-boiled large eggs, size 1 or 2
5 ml (1 tsp) lemon juice, or to taste	30 ml (2 tbsp) chopped spring onions or red onion
salt and freshly ground pepper or cayenne pepper	(optional)

Halve the avocado and remove stone by hitting it forcefully with the heel of a heavy knife, so knife sticks in stone. Remove avocado flesh and mash with a fork. Add lemon juice, salt and pepper.

Coarsely grate the hard-boiled eggs. Add eggs and onion to avocado and mix lightly. Taste and adjust seasoning.

PIROSHKI WITH SALMON AND CABBAGE

With the influx of Russian immigrants in recent years, piroshki have become popular in Israel. Other fillings include cabbage on its own, meat, chicken, buckwheat and liver. Piroshki are served as an appetizer or as an accompaniment for soup. These piroshki are baked, but some versions are fried.

MAKES ABOUT 40 PIROSHKI

---

about 30 ml (2 tbsp) dried
cèpes, porcini or Polish
mushrooms
½ green cabbage, about 450 g
(1 lb), cored, rinsed and
finely chopped
40 g (1½ oz) unsalted butter
salt and pepper
100 g (4 oz) salmon fillet, cut
in tiny dice

25 ml (5 tsp) soured cream
Piroshki Dough (recipe
follows), prepared a day
before baking
1 large egg, size 1 or 2,
beaten with a pinch of
salt, for glaze

Soak mushrooms in a bowl of hot water for 30 minutes. Drain and chop. In a large pan of boiling salted water, boil cabbage for 3 minutes or until tender. Drain, rinse with cold water, then drain thoroughly. Squeeze out excess liquid. Melt butter in a large frying pan and add cabbage with salt and pepper to taste. Cover and cook over low heat for 10 minutes or until tender. Add salmon and cook for another ½ minute, until barely tender. Stir in cèpes. Transfer mixture to a bowl and cool to room temperature. Stir in soured cream and taste for seasoning. Refrigerate for 15 minutes.

Lightly butter 2 or 3 baking sheets. Cut dough into 4 equal parts and return 3 parts to refrigerator. Shape fourth part into a round. Roll it about 0.3 cm (⅛ inch) thick and stamp out 7.5-cm (3-inch) rounds with a cutter, reserving scraps. Brush each round lightly with egg glaze. Place 7.5 ml (1½ tsp) filling in centre of each round and shape filling in an oval across centre of round to about 1 cm (⅜ inch) from each edge. Bring up 2 long opposite edges around filling and mould dough around it to a boat shape, joining 2 edges at top over filling. Pinch edges together along top, fluting them neatly. Arrange piroshki 4 cm (1½ inches) apart on baking sheets, cover with a tea towel, and leave to rise in a warm place for 15 minutes. Continue with remaining dough and filling.

Preheat oven to 200°C (400°F) mark 6. Brush risen piroshki with egg glaze and bake for 15 minutes or until golden brown.

Knead dough scraps together and refrigerate for 2 hours. Refrigerate remaining filling. Shape and bake more piroshki. (Piroshki can be baked up to 8 hours ahead and reheated for serving; refrigerate them, covered. They can also be frozen.) Serve them warm.

PIROSHKI DOUGH

Although some people prepare piroshki from shortcrust pastry, I prefer this rich, traditional yeast-risen dough.

MAKES ENOUGH FOR 40 PIROSHKI

12.5 ml (2½ tsp) dried yeast	150 ml (¼ pint) lukewarm
15 ml (1 tbsp) sugar	milk
60 ml (4 tbsp) lukewarm	90 g (3½ oz) unsalted butter,
water	melted and cooled
375 g (13 oz) plain flour	2 large eggs, size 1 or 2
8.75 ml (1¾ tsp) salt	

In a small bowl mix yeast with sugar and lukewarm water and leave for 10 minutes, or until foamy. In a large bowl combine 350 g (12 oz) flour with salt; make a well in centre and add yeast mixture, milk, butter, eggs and remaining sugar. Combine mixture until a soft dough is formed and knead dough on a lightly floured surface, adding more of remaining flour as necessary to keep it from sticking, for 10–15 minutes, or until smooth. Form dough into a ball, put it in an oiled bowl and turn to coat with oil. Cover and leave to rise in a warm place for 1–1½ hours or until it is doubled in bulk. Knock back, cover and refrigerate overnight.

MUSHROOM TURNOVERS

Lately cooks have been preparing bourekas with fillings other than the traditional spinach and cheese. Mushroom filling is now fashionable, and so is potato, with or without cheese. Instead of using filo dough, many home cooks use puff pastry, as in this version.

These turnovers are good as an hors d'oeuvre, but they can be made larger and served as a first course.

MAKES ABOUT 40 PASTRIES

MUSHROOM FILLING

15 g (½ oz) butter or margarine	*salt and freshly ground pepper*
2 shallots or white part of 2 spring onions, finely chopped	*60 ml (4 tbsp) double cream or chicken soup*
	30 ml (2 tbsp) finely chopped fresh parsley
225 g (8 oz) button mushrooms, chopped	*15 ml (1 tbsp) breadcrumbs*
	1 large egg yolk, size 1 or 2

---

900 g (2 lb) good-quality puff pastry, well chilled	*about 10 ml (2 tsp) sesame seeds (optional)*
1 large egg, size 1 or 2, beaten with a pinch of salt, for glaze	

Melt butter in a medium frying pan over low heat. Add shallots and cook for 1 minute. Add mushrooms and a small pinch of salt and pepper. Cook over medium–high heat, stirring often, for 7 minutes or until liquid that comes out of mushrooms evaporates. Stir in cream or soup and bring to the boil. Simmer, stirring often, for about 2 minutes or until mixture is thick and liquid is absorbed.

Transfer mixture to a bowl. Stir in parsley and breadcrumbs. Cool to lukewarm, then add egg yolk and beat until blended. Taste and adjust seasoning. Cover and refrigerate for 30 minutes. (Filling can be kept for 1 day in refrigerator.)

Sprinkle 2 baking sheets with water. Roll out half the dough on a cool, lightly floured surface until about 0.3 cm (⅛ inch) thick. Using a 7.5-cm (3-inch) round cutter, cut rounds of dough. Separate rounds from rest of dough, reserving scraps. Roll each round to elongate it slightly to an oval. Put 5 ml (1 tsp) filling in centre of each oval. Brush half of oval, around a narrow end, with beaten egg. Fold oval in half to enclose filling, joining second side to egg-brushed side. Press to seal well. Set turnovers on a prepared baking sheet. Refrigerate for at least 30 minutes, or wrap and keep pastries in freezer until ready to bake. Shape turnovers from remaining pastry and filling. Refrigerate scraps for at least 30 minutes and make turnovers from them also.

Preheat oven to 220°C (425°F) mark 7. Brush turnovers with beaten egg. Sprinkle with sesame seeds, if desired.

Bake pastries for about 10 minutes. Reduce oven temperature to 190°C (375°F) mark 5 and bake for about 12 minutes or until puffed and brown. (Pastries can be kept for 2 days in an airtight container or they can be frozen.) Serve warm or at room temperature.

NOTE: As with all filled pastries, avoid the temptation to put too generous an amount of filling in the turnovers or they will burst.

ARTICHOKES WITH LEMON DRESSING

Jews from Mediterranean countries frequently prepare this appetizer for Passover, when artichokes are in season.

MAKES 8 SERVINGS

8 fairly small artichokes	10 ml (2 tsp) chopped fresh
30 ml (2 tbsp) strained fresh	thyme, or 3.75 ml (¾ tsp)
lemon juice	dried thyme, crumbled
salt and pepper	15 ml (1 tbsp) chopped fresh
90 ml (6 tbsp) olive oil	parsley

Break off stalk of each artichoke. With scissors cut off sharp point of each leaf. Add artichokes to a large saucepan of boiling salted water, cover with a slightly smaller lid to keep them submerged, and cook over medium heat for about 45 minutes or until a leaf can be pulled out easily. Remove them and drain thoroughly, upside down.

For dressing, whisk lemon juice with salt and pepper. Whisk in oil and thyme and taste for seasoning. Whisk dressing again before using and add parsley. Serve artichokes warm or at room temperature, accompanied by dressing.

CRISP MEAT-FILLED PASTRIES (KUBEH)

These football-shaped pastries of a brown, delicately crunchy bulgar wheat shell enclosing a meat and pine nut filling are absolutely irresistible.

Kubeh do require practice to give them a perfect shape so that the shell is fine and even, but in the note there is an easier method.

Kubeh are made in much of the Middle East, and the pastry and seasonings vary from place to place. Besides bulgar wheat, the shell might be made from rice, semolina or mashed potatoes, and the kubeh might be poached instead of fried. For Passover, kubeh are made with a matzo meal shell instead of one of bulgar wheat.

MAKES ABOUT 14 PIECES; 6 OR 7 PORTIONS

MEAT AND PINE NUT FILLING

30 ml (2 tbsp) vegetable oil	30 ml (2 tbsp) water
1 medium onion, chopped	salt and freshly ground pepper
150 g (5 oz) extra-lean minced beef	30 ml (2 tbsp) pine nuts

BULGAR WHEAT DOUGH

175 g (6 oz) bulgar wheat, finest grind, soaked in 750 ml (1¼ pints) cold water for 1 hour or until softened	45 ml (3 tbsp) plain flour
	5 ml (1 tsp) salt
	2.5 ml (½ tsp) paprika
	45–60 ml (3–4 tbsp) water
30 ml (2 tbsp) fine dry unseasoned breadcrumbs	

about 250 ml (8 fl oz) vegetable oil for frying	Tahini Sauce with parsley (page 177), as an accompaniment

Heat oil for filling in a heavy medium frying pan over medium heat. Add onion and sauté for about 10 minutes or until golden brown. Add beef, water, salt and pepper and sauté, stirring often, until meat is thoroughly cooked, about 10 minutes. Transfer mixture to a strainer to thoroughly drain excess fat. Transfer to a bowl. Add pine nuts.

Drain bulgar wheat thoroughly in a strainer. Squeeze out excess liquid then return to bowl. Add dry ingredients for dough and mix well. Gradually add water, kneading mixture with your hands, until it is just moist enough to form a stiff dough; it will be sticky.

Taste both dough and filling and adjust seasoning. Both should be well seasoned.

Take about 30 ml (2 tbsp) dough and squeeze together into a patty shape between both hands about 15 times to knead further, pressing to make dough compact. Then roll between your palms to a smooth ball. Put balls on a plate.

Prepare a bowl of water. Line a baking sheet with greaseproof paper. Moisten the palm of your left hand and the index finger of your right hand. Put a ball of dough in your left palm. With your right index finger, make a hole in ball of dough and gradually push it to elongate it and to form a cavity in it, at the same time squeezing and turning the dough around your finger with your left hand. Try to form a thin, even shell without any cracks. If cracks form, make a ball of the piece of dough and start again. Put in enough filling to come nearly to top. Wet your right thumb and index finger and pinch open end of dough closed, completely enclosing filling. (Try not to use too much water when working because kubeh then become wet and sticky, and will make frying oil splatter.) Shape each end into a point, so pastry is shaped like a long football. Set aside on prepared baking sheet. Continue with remaining dough and remaining filling. Refrigerate, uncovered, for 1 hour. (Kubeh can be prepared to this point and refrigerated overnight.)

Heat oil in a large, deep heavy frying pan over medium-high heat; when oil is hot enough, it should sizzle when the end of kubeh is touched to it. Fry kubeh in batches, without crowding, for about 4 minutes per side or until deep golden brown; reduce heat if they brown too fast. Stand back while frying, as oil tends to splatter. Use 2 slotted spatulas to turn them carefully. Drain well on several layers of paper towels. Serve hot, warm or at room temperature, accompanied by Tahini Sauce with parsley.

NOTE: An easier, if less traditional, way to shape kubeh is as flat cakes. Prepare balls of dough as before. With moistened hands, flatten dough to a round, then press to flatten further in your palm. Cup your palm so there is a hollow in middle of dough. Place about 7.5 ml (1½ tsp) filling in the hollow. Bring dough around it and press to join edges to completely enclose filling. Pat again to a round. Fry as before.

MARINATED AUBERGINE SLICES

Marinated aubergine slices are loved throughout the Mediterranean basin and are an important part of Sephardic cooking. In this recipe, which is inspired by a dish I enjoyed at a small restaurant in Tel Aviv, the zesty spiced vinegar penetrates the sautéed aubergine and balances its richness. Herbs such as coriander can be used to flavour the marinade instead of spices. Generally the marinated slices are served as an appetizer or a side dish, but they are also wonderful in a sandwich with cold meats or with sliced cheese.

MAKES 4 TO 6 SERVINGS

2 medium aubergines, 900 g
  (2 lb)
10 ml (2 tsp) salt
175 ml (6 fl oz) olive oil
freshly ground black pepper
1 medium red pepper, roasted
  and peeled

quartered pita or sliced French
  or Italian bread, for
  accompaniment

GARLIC-CHILLI MARINADE
6 medium garlic cloves
30 ml (2 tbsp) olive oil
1 fresh serrano chilli, halved
  lengthways, cored and
  seeded

5 ml (1 tsp) sweet paprika
5 ml (1 tsp) ground cumin
salt
45 ml (3 tbsp) mild white
  wine vinegar

Cut aubergines in 1-cm (½-inch) slices crossways, discarding ends. Arrange slices in 1 layer on a rack set over a tray. Sprinkle each side evenly with about 5 ml (1 tsp) salt. Leave slices to drain for 1 hour, turning them over after 30 minutes. Pat them dry very thoroughly with several changes of paper towels.

In a large heavy frying pan, heat 45 ml (3 tbsp) oil over medium heat. Quickly add enough aubergine slices to make 1 layer. Sauté aubergine for about 2½ minutes on each side, or until tender when pierced with a fork. Transfer slices to a plate. Add 45 ml (3 tbsp) oil to frying pan, heat oil and sauté remaining aubergine in batches, adding remaining oil between batches as necessary. Transfer aubergine to a large shallow serving dish or baking dish, such as a 38-cm (15-inch) oval gratin dish.

Peel 2 garlic cloves without crushing them. Cut them into very thin slices lengthways, then peel and finely chop remaining garlic cloves. Heat oil in a small saucepan, add chopped garlic and halved chilli, and cook over low heat for 2 minutes. Stir in paprika, cumin and a small pinch of salt. Add vinegar and sliced garlic, bring to the boil and cook over low heat for 1 minute. Remove marinade from heat and discard chilli.

Pour marinade evenly over aubergine slices and sprinkle them with black pepper to taste.

Turn slices over so that all come in contact with marinade. Halve the roasted pepper crossways and cut halves lengthways in 1-cm (½-inch) wide strips. Put pepper strips on top of aubergine. Leave to stand at room temperature for 30 minutes before serving. (Slices can be kept, covered, for 3 days in refrigerator.)

When serving, set a pepper strip on each aubergine slice, with skinned side of pepper facing up, and top strip with a garlic slice. Serve aubergine cold or at room temperature, accompanied by fresh pita or bread.

NOTE: If you are sensitive to chillies, wear rubber gloves when handling them. If you do not wear gloves, wash your hands immediately after handling chillies.

HUMMUS
(CHICK PEA DIP)

Hummus is a golden chick pea purée flavoured with tahini (sesame paste), garlic and lemon juice and served as an appetizer, spread or dip. Generally it is served on a flat plate and garnished with olive oil or more tahini sauce, then with paprika and chopped parsley. It is an inexpensive, easy to make party dish.

In Jerusalem you can buy two other types of hummus: a country-style hummus of whole chick peas mixed into tahini with red pepper flakes and parsley or coriander; and 'Jerusalem hummus', the smooth type sprinkled with pine nuts, olive oil and paprika.

MAKES 4 TO 6 SERVINGS

225 g (8 oz) dried chick peas
or 2 × 439-g (15½-oz)
cans, rinsed
scant 1.3 litres (2¼ pints)
water
3 medium garlic cloves

60 ml (4 tbsp) strained fresh
lemon juice
60 ml (4 tbsp) tahini (stirred
before measuring)
salt to taste
cayenne pepper

GARNISH
60–90 ml (4–6 tbsp) extra-
virgin olive oil or Tahini
Sauce (opposite)

paprika or cayenne pepper
15 ml (1 tbsp) chopped fresh
parsley
pita, for serving

Pick over dried chick peas, discarding pebbles and broken or discoloured peas. Soak chick peas for 8 hours or overnight in water to cover generously; or quick-soak by putting them in a medium saucepan with 1 litre (1¾ pints) water, bringing to the boil, and boiling uncovered for 2 minutes; remove from heat, cover and leave to stand for 1 hour.

Drain chick peas and rinse. Put in a medium saucepan and add 1.1 litres (2 pints) water. Bring to a simmer, cover and cook over low heat for about 2 hours or until very tender. Drain well. Cool slightly.

Set aside about 50 g (2 oz) whole cooked or canned chick peas. Finely chop garlic in a food processor. Add remaining chick peas and process coarsely. Add lemon juice, tahini, and 60 ml (4 tbsp) water and purée until finely blended. Transfer to a bowl. Stir in enough additional water so that mixture has consistency of a smooth spread. Season with salt and cayenne to taste. (Spread can be kept for 4 or 5 days in refrigerator.)

To serve, spread hummus about 0.5 cm (¼ inch) thick on a platter or serving plates. Make a hollow in centre with back of a spoon and fill with olive oil or tahini. Sprinkle hummus with paprika or a little cayenne, then sprinkle parsley on hummus or on tahini for garnish (but not on olive oil). Garnish with reserved chick peas and serve with fresh or warmed pita.

TAHINI SAUCE
(SESAME DIP)

Tahini, or sesame paste, is used in Israel and in much of the eastern Mediterranean as the basis for a sauce, a dip and a flavouring. Tahini Sauce is rich with a slight touch of bitterness. Some people use is as an all-purpose sauce instead of mayonnaise, and spoon it over fish or meat. It is sometimes mixed with diced tomato and cucumber or simply with plenty of parsley and served as a salad. But most often it is served on its own, accompanied by pita for dipping.

The proportions of water used for Tahini Sauce vary; add water to the paste gradually to obtain the thickness you want. Tahini Sauce is made thinner if used as a pouring sauce to serve over food than if served as a dip to be scooped up with pita.

MAKES 250 ML (8 FL OZ); 4 TO 6 SERVINGS

120 ml (4 fl oz) tahini (sesame paste)	30 ml (2 tbsp) strained fresh lemon juice
120 ml (4 fl oz) water	3 large garlic cloves, finely chopped
1.25 ml (¼ tsp) salt, or to taste	pinch of cayenne (optional)

GARNISH

30–45 ml (2–3 tbsp) olive oil (optional)	45 ml (3 tbsp) chopped fresh parsley
paprika or cayenne, for sprinkling	pita, for serving

In a medium bowl, stir tahini to blend in its oil. Stir in 120 ml (4 fl oz) water. Add salt, lemon juice, garlic and cayenne. If sauce is too thick, gradually stir in more water. Taste, and add more salt or lemon juice if desired. (Tahini Sauce can be kept for 2 days in refrigerator; it thickens on standing, and may need a little water when served.)

To serve as a dip, spread tahini on a serving plate. If desired, make a small hollow in centre and spoon in a little olive oil. Sprinkle Tahini Sauce lightly with paprika or cayenne and with chopped parsley. Serve with fresh or warmed pita.

SALADS

Living in Israel introduced me to new ideas for light, healthy Mediterranean eating. One is that a meal is not complete unless it includes *salat*, or Israeli salad. But this salad is quite specific: it is nothing like our green salad or restaurant-style dinner salads. Rather, it consists of a colourful mixture of diced tomatoes, peppers and cucumbers. Israelis insist that these cubes be very small.

Usually served as an accompaniment, this quick-to-make salad adds a lively note to any menu. It can be served as is, or can be embellished with parsley or other herbs; my Israeli mother-in-law likes to stir in chopped fresh coriander and onions, for example. A dash of extra-virgin olive oil gives a nice touch and, because it is so flavourful, a little goes a long way.

Of course, there are many other salads in the Jewish repertoire. Some are of raw vegetables like the Cucumber Salad with Yogurt and Mint or Fresh and Tangy Carrot Salad in this chapter. Others are based on steamed or boiled vegetables, like Beetroot Salad with Apples (page 100). There is a wealth of potato salads – both creamy Ashkenazic and tangy Sephardic styles. For some Middle Eastern-style salads the vegetables are grilled, as in Aubergine Salad with Tahini or Grilled Pepper and Tomato Salad.

Salads are served as appetizers or accompaniments, and at least one salad appears at every meal, sometimes even for breakfast. For a sumptuous dinner in the Mediterranean style, a great assortment of colourful salads, along with olives and pickles, plays the role of an enticing beginning to the feast.

CREAMY POTATO SALAD WITH GHERKINS

Pickles are an important staple of the Jewish table. Although those made from cucumbers are the most common, at a typical Jerusalem market you can also find pickled green tomatoes, small aubergines, beetroots, baby onions, lemon slices and mixed vegetables. Most often they are served as accompaniments but they also add zest to salads like this one.

MAKES 6 SERVINGS

900 g (2 lb) red-skinned potatoes of uniform size, scrubbed but not peeled
salt
30 ml (2 tbsp) dry white wine
15 ml (1 tbsp) mild white wine vinegar
15 ml (1 tbsp) vegetable oil
freshly ground pepper
25 g (1 oz) red onion, finely chopped

55 ml (2 tbsp plus 1 tsp) Dijon mustard, or to taste
300 ml (½ pint) mayonnaise
3 hard-boiled large eggs, size 1 or 2
1 medium gherkin, cut into tiny dice
45 ml (3 tbsp) chopped fresh parsley

Put potatoes in a large saucepan, cover with water by about 1 cm (½ inch) and add salt. Bring to the boil. Cover and simmer over low heat for about 25 minutes, or until a knife can pierce the centre of largest potato easily and potato falls from knife when lifted. Meanwhile, combine wine, vinegar, oil, salt and pepper in a small bowl and whisk until blended.

Drain potatoes and peel while hot. Cut into fairly small dice, then put potatoes in a large bowl. Rewhisk wine mixture until blended and pour over potatoes. Toss or fold gently to mix thoroughly. Fold in onion. Cool to room temperature.

Whisk mustard into mayonnaise and fold into potatoes. Chop 2 eggs; cut third egg in 6 wedges. Add chopped eggs, gherkin and 30 ml (2 tbsp) parsley to salad and fold in gently. Taste and adjust seasoning. (Salad can be kept, covered, overnight in refrigerator.) Garnish with remaining parsley and egg wedges. Serve at cool room temperature.

POTATO AND LOX SALAD

If you are fond of that 'all-American' Jewish sandwich of bagel with lox and cream cheese, you will like this colourful salad. It is a great way to use small, less expensive pieces of lox.

MAKES 4 SERVINGS

---

900 g (2 lb) red-skinned potatoes of uniform size, scrubbed but not peeled
salt
30 ml (2 tbsp) dry white wine
15 ml (1 tbsp) mild white wine vinegar
15 ml (1 tbsp) vegetable oil

freshly ground pepper
120–150 ml (4–5 fl oz) Mustard Vinaigrette (page 192)
75 g (3 oz) lox, thinly sliced
30 ml (2 tbsp) sliced or snipped chives

Put potatoes in a large saucepan, cover with water by about 1 cm (½ inch), and add salt. Bring to the boil, cover and simmer over low heat for about 25 minutes, or until a knife can pierce centre of largest potato easily and potato falls from knife when lifted. Meanwhile, combine wine, vinegar, oil, salt and pepper in a small bowl and whisk until blended.

Drain potatoes and peel while hot. Cut into fairly small dice, then put potatoes in a large bowl. Rewhisk wine mixture until blended and pour it over potatoes. Toss or fold gently to mix thoroughly. Cool to room temperature.

Whisk vinaigrette until blended. Add about 120 ml (4 fl oz) vinaigrette to salad and fold it in gently using a spatula. (Salad tastes best on day it is made but it can be prepared 1 day ahead, covered, and refrigerated.)

Bring salad to cool room temperature. Cut lox lengthways in 5 × 1-cm (2 × ½-inch) strips, using thin-bladed knife. Reserve 6 strips for garnish. Fold chives and remaining lox into salad. Taste and adjust seasoning, adding 15–30 ml (1–2 tbsp) more vinaigrette if desired. Transfer to serving dish. Garnish with reserved lox strips.

180

POTATO SALAD WITH SMOKED TURKEY

Smoked turkey has long been a favourite of the kosher cold meats, and today its lean meat makes it a frequent choice for sandwiches. It is also good in salads and can turn a potato salad like this one into a main course.

MAKES 4 SERVINGS

900 g (2 lb) red-skinned potatoes of uniform size, scrubbed but not peeled
salt
30 ml (2 tbsp) dry white wine
15 ml (1 tbsp) mild white wine vinegar
15 ml (1 tbsp) vegetable or olive oil
freshly ground pepper
75 g (3 oz) smoked turkey, thinly sliced
45 ml (3 tbsp) snipped fresh dill or finely chopped parsley
30 ml (2 tbsp) finely chopped spring onions
300 ml (½ pint) mayonnaise

Put potatoes in a large saucepan, cover with water by about 1 cm (½ inch) and add salt. Bring to the boil, cover and simmer over low heat for about 25 minutes, or until a knife can pierce centre of largest potato easily and potato falls from knife when lifted. Meanwhile, combine wine, vinegar, oil, salt and pepper in a small bowl and whisk until blended.

Drain potatoes and peel while hot. Cut into fairly small dice, then put potatoes in a large bowl. Rewhisk wine mixture until blended and pour it over potatoes. Toss or fold gently to mix thoroughly. Cool to room temperature.

Cut turkey slices in half crossways, then lengthways into 5 × 1-cm (2 × ⅜-inch) strips. Add turkey, dill or parsley, spring onions and mayonnaise to potatoes and fold gently. Taste and adjust seasoning. (Salad tastes best on day it is made but it can be prepared 1 day ahead, covered and refrigerated.) Serve at cool room temperature.

AUBERGINE SALAD
WITH TAHINI

For this Middle Eastern salad, the aubergine is barbecued so that it acquires a smokey taste. This is the preferred way of preparing aubergine salad in Israel. In addition to the tahini, garlic and lemon juice, some cooks flavour this salad with 2.5–5 ml (½–1 tsp) ground cumin.

If you want to cook the aubergines by grilling, choose long, fairly slender ones.

MAKES 4 SERVINGS

---

1 medium aubergine, about
  550 g (1¼ lb)
3 medium garlic cloves, finely
  chopped
45 ml (3 tbsp) strained fresh
  lemon juice
15 ml (1 tbsp) water

60 ml (4 tbsp) tahini (sesame
  paste), stirred before
  measuring
salt and freshly ground black
  pepper
30 ml (2 tbsp) chopped fresh
  parsley, for garnish
  (optional)

Prick aubergine a few times with fork. Barbecue aubergine above medium-hot coals about 1 hour or grill for about 40 minutes, turning often, until skin blackens, flesh is tender and aubergine looks collapsed. Remove aubergine peel and cut off stalk. Drain off any liquid from inside aubergine. Chop flesh very fine with knife; there should still be small chunks. Transfer to a bowl and add garlic.

Stir lemon juice and water into tahini until smooth. Add to aubergine and mix well. Add salt and pepper to taste. To serve, spread on a plate and sprinkle with parsley.

BULGARIAN AUBERGINE SALAD WITH GRILLED PEPPERS

When I lived in Bat Yam, a suburb of Tel Aviv, a neighbour gave me the recipe for this hot, delicious salad, a speciality of Bulgarian Jews. Bulgarian cuisine is part of the Balkan style and bears a certain similarity to that of Greece and Turkey. Some people omit the chillies in the salad, but in my family we love it this way.

MAKES 6 SERVINGS

2 long, fairly slender aubergines, about 450 g (1 lb) each	2 medium garlic cloves, finely chopped
1 medium green pepper	30 ml (2 tbsp) chopped fresh parsley
1 medium red pepper	15 ml (1 tbsp) vinegar
2 jalapeño chillies	15 ml (1 tbsp) olive oil
	salt to taste

Prick aubergine a few times with fork. Grill aubergine for about 40 minutes or cook above medium-hot coals for about 1 hour, turning often, until skin blackens and flesh is tender. Remove aubergine peel and cut of stalk. Drain off any liquid from inside aubergine. Chop flesh very fine with knife; there should still be small chunks. Transfer to a bowl.

Grill peppers and chillies about 5 cm (2 inches) from heat source, turning them often, until skins are blistery all over, about 5 minutes for chillies and 15–20 minutes for peppers. Transfer them to plastic bags and close bags. Leave to stand for 10 minutes. Peel peppers using paring knife, handling chillies with rubber gloves if you are sensitive. Remove seeds from peppers and chillies. Dice peppers. Finely chop chillies.

Add chillies, garlic and parsley to aubergine and mix well. Add vinegar, oil and salt to taste. Stir in peppers. Taste and adjust seasoning. (Salad can be kept, covered, for 2 days in refrigerator.) Serve cold or at room temperature.

CREAMY AUBERGINE SALAD

This easy to make version of aubergine salad, a favourite delicatessen item in Israel, combines Middle Eastern and European influences with the addition of mayonnaise to the salad. To give it a more 'Mediterranean' flavour, barbecue the aubergine as in the previous recipe instead of baking it.

MAKES 8 TO 10 SERVINGS

4 medium aubergines, about
  2 kg (4½ lb) total
2 medium garlic cloves, finely
  chopped
30 ml (2 tbsp) finely chopped
  onion
175 ml (6 fl oz) mayonnaise

10 ml (2 tsp) strained fresh
  lemon juice
salt and pepper to taste
parsley sprigs, for garnish
black olives, for garnish
quartered pita or sliced
  French or Italian bread,
  for accompaniment

Preheat oven to 200°C (400°F) mark 6. Pierce each aubergine a few times with a fork to prevent it from bursting. Bake whole aubergines on a large baking sheet lined with foil for 30 minutes. Turn aubergines over and bake for 30–40 minutes, or until they are very tender. Leave aubergines until cool enough to handle. Holding stalk end, peel off skin of each aubergine. Drain aubergines in a colander for 1 hour.

Cut off tops. Chop aubergine flesh, using a knife, until it is a chunky purée. In a large bowl combine aubergine, garlic, onion, mayonnaise, lemon juice and salt and pepper to taste and mix well; salad should be highly seasoned. Refrigerate for at least 30 minutes before serving. (Salad can be kept for 3 days in refrigerator.)

Spoon salad into a shallow bowl or plate, garnish with parsley sprigs and olives, and serve it with fresh pita or bread.

CHICKEN SALAD WITH AVOCADO AND ALMONDS

Chicken salad makes frequent appearances on the tables of traditional Jewish cooks, since the essential ingredient is a natural by-product of making chicken soup. This recipe is inspired by a chicken salad I enjoyed at the home of Betty Solomon, a popular hostess in Jerusalem. She garnished the edge of the salad with a row of sliced peaches, but you can use orange segments as a substitute in winter; or if you prefer a vegetable garnish, surround the salad with lightly cooked broccoli florets or cherry tomatoes.

MAKES 4 SERVINGS

40 g (1½ oz) slivered almonds
1 hard-boiled large egg,
* chopped, size 1 or 2*
* (optional)*
700 g (1½ lb) cooked chicken,
* diced*
15 ml (1 tbsp) chopped fresh
* tarragon or snipped chives*

30 ml (2 tbsp) chopped fresh
* parsley*
10–15 ml (2–3 tsp) prepared
* mustard (optional)*
90–120 ml (8–9 tbsp)
* mayonnaise, or more to*
* taste*
1 ripe avocado
about 16 leaves tender lettuce

Preheat oven to 180°C (350°F) mark 4. Toast almonds on a small baking sheet until light brown, about 4 minutes. Transfer to a plate and cool.

In a medium bowl combine egg, chicken, tarragon and parsley. Mix mustard with 90 ml (6 tbsp) mayonnaise and add to salad. (Salad can be kept, covered, for 1 day in refrigerator.)

A short time before serving, halve the avocado and remove stone. Scoop out flesh and dice it. Reserve a few avocado dice and about half the almonds for a garnish. Fold remaining avocado and almonds into salad. Taste and add more mayonnaise, salt and pepper if desired.

Make a bed of lettuce on each of 4 plates or on a platter. Spoon salad onto lettuce. Garnish with avocado dice and sprinkle top with remaining toasted almonds.

NOTE: About 40 g (1½ oz) diced oil-packed sun-dried tomatoes are a nice addition to this salad.

FRESH AND TANGY CARROT SALAD

Here is proof that a salad of grated carrots can be exciting, as the lemony dressing provides a delightful balance to the sweetness of the vegetable. This Moroccan salad is often featured on menus of Middle Eastern restaurants in Tel Aviv. It makes a pretty addition to a selection of salads for a colourful first course, or a good accompaniment for cold meats.

MAKES 4 SERVINGS

---

450 g (1 lb) carrots, about 6 medium

1 medium garlic clove, finely chopped

2.5 ml (½ tsp) Tabasco sauce, or freshly ground black pepper to taste

30 ml (2 tbsp) chopped fresh coriander or parsley

60 ml (4 tbsp) strained fresh lemon juice

60 ml (4 tbsp) extra-virgin olive oil

pinch of salt

coriander or parsley sprigs, for garnish

Peel carrots and coarsely grate them. Mix with garlic, Tabasco sauce, coriander, lemon juice, oil and salt. Taste and adjust seasoning; be generous with pepper. Serve on a flat plate. Garnish with coriander sprigs around edges.

GRILLED PEPPER AND TOMATO SALAD

When you are barbecuing, it is convenient to put a few peppers and tomatoes on the barbecue to prepare this easy salad, a speciality of Jews from North Africa. At other times, use the cooker grill.

MAKES 4 SERVINGS

---

4 ripe fairly small tomatoes

4 medium garlic cloves, unpeeled

2 medium green peppers

22.5 ml (1½ tbsp) lemon juice

22.5 ml (1½ tbsp) extra-virgin olive oil

salt and pepper

Preheat grill. Put tomatoes, garlic cloves and peppers on grill rack and grill, turning them often. Grill tomatoes for 4–5 minutes or until their skin begins to wrinkle; grill garlic for about 12 minutes; grill peppers for about 15–20 minutes or until their skin turns blistery all over and is black in spots.

Core tomatoes and peel with aid of a small knife. Put peppers in a plastic bag, close bag and leave to 10 minutes. Peel peppers and remove their cores and seeds.

Peel garlic cloves and chop the pulp until very fine and practically a purée. Put garlic in a small bowl. Stir in lemon juice, oil and salt and pepper to taste.

Quarter the tomatoes and cut the peppers into wide lengthways strips. Arrange them on a serving plate. Pour sauce over them and leave for 1 hour for flavours to blend. Serve cold or at room temperature.

NOTE: The vegetables can be grilled on a barbecue instead of under a grill. Put garlic on a fine-meshed barbecue screen so it won't fall into coals.

PIQUANT COOKED CARROT SALAD

My friend Hannah, who lives near Tel Aviv, prepares wonderful North African dishes like this spicy salad, for which she sometimes cooks pieces of pumpkin with the carrots. In the authentic version the carrots are mashed before being seasoned, but I leave the slices whole so they retain an attractive shape and a more interesting texture.

MAKES 4 SERVINGS

450 g (1 lb) medium carrots, sliced (about 5)
salt
45 ml (3 tbsp) vegetable oil
3 medium garlic cloves, finely chopped
45 ml (3 tbsp) red or white wine vinegar

60 ml (4 tbsp) water
2.5 ml (½ tsp) Tabasco sauce
1.25 ml (¼ tsp) caraway seeds
1.25 ml (¼ tsp) paprika

In a saucepan cover carrots with water and add salt. Bring to the boil and simmer over medium heat for 20–25 minutes or until tender.

Heat oil in a frying pan over medium heat. Stir in garlic and sauté for just a few seconds. Add vinegar, water, Tabasco sauce, caraway seeds, paprika and a pinch of salt. Bring to the boil, stirring. Reduce heat to low.

When carrots are tender, drain them thoroughly. Add them to vinegar mixture. Simmer, uncovered, for 5 minutes or until sauce is reduced and coats carrots thoroughly. Taste and add more salt if necessary. Serve hot or cold.

CUCUMBER SALAD WITH YOGURT AND MINT

Garlic-scented cucumber salad with yogurt is prepared in many Mediterranean countries, such as Turkey and Lebanon, and is a favourite among Sephardic Jews in general. It is similar to some versions of an Indian salad called *raita*. Sometimes the yogurt quantity is increased, then the dish is served as a cold soup.

If you wish to serve this salad to accompany the rice and lentil stew called Majadrah (page 279) in a traditional manner, finely dice the cucumbers and substitute 5–10 ml (1–2 tsp) dried mint for the fresh.

MAKES 6 SERVINGS

1 small clove garlic, crushed	1 large cucumber, about 450 g
5 ml (1 tsp) salt	(1 lb)
37.5 ml (2½ tbsp) coarsely	small sprigs of mint, for
chopped mint	garnish
900 ml (1½ pints) natural	
yogurt	

Mash garlic with salt and mint in a bowl, using back of a spoon. Add yogurt and blend well. Be sure to mix garlic mixture from bottom of bowl into yogurt.

Peel cucumber and halve it lengthways. Cut it into thin slices and add to yogurt mixture. Fold in gently. Taste for seasoning. Refrigerate for at least 15 minutes or up to 4 hours before serving. Serve garnished with small sprigs of mint.

BULGAR WHEAT AND PARSLEY SALAD WITH MINT AND TOMATOES (TABBOULEH)

This is a great party dish. I received the recipe from Ronnie Venezia, a talented cook who lives in Jerusalem and was born in Lebanon. There are many versions of this Middle Eastern salad but I find hers is the best: colourful, tangy and with generous quantities of herbs. It is vibrant with the fresh flavours of the market, and should be made with the best ingredients – fresh herbs, ripe tomatoes, freshly squeezed lemon juice and extra-virgin olive oil.

MAKES ABOUT 8 APPETIZER OR 4 TO 6 MAIN-COURSE SERVINGS

250 g (9 oz) fine bulgar wheat	2 bunches mint
1.1 litres (2 pints) cold water	1 bunch spring onions
5 plum tomatoes	juice of 2½–3 lemons
4 small pickling cucumbers or ½ cucumber	175 ml (6 fl oz) extra-virgin olive oil
1 bunch parsley	salt and freshly ground black pepper

Soak bulgar wheat in cold water overnight or for about 8 hours or until tender; taste it to check. (If you are in a hurry, pour hot water over the bulgar wheat instead and soak it until completely cool and tender.) Transfer bulgar to a colander and drain off excess water. Squeeze wheat dry and transfer to a large bowl.

Dice tomatoes and cucumbers until very small. Chop parsley and mint leaves. Cut spring onions into thin slices. Mix diced vegetables with herbs and wheat. Add lemon juice to taste and olive oil; salad should be fairly sharp. Season to taste with salt and pepper. (Salad can be kept, covered, for 1 day in refrigerator.) Serve cold or at cool room temperature.

CAULIFLOWER AND GREEN BEAN SALAD WITH LOX VINAIGRETTE

This pretty, easy-to-prepare salad is perfect for summer, and is a good way to make use of a tiny amount of lox. In America lox is associated with Jewish cooking, and indeed the word *lox* came into English from Yiddish.

MAKES 2 OR 3 SERVINGS

1 small cauliflower, cut into medium florets	*45 ml (3 tbsp) vegetable oil*
salt	*freshly ground pepper*
100 g (4 oz) green beans, trimmed and cut in half	*10 ml (2 tsp) snipped fresh dill*
15 ml (1 tbsp) white wine vinegar	*15–30 ml (1–2 tbsp) finely diced lox or smoked salmon, about 15 g (½ oz)*

Boil cauliflower, uncovered, in a large saucepan of boiling salted water for about 7 minutes or until just tender. Drain, rinse gently with cold water and drain well. Boil green beans, uncovered, in a medium saucepan of boiling salted water for about 5 minutes or until just tender. Drain and rinse in same manner.

To make vinaigrette, whisk vinegar with oil, salt and pepper until blended.

Arrange cauliflower in centre of a serving plate, with florets facing up and outwards, reforming the shape of a cauliflower. Arrange green beans around it. Spoon 15 ml (1 tbsp) vinaigrette over green beans. Add dill and lox to remaining vinaigrette and spoon over cauliflower. Serve at room temperature.

COUNTRY-STYLE HUMMUS WITH TAHINI

Unlike the usual hummus, which is served as a spread, this is a salad of whole chick peas in a rich, white tahini dressing. It is quick and easy to make. Serve it as a first course, accompanied by pita and, if you wish, by plum tomato slices.

MAKES 4 TO 6 SERVINGS

---

150 ml (¼ pint) tahini (sesame paste), stirred before measuring
120 ml (4 fl oz) water, or more as needed
1.25 ml (¼ tsp) salt, or to taste
1.25 ml (¼ tsp) dried red chilli flakes

30 ml (2 tbsp) strained fresh lemon juice
1 medium garlic clove, finely chopped
1 × 439-g (15½-oz) can chick peas, drained and rinsed
30 ml (2 tbsp) chopped fresh coriander or parsley

In a medium bowl, stir tahini with 120 ml (4 fl oz) water. Add salt, chilli flakes, lemon juice and garlic. Dressing should be thick enough to flow from spoon, but should not run from spoon. If it is too thick, gradually stir in another 15 ml (1 tbsp) water.

Drain chick peas in a strainer, rinse thoroughly with cold water and drain well. Reserve a few chick peas and a pinch of coriander for garnish. Add remaining chick peas and coriander to tahini dressing. Taste and add more salt or lemon juice if desired. Spoon into a fairly shallow bowl. Garnish with reserved chick peas and coriander and serve.

NOTE: If you wish, soak and cook 150 g (5 oz) dried chick peas as for Hummus (page 175) instead of using canned ones; or, if you happen to have cooked chick peas, use 250 g (9 oz) for this recipe.

SEPHARDIC BEETROOT SALAD WITH CORIANDER

My sister-in-law from India often prepares a beetroot salad like this as a first course for *Shabbat* dinner. It's easy to make and delicious.

MAKES 6 SERVINGS

10 small beetroots, about 4 cm (1½ inches) in diameter	salt and freshly ground pepper 75–90 ml (5–6 tbsp) vegetable oil
30 ml (2 tbsp) lemon juice or vinegar	30 ml (2 tbsp) chopped fresh coriander

Rinse beetroots, taking care not to pierce skin. Put 2.5 cm (1 inch) of water in a steamer and bring to the boil. Place beetroots on steamer rack or on another rack or in a colander above boiling water. Cover tightly and steam for 50–60 minutes or until tender. Leave to cool. Rinse beetroots with cold water and slip off skins.

In a small bowl whisk lemon juice with salt and pepper. Whisk in 75 ml (5 tbsp) oil. Adjust seasoning. Stir in 15 ml (1 tbsp) coriander.

Dice the beetroots. Put in a bowl and add enough dressing to moisten. Toss gently. Taste and adjust seasoning; add remaining 15 ml (1 tbsp) oil if needed. Sprinkle with remaining coriander.

MUSTARD VINAIGRETTE

This dressing is good for potato salads, other salads of cooked vegetables and green salads. Use your favourite mustard; I like to use the smooth Dijon type. Add extra mustard if preferred.

MAKES ABOUT 175 ML (6 FL OZ)

45 ml (3 tbsp) white wine vinegar	7.5 ml (1½ tsp) mustard 135 ml (4½ fl oz) vegetable or olive oil
salt and freshly ground pepper	

Whisk vinegar with salt, pepper and mustard in a small heavy bowl until well blended. Gradually whisk in oil. Taste and adjust seasoning. (Can be prepared 1 week ahead, covered and refrigerated.)

SOUPS

 Chicken soup is so thoroughly identified with Jewish cooking that food writers and chefs occasionally try to prove that other cuisines have it, too! A bowl of steaming chicken soup has long been known as 'Jewish mothers' penicillin' and as the ultimate comfort food with which Jewish women pamper their families. When I was growing up, my mother made chicken soup with matzo balls every Friday, a tradition she still cherishes.

Most versions of chicken soup are fairly delicate in seasoning and uncomplicated. My mother adds onions, carrots and dill; my mother-in-law adds cumin, turmeric and tomato; my Moroccan cousin adds onion, rice and Italian parsley or coriander. But for all of them the most important thing is to use plenty of chicken for the amount of water and to simmer it until the soup is well flavoured.

Hearty soups are part of the culinary repertoire of Jewish cooks from all over the world, from the robust Polish mushroom-barley soups to the aromatic lentil soups of Indian Jews to the spicy Yemenite meat soups. For dairy meals, lighter soups are generally the rule. Most of these are vegetable soups, which are made in countless versions.

Often, chicken or meat soup is prepared for *Shabbat* in generous quantities, and some is left for later in the week. This proves to be an efficient way of cooking, since the soup can be quickly reheated, making it easy to put a quick, home-cooked meal on the table.

Besides matzo balls, the most common soup additions are noodles and rice; and some cooks serve chicken soup with both matzo balls and fine noodles.

For Passover, there are matzos for crumbling into the soup, or packaged matzo farfel, which is matzo cut in small squares. During the rest of the year, the standard accompaniment for soups is fine-quality bread.

MAIN-COURSE CHICKEN SOUP WITH VEGETABLES

This is a dish my husband and I prepare often at home – it's convenient to reheat, easy to make, light and low in fat. We call a few days of menus built around this soup our 'chicken soup diet'.

We have expanded this idea by adding a large amount of vegetables, for good flavour and nutrition. Instead of bread, we sometimes serve the soup with separately cooked white, brown or wild rice, fine noodles or couscous. Sometimes we briefly cook fresh or frozen vegetables, such as corn, peas, courgettes and carrots, in a separate pan to keep their colour, taste and texture, and spoon a generous helping of these vegetables into each bowl before adding the soup.

MAKES ABOUT 6 MAIN-COURSE SERVINGS

1 whole chicken, about 1.6 kg (3½ lb) or 1.1–1.4 kg (2½–3 lb) chicken pieces
salt and freshly ground pepper
30 ml (2 tbsp) ground cumin
5 ml (1 tsp) turmeric
1 large onion, whole or sliced
4 medium carrots, 350 g (12 oz), peeled and cut in 5-cm (2-inch) lengths
about 1.7 litres (3 pints) water

4–6 medium boiling potatoes, about 550 g (1¼ lb)
6 garlic cloves, coarsely chopped
4 medium courgettes, about 450 g (1 lb), cut in 5-cm (2-inch) lengths
225 g (8 oz) button mushrooms, quartered
30 ml (2 tbsp) chopped fresh parsley or coriander

Remove fat from chicken. Put chicken in a large casserole or pan. If chicken giblets are available, add neck and other giblets, except liver. Sprinkle with salt, pepper and spices on both sides. Leave to stand while preparing vegetables.

Add onion and carrots to casserole and cover ingredients generously with water. Bring to the boil, skim excess foam from surface, cover and cook over low heat for 1 hour.

Peel potatoes. Add potatoes and garlic to casserole, cover and cook over low heat for 45 minutes. Add courgettes and mushrooms, sprinkle with salt and bring to a simmer. Cover and cook over low heat for 30 minutes.

Skim off fat. (This is easier to do when soup is cold.) Taste and adjust seasoning. If desired, remove skin from chicken and cut meat from bones; return chicken to soup. (Soup can be kept, covered, for 3 days in refrigerator.) Serve soup in fairly shallow bowls with chicken and vegetables. If desired, add parsley or coriander to each bowl when serving.

CHICKEN SOUP WITH RICE, TOMATOES AND CORIANDER

In this zesty North African version of Jewish chicken soup, the chicken can be served in the soup or reserved for other uses.

MAKES 4 TO 6 MAIN-COURSE OR 8 FIRST-COURSE SERVINGS

30 ml (2 tbsp) olive or vegetable oil	2.8 litres (5 pints) water
1 medium onion, chopped	1 celery stalk, cut in thin strips
1.1 kg (2½ lb) chicken pieces (legs, thighs or wings)	2 medium garlic cloves, chopped
salt and freshly ground black pepper	175 g (6 oz) long-grain white rice
225 g (8 oz) ripe plum tomatoes, peeled and diced	15 g (½ oz) fresh coriander, coarsely chopped

Heat oil in a large, heavy casserole. Add onion and sauté over medium heat until golden, about 7 minutes. Add chicken, sprinkle with salt and pepper, and sauté for 7 minutes. Add tomatoes and sauté lightly. Add water, celery and garlic and bring to a simmer. Skim foam from surface. Cover and simmer for 45 minutes, skimming fat occasionally.

Rinse rice with cold water, drain and add to soup. Stir once, cover and cook over low heat for 20 minutes or until rice is tender. (Soup can be kept, covered, for 2 days in refrigerator; since it thickens on standing, add a little water when reheating it.) Add coriander. Either serve as is, adding chicken pieces to soup bowls; or remove chicken meat from bones and return meat to casserole; or reserve chicken meat for other uses. Taste soup and adjust seasoning. Serve hot.

MUSHROOM-BARLEY CHICKEN SOUP

This chicken-based version of mushroom-barley soup, which eastern European Jews have popularized in both America and Israel, is substantial enough to be a main course. For a first course the soup can be made with vegetables alone or with strained meat or chicken stock or soup but without the pieces of chicken. The seasoning is delicate so the taste of the mushrooms comes through. In Hungary the soup is flavoured generously with both hot and sweet paprika. We sometimes add spicy beef sausages to the soup to make it a hearty main-course soup.

MAKES 4 MAIN-COURSE OR 6 FIRST-COURSE SERVINGS

25 g (1 oz) dried porcini or Polish mushrooms	1 large leek, with 5 cm (2 inches) green tops, split, cleaned and sliced
250 ml (8 fl oz) hot water	3 celery stalks, diced
700 g (1½ lb) chicken wings	salt and freshly ground pepper
225 g (8 oz) (about 3 medium) carrots, diced	100–225 g (4–8 oz) fresh button mushrooms, halved and sliced (optional)
1 parsnip, diced	
1 medium onion, diced	
1.7 litres (3 pints) water	30–40 ml (2–3 tbsp) chopped fresh parsley, dill or mixture
90 g (3½ oz) pearl barley	

Rinse mushrooms and soak for 20 minutes in hot water. Remove mushrooms, reserving liquid. Dice any large ones.

In a large casserole combine chicken, carrots, parsnip, onion and 1.7 litres (3 pints) water and bring to the boil. Skim foam from surface and reduce heat to low. Add barley, leek, celery, salt and pepper. Add fresh and dried mushrooms. Pour mushroom soaking water into another bowl, leaving behind and discarding the last few spoonfuls of liquid, which may be sandy, then add mushroom liquid to soup. Cover and cook for about 1½ hours or until chicken is tender and soup is well flavoured. Skim off excess fat. Taste and adjust seasoning.

Remove chicken meat from bones and add it to soup. (Soup can be kept, covered, for 2 days in refrigerator. When reheating, add a little water if soup is too thick.) When serving, sprinkle each bowl with chopped herbs.

YEMENITE CHICKEN SOUP

This aromatic chicken soup is quite a change from the usual 'Jewish' chicken soup familiar in America. I learned how to make it from my husband's aunt, who is an expert in old-fashioned Yemenite cooking. To make sure the soup has its fresh, authentic taste, we grind the cumin seeds in a spice grinder. The spices give the soup a golden hue and seem to intensify the natural soup colour.

This soup has become so popular in Israel that now it often appears on menus of 'Israeli' restaurants, even those that do not specialize in Yemenite food. Yemenite beef soup is equally well loved and is made the same way, with meaty beef bones instead of chicken.

MAKES 8 FIRST-COURSE OR
4 TO 6 MAIN-COURSE SERVINGS

30 ml (2 tbsp) ground cumin	*1 large onion*
10 ml (2 tsp) turmeric	*2 ripe, medium tomatoes, or*
1.25 ml (¼ tsp) ground pepper	*4 plum tomatoes*
1.1–1.4 kg (2½–3 lb)	*about 1.7 litres (3 pints)*
chicken pieces, or 1 medium	*boiling water*
chicken, cut into pieces	*4–6 fairly small boiling*
salt to taste	*potatoes, peeled (optional)*

Mix cumin, turmeric and black pepper. Put chicken in a large heavy casserole and heat over low heat. Sprinkle with salt and spice mixture and heat over low heat for about 7 minutes, turning pieces occasionally so they are well coated with spices.

Cut a deep X in the onion and in each tomato and add whole to casserole. Add boiling water to cover, pouring it in along side of casserole so spices are not washed off chicken. Add potatoes, push them into liquid and add more water if necessary so they are covered. Bring to the boil, then skim foam from surface. Cover and cook over low heat for 2 hours or until soup is well flavoured. (Soup can be kept, covered, for 3 days in refrigerator.) Skim excess fat. Taste and adjust seasoning. Serve hot, in shallow bowls.

VARIATION
Yemenite Beef Soup

Use 1.1–1.4 kg (2½–3 lb) meaty beef bones, such as shin bones, instead of chicken. Cook soup for 3–4 hours.

HEARTY MEAT SOUP WITH GREEN BEANS

This is a spicy meat soup like my Yemen-born mother-in-law makes, with chunks of beef, chick peas and green beans. It is seasoned with a curry-like spice mixture that gives it a wonderful aroma and intriguing flavour. For a touch of heat, the fiery chilli chutney called Zehug (page 154) can be served on the side.

MAKES 6–8 FIRST COURSE SERVINGS

1 veal or beef soup bone (optional)
about 1.4 litres (2½ pints) water
450 g (1 lb) chuck steak or stewing steak, excess fat removed
30 ml (2 tbsp) vegetable oil
2 medium onions, chopped
15 ml (1 tbsp) ground cumin
2.5 ml (½ tsp) turmeric
salt and freshly ground pepper

100 g (4 oz) green beans, ends removed, broken into 2.5-cm (1-inch) pieces
4 large garlic cloves, finely chopped
175 g (6 oz) small pasta shapes, such as wheels, medium shells or elbow macaroni
pinch of cayenne pepper
45 ml (3 tbsp) chopped fresh coriander or parsley

If using a soup bone, put it in a large saucepan, add water and bring to the boil. Skim foam from surface. Simmer uncovered over low heat for 2 hours. Remove bone and reserve. Measure stock and add enough water to make 1.4 litres (2 ½ pints).

Cut beef into 2.5-cm (1-inch) cubes. Heat oil in a large saucepan. Add onions and sauté over medium heat for 5 minutes. Add beef cubes, cumin, turmeric and a pinch of salt and pepper. Sauté for 5 minutes, stirring. Add bone and measured liquid and bring to the boil. Cover and simmer over low heat for 1½–2 hours or until beef is very tender. (Soup can be kept, covered, for 2 days in refrigerator. Reheat over medium-low heat, covered.)

Add green beans to soup and simmer, uncovered, for 7 minutes. Remove soup bone and add any meat from it to soup. Add garlic, sprinkle in pasta and stir to submerge it. Simmer, uncovered, over medium-low heat, stirring occasionally, for 7–9 minutes or until pasta and beans are tender. Stir in cayenne pepper and coriander or parsley. Taste and adjust seasoning. Serve hot.

IRANIAN MEATBALL SOUP FOR SHABBAT (GUNDI)

In recent years southern California has become one of the world's largest centres of Jews from Iran. In fact, during the last few years several Iranian kosher grocery shops have opened in my hometown of Santa Monica. For *Shabbat* a traditional Iranian dish is gundi, a spicy chicken soup containing meatballs made with chick peas, accompanied by rice. Iranians use chick pea flour, but this recipe uses the more available canned chick peas. The meatball mixture can also be sautéed in small cakes, as in the variation, and served as an appetizer.

MAKES 4 MAIN-COURSE OR 6 FIRST-COURSE SERVINGS

700 g (1½ lb) chicken wings or legs
1 medium onion

salt and freshly ground pepper
1.5 litres (2¾ pints) water

MEATBALLS
scant 15 g (½ oz) parsley sprigs
1 × 227–250-g (8–9-oz) can chick peas, drained and rinsed

½ large onion, cut in chunks
225 g (8 oz) lean minced beef
1.25 ml (¼ tsp) salt
1.25 ml (¼ tsp) black pepper

2 large boiling potatoes, about 350 g (12 oz), peeled and cut in large dice
2 large carrots, diced
15 ml (1 tbsp) tomato purée
5 ml (1 tsp) ground cumin
1.25 ml (¼ tsp) turmeric

2.5 ml (½ tsp) red pepper flakes, or cayenne pepper to taste
200–275 g (7–10 oz) long-grain white rice, preferably basmati
30 ml (2 tbsp) chopped fresh parsley

Cook chicken with onion, salt and pepper in water for 1 hour, partly covered. Discard onion and remove chicken; reserve meat for other dishes.

Mince parsley in a food processor and remove. Add chick peas to food processor and chop them, then remove them. Mince onion in processor. Mix beef, chick peas, onion, salt, pepper and parsley.

Shape spoonfuls of mixture into small meatballs. Squeeze each well so it will be compact, then roll it between your palms to a smooth ball. Put on a plate and refrigerate.

Add potatoes to soup along with carrots and cook, covered, for 20 minutes. Add tomato purée, cumin, turmeric and pepper flakes. Stir to blend. Add meatballs, cover and simmer over low heat for 30 minutes. (Soup can be kept, covered, for 2 days in refrigerator.)

Add rice to a large saucepan of 1.7 litres (3 pints) boiling salted water. Boil, uncovered, for 14 minutes or until tender. Drain well.

Add parsley to hot soup. Taste and adjust seasoning. To serve, spoon a generous amount of rice into each bowl and top with soup and meatballs.

NOTE: Instead of canned chick peas, you can use 50 g (2 oz) dried chick peas, soaked for 8 hours or overnight and drained.

HERBED BEAN AND PASTA SOUP

Jews from Italy prepare this thick chunky soup, which is similar to the well-known dish, *pasta e fagioli*. It is flavoured with rosemary, sage, garlic and vegetables and makes a warming first course.

MAKES 4 OR 5 FIRST-COURSE SERVINGS

---

about 275 g (10 oz) small dried white beans
1.4 litres (2½ pints) plus 1 litre (1¾ pints) water
1 large sprig fresh rosemary or 10 ml (2 tsp) dried, crumbled
450 ml (¾ pint) chicken soup or stock
30 ml (2 tbsp) olive oil
1 medium onion, finely chopped
1 celery stalk, diced
40 g (1½ oz) carrot, finely chopped

450 g (1 lb) fresh tomatoes, peeled, seeded, chopped; or 1 × 794-g (28-oz) can plum tomatoes, drained and chopped
2 large garlic cloves, finely diced
100 g (4 oz) small pasta shapes – shells, bow ties, squares or wheels
45 ml (3 tbsp) chopped fresh parsley
30 ml (2 tbsp) chopped fresh sage or basil, or 10 ml (2 tsp) dried, crumbled

---

Pick over beans, discarding any pebbles and broken or discoloured beans. Rinse beans, drain and place in a large bowl; add 1.4 litres (2½ pints) water. Cover and leave to stand for at least 8 hours or overnight. Or, for quicker soaking, place beans in a large saucepan with 1.4 litres (2½ pints) water, bring to the boil and boil briskly, uncovered, for 2 minutes. Remove from heat, cover and leave to stand for 1 hour.

Drain beans, discarding soaking liquid. Combine beans, rosemary, chicken soup and 1 litre (1¾ pints) water in a large saucepan. Bring to the boil, then regulate heat to medium or medium-low so soup simmers and cook, uncovered, adding hot water occasionally so beans remain covered, for 1¼ hours or until beans are tender. Drain beans, reserving cooking liquid. Measure liquid; add enough water to make 1 litre (1¾ pints). Discard rosemary.

Heat oil in a heavy medium saucepan over medium-low heat. Add onion, celery and carrot and sauté, stirring often, for about 10 minutes or until onion is soft. Add tomatoes and bring to the boil. Cook, uncovered, over medium heat for about 15 minutes or until vegetables are tender. Add cooked beans and measured liquid. (Soup can be kept, covered, for 2 days in refrigerator.)

Bring soup to the boil. Add garlic and pasta and cook uncovered over medium-high heat, stirring occasionally, for 5–8 minutes or until pasta is tender but firm to the bite. Stir in parsley and sage or basil. Taste and adjust seasoning. Serve hot.

FRESH MUSHROOM SOUP WITH DILL DUMPLINGS

This winter treat features a Hungarian touch – hearty dumplings that cook directly in the soup. A two-way soup, it can be made with chicken or vegetable stock.

MAKES 4 SERVINGS

DILL DUMPLINGS

1 large egg, size 1 or 2	1.25 ml (¼ tsp) paprika
0.75 ml (⅛ tsp) salt	2.5 ml (½ tsp) dried dill
pinch of cayenne	25 g (1 oz) plain flour

---

40 g (1½ oz) non-dairy margarine	5 ml (1 tsp) paprika
	salt and freshly ground pepper
50 g (2 oz) onion, finely chopped	30 ml (2 tbsp) plain flour
	750 ml (1¼ pints) chicken soup or stock
350 g (12 oz) small white mushrooms, halved and thinly sliced	30 ml (2 tbsp) snipped fresh dill or 10 ml (2 tsp) dried

---

Whisk egg with salt, cayenne, paprika and dill. Gradually stir in flour with whisk until mixture forms a smooth thick mixture. Do not beat.

Melt margarine in medium, heavy saucepan over medium heat. Add onion and cook for 10 minutes, stirring often. Stir in mushrooms and add paprika and a small pinch of salt and pepper. Cover and cook, shaking pan occasionally, for 10 minutes. Uncover and cook, stirring, for about 5 minutes or until liquid evaporates.

Reduce heat to low. Add flour and cook, stirring constantly, for about 3 minutes or until mixture is well blended and bubbly. Remove from heat. Pour in chicken soup, stirring and scraping bottom of saucepan thoroughly. Bring to the boil over medium–high heat, stirring constantly. Reduce heat to low so soup simmers.

Add a little dumpling mixture to simmering soup, about 1.25 ml (¼ tsp) at a time. Simmer, uncovered, occasionally shaking pan, for about 5 minutes or until dumplings no longer taste floury; taste one to check. (Soup can be kept, covered, for up to 2 days in refrigerator. Reheat, uncovered, over low heat.)

Stir in 15 ml (1 tbsp) fresh or 10 ml (2 tsp) dried dill. Taste, and add salt and pepper if needed. Serve hot, sprinkled with dill.

SPICY WINTER BEAN SOUP

B eef and bean soup is popular in most Jewish ethnic groups. Ashkenazic versions are flavoured with onion, carrot and parsley rather than the garlic and tomatoes in this North African version. In some Sephardic families, the soup is made with saffron instead of turmeric and chopped fresh coriander is sprinkled over each serving.

MAKES 6 TO 8 MAIN-COURSE SERVINGS

450 g (1 lb) dried white beans, such as haricot
45 ml (3 tbsp) vegetable oil
2 large onions, sliced
700 g (1½ lb) beef with bones, such as shin
4 medium garlic cloves, chopped
15 ml (1 tbsp) tomato purée
10 ml (2 tsp) paprika
5 ml (1 tsp) turmeric

1.7 litres (3½ pints) water
700 g (1½ lb) boiling potatoes
salt to taste
4 large eggs in shell, size 1 or 2, rinsed (optional)
1.25 ml (¼ tsp) cayenne pepper
scant 15 g (½ oz) fresh parsley or coriander, chopped

Sort beans, discarding any broken ones and any stones. In a large bowl soak beans overnight in cold water to generously cover. Or, for a quicker method, cover beans with 1.7 litres (3½ pints) water in a large saucepan, bring to the boil and boil for 2 minutes; cover and leave to stand off heat for 1 hour.

Rinse beans and drain. Heat oil in large saucepan over medium heat, add onions and sauté for about 10 minutes. Add beef, beans, garlic, tomato purée, paprika, turmeric and water and bring to the boil. Cover and cook over low heat for 1 hour.

Peel and halve potatoes and add to saucepan. Add salt and eggs in their shells and continue to cook for 1 hour or until meat is very tender. (Soup can be kept, covered, for 2 days in refrigerator.)

To serve, remove meat. Dice any meat from bone and add to soup. Serve any marrow bones, if desired. Shell eggs and halve them lengthways. Stir cayenne pepper and parsley into soup. Garnish with eggs.

VEGETABLE SOUP WITH MATZO BALLS AND FRESH HERBS

Kneidlach, or matzo balls, are a treat not only in chicken soup but also in *milchig* (dairy) vegetable soups like this one. My mother began making this quick, light, colourful soup with small matzo balls when our family moved to Jerusalem from Washington, D.C. The lavish use of fresh dill and parsley are characteristic of the style of cooking she learned from her Israeli friends.

MAKES 4 FIRST-COURSE SERVINGS

25 g (1 oz) butter, margarine, or vegetable oil	450 g (1 lb) courgettes, coarsely grated
1 medium onion, chopped	1 ripe, medium tomato, diced
1 large carrot, grated	1 litre (1¾ pints) water

MATZO BALLS	
25 g (1 oz) matzo meal	1.25 ml (¼ tsp) baking
1.25 ml (¼ tsp) salt	powder
pinch of pepper	1 large egg, size 1 or 2

250 ml (8 fl oz) milk	30 ml (2 tbsp) snipped or
45 ml (3 tbsp) chopped fresh parsley	chopped fresh dill, or 10 ml (2 tsp) dried

Melt butter in a medium saucepan over medium-low heat. Add onion and sauté for 7 minutes. Add carrot, courgettes, tomato, water, salt and pepper. Bring to the boil, then simmer for 10 minutes.

Meanwhile make small matzo balls. Stir together the matzo meal, salt, pepper and baking powder in a small bowl. Add egg and stir until blended. Take 5 ml (1 tsp) of mixture, roll gently between your palms to a ball and transfer to a plate. Repeat with remaining mixture.

Add matzo balls to soup after it has simmered for 10 minutes. Cover and cook for 10 minutes. Stir in milk and heat briefly; do not boil. Just before serving, add chopped parsley and dill. Taste and adjust seasoning.

SOUPS

BORSCHT WITH POTATOES AND SOURED CREAM

This refreshing soup of Polish origin is a great favourite among Jews from eastern Europe. Traditional recipes call for thickening the soup with eggs or egg yolks, but this is a lighter version that is good warm or cold. I like to serve garnishes of snipped dill, soured cream, diced hard-boiled egg, diced cucumber and warm potatoes so that the soup makes a colourful first course, and each person can choose what to add to his or her bowl.

MAKES 5 OR 6 FIRST-COURSE SERVINGS

9 beetroots, each 4–5 cm (1½–2 inches) in diameter, 700 g (1½ lb) total, including 5–7.5 cm (2–3 inches) of beetroot tops	1 medium onion, halved 1.4 litres (2½ pints) water 2.5 ml (½ tsp) salt 15 ml (1 tbsp) sugar 30 ml (2 tbsp) strained fresh lemon juice

ACCOMPANIMENTS
6 small boiled potatoes, hot or at room temperature soured cream diced cucumber	snipped fresh dill diced or sliced hard-boiled eggs

Scrub beetroots clean with a stiff brush under cold water. Leave 5–7.5 cm (2–3 inches) of tops on. Combine beetroots, onion and water in a medium saucepan and bring to the boil. Cover and simmer over low heat for about 1 hour or until beetroots are tender. Discard onion. Remove beetroots and slip off their skins. Pour soup into a bowl. Rinse saucepan. Slowly pour beetroot cooking liquid back into pan, leaving last few spoonfuls soup, which may be sandy, behind in bowl; discard this liquid.

Grate beetroots coarsely in food processor or with grater. Return to soup and add salt and sugar. Cook for 2 minutes, stirring, over low heat. Remove from heat and add lemon juice. Taste and adjust seasoning; soup should be slightly sweet and sour.

Serve hot or cold. If serving hot, garnish with potato and soured cream. If serving cold, taste again before serving; serve plain, or with any or all of the accompaniments in separate bowls.

205

BLINTZES, PANCAKES AND EGG DISHES

 Blintzes are the most famous type of pancake in Jewish cooking, and in Israel are often the highlight of restaurants specializing in dairy foods.

Cheese blintzes filled with soft cheeses like cottage cheese and curd cheese are the best known and are especially popular for the holiday of Shavuot, but there are many other fillings. Dessert blintzes contain apples, blueberries, cherries or other fruit, while savoury blintzes are wrapped around fillings of mushrooms, cabbage, potatoes or meat.

The batter for making blintzes resembles that of French crêpes, except that for meat blintzes water replaces the milk in the batter. The cooking technique for blintzes is different from that of crêpes, however. Blintzes are sautéed on only one side before being filled. After the filling is added, the blintzes are folded so the uncooked side faces outwards, and then are baked or sautéed, thus heating the filling and lightly browning the second side of each blintze. The folding technique is different also. Two opposite sides of the blintze are folded lightly over the filling, and then the blintze is rolled up in a cylindrical shape with both ends closed so the filling will not come out.

Jews from Yemen prepare a special type of pancake known as *melawah*. Unlike other pancakes, they are made from a pastry somewhat resembling puff pastry rather than a batter and are sautéed until crisp outside and tender inside. These pancakes are served for breakfast or supper, sometimes accompanied by Browned Eggs (see 216), but I find them wonderful for brunch. They have become à la mode in Israeli cafés as a rich, savoury snack.

Eggs play an important role on the Jewish menu, since they are pareve, or neutral, and can thus be combined in a meal with either *milkchig* (dairy) or *fleishig* (meat) ingredients. A typical supper in Israel is an omelette with Mediterranean diced vegetable salad and a pita. The omelette is most frequently prepared in the Sephardic style – flat and resembling an Italian *frittata*. Also popular among Jewish cooks are scrambled eggs, either with lox in the American-Ashkenazic style, with tomatoes and onions in the Moroccan fashion, or with sautéed mushrooms, which are well liked by everyone.

A special type of egg dish, known simply as Browned Eggs, is a favourite among Sephardic Jews and is made for *Shabbat*, Passover, and other festive occasions. Basically these are eggs cooked in their shells for a long time until the shells turn deep brown, the whites become light brown, and the yolks acquire a rich, creamy texture. There are several ways to prepare them. Often a few eggs are simply added to a meat soup or stew dish and simmered with the meat. Yemenite cooks sometimes place eggs in their shells on top of a special bread called *Shabbat* Breakfast Bread (page 293) that is baked in a covered pot. When cooks wish to prepare browned eggs without making stew or bread, they simply cook the eggs with onion skins, as on page 216.

BASIC BLINTZES

The word *blintze* comes from Yiddish and blintzes are one of the great specialities of the Ashkenazic kitchen. Like crêpes, blintzes can be wrapped around a mixture that is sweet or savoury, and they can play the role of appetizer, main course or dessert. Cheese filling is the favourite, but other well-liked sweet fillings are apple, cherry and blueberry. Frequent savoury filling choices are meat, chicken, mushroom and potato-onion.

MAKES 12 TO 15 BLINTZES

3 large eggs, size 1 or 2	*25 g (1 oz) butter or*
300 ml (½ pint) milk or	*margarine*
water, or more as needed	*5–15 ml (1–3 tsp)*
75 g (3 oz) plain flour	*vegetable oil, for brushing*
2.5 ml (½ tsp) salt	*pan*

To prepare batter in food processor: combine eggs, 60 ml (4 tbsp) milk, flour and salt in bowl and mix using several on/off turns; batter will be lumpy. Scrape down sides and bottom of bowl. With machine running, pour 250 ml (8 fl oz) milk through feed tube and process batter for about 15 seconds. Scrape down sides and bottom of container thoroughly. Blend batter for about 15 seconds.

To prepare batter in blender: combine eggs, 300 ml (½ pint) milk, flour and salt in blender. Mix for about 1 minute until smooth.

To prepare batter in a bowl: Sift flour into medium bowl. Push flour to sides of bowl, leaving large well in centre of flour. Add eggs, salt and 60 ml (4 tbsp) milk to well and whisk ingredients in well briefly until blended. Using a whisk, stir flour gently and gradually into egg mixture until mixture is smooth. Gradually whisk in 250 ml (8 fl oz) milk.

Strain batter if it is lumpy. Cover and refrigerate for about 1 hour. (Batter can be refrigerated, covered, for up to 1 day.)

Melt butter in small saucepan over low heat. Stir batter well. Gradually whisk melted butter into batter. (Batter should have consistency of whipping cream. If it is too thick, gradually whisk in more milk, about 5 ml (1 tsp) at a time.)

Heat a 15–16-cm (6–6½-inch) crêpe pan or frying pan (for small blintzes) or a 20–23-cm (8–9-inch) frying pan (for larger blintzes) over medium-high heat. Sprinkle with a few drops of water. If water immediately sizzles, pan is hot enough. Brush pan lightly with oil; if using a non-stick pan, no oil is needed. Remove pan from heat and hold it near bowl of batter. Working quickly, add 30 ml (2 tbsp) batter to small pan, or 45 ml (3 tbsp) to large pan, adding batter to edge and tilting and swirling pan until its base is covered with thin layer of batter. Immediately pour any excess batter back into bowl.

Return pan to medium-high heat. Loosen edges of blintze with palette knife, discarding any pieces clinging to sides of pan. Cook blintze until underneath browns lightly. Slide blintze out onto plate, with uncooked side facing up. Top with sheet of greaseproof paper or foil if making them a few days ahead or if freezing them. Reheat pan a few seconds. Continue making blintzes, stirring batter occasionally with whisk. Adjust heat and brush pan with more oil if necessary. If batter thickens on standing, very gradually whisk in a little more milk, about 5 ml (1 tsp) at a time. Pile blintzes on plate, each separated with paper or foil, as they are done. (Blintzes can be kept, wrapped tightly, for up to 3 days in refrigerator; or they can be frozen. Bring to room temperature before using, to avoid tearing).

CHIVE BLINTZES WITH CABBAGE AND SOURED CREAM

In this luscious Polish-style dish, soured cream enriches the filling of sautéed cabbage and onions, and is also served as a topping. Chives add a modern, fresh touch to the blintz batter. Add 10 ml (2 tsp) snipped fresh chives to blintze batter.

MAKES 6 SERVINGS

CABBAGE FILLING

½ large green cabbage, 700 g
  (1½ lb), cored and rinsed
salt and freshly ground pepper
40 g (1½ oz) butter
½ large onion, finely chopped

1 hard-boiled large egg, size 1
  or 2, chopped
120 ml (4 fl oz) soured cream,
  at room temperature

---

12 chive Blintzes, each
  about 23 cm (9 inches) in
  diameter (opposite)
40 g (1½ oz) butter, cubed

120 ml (4 fl oz) soured cream
20 ml (4 tsp) snipped fresh
  chives
salt and freshly ground pepper

Chop cabbage as fine as possible, preferably in a food processor in batches. In a large pan of boiling salted water, boil cabbage for 3 minutes. Drain, rinse under cold water and drain thoroughly. Squeeze out excess liquid. Melt butter in a large frying pan, add onion and cook over low heat for 7 minutes or until soft but not browned. Stir in cabbage and sprinkle with salt and pepper. Cover and cook over low heat, stirring occasionally, for 15 minutes or until tender. Transfer mixture to a bowl and cool to room temperature. Stir in egg and soured cream and taste for seasoning.

Spoon about 30 ml (2 tbsp) filling onto the cooked side near one edge of each blintze. Fold sides over so that each covers about half the filling; roll up, beginning at filling edge. Arrange rolls in one layer in a shallow buttered baking dish. Dot with cubes of butter.

Preheat oven to 220°C (425°F) mark 7. Bake blintzes for 15 minutes, or until heated through and lightly browned. Mix soured cream with 15 ml (1 tbsp) chives and salt and pepper. Spoon soured cream mixture over centre of each. Sprinkle with chives.

MUSHROOM BLINTZES

Creamy mushroom-filled blintzes originated in Europe and now are relished by Jews of all origins. In Tel Aviv you can order them at a special blintze restaurant, the Jewish counterpart of the French crêperie.

MAKES 10 TO 12 BLINTZES; 5 OR 6 SERVINGS

MUSHROOM FILLING

40 g (1½ oz) butter
225 g (8 oz) small mushrooms, halved and sliced
salt and freshly ground white pepper
2.5 ml (½ tsp) paprika

30 ml (2 tbsp) plain flour
300 ml (½ pint) milk
freshly grated nutmeg
75 ml (5 tbsp) double cream
pinch of cayenne pepper
30 ml (2 tbsp) chopped fresh parsley

10–12 small Basic Blintzes (page 208) or chive Blintzes (page 209)
25 g (1 oz) butter, for dotting blintzes

soured cream, for serving (optional)
snipped fresh dill or chives or chopped parsley, for garnish (optional)

Melt 15 g (½ oz) butter in a large frying pan over medium heat. Add mushrooms, salt, pepper and paprika and sauté for 5 minutes.

Melt remaining 25 g (1 oz) butter in a heavy medium saucepan over low heat. Whisk in flour and cook, whisking constantly, for about 2 minutes or until foaming but not browned. Remove from heat and whisk in milk. Bring to the boil over medium–high heat, whisking, then add a small pinch of salt, white pepper and nutmeg. Cook over low heat for 3 minutes, then whisk in cream and bring to the boil. Cover over low heat, whisking often, for about 5 minutes or until thick. Add cayenne, stir in mushrooms and parsley, taste and adjust seasoning.

Preheat oven to 220°C (425°F) mark 7. Butter a large shallow baking dish or two 20-cm (8-inch) gratin dishes or other shallow baking dishes. Spoon 45 ml (3 tbsp) filling onto cooked side of each blintze, across lower third. Fold sides over so that each covers part of filling, then roll up in cigar shape, beginning at edge with filling.

Arrange blintzes in single layer in dish. Cut butter into small cubes and dot blintzes with butter. (Blintzes can be prepared to this point and kept, covered, for 1 day in refrigerator. Bring blintzes to room temperature and preheat oven before continuing.)

Bake blintzes for about 15 minutes or until heated through and lightly browned. Serve immediately. If desired, top each with a small spoonful of soured cream and a pinch of chopped herbs.

RICH YEMENITE PANCAKES (MELAWAH)

My mother-in-law taught me to prepare these pancakes, which are made from a pastry dough, rather than from a pourable batter. The pancakes are composed of thin layers of dough and are very rich; they are served at breakfast, brunch or supper, either plain or with honey. They are a delicious treat, and are well known in Israel as a unique speciality of the Jews from Yemen. Imagine my surprise when I found a nearly identical pastry on the other side of the globe – Chinese spring onion pancakes, which I tasted in Taiwan! When I saw them demonstrated in a cooking course in Taipei, the chef made the dough using a very similar technique to my mother-in-law's, but sprinkled the dough with chopped spring onions before rolling it.

MAKES 6 GENEROUS SERVINGS

425 g (15 oz) plain flour	300 ml (½ pint) water
5 ml (1 tsp) baking powder	175 g (6 oz) margarine,
7.5 ml (1½ tsp) salt	cut in 6 pieces, plus 25 g
1 large egg, size 1 or 2	(1 oz) for frying

Combine flour, baking powder and salt in food processor and process to blend. Add egg and 250 ml (8 fl oz) water and process with on/off turns to mix. With motor running, gradually add enough remaining water so mixture comes together to a smooth, fairly stiff dough. It will be sticky.

Remove dough from processor and knead well by slapping it vigorously on a work surface. Divide into 6 pieces and knead each with a slapping motion until smooth. Roll each in your palm to a ball. Put on an oiled plate, cover and refrigerate for 4 hours or overnight.

Oil a work surface and rolling pin. Leave the 175 g (6 oz) margarine to stand at room temperature until very soft. Roll out 1 ball of dough as thin as possible, so you can almost see through dough, to about 30-cm (12-inch) square. If dough tears, simply press it together. Spread dough with about one-sixth of the soft margarine. Roll up as for a Swiss roll. Tap the roll with your knuckles to flatten it and roll it up in a spiral. Put on a plate, cover and refrigerate overnight or up to 2 days. (Dough can also be frozen; thaw overnight in refrigerator before using.)

Set a ball of dough on a lightly oiled plate and flatten it with your lightly oiled hands to a round as large as the frying pan. Heat 5 ml (1 tsp) margarine in a heavy 23-cm (9-inch) frying pan and add the round of dough. Cover and fry over medium-high heat for 30 seconds, then over medium-low heat for about 5 minutes per side or until brown on both sides and cooked through. Repeat for remaining balls of dough, adding margarine to pan as needed.

LOX AND EGGS WITH SAUTÉED ONIONS

This deluxe version of scrambled eggs is easy and inexpensive to prepare at home. At some fish markets you can purchase small pieces of lox that are perfect for this dish and make it more economical. If you prefer larger pieces of lox with the eggs, cut it into strips instead of dicing it.

MAKES 4 OR 5 SERVINGS

---

40 g (1½ oz) butter or	*pinch of freshly ground white*
margarine	*pepper*
75 g (3 oz) onion, chopped	*175 g (6 oz) lox, diced*
10 large eggs, size 1 or 2	*parsley sprigs, for garnish*
1.25 ml (¼ tsp) salt	

Melt butter in a large frying pan. Add onion and sauté over medium-low heat, stirring often, for about 7 minutes until tender and golden.

Whisk eggs with salt and pepper in a large bowl until well blended. Add to frying pan and scramble over low heat, stirring often, until eggs are set to taste. Remove from heat and gently stir in lox. Taste and adjust seasoning. Serve immediately, with parsley.

EGGS WITH PEPPERS AND TOMATOES (SHAKSHUKA)

Shakshuka is the name of a whole class of egg and vegetable dishes typical of the North African Jewish kitchen. Potatoes, cauliflower, courgettes or other cooked vegetables might be used. The technique can vary, too. Some people cook the mixture over low heat without stirring, and the result is similar to a flat omelette or an Italian *frittata*. Others add the eggs whole and poach them in the vegetable mixture.

The most popular version is of eggs scrambled with tomatoes, peppers and onions and is rather similar to the French Basque recipe, *piperade*, except in the seasoning. This recipe is from Mazal Cohen, by husband's aunt from Yemen, who flavours the eggs with cumin and turmeric. It is fairly delicate, but you can add chopped chilli and garlic with the tomatoes if you like. In Israel Shakshuka is a supper dish, but it's good for a light lunch too. Serve it with fresh or toasted pita or sesame bread.

MAKES 2 SERVINGS

30–45 ml (2–3 tbsp) vegetable oil	2.5 ml (½ tsp) ground cumin
1 small onion, chopped	1.25 ml (¼ tsp) turmeric
½ medium green pepper, diced	cayenne pepper to taste (optional)
3 ripe, medium tomatoes, 350 g (12 oz) total, diced	3 large eggs, size 1 or 2, beaten
salt and freshly ground black pepper	30 ml (2 tbsp) chopped fresh parsley (optional)

Heat oil in a medium frying pan over medium heat. Add onion and sauté for about 5 minutes or until golden brown. Add green pepper and sauté for 2 minutes. Add tomatoes, salt and spices and cook for about 2 minutes. Add beaten eggs and parsley and scramble over low heat until set. Taste and adjust seasoning. Serve immediately.

NORTH AFRICAN BAKED EGGS WITH TOMATOES AND ONIONS

This baked version of the North African egg dish, Shakshuka (page 213), bears a certain resemblance to the French *oeufs au plat*. In Israel the eggs are usually cooked thoroughly.

MAKES 4 SERVINGS

30 ml (2 tbsp) vegetable or olive oil

1 medium onion, sliced

1 small garlic clove, finely chopped

1.1 kg (2½ lb) ripe tomatoes, peeled, seeded and chopped; or 2 × 794-g (28-oz) cans plum tomatoes, drained and chopped

1.25 ml (¼ tsp) dried thyme

1 bay leaf

salt and freshly ground pepper

pinch of cayenne pepper or Tabasco sauce to taste

30–45 ml (2–3 tbsp) chopped fresh coriander (optional)

4 large eggs, size 1 or 2

30 ml (2 tbsp) vegetable oil or melted butter or margarine

Preheat oven to 220°C (425°F) mark 7. Heat oil in a heavy large frying pan over medium heat. Add onion and sauté for about 10 minutes or until soft and beginning to brown; remove with slotted spoon. Add garlic to frying pan and cook over low heat, stirring, for about ½ minute. Add tomatoes, thyme, bay leaf, salt and pepper. Bring to the boil, then cook over medium heat, stirring often, until tomatoes are soft and mixture is thick and smooth, for about 20 minutes. Discard bay leaf. Stir in onion. Add cayenne or Tabasco sauce and coriander, reserving a little for garnish. Taste and adjust seasoning. (Mixture can be kept, covered, for 2 days in refrigerator.)

Reheat the tomato mixture if necessary. Grease 4 individual 15-cm (6-inch) shallow baking dishes or one 1.1-litre (2-pint) shallow dish of about 22-cm (8½-inch) diameter. Spread tomato mixture in dishes. With a spoon make a hollow in centre of mixture in each small dish, or make 4 hollows in large dish, each large enough to contain 1 egg. Break egg carefully into each hollow. Sprinkle a little oil or melted butter over each egg.

Bake for about 10 minutes or until eggs are done to taste. Set individual dishes on plates, sprinkle eggs with coriander and serve.

SALAMI WITH VEGETABLES AND EGGS

I prefer this Mediterranean-style version of salami and eggs, because it is lighter, and the diced aubergine, courgette and tomatoes provide a pleasing contrast to the salami's salty taste. The dish is very easy to make, since the eggs poach directly in the vegetable mixture.

MAKES 2 TO 4 SERVINGS

2 slices salami, finely diced	30 ml (2 tbsp) chopped spring
1 small aubergine, finely diced	onions
3 small courgettes, finely diced	salt and pepper
1 medium tomato, finely diced	2.5 ml (½ tsp) dried oregano
	4 large eggs, size 1 or 2

Heat salami in a large frying pan until the fat runs. Add aubergine, cover and cook for 8–10 minutes. Add courgettes and cook for 5 minutes. Add tomato, spring onions, salt and pepper and oregano and cook for 5 minutes or until vegetables are tender. Taste and adjust seasoning. Make 4 hollows in mixture. Add 1 whole egg to each hollow and sprinkle lightly with salt and pepper. Cover and cook for 4–5 minutes or until eggs are done to taste. Serve at once.

SCRAMBLED EGGS WITH SPICED MUSHROOMS

A zesty change from the usual scrambled eggs, this dish is great for brunch, lunch or supper, accompanied by fresh pita and Israeli Vegetable Salad (page 34).

MAKES 2 SERVINGS

30 ml (2 tbsp) olive oil,	2.5 ml (½ tsp) ground cumin
butter or a mixture of both	4 large eggs, size 1 or 2
225 g (8 oz) small	cayenne pepper to taste
mushrooms, quartered	15 ml (1 tbsp) chopped fresh
salt and pepper	parsley (optional)

Heat oil in a medium frying pan over medium-high heat. Add mushrooms, salt, pepper and cumin. Sauté, stirring often, for 7–10 minutes or until tender and lightly browned.

Beat eggs with a pinch of salt and cayenne. Reduce heat under frying pan to low. Add eggs and scramble them, stirring often, until they are set to taste. Remove from heat and stir in parsley. Taste, adjust seasoning and serve.

BROWNED EGGS (HUEVOS HAMINADOS)

A Sephardic treat for *Shabbat* and Passover, these eggs cook gently over a very low heat until they are light brown, creamy textured and rich in flavour, in a technique somewhat similar to preparing Chinese tea eggs. They are enjoyed during the rest of the year, too, especially to accompany Spinach or Cheese Bourekas (pages 162 and 70). Browned Eggs are often made as part of meaty soups or stews like Hamin (page 156), but this is the way to prepare them on their own.

If you think onion skins have no use, here's proof that they do! To make this dish, you'll need to save the skins when you're using several onions. The onions impart a bright Burgundy colour to the egg shells; some cooks add coffee to the cooking liquid to give them a dark brown hue. For people who leave a low oven or a hot plate on all night for *Shabbat* to keep other dishes warm, these eggs are convenient to prepare.

MAKES 8 SERVINGS

skins of 6 onions	30 ml (2 tbsp) olive or
8 large eggs, with no cracks,	vegetable oil
size 1 or 2	2.5 ml (½ tsp) black
5 ml (1 tsp) salt	pepper
1.7 litres (3 pints) water	

Put half the onion skins in a medium saucepan in which the eggs will fit in a single layer. Set eggs on top. Add remaining ingredients and bring to the boil. Cover and cook over very low heat for 6 hours or overnight. Serve eggs hot or warm.

FISH

Fish is a traditional first course for *Shabbat* and holiday dinners, and therefore Jewish cooks all over the world have developed festive fish dishes. Often these appetizer dishes are served cold, because of the prohibition of cooking food on *Shabbat*.

Although fish is pareve, or suitable for dairy or meat meals, many Jewish fish specialities do not contain dairy products because the fish usually begins a menu that features a meat or poultry main course. As a main course, however, fish is a frequent choice for dairy meals, and in these cases the recipe might contain butter or cream, as in Sole with Mushrooms in Paprika Cream.

In the United States the most famous Jewish fish dish is Polish-style gefilte fish served with a dab of spicy red horseradish. When I was growing up, my mother worked for hours to prepare it every week, chopping the fish in a wooden bowl with a round-bladed knife. Today gefilte fish is easy to make in a food processor.

The seasonings popular among Jews from Mediterranean and Middle Eastern lands also result in delicious fish dishes. Sephardic fish with lemon, and hot and spicy Moroccan fish with garlic and peppers, for example, are time-honoured appetizers that appear regularly on the *Shabbat* table. For weekday meals, fish shows up as a main course. It will often be sprinkled with cumin and either turmeric or thyme, then grilled, barbecued or fried; or it might be served in a zesty sauce, as in Yemenite-style haddock in a coriander-spring onion tomato sauce.

Most classic Ashkenazic fish recipes feature freshwater fish because these were the varieties found in the rivers and lakes of eastern and central Europe. Traditional Sephardic dishes make use of Mediterranean fish.

Do try to go to the best fish market so you can buy the freshest and best quality fish.

SWEET AND SOUR SALMON

Salmon with currants, walnuts and parsley makes a colourful, low-fat appetizer or a refreshing summer main course. The fish is served cold, and its sweet-and-sour taste is delicate.

Sweet-and-sour fish is traditionally prepared with carp and is popular among Jews from Poland, Germany and much of eastern Europe. The carp recipe has even become part of classic French cuisine, in which it is known as *carpe à la juive* (Jewish-style carp). It appears in four versions in Escoffier's authoritative *Guide Culinaire* – carp with white wine, garlic and shallots; with wine, shallots, garlic and lots of fresh parsley; with saffron and almonds; and with sugar, vinegar, raisins and currants.

Many old-fashioned versions of the recipe specify adding crumbled gingernuts or a pinch of dried ginger to the cooking liquid, but I like the zing of fresh ginger.

MAKES 4 FIRST-COURSE SERVINGS OR
2 MAIN-COURSE SERVINGS

2 salmon steaks, 2.5 cm (1 inch) thick, about 700 g (1½ lb) total	120 ml (4 fl oz) dry white wine
salt and freshly ground pepper	30 ml (2 tbsp) vegetable oil
1 medium onion, sliced	10 ml (2 tsp) white wine vinegar
2 medium carrots, sliced in rounds	5 ml (1 tsp) sugar
2 bay leaves	45 ml (3 tbsp) currants
2 slices fresh ginger, 1-cm (½-inch) cube	30 ml (2 tbsp) chopped fresh parsley
2 whole cloves	25 g (1 oz) walnut halves or pieces
450 ml (¾ pint) water	lemon wedges, for garnish

Sprinkle salmon lightly with salt and pepper and set aside.

Combine onion, carrots, bay leaves, ginger, cloves, salt and pepper to taste, and water in a sauté pan or deep frying pan in which salmon can just fit. Bring to the boil, cover and simmer for 15 minutes. Add wine and oil and bring to a simmer. Add salmon, cover and cook over low heat for 10–12 minutes or until fish is tender; check near bone – flesh should have turned a lighter shade of pink. Transfer fish carefully to a deep serving dish.

Boil the cooking liquid for 5 minutes or until it is reduced to 450 ml (¾ pint). Strain, reserving a few carrot slices for garnish, and return strained liquid to pan. Add vinegar, sugar and currants and simmer for 1 minute. Add parsley, taste and adjust seasoning. Add walnuts and pour or spoon mixture over fish.

Serve fish cold. When serving, spoon a little of the liquid over fish. Garnish with a few carrot slices and lemon wedges.

GRILLED SALMON WITH MOROCCAN SEASONINGS

Although Moroccan-Jewish cooking has a reputation in Israel for being rather hot, each cook adds only the amount of seasoning liked by his or her family. And there are plenty of delicate dishes too, because of the French influence. This is an example of such a dish, subtly spiced with the popular combination of cumin, paprika and olive oil. It's very quick and easy, and is wonderful with rice or couscous.

MAKES 2 MAIN-COURSE SERVINGS

2 salmon steaks, 2.5 cm (1 inch) thick, about 550 g (1¼ lb) total	2.5 ml (½ tsp) dried leaf thyme, crumbled
2.5 ml (½ tsp) ground cumin	salt and freshly ground pepper
1.25 ml (¼ tsp) paprika	15–30 ml (1–2 tbsp) olive oil
	cucumber slices
	tomato slices

Line grill rack with foil if desired. Preheat grill with rack about 10 cm (4 inches) from heat source. Lightly oil grill rack or foil.

Remove any scales from salmon steaks. Mix cumin, paprika and thyme in a small bowl. Sprinkle about half the mixture on one side of salmon, then sprinkle with salt and pepper. Drizzle with half the oil. Set salmon on grill rack and grill for 4 minutes. Turn over, sprinkle with remaining spice mixture, a pinch more of salt and pepper, and remaining oil. Grill for 4–5 more minutes. To check whether salmon is done, make a small cut with a sharp knife near bone; colour of flesh should have become lighter pink all the way through, or nearly all the way through if you like fish a bit less done.

Serve hot, with cucumber and tomato slices.

COLD OVEN-POACHED TROUT WITH HORSERADISH SAUCE

In the Jewish kitchen, horseradish is a favourite with fish. Here it flavours an easy, mayonnaise-based sauce to slightly tone down its sharpness, making it a fitting, but still very zesty, partner for the delicate trout. The dish will be prettiest if pink salmon trout are used.

This recipe features a mayonnaise and yogurt or soured cream sauce, but you can omit the yogurt or soured cream for a *fleishig* meal. A refreshing accompaniment for the fish is thinly sliced cucumber.

MAKES 4 MAIN-COURSE SERVINGS

1 medium carrot, sliced	1.1 litres (2 pints) water
1 medium onion, sliced	120 ml (4 fl oz) dry white
1 bay leaf	wine
2.5 ml (½ tsp) dried thyme	4 small trout, 225 g (8 oz)
5 ml (1 tsp) salt	each
1.25 ml (¼ tsp) black	
peppercorns	

HORSERADISH SAUCE

150 ml (¼ pint) mayonnaise	15 ml (1 tbsp) chopped fresh
120 ml (4 fl oz) natural	parsley (optional)
yogurt or soured cream	salt and white pepper
1.25 ml (¼ tsp) strained fresh	10–15 ml (2–3 tsp) water
lemon juice	(optional)
30 ml (2 tbsp) prepared	
horseradish, or to taste	

Combine carrot, onion, bay leaf, thyme, salt, peppercorns and water in a large saucepan. Cover and bring to the boil. Simmer over low heat for 20 minutes, then strain into a bowl and add wine. Leave to cool slightly.

Preheat oven to 200°C (400°F) mark 6. Snip fins off fish and trim tails straight, using sturdy scissors. Rinse fish inside and out, removing any scales and pat dry. Leave on heads and tails. Season fish inside and out with salt and pepper.

Set fish in one layer in a large, heavy, flameproof baking dish.

Pour enough of wine mixture over fish to cover them and bring to a simmer. Cover with foil, transfer to oven and bake until a thin skewer inserted into thickest part of fish comes out hot to touch, about 12 minutes. Uncover fish and leave to cool in liquid until lukewarm.

Whisk mayonnaise with yogurt in a bowl until smooth. Whisk in lemon juice, then stir in horseradish and parsley. Taste, and add salt and pepper if needed. If sauce is too thick, gradually whisk in 10–15 ml (2–3 tsp) water.

Transfer fish carefully to a plate lined with paper towels, using 2 fish slices. Remove skin of each fish by scraping gently with paring knife; leave skin on head and tail. Leave fish to cool to room temperature. (Fish can be kept, covered, for up to 1 day in refrigerator; refrigerate sauce in separate dish, covered.)

Serve fish with horseradish sauce.

BRAISED COD WITH CHICK PEAS AND OLIVE OIL

I first tasted this dish in Florence, Italy. Later I learned that it is also characteristic of the cuisine of Moroccan Jews. Dried chillies and garlic cook with the chick peas, and these cooking juices then flavour the fish but do not make it excessively hot. It's a simple and delicious dish, especially when made with superior quality olive oil. Some cooks add fresh coriander, paprika, cumin and turmeric to the fish.

MAKES 4 MAIN-COURSE SERVINGS

about 550 g (1¼ lb) cooked chick peas or 2 × 439-g (15½-oz) cans
5 large garlic cloves, sliced
4 dried red chillies
salt
75–90 ml (5–6 tbsp) extra-virgin olive oil
freshly ground pepper

60 ml (4 tbsp) chick pea cooking liquid or water
900 g (2 lb) cod steaks or fillets, about 2.5 cm (1 inch) thick
coriander or parsley sprigs, for garnish
lemon wedges, for garnish (optional)

Preheat oven to 200°C (400°F) mark 6. If using canned chick peas, rinse and drain them. Combine chick peas with garlic, chillies, pinch of salt and 45–60 ml (3–4 tbsp) oil in a medium saucepan. Add 60 ml (4 tbsp) cooking liquid from chick peas, or 60 ml (4 tbsp) water if using canned ones. Push peppers to bottom of pan and bring liquid to a simmer. Cover tightly and cook over medium-low heat for 20 minutes.

Transfer half the chick pea mixture to a 23-cm (9-inch) square baking dish. Set fish on top and sprinkle with salt and pepper. Top fish with remaining chick pea mixture. Sprinkle with remaining 30 ml (2 tbsp) oil. Cover and bake for 30–35 minutes or until fish can just be flaked but is not falling apart.

Discard the chillies. Serve fish hot or lukewarm. Spoon a few spoonfuls of juices over fish and chick peas when serving. Garnish with coriander or parsley sprigs and lemon wedges.

NOTE: If using dried chick peas, use 225 g (8 oz). Soak overnight or quick-soak (see the recipe for Hummus, page 175). Drain, rinse and cook in water to generously cover for 1¼–1½ hours.

SAFFRON FISH BALLS
IN TOMATO SAUCE

I received this recipe from Paule Tourdjman, a Jewish woman from Morocco who worked with me at La Varenne Cooking School in Paris. The fish balls in their aromatic tomato sauce are good as an appetizer, or a light main course with white rice. Some cooks use cumin instead of the saffron, or a combination of dried ginger and grated orange rind.

MAKES 4 MAIN-COURSE OR
6 OR 7 FIRST-COURSE SERVINGS

0.75 ml (⅛ tsp) saffron
threads, or good pinch

45 ml (3 tbsp) extra-virgin
olive oil

SAUCE

900 g (2 lb) ripe tomatoes or
2 × 794-g (28-oz) cans
plum tomatoes
30 ml (2 tbsp) olive oil
1 medium onion, chopped

50 g (2 oz) red pepper, diced
(optional)
3 sprigs fresh thyme or 2.5 ml
(½ tsp) dried
1 bay leaf
salt and freshly ground pepper

FISH BALLS

1 medium onion, quartered
450 g (1 lb) cod fillet, any
bones removed, cut into
pieces
5 ml (1 tsp) salt
1.25 ml (¼ tsp) ground white
pepper

1 slice white bread, crust
removed, torn into pieces
1 large egg, size 1 or 2
1 large egg white, size 1 or 2
15 g (½ oz) fresh parsley,
chopped

Slightly crush the saffron with your fingers and soak in oil for about 30 minutes.

Peel and seed the fresh tomatoes, reserving juice; if using canned tomatoes, drain and reserve juice. Coarsely chop the tomatoes. In a medium saucepan, heat oil, add onion and red pepper and sauté over medium-low heat for 7 minutes. Add tomatoes, thyme, bay leaf, salt and pepper. Bring to the boil, cover and cook over low heat for 20 minutes. Remove bay leaf and thyme sprigs. Set aside.

In a food processor, finely chop onion and remove. Chop fish in processor. Add salt, pepper, bread, egg, egg white and 15 ml (1 tbsp) saffron oil. Transfer to a bowl. Stir in chopped parsley and onion. Form mixture into small balls, using 15 ml (1 tbsp) mixture for each, and roll them between your palms until smooth. Put on a plate.

Measure the reserved tomato juice, adding water if necessary to make 250 ml (8 fl oz). Add measured juice and remaining saffron oil to sauce. Transfer sauce to a sauté pan or deep frying pan. Put half the fish balls in sauce, cover and cook, without stirring, for 20 minutes. Carefully remove them with a slotted spoon. Cook remaining fish balls in sauce. Return all fish balls to sauce. Taste sauce and adjust seasoning. Serve hot or cold.

HADDOCK IN CORIANDER–SPRING ONION TOMATO SAUCE

This aromatic dish features an easy-to-make sauce based on puréed fresh tomatoes. In Israel the dish is made with mullet or tilapia, which are commonly available fresh, but I use haddock, sea bass, halibut, cod or sometimes salmon. Simply cooked rice is a good accompaniment for the flavourful sauce.

MAKES 4 MAIN-COURSE SERVINGS

450 g (1 lb) ripe tomatoes, cored and cut in large chunks
30 ml (2 tbsp) vegetable oil
½ large onion, diced
6 large garlic cloves, chopped
30 ml (2 tbsp) tomato purée
about 11.25 ml (2¼ tsp) ground cumin
2.5 ml (½ tsp) turmeric

1.25 ml (¼ tsp) paprika
pinch of cayenne pepper
15 g (½ oz) fresh coriander, chopped
800 g (1¾ lb) haddock, cod or other fish fillets, about 2.5 cm (1 inch) thick
salt and pepper
45 ml (3 tbsp) chopped spring onions

Purée the tomatoes in a food processor or blender. Heat oil in a large sauté pan, add onion and sauté over medium heat until golden brown. Add tomatoes, garlic, tomato purée, 1.25 ml (¼ tsp) cumin, turmeric, paprika, cayenne and half the coriander. Bring to the boil, cover and simmer for 10 minutes.

Sprinkle fish lightly on both sides with salt, pepper and remaining cumin. Add fish to sauce and sprinkle with 30 ml (2 tbsp) chopped spring onions. Cover and cook over low heat for 15 minutes. Turn over and cook for 10–15 more minutes or until it can flake easily.

Sprinkle fish with remaining coriander and remaining spring onions. Serve hot or at room temperature.

FISH WITH LIGHT LEMON AND DILL SAUCE

Cold fish in lemon sauce is a favourite first course among Jews from Greece and Turkey. Most versions of the dish use an egg-based sauce, but this eggless recipe is lighter and simpler to prepare. I like it because the fresh taste of the dill balances the lemon flavour. The fish can be either poached, as here, or sautéed.

MAKES 3 OR 4 MAIN-COURSE OR 6 FIRST-COURSE SERVINGS

30 ml (2 tbsp) lemon juice	700 g (1½ lb) halibut fillet,
45 ml (3 tbsp) olive oil	1–2.5 cm (½–1 inch)
175 ml (6 fl oz) water	thick
salt and pepper	

LEMON-DILL SAUCE

30 ml (2 tbsp) lemon juice	30 ml (2 tbsp) snipped fresh
90 ml (6 tbsp) olive oil,	dill
preferably extra-virgin	salt and cayenne pepper to
1 medium garlic clove, very	taste
finely chopped	1.25 ml (¼ tsp) paprika

lettuce leaves and lemon
wedges, for serving

Combine lemon juice, oil, water and a pinch of salt and pepper in a sauté pan or deep frying pan. Bring to a simmer. If fish is 1 cm (½ inch) thick or less, fold it in half. Add fish to simmering liquid and sprinkle with salt and pepper. Cover and cook over low heat for 10 minutes or until fish changes colour throughout. Cool slightly in the liquid, then transfer carefully to a plate to cool.

Combine sauce ingredients in a bowl and whisk until blended. Arrange lettuce leaves on a serving plate or plates and set fish on top. Whisk sauce again and spoon a little over fish. Garnish with lemon wedges. Serve any remaining sauce separately.

SEPHARDIC FISH STEAKS WITH CUMIN AND GARLIC

Jews from Morocco and other North African countries often marinate fish in this savoury cumin-garlic-olive oil marinade, called *tchermela*, before cooking. The fish can be cooked directly in the marinade, as here, or can be drained and then baked, grilled, barbecued or fried.

MAKES 4 MAIN-COURSE SERVINGS

4 steaks of halibut or other
firm lean fish, about 2.5 cm
(1 inch) thick, about 700 g
(1½ lb)

MARINADE

15 ml (1 tbsp) chopped fresh
coriander
1 medium garlic clove, finely
chopped
5 ml (1 tsp) ground cumin

5 ml (1 tsp) paprika
pinch of cayenne pepper
30 ml (2 tbsp) olive oil
pinch of salt

SAUCE

5 ml (1 tsp) paprika
2.5 ml (½ tsp) ground
cumin
75 ml (5 tbsp) water
5 ml (1 tsp) tomato purée

15 ml (1 tbsp) fresh lemon
juice
30 ml (2 tbsp) vegetable oil
2 medium garlic cloves, finely
chopped
pinch of salt

Put fish steaks in a tray in one layer. Mix the marinade ingredients and rub them over both sides of fish steaks. Cover and marinate in refrigerator for 1–3 hours, turning steaks occasionally.

Mix paprika and cumin in a small dish. In a cup, stir water into tomato purée until smooth. Add lemon juice. Heat oil in a large deep frying pan and add garlic and spice mixture. Sauté for 30 seconds over medium heat, stirring, then remove from heat and add tomato purée mixture. Bring to a simmer, stirring.

Add fish steaks to sauce with their marinade and a pinch of salt. Reduce heat to low, cover and simmer, basting fish occasionally, for about 10 minutes or until flesh of fish can be flaked easily with a fork.

With a slotted spoon, transfer fish to a serving plate; keep it warm. Boil sauce, stirring constantly, until it measures about 60 ml (4 tbsp). Taste sauce for seasoning, spoon it over fish and serve immediately.

MOROCCAN SEA BASS WITH PEPPERS AND TOMATOES

Moroccan-Jewish cooks are talented in cooking fish, and this easy dish of exuberant flavours is one of their best known. The fish is arranged in layers with sliced tomatoes, peppers and chillies, and sprinkled with fine olive oil.

MAKES 3 OR 4 MAIN-COURSE OR
6 FIRST-COURSE SERVINGS

---

900 g (2 lb) fish steaks or fillets, such as sea bass, cod or halibut, 2.5 cm (1 inch) thick

2 jalapeño chillies, seeded and chopped

1 red or green pepper, cut into thin strips

3 large ripe tomatoes, about 550 g (1¼ lb), sliced 0.5 cm (¼ inch) thick

salt and freshly ground pepper

6 medium garlic cloves, chopped

scant 15 g (½ oz) fresh coriander or Italian parsley, chopped

75 ml (5 tbsp) olive oil, preferably extra-virgin

cayenne pepper (optional)

Rinse fish and pat dry. Put chillies and pepper in a sauté pan. Cut any large tomato slices in half, then top peppers with tomatoes in one layer. Sprinkle with salt, pepper, 15 ml (1 tbsp) garlic and 30 ml (2 tbsp) coriander. Top with fish in one layer. Sprinkle fish with salt and pepper. Pour oil evenly over fish, then sprinkle with remaining garlic and 30 ml (2 tbsp) coriander.

Cover and cook over low heat for 30 minutes or until fish can be easily flaked with a fork. Remove fish and vegetables with a slotted spatula. Boil liquid to reduce it until slightly thickened. Taste liquid and adjust seasoning. Add cayenne pepper if desired. To serve, spoon sauce over fish and sprinkle with remaining coriander. Serve hot or cold.

SPICY SAUTEED SOLE

Sautéed fish with a crisp coating is a delicious dish, but with the typical Yemenite-Jewish spice mixture of cumin and turmeric, it is irresistible. In fact, this Yemenite-Jewish spice mixture, known as *hawaij marak* (soup spice) and which sometimes also includes cardamom seeds, has become so much in demand in Israel that it is now sold at the markets.

MAKES 4 MAIN-COURSE SERVINGS

700 g (1½ lb) sole fillets	*2.5 ml (½ tsp) turmeric*
2.5 ml (½ tsp) salt	*25 g (1 oz) plain flour*
1.25 ml (¼ tsp) ground black	*75 ml (5 tbsp) vegetable or*
pepper	*olive oil*
7.5 ml (1½ tsp) ground cumin	

Run your fingers over the fillets to check for bones. Gently remove any bones using tweezers, pastry crimper or small sharp knife. Cut each fillet in 2 pieces crossways. Arrange them in one layer on plate.

Mix salt, pepper, cumin and turmeric. Sprinkle 6.75 ml (1¼ tsp) spice mixture as evenly as possible over top of fish. Rub spices thoroughly into fish. Turn fish over. Sprinkle remaining spice mixture over fish and rub thoroughly into it. Leave to stand for 10 minutes. Preheat oven to 150°C (300°F) mark 2.

Spread flour on a plate. Lightly coat fish with flour on both sides. Tap and shake to remove excess flour. Transfer fish to a large plate and arrange side by side.

Heat oil in heavy large frying pan over medium-high heat. Add enough fillet pieces to make one layer. Sauté until coating is golden brown and flesh is opaque, about 1 minute on each side; turn fish carefully using 2 fish slices. If oil in frying pan begins to brown, reduce heat to medium. Transfer fish pieces to ovenproof platter, arrange side by side and keep them warm in oven while you sauté remaining pieces. Serve immediately.

SOLE WITH MUSHROOMS IN PAPRIKA CREAM

This rich Hungarian-style dish is a festive main course for a *milchig* dinner – that is, one featuring dairy products. Spaetzle (page 278), fresh noodles or steamed potatoes are the perfect accompaniment.

MAKES 4 MAIN-COURSE SERVINGS

100 g (4 oz) small mushrooms
25 g (1 oz) butter
salt and freshly ground pepper
700 g (1½ lb) sole fillets
about 25 g (1 oz) plain flour
30 ml (2 tbsp) vegetable oil
30 ml (2 tbsp) chopped spring onions (mostly white part)

120 ml (4 fl oz) double cream
5 ml (1 tsp) paprika
120 ml (4 fl oz) soured cream, at room temperature
pinch of hot paprika or cayenne pepper (optional)
30 ml (2 tbsp) chopped fresh parsley (optional)

Quarter the mushrooms. Melt 15 g (½ oz) butter in a medium frying pan, add mushrooms, salt and pepper and sauté over medium-high heat for about 5 minutes or until tender and lightly browned. Set aside.

Check fillets and remove any bones. Sprinkle fillets with salt and pepper on both sides. Dredge them lightly with flour and tap them to remove excess.

Heat oil and remaining 15 g (½ oz) butter in a large frying pan over medium–high heat. Add fillets and sauté for about 2 minutes per side, or until they can be pierced easily with a skewer. Transfer them to a serving plate and keep warm.

Add spring onions to frying pan and sauté for 2 minutes. Stir in cream, paprika and a little salt and pepper. Simmer over medium heat, stirring, until sauce is thick enough to coat a spoon. Add mushrooms and soured cream, and heat gently without boiling. Add hot paprika or cayenne. Taste and adjust seasoning, then remove from heat. Pour sauce and mushrooms over fillets, sprinkle with parsley and serve immediately.

POULTRY AND MEAT

 Roast chicken, quickly sautéed turkey schnitzel and aromatic meat patties are frequently prepared by Jewish cooks. Yet it is for gently simmered stews and braised dishes that Jewish cuisine is best known.

There are several reasons for this. First, the rules for *Shabbat*, for which the most festive dinner of the week is prepared, prohibit cooking during the day on Saturday. Everything must be cooked before sundown on Friday and kept hot for the main meal on Saturday, which is served around noon.

The types of dishes most suited to this cooking schedule are braised or stewed dishes. Jewish communities all over the world have developed delicious stews; some have surprising similarities, even though they originate in places far away from each other. The most celebrated example is the flavourful meat and bean stew called *hamin*, which is prepared in different versions by Ashkenazic and Sephardic Jews from many localities. The dried beans used differ from place to place, and so do the meats and seasonings, but the method is the same – the ingredients are combined in a covered casserole, which is then left over the lowest heat or baked slowly all night.

Stews are especially popular among Jews of Mediterranean and Middle Eastern origin. 'The secret to good cooking,' a Sephardic chef once told me, 'is very slowly simmering the ingredients together for a long time, so the seasonings penetrate the meat as much as possible. If you treat the ingredients gently, you will get the most out of them, but if you heat them violently over a high flame, you will ruin them'. The technique of long cooking over low heat promotes an exchange of flavours among the meat, the sauce and the vegetables. The result is a wonderful aroma and a rich harmony of tastes, which intensify if the dish is reheated the next day, because the ingredients have been in contact for a longer time. In addition, stewing is especially suitable to many of the kosher cuts of meat, which come from the front of the animal and many of which require long, gentle simmering to tenderize them.

Many Sephardic stews contain a relatively large quantity of vegetables for a small amount of meat. This practice, which began for reasons of economy, also makes sense from the point of view of nutrition and produces dishes that are colourful and not heavy. Aromatic vegetables, such as onions and carrots, are often put in the pan from the beginning, while tender vegetables may be added later. In addition to the Mediterranean favourites of tomatoes, onions and peppers, numerous green vegetables enliven the stews. A perfect example is Msouki (page 63), the Tunisian Passover stew, which includes spinach, artichokes, courgettes, leeks, carrots and many other vegetables.

Flavourings of stews and other meat dishes vary tremendously, according to the cook's country of origin. A variety of herbs such as mint, dill, flat-leaf parsley and fresh coriander, and spices such as saffron, cumin, turmeric and cinnamon, give Sephardic stews their liveliness. Because they are enhanced by so many flavours, most of these stews do not usually require stock.

For Rosh Hashanah and other occasions, many Jews prepare dishes with a sweet touch, combining meat and fruit. There are the meat and dried fruit tzimmes of Ashkenazic Jews, and the Moroccan sweet tajines.

Many of the traditional Jewish stews thicken naturally by reduction during the long, slow cooking and are not usually thickened with flour. These stews vary in consistency and in many cases there is no need for the sauce to be so thick that it clings to the meat. Often there is a generous amount of sauce. Some are designed to moisten the rice, potatoes, noodles or couscous served as an accompaniment.

These savoury stews have withstood the test of time and have remained the basis of home cooking of many Jewish cooks. Because they can be more or less left alone, can be prepared ahead and require little or no last-minute work, they are often the most convenient choice for both everyday meals and for entertaining.

ROAST CHICKEN WITH NOODLE-MUSHROOM-WALNUT STUFFING

Instead of serving chicken with a noodle kugel, you can roast the bird with a stuffing that includes kugel ingredients but does not contain egg. For the tasty stuffing used here, the mushrooms are made into a French preparation known as *duxelles* – they are finely chopped and then sautéed to intensify their flavour.

MAKES 4 SERVINGS

---

65 g (2½ oz) walnut halves

DUXELLES AND PASTA STUFFING

50 g (2 oz) non-dairy margarine, at room temperature

2 small shallots, finely chopped

100 g (4 oz) button mushrooms, finely chopped

salt and freshly ground pepper to taste

100 g (4 oz) fresh or 75 g (3 oz) dried egg noodles or fettuccine

30 ml (2 tbsp) finely chopped fresh parsley

1.8-kg (4-lb) chicken

75 g (3 oz) non-dairy margarine, softened

salt and freshly ground pepper to taste

100 g (4 oz) mushrooms, halved and sliced

225 g (8 oz) fresh or 175 g (6 oz) dried egg noodles or fettuccine

30 ml (2 tbsp) finely chopped fresh parsley

Preheat oven to 200°C (400°F) mark 6. Toast walnuts in a baking dish in oven, shaking it occasionally, for about 7 minutes or until lightly browned. Transfer to a bowl and cool. Break 90 ml (6 tbsp) toasted walnut halves in pieces and reserve for stuffing.

Melt 25 g (1 oz) margarine for stuffing in a medium frying pan over low heat. Add shallots and cook for 2 minutes or until soft but not browned. Add chopped mushrooms, salt and pepper and cook over high heat, stirring often, for about 5 minutes or until mixture is thick and dry.

Cook noodles uncovered in a medium saucepan of boiling salted water over high heat for about 1–2 minutes for fresh or 2–5 minutes for dried, or until tender but firm to the bite. Drain, rinse with cold water and drain again. Transfer to a large bowl. Add chopped mushroom mixture, remaining 25 g (1 oz) margarine, reserved walnut pieces and parsley, and toss mixture. Taste and adjust seasoning. Leave stuffing to cool completely.

Preheat oven to 200°C (400°F) mark 6. Discard excess fat from chicken. Rub chicken with 15 ml (1 tbsp) soft margarine and sprinkle it lightly with salt and pepper. Spoon stuffing into chicken, packing it in gently. Set chicken in a roasting tin or shallow baking dish just large enough to contain it. Roast chicken, basting it occasionally, for about 1 hour 10 minutes or until thickest part of drumstick is tender when pierced with a skewer and juices that run from chicken are clear; if juices are pink, roast chicken for a few more minutes and check again.

Melt 25 g (1 oz) margarine in a large frying pan over medium-high heat. Add sliced mushrooms, salt and pepper and sauté for about 3 minutes or until lightly browned.

Cook noodles in boiling salted water as before. Drain them well and transfer to pan of mushrooms. Add remaining 40 g (1½ oz) margarine, 45 ml (3 tbsp) toasted walnut halves and parsley and toss mixture. Season to taste with salt and pepper.

To serve, set chicken on a heated serving plate and spoon noodle and sliced mushroom mixture around it. Sprinkle pasta with remaining toasted walnut halves. Carve chicken at the table and serve with stuffing.

SPICY ROAST CHICKEN WITH MATZO-ONION STUFFING

'East meets West' or combination cuisine, is a theme that is very much in vogue in America today, but this dish, like many others, was created in this fashion in Israel years ago as a natural result of neighbours' exchanging recipes. It has a typical Ashkenazic onion-flavoured matzo stuffing served inside an aromatic, Middle Eastern spiced chicken. Serve the chicken with colourful vegetables, such as asparagus, broccoli or carrots, and with Garlic-Scented Roast Potatoes (page 266). The chicken is also delicious without stuffing.

MAKES 4 SERVINGS

MATZO AND ONION STUFFING

2 matzos	salt and pepper
120 ml (4 fl oz) hot chicken soup or broth	2.5 ml (½ tsp) ground cumin
30 ml (2 tbsp) vegetable oil	1.25 ml (¼ tsp) turmeric
1 large onion, chopped	1 large egg, size 1 or 2, beaten

1.6-kg (3½-lb) chicken	5 ml (1 tsp) ground cumin
1.25 ml (¼ tsp) salt	1.25 ml (¼ tsp) turmeric
1.25 ml (¼ tsp) pepper	15 ml (1 tbsp) vegetable oil

Crumble matzos into a bowl and pour chicken soup over them. Heat oil in a frying pan and add onion, salt, pepper, cumin and turmeric. Sauté over medium heat, stirring often, until tender and golden brown. Add onion to matzo mixture and leave to cool. Stir in egg and taste for seasoning.

Preheat oven to 200°C (400°F) mark 6. Discard excess fat from chicken. Mix salt, pepper, cumin, turmeric and oil. Rub chicken all over with mixture.

Spoon stuffing into chicken. Set in a roasting tin and roast for about 1¼ hours, basting occasionally if desired. Chicken is done when juices that run from thickest part of leg are clear when meat is pierced, and a skewer inserted into stuffing comes out hot. Spoon stuffing into a serving dish. Transfer chicken to a carving board or serving plate. Serve hot, with stuffing.

STUFFED CHICKEN WITH COUSCOUS, RAISINS AND PECANS

Moroccan Jews make a delicious couscous stuffing for chicken. I love the taste of fresh ginger and toasted pecans in the saffron-scented stuffing in this recipe, but if you wish to prepare a more authentic Moroccan version, use 5 ml (1 tsp) dried ginger instead of fresh and substitute almonds for the pecans.

MAKES 4 SERVINGS

COUSCOUS STUFFING

2 pinches of saffron threads, about 1.25 ml (¼ tsp)
300 ml (½ pint) boiling water
10 ml (2 tsp) olive oil
50 g (2 oz) pecan halves, broken in pieces
salt
50 g (2 oz) unsalted non-dairy margarine

35 ml (2 tbsp plus 1 tsp) peeled and finely chopped fresh ginger
215 g (7½ oz) couscous
freshly ground pepper
40 g (1½ oz) raisins
30 ml (2 tbsp) finely chopped fresh parsley leaves

1.8-kg (4-lb) chicken
1.25 ml (¼ tsp) salt
1.25 ml (¼ tsp) pepper

2.5 ml (½ tsp) ground ginger
2.5 ml (½ tsp) paprika
15 ml (1 tbsp) olive oil

Crush saffron between your fingers. In a small saucepan add saffron to boiling water; cover and leave to stand for 20 minutes.

In a small heavy frying pan, heat oil, add pecan pieces with a pinch of salt and sauté over medium heat, stirring, for 2 minutes, or until lightly browned. Transfer nuts to a plate and leave to cool.

In a large frying pan melt 25 g (1 oz) margarine, add ginger and sauté over medium heat, stirring, for 1 minute. Add couscous with salt and pepper and stir mixture with a fork until blended. Scatter raisins on top. Remove frying pan from heat and and shake it to spread couscous in an even layer. Bring saffron-flavoured water to the boil, pour it evenly over couscous, immediately cover frying pan tightly and leave mixture to stand for 3 minutes. Fluff couscous with a fork. Cut remaining margarine in small pieces and add them. Add pecans and parsley and toss mixture to combine it. Season and cool.

Preheat oven to 200°C (400°F) mark 6. Discard excess fat from chicken. In a small bowl mix salt, pepper, ginger, paprika and oil. Rub chicken all over with mixture. Spoon about 175 g (6 oz) stuffing into chicken, packing it in gently. Keep remaining couscous mixture at room temperature. Set chicken in a roasting tin or shallow baking dish just large enough to contain it. Roast chicken, basting it occasionally, for 1¼ hours, or until thickest part of drumstick is tender when pierced with a skewer and juices that run from chicken are clear. If juices are pink, roast chicken for a little longer.

To serve, spoon stuffing from chicken onto a serving plate. Carve chicken and arrange pieces over stuffing. Add 30 ml (2 tbsp) pan juices to remaining couscous mixture and reheat it gently, stirring with a fork, for 2 minutes. Fluff couscous mixture with a fork. Serve couscous in a separate dish.

ISRAELI
BARBECUED CHICKEN

Barbecued meats and poultry are as popular in Israel as in America, and are often the star of Israeli Independence Day barbecue menus.

MAKES 6 TO 8 SERVINGS

2–2.3 kg (4½–5 lb) chicken pieces	30 ml (2 tbsp) cumin, preferably freshly ground
30 ml (2 tbsp) olive oil	10 ml (2 tsp) turmeric
pinch of salt (optional)	about 1.25 ml (¼ tsp) freshly ground black pepper
,	

Rub chicken with oil and sprinkle lightly with salt. Mix cumin, turmeric and pepper and sprinkle on both sides of chicken. Leave to stand while coals are heating.

Set chicken on rack about 10–15 cm (4–6 inches) above glowing coals. Barbecue breast pieces for about 10 minutes per side, and leg and thigh pieces for 15–18 minutes per side or until thickest part of meat near bone is no longer pink when cut. Serve immediately.

NOTE: If you are using koshered chicken (that has been salted), salt is not needed for this recipe.

EASY LEMON CHICKEN

From a Moroccan-Jewish friend in Paris I learned this simple version of a traditional North African recipe. The slowly cooked onions give the sauce a wonderfully rich flavour, while the slight tartness of the lemon slices impart a refreshing quality. In its homeland the recipe is made with preserved lemons, and if you find some in a Middle Eastern shop, you can chop a few slices and add them to the dish after browning the chicken, rather than using fresh lemons. Some people add black or green olives to the dish during the last five minutes of cooking.

MAKES 4 SERVINGS

1.4-kg (3-lb) chicken, cut into pieces, or 1.1–1.4 kg (2½–3 lb) chicken pieces
30 ml (2 tbsp) vegetable oil
salt and freshly ground pepper
2 large onions, halved and thinly sliced
1 large garlic clove, chopped

175 ml (6 fl oz) homemade chicken stock or soup (page 345)
1 lemon, unpeeled, rinsed and thinly sliced
15 ml (1 tbsp) chopped fresh parsley or coriander

Pat chicken dry. Heat oil in large deep frying pan or sauté pan over medium-high heat. Sprinkle chicken pieces with salt and pepper and brown them in 2 batches in oil, about 3 minutes per side. Remove with tongs to a plate. Add onions and cook over medium-low heat until softened and golden, 10–15 minutes. Return chicken to pan and add any juices from plate. Sprinkle garlic over chicken and pour stock into pan. Cover and simmer for 30 minutes. Remove breast pieces. Cover and simmer remaining pieces for 5 minutes.

Remove any pips from lemon slices with point of sharp knife. Discard end slices of lemon. Put lemon slices in a saucepan and cover with cold water. Bring to a simmer, cover and cook over medium-low heat for 5 minutes. Drain slices; don't worry that some will not remain whole.

Remove chicken pieces from pan but leave in onion. Boil juices for 3–5 minutes to thicken. Return chicken to pan. Top with lemon slices, cover and warm over low heat for 5 minutes. (Chicken can be kept, covered, for 1 day in refrigerator. Reheat in covered pan over low heat.) Taste sauce and adjust seasoning. Sprinkle with parsley.

EXOTIC ROAST CHICKEN

This unusual recipe for chicken with a stuffing studded with almonds and pine nuts and flavoured with fresh coriander and cinnamon is inspired by a recipe called Jewish partridge, from a thirteenth-century book on the cooking of Spain and the Maghreb area of North Africa. Culinary historian Charles Perry gave me the Jewish recipes from the book, known simply as 'Anonymous Manuscript', which was written in Arabic and published in translation in Madrid. The translated version is *Traduccion Espanola de un Manuscrito Anonimo del Siglo XIII sobre la Cocina Hispano-Magaribi.*

MAKES 4 SERVINGS

ALMOND – PINE NUT STUFFING

40 g (1½ oz) almonds
25 g (1 oz) pine nuts
about 100–150 g (4–5 oz) day-old or stale white bread, preferably challah or French or Italian bread
60 ml (4 tbsp) vegetable oil
1 medium onion, finely chopped
salt and freshly ground pepper

225 g (8 oz) chicken or turkey meat, minced
1.25 ml (¼ tsp) ground cinnamon
15 g (½ oz) fresh coriander, chopped
15 g (½ oz) fresh parsley, chopped
60–120 ml (2–4 fl oz) chicken soup or stock
15–25 g (½–1 oz) non-dairy margarine

1.6–1.8-kg (3½–4-lb) chicken
1.25 ml (¼ tsp) salt
1.25 ml (¼ tsp) pepper
10 ml (2 tsp) vegetable oil
60–120 ml (2–4 fl oz) chicken soup or stock, for basting

about 40 g (1½ oz) mixed toasted nuts (pistachios, almonds and pine nuts), for garnish
coriander or parsley sprigs, for garnish

Preheat oven to 180°C (350°F) mark 4. Toast almonds and pine nuts in small baking dish in oven until lightly browned, about 4 minutes. Cool nuts and coarsely chop.

If using challah, remove crust. Slice bread. Grind it, a few slices at a time, in food processor to make crumbs. Transfer to a large bowl.

Heat 45 ml (3 tbsp) oil in medium frying pan over medium heat. Add onion, salt and pepper. Sauté until onion is soft and light brown, about 10 minutes. Remove onion with slotted spoon and add remaining oil to frying pan. Heat briefly, then add minced chicken, cinnamon and a small pinch of salt and pepper. Cook over medium-high heat, breaking up meat with wooden spoon, for about 5 minutes. Return onion to frying pan and mix well with chicken.

Add onion-chicken mixture and toasted nuts to breadcrumbs and toss lightly until blended. Add coriander and parsley and toss. Gradually add 60 ml (4 tbsp) soup, tossing lightly. Mixture may appear dry, but juices in bird will moisten it. Taste and adjust seasoning. (Stuffing can be refrigerated for up to 1 day in covered container. Do not stuff bird in advance.)

Preheat oven to 190°C (375°F) mark 5. Discard excess fat from chicken. Mix salt, pepper and oil. Rub chicken all over with seasoning mixture. Spoon stuffing lightly into chicken; do not pack it tightly. Fold skin over stuffing; truss or skewer closed, if desired. Set chicken in a roasting tin.

Add a little more soup, if necessary, to extra stuffing so that most of bread is very lightly moistened. Grease a 750 ml–1 litre (1¼–1¾ pint) casserole and spoon stuffing into it. Dot with margarine. Cover and refrigerate.

Roast chicken for 45 minutes, then put dish of extra stuffing in oven, cover it and roast both together for about 45 minutes, basting chicken occasionally with pan juices if desired, and basting stuffing occasionally with a few spoonfuls stock. To check whether chicken is done, insert a skewer into thickest part of drumstick; it should be tender and juices that run from chicken should be clear. If juices are pink, roast chicken a few more minutes and check it again. Insert a skewer into stuffing inside chicken; it should come out hot.

Carve the chicken. Spoon stuffing onto serving plate with chicken pieces and garnish with toasted nuts and with coriander or parsley sprigs.

SAUTEED CHICKEN LIVERS WITH RED PEPPERS

Chicken livers with onions are enjoyed by Jews of most origins. According to the Ashkenazic custom, livers must be grilled until done in order to be kosher. Thus after grilling here, the livers should be only briefly sautéed for this dish, just until heated through.

Like the French, the Jews prize *foie gras*, or the rich livers of fattened geese or ducks. Israel is now a major exporter of *foie gras* to France. Israeli chefs have developed a unique *foie gras* speciality barbecued on skewers, which is very rich, tender and melts in your mouth. I'm not going to give a recipe for this expensive luxury. Instead try it at restaurants that specialize in this delicacy.

MAKES 4 MAIN-COURSE OR 6 FIRST-COURSE SERVINGS

450 g (1 lb) chicken livers	freshly ground black pepper
salt	pinch of cayenne pepper
75 ml (5 tbsp) vegetable oil	2.5 ml (½ tsp) ground cumin
1 large onion, halved and cut into thin slices	15 ml (1 tbsp) chopped fresh parsley (optional)
1 large red pepper, cut into about 5 × 1-cm (2 × ½-inch) strips	hot cooked rice, for serving (optional)

Preheat grill with rack about 7.5 cm (3 inches) from flame. Rinse livers and pat dry on paper towels; cut off any green spots. Put livers on foil under grill and sprinkle with salt. Grill for 3 minutes or until top is light brown. Turn livers over, sprinkle second side with salt and grill for 3–4 more minutes or until cooked. Discard juices from foil. Cut livers in half.

Heat 45 ml (3 tbsp) oil in a large heavy frying pan over medium heat. Add onion, pepper, salt and pepper and cook, stirring occasionally, for about 15 minutes or until vegetables are very tender and onion is lightly browned. Leave in frying pan for reheating.

In another frying pan heat remaining 30 ml (2 tbsp) oil over medium-high heat. Add livers and sprinkle with black pepper, cayenne and cumin. Toss over heat for 1 minute until hot.

Reheat onion mixture. Taste and adjust seasoning. Add livers and heat briefly together. Sprinkle with parsley and serve on heated plates; for a main course, serve on a bed of cooked rice.

CHICKEN WITH PEPPERS AND RICE

Jewish cooks in both Latin America and the Middle East prepare this colourful 'all-in-one-pan' main course, a distant cousin of paella.

MAKES 4 SERVINGS

1.6-kg (3½-lb) chicken, cut into 8 serving pieces
salt and freshly ground pepper
7.5 ml (1½ tsp) ground cumin
15 ml (1 tbsp) vegetable oil
1 medium onion, thinly sliced
1 medium green pepper, cut into thin strips
1 medium red pepper, cut into thin strips

1 large garlic clove, finely chopped
200 g (7 oz) long-grain white rice
2 ripe medium tomatoes, peeled, seeded and chopped
350 ml (12 fl oz) hot chicken soup, stock or water

Sprinkle chicken pieces with salt, pepper and 2.5 ml (½ tsp) cumin. Rub seasonings into chicken. Turn pieces over and sprinkle again with salt, pepper and 2.5 ml (½ tsp) cumin. Rub again into chicken.

Heat oil in a very large, frying pan, at least 30 cm (12 inches) in diameter. Add chicken leg and thigh pieces and brown them on all sides over medium–low heat for about 15 minutes. Remove them and brown remaining chicken pieces for 5 minutes; remove.

Add onion to frying pan and cook over low heat until soft but not browned. Stir in peppers and garlic and cook, stirring often, for about 5 minutes. Add rice and remaining cumin to frying pan and sauté over low heat, stirring, for 2 minutes. Stir in tomatoes. Set chicken pieces on top, putting in leg and thigh pieces first.

Pour hot stock over all and add another pinch of salt and pepper. Reduce heat to very low and cook, covered tightly, for 45–50 minutes or until chicken and rice are tender and liquid is absorbed. If all of liquid is absorbed but rice is not yet tender, add a few more spoonfuls stock or water and simmer a few more minutes.

NOTE: All drumsticks or all breast pieces with bone cut out can be substituted for the cut chicken. For a lovely orange hue rub chicken with 2.5 ml (½ tsp) turmeric along with other seasonings.

241

CRISP TURKEY SCHNITZEL

One of the most frequently prepared dishes in Israel, whether for fancy weddings or for a quick lunch for the children, is schnitzel.

Unlike the Austrian wiener schnitzel made with veal, in Israel schnitzel is made with turkey or chicken breast and the meat is spiced before being coated. This is my favourite way to prepare them because the lean meat remains juicy and the coating is crisp.

MAKES 4 SERVINGS

---

550 g (1¼ lb) turkey breast slices, about 8 slices, about 0.5 cm (¼ inch) thick
7.5 ml (1½ tsp) ground cumin
2.5 ml (½ tsp) paprika
2.5 ml (½ tsp) turmeric
2.5 ml (½ tsp) salt
1.25 ml (¼ tsp) ground pepper

pinch of cayenne pepper
75 g (3 oz) unseasoned dry breadcrumbs
2 large eggs, size 1 or 2
75 ml (5 tbsp) vegetable oil
lemon wedges, for serving

If any of the turkey slices is thicker than 0.5 cm (¼ inch), pound it between 2 pieces of cling film to an even thickness of 0.5 cm (¼ inch) using a flat meat pounder or rolling pin.

Arrange turkey in one layer on plate. Mix cumin, paprika, turmeric, salt, black pepper and cayenne in a small bowl. Sprinkle spice mixture as evenly as possible over one side of turkey pieces and rub second side with remaining spice mixture.

Preheat oven to 140°C (275°F) mark 1. Spread flour in plate. Spread breadcrumbs in second plate. Beat eggs in shallow bowl. Lightly coat a turkey slice with flour on both sides. Tap and shake to remove excess flour. Dip slice in egg. Lastly dip both sides in bread-crumbs so turkey is completely coated; pat and press lightly so crumbs adhere. Repeat with remaining slices. Set pieces side by side on large plate. Handle turkey lightly at all stages to preserve coating.

Heat oil in heavy large frying pan over medium-high heat. Add enough turkey to make one layer and sauté until golden brown on both sides, about 1 minute per side. Turn carefully using 2 wide spatulas. If oil begins to brown, reduce heat to medium. Set turkey slices side by side on an ovenproof plate and keep them warm in oven while sautéing remaining slices. Garnish with lemon wedges.

ROAST GOOSE

Goose is an important bird in Alsace, and Jews there pair it with fruit, as in this recipe, or with sauerkraut. A roast goose makes a festive main course for Hanukkah.

MAKES 6 TO 8 SERVINGS

1 young goose, about 3.6–4 kg (8–9 lb), thawed if frozen
salt and freshly ground pepper
5 large sharp apples
1 medium onion, quartered
40 g (1½ oz) non-dairy margarine

60 ml (4 tbsp) dry white wine
350 ml (12 fl oz) chicken soup or stock, preferably homemade (page 345)
15 ml (1 tbsp) potato flour
45 ml (3 tbsp) apple juice or water

Preheat oven to 230°C (450°F) mark 8. Remove excess fat from goose. Cut off fatty flap of skin near tail. Prick goose skin a few times with a fork or skewer; do not pierce meat. Season goose inside and outside with salt and pepper. Peel 1 apple and put it and quartered onion inside goose. Put goose on its back on a rack in a roasting tin.

Roast goose for 30 minutes or until it begins to brown. Baste occasionally. Remove fat from pan as it accumulates.

Reduce oven temperature to 180°C (350°F) mark 4. Turn goose over onto its breast and roast for 1½ hours. If tin becomes dry, add a little water. Cover goose with foil and continue roasting, removing fat from tin occasionally and basting goose once or twice, for about 1–1½ more hours. To check whether it is done, pierce thickest part of drumstick; juices should be pale yellow.

Meanwhile, peel remaining apples. Core and cut them into eighths. Melt margarine in a large frying pan over medium heat. Add apples in batches and sauté for about 5 minutes on each side.

When goose is cooked, discard fat from tin. Add wine and 120 ml (4 fl oz) soup to tin. Bring to the boil, stirring and scraping. (If roasting tin is large, place it over 2 burners.) Strain mixture into a medium saucepan. Add remaining soup and bring to the boil. Season it lightly with salt and pepper, then reduce heat to low. Whisk potato flour with apple juice until smooth, then gradually whisk juice mixture into simmering stock mixture. Season.

Discard onion and apple from inside goose. Carve goose. Reheat sautéed apples and serve with goose. Serve sauce separately.

MEDITERRANEAN BEEF STEW WITH CHILLIES AND GREEN BEANS

With its selection of jalapeño and Anaheim chillies, this might sound like a Mexican recipe; but hot and mild chillies are often used by Jews from Morocco and other southern Mediterranean countries to flavour beef stews. Anaheim chillies are long, mild green chillies; if they are not available, substitute a green pepper.

MAKES 4 SERVINGS

30 ml (2 tbsp) vegetable oil	salt and freshly ground pepper
1 medium onion, halved and thinly sliced	2 ripe plum tomatoes, diced (optional)
900 g (2 lb) chuck or blade steak, fat removed, cut into 2.5-cm (1-inch) cubes	30 ml (2 tbsp) tomato purée
	250 ml (8 fl oz) water, plus additional as needed
2 green or red Anaheim chillies, cut into 1-cm (½-inch) dice	450 g (1 lb) small or medium potatoes
2 jalapeño chillies, chopped	450 g (1 lb) green beans
7.5 ml (1½ tsp) ground cumin	cayenne pepper (optional)
4 medium garlic cloves, chopped	30 ml (2 tbsp) chopped fresh parsley or coriander (optional)

Heat oil in a large casserole, add onion and sauté for about 7 minutes over medium-low heat. Add beef, chillies and cumin, and sauté for about 7 minutes, stirring often. Add garlic, salt, pepper, tomatoes, tomato purée and water. Stir and bring to the boil. Cover and cook over low heat for 1½ hours.

Peel potatoes and cut into chunks about 2.5 cm (1 inch) thick. Add to stew. If stew appears dry, add about 60 ml (4 tbsp) water. Cover and cook for 40 minutes or until potatoes are tender.

Meanwhile, remove ends from beans and break them in half. Cook beans in boiling salted water for about 7 minutes or until tender. Rinse with cold water.

When potatoes are tender, add beans to stew and heat gently for 2–3 minutes. Add cayenne if desired. (Stew can be kept for 2 days in refrigerator. Reheat in covered pan.) Sprinkle with parsley.

JEWISH GOULASH

Although goulash is actually a soup in Hungarian cooking, Jewish cooks prepare goulash as a paprika-flavoured beef stew. This became the most common way of making goulash in the United States and Israel. Like many simple recipes, it can be one of the very best. Goulash can be surprisingly spicy, since both sweet and hot paprika are used. If light-green Hungarian peppers, which resemble peppers but are slightly longer, are available, you can substitute them for the peppers in this recipe. Serve the goulash with boiled potatoes, Spaetzle (page 278), noodles or with plain or toasted egg barley.

MAKES 6 SERVINGS

45 ml (3 tbsp) vegetable oil	5 medium garlic cloves,
2 large onions, halved and	chopped
thinly sliced	1.25 ml (¼ tsp) caraway seeds
1.4 kg (3 lb) chuck steak,	freshly ground black pepper
excess fat removed, cut into	2 medium green peppers, diced
2.5-cm (1-inch) cubes	2 ripe medium tomatoes,
20 ml (4 tsp) paprika,	350–450 g (¾–1 lb),
preferably good quality	peeled and diced
Hungarian sweet paprika	hot paprika or cayenne pepper
salt	to taste
120 ml (4 fl oz) water	

Heat oil in a wide saucepan or casserole. Add onions and cook over medium-low heat for about 12 minutes or until softened and lightly browned. Remove with slotted spoon. Add meat in batches and sauté over medium heat for about 10 minutes or until meat is lightly browned; remove each batch after browning it.

Return onions and meat to pan. Add paprika, sprinkle lightly with salt and sauté, stirring, for 5 minutes. Add water, garlic, caraway seeds and black pepper. Cover and simmer over low heat, stirring occasionally, for 1 hour, adding water in small amounts, about 60 ml (4 tbsp) at a time, if pan becomes dry. Add green pepper and tomatoes and simmer for 1 hour or until meat is tender when pierced with knife. Add hot paprika or cayenne. Taste and adjust seasoning. Serve hot.

AROMATIC MEAT PATTIES

If you like hamburgers, wait till you try these flavourful patties! Seasoned with thyme, oregano, coriander and garlic, as well as a hint of cinnamon, they make a good and easy main course. Jews from Tunisia serve them as one of several accompaniments for a couscous feast. The meat mixture is also used as a filling for vegetables.

MAKES 15 OR 16 PATTIES; 6 TO 8 SERVINGS

2 medium onions, finely chopped
6.25 ml (1¼ tsp) salt
4 slices stale white bread
450 g (1 lb) lean minced beef
30 ml (2 tbsp) chopped celery leaves
30 ml (2 tbsp) chopped fresh parsley
45 ml (3 tbsp) chopped fresh coriander
5 ml (1 tsp) dried leaf thyme, crumbled

5 ml (1 tsp) dried leaf oregano, crumbled
2.5 ml (½ tsp) ground cinnamon
2.5 ml (½ tsp) cayenne pepper
5 ml (1 tsp) paprika
pinch of freshly ground pepper
3 medium garlic cloves, chopped
2 large eggs, size 1 or 2
about 60 ml (4 tbsp) vegetable oil, for frying

Put onions in a strainer and sprinkle with 2.5 ml (½ tsp) salt. Leave to stand for about 5 minutes, then rinse onions in strainer. Dip each bread slice in a bowl of water to moisten. Add soaked bread to onions and squeeze both dry.

Mix beef with onions, bread, celery leaves, herbs, spices, garlic and 3.75 ml (¾ tsp) salt. Add eggs. Mix very well with your hands to be sure mixture is evenly combined. Shape mixture in patties, using about 75 g (3 oz) mixture for each. Compact the patties between your hands and flatten them.

Heat vegetable oil in a large heavy frying pan over medium-low heat. Add enough patties to make 1 layer and sauté for about 5 minutes per side or until cooked through. Fry remaining patties in same way, adding oil to frying pan if necessary and heating it before adding more patties. Drain patties on paper towels before serving.

NOTE: The technique of salting the onions and rinsing off the salt gives them a more delicate flavour.

VEAL STEW WITH SAFFRON AND CAULIFLOWER

This light, aromatic veal dish is made in the style of Moroccan Jews. Serve it with its traditional accompaniment of couscous or with rice. A salad of grilled tomatoes and peppers makes a good starter, in keeping with the Mediterranean character of the main course.

MAKES 4 SERVINGS

large pinch of saffron threads
60 ml (4 tbsp) hot water
45 ml (3 tbsp) olive oil
2 medium onions, sliced
3 medium garlic cloves, chopped
900 g (2 lb) boneless veal shoulder or veal stewing meat, cut into 4-cm (1½-inch) pieces
2.5 ml (½ tsp) salt
1.25 ml (¼ tsp) ground pepper
3.75 ml (¾ tsp) ground ginger

600–750 ml (1–1¼ pints) water
1 large or 2 small cauliflowers, about 900 g (2 lb), divided into medium florets
10 ml (2 tsp) paprika
2.5 ml (½ tsp) ground cumin
15 ml (1 tbsp) chopped fresh coriander
15 ml (1 tbsp) chopped fresh parsley
steamed rice or couscous, for accompaniment

Add saffron to hot water and leave to soften for 20 minutes.

Heat oil in a large heavy casserole, add onions and garlic, and cook over low heat, stirring, for 2 minutes. Add veal, salt, pepper, ginger and saffron in its liquid and mix well. Pour in enough water to barely cover veal, about 600–750 ml (1–1¼ pints). Bring to the boil, cover and simmer over low heat, stirring occasionally, for 1 hour. (Veal can be kept, covered, for 1 day in refrigerator. Reheat it over low heat, covered.)

In a large saucepan of boiling salted water, cook cauliflower, uncovered, for 2 minutes. Drain immediately in a colander.

Stir paprika, cumin and coriander into stew. Add cauliflower and stir gently; be sure cauliflower stalks are immersed in liquid. Cover and simmer over low heat without stirring for 30 minutes, or until veal and cauliflower are tender but cauliflower is not falling apart. Transfer veal and cauliflower with a slotted spoon to a heated plate,

247

leaving most of the onions in casserole. Cover plate and keep veal and cauliflower warm.

Boil cooking liquid, including onions, stirring occasionally, until mixture is reduced to about 350 ml (12 fl oz). Taste for seasoning.

Remove onions from sauce with a slotted spoon and spoon them onto a serving plate. Set veal on top and cauliflower around it, with florets pointing outwards. Spoon sauce over veal and cauliflower. Sprinkle with parsley and serve with steamed rice or couscous.

VEAL WITH OLIVES, TOMATOES AND FRESH HERBS

Olive trees have been prized in Israel since biblical times, and their fruit and its oil are treasured today also. Both enter this flavourful stew, an ideal main course for Succot, when tomatoes are in their prime.

MAKES 4 SERVINGS

900 g (2 lb) boneless veal shoulder
30 ml (2 tbsp) olive oil
1 medium onion, finely chopped
4 large garlic cloves, finely chopped
salt and freshly ground pepper
900 ml (2 lb) ripe tomatoes, peeled, seeded and chopped; or 2 × 794-g (28-oz) cans plum tomatoes, drained and chopped

15 ml (1 tbsp) finely chopped fresh marjoram, or 5 ml (1 tsp) dried, crumbled
10 ml (2 tsp) fresh thyme leaves or 3.75 ml (¾ tsp) dried, crumbled
250 ml (8 fl oz) water
1 bay leaf
175 g (6 oz) brine-cured black olives, drained
30 ml (2 tbsp) finely chopped fresh parsley leaves

Cut veal into 2.5–3-cm (1–1¼-inch) pieces and pat dry. In a heavy casserole heat oil over medium-high heat. Add veal in batches and brown lightly on all sides. Transfer veal pieces as they brown to a plate. Add onion to casserole and cook over low heat, stirring often, for 5 minutes or until softened.

Return veal to casserole, reserving any juices on plate. Add garlic and pinch of salt and pepper and cook over low heat, stirring, for ½ minute. Stir in tomatoes, marjoram and thyme and bring to the boil. Add juices from plate, water and bay leaf and bring again to the boil, stirring. Cover and cook for about 1 hour, or until veal is just tender when pierced with a knife.

Remove veal from casserole with a slotted spoon. Boil cooking liquid, stirring, until it is reduced to 450 ml (¾ pint). Drain liquid from meat a few times and add to casserole as liquid reduces. Discard bay leaf.

Return meat to sauce, add olives and heat over low heat for 1–2 minutes. (Stew can be kept, covered, for 2 days in refrigerator. Reheat it over low heat, covered.) Remove casserole from heat and sprinkle with parsley. Taste and adjust seasoning. Serve stew from enamelled casserole or from a heated deep serving dish.

COUSCOUS WITH LAMB AND SEVEN VEGETABLES

This is the time-honoured way to prepare couscous, by steaming it several times in a special couscous cooker called a *couscoussier*, in which the stew simmers in the pan at the bottom and the couscous cooks in the steamer above it. If you don't have one, you can substitute a vegetable steamer that sits snugly in or above a deep pan.

Steaming is necessary to cook the raw couscous that comes in bulk and that can be purchased at some Middle Eastern shops. Most of the packaged couscous, however, is precooked. It can be steamed as in this recipe but to save time, it can be cooked according to the quick method in Stuffed Chicken with Couscous, Raisins and Pecans (page 235).

Raisins impart a hint of sweetness to this sumptuous main course, a Moroccan tradition for the Jewish New Year. In some families, a platter with a few of each of the seven 'vegetables' – chick peas, turnips, carrots, onions, courgettes, winter squash or pumpkin and raisins, all sprinkled with sugar and cinnamon, is set out to begin the Rosh Hashanah meal.

This dish is also prepared with beef. Sometimes chicken pieces are substituted for the meat; in this case the cooking time should be reduced by 30 minutes.

MAKES 5 OR 6 SERVINGS

150 g (5 oz) dried chick peas
  or 225–250 g (8–9 oz)
  canned
750 ml (1¼ pints) cold water
  (for dried chick peas)

salt
450 g (1 lb) couscous
120 ml (4 fl oz) water
5 ml (1 tsp) salt

MEAT BROTH
700–900 g (1½–2 lb) bone-
  less shoulder of lamb or
  chuck steak, fat removed
a few lamb or beef bones
2 medium onions, sliced
30 ml (2 tbsp) vegetable oil

1.25 ml (¼ tsp) saffron
  threads
salt and pepper
1.6 litres (2¾ pints) water
1 fresh chilli, chopped, or
  1 whole dried chilli

SEVEN 'VEGETABLES'
225 g (8 oz) winter squash or
  pumpkin, peeled and cut
  into 5-cm (2-inch) chunks
225 g (8 oz) carrots, halved
  lengthways and cut into
  5-cm (2-inch) pieces
2 medium tomatoes, quartered
1 small turnip, peeled
1 medium onion, quartered

2 celery stalks, cut into 5-cm
  (2-inch) lengths
225 g (8 oz) courgettes, cut
  into 5-cm (2-inch) pieces
2 medium garlic cloves, peeled
30 ml (2 tbsp) chopped fresh
  coriander
100 g (4 oz) raisins

60–120 ml (2–4 fl oz)
  vegetable oil or margarine
cinnamon, for garnish

hot pepper sauce, for
  accompaniment (optional)

To prepare dried chick peas, sort through them, discarding any pebbles or other foreign material; rinse well. Either soak overnight in water to cover generously, or use this quicker method: put them in a saucepan with 450 ml (¾ pint) water and bring to the boil, boil for 2 minutes, cover and leave for 1 hour.

Drain soaked chick peas and place in saucepan. Add 750 ml (1¼ pints) cold water and bring to the boil. Cover and simmer for about 1½ hours, adding hot water occasionally to keep them covered with water. Add a pinch of salt and continue simmering for 30–45 minutes more or until tender.

Rinse couscous in a bowl and drain in a fine strainer. Transfer to a shallow bowl and rub grains to be sure they are separate. Leave to dry while preparing meat.

Cut meat into 4-cm (1½-inch) cubes. Put meat and bones in pan of couscous cooker or pan of vegetable steamer and add onions, oil, saffron, salt and pepper. Cover and heat for 5 minutes over low heat, stirring. Add water and chilli and bring to the boil.

Put couscous in a steamer part of couscous cooker or in a muslin-lined vegetable steamer. Tie a damp towel around base of steamer part of couscous pot so steam won't escape from sides. Steam couscous uncovered above simmering stew for 30 minutes. (If using a vegetable steamer, cover couscous during steaming.)

Remove couscous, put it in a large bowl and leave to cool. Mix water and salt; then sprinkle couscous lightly with salted water, rubbing and tossing it between your fingers to prevent grains from sticking together.

After meat has simmered for 1½ hours, add winter squash, carrots, tomatoes, turnip, onion, celery, courgettes, cooked or canned chick peas, garlic and half the coriander. Bring to the boil, then simmer for 30 minutes or until meat and vegetables are tender. Simmer raisins separately in about 250 ml (8 fl oz) broth from the meat for 10 minutes or until tender. Cover and keep them warm.

About 30 minutes before serving (or after meat has simmered for 2 hours), put couscous in steamer and set it above simmering broth. Steam uncovered (but cover if using vegetable steamer) for about 30 minutes or until steam comes through couscous. Transfer to a large bowl.

Taste meat broth for seasoning. Discard dried chilli.

Sprinkle oil over couscous in bowl. Slowly add 60 ml (4 tbsp) meat broth. Mix lightly with a fork or with your fingers.

To serve, pile couscous in a cone shape on a large serving dish. Decorate by sprinkling cinnamon in a few lines going from top to bottom of cone of couscous, or by spooning raisins on top of and around couscous. Place meat and vegetables on a serving plate and sprinkle them with remaining coriander. Serve broth from a tureen. Serve in shallow bowls. Accompany with hot pepper sauce.

BAKED LAMB WITH ORZO

Orzo was once nicknamed for Israel's leader, 'Ben Gurion rice', during a recession in the country because this rice-shaped pasta was supplied instead of rice, which was scarce. But today orzo is a well-liked accompaniment for lamb, as in this Sephardic-style dish delicately perfumed with cinnamon, oregano and white wine.

MAKES 6 SERVINGS

about 1 kg (2–2½ lb) lamb chops, 2.5–3 cm (1–1¼ inches) thick, trimmed of skin and excess fat
45 ml (3 tbsp) olive oil
15 ml (1 tbsp) strained fresh lemon juice
salt and freshly ground pepper
1.25 ml (¼ tsp) dried red chilli flakes (optional)
250 ml (8 fl oz) dry white wine
1 small cinnamon stick

1 large onion, halved and thinly sliced
2 large garlic cloves, finely chopped
250 ml (8 fl oz) smooth Basic Tomato Sauce (page 345),or from jar
10 ml (2 tsp) dried leaf oregano, crumbled
450 ml (¾ pint) boiling water
450 g (1 lb) orzo (rice-shaped pasta)
15 ml (1 tbsp) chopped fresh parsley

Preheat oven to 230°C (450°F) mark 8. Put chops in a 2.3-litre (4-pint) gratin dish or other large baking dish. Sprinkle lamb with oil, lemon juice, salt, pepper and chilli flakes and turn to coat evenly with flavourings. Bake for 10 minutes, turning once. Reduce heat to 180°C (350°F) mark 4. Add wine, cinnamon stick, onion and garlic to dish. Bake for about 15 minutes or until meat is still pink, but not red, inside when cut; it will be returned to oven to cook further.

Remove chops and cut meat from bones, keeping meat in large pieces and reserving bones. Reserve meat on plate and cover. Return bones to pan, stir and return to oven. Bake for 25 minutes or until onion is tender. Discard cinnamon stick and bones.

Add tomato sauce, oregano and boiling water to pan. Season well with salt and pepper. Add pasta and stir. Bake for 20 minutes without stirring. Set meat pieces on top in 1 layer and press gently into mixture. Return to oven and bake for 10 minutes or until orzo is tender but firm to the bite and meat is cooked. Sprinkle with parsley.

VEGETABLES

In the area of vegetable cookery, Jewish cooks have made notable contributions in several categories – kugels, latkes and stuffed vegetables.

For as long as I can remember, kugel has been one of my favourite types of dishes. Kugels are made from vegetables, rice, noodles or matzo and come in many shapes, colours and textures. They can be sweet or savoury, and can play the role of side dish or dessert. Nearly all are baked. Some kugels are smooth and creamy, almost like a pudding, while others are firm and rather cakelike. Some are served with a spoon; others are cut in squares or slices for serving. Most are served from their baking dish, but some are unmoulded like a cake.

Kugels are sometimes translated as soufflés, but they are firmer than the French speciality. Vegetable kugels are often made from single vegetables like carrots or courgettes, or from a mixture of vegetables, as in Cauliflower Kugel with Mushrooms. The most common vegetable kugel is made of potatoes, either grated, as in Passover Potato and Vegetable Kugel (page 37), or mashed, as in Potato Kugel with Asparagus and Broccoli.

Latkes, or pancakes, are also best known when made of potatoes but can be prepared from many other vegetables as well. In fact, my mother taught me to use the same mixtures to either bake as a kugel or to sauté as latkes. Latkes are popular Hanukkah fare; for more information on these delicious pancakes, see Hanukkah.

When I lived in Israel, I loved learning to prepare vegetable recipes in the Mediterranean style. Jews from this region brought with them a repertoire of delightful dishes for making good use of courgettes, peppers, leeks and aubergines, all of which were exotic vegetables to me twenty years ago.

Stuffed vegetables, the most popular of these Sephardic vegetable dishes, are festive fare. Eating the vegetable, stuffing and sauce

253

together is a gratifying taste sensation. But stuffed vegetables have other advantages as well: they are economical, they can be prepared with easily available ingredients, and they lend themselves to many variations.

Fillings for vegetables, whether for aubergines, courgettes, onions, peppers, celery stalks or grape leaves, consist generally of rice as the main ingredient, usually combined with beef or lamb. Cooks in Israel add fragrant herbs – always flat-leaved parsley, and sometimes coriander or mint. Spices, especially cinnamon, cumin, turmeric and plenty of pepper, might also be mixed into the stuffing. For a pleasant flavour and texture contrast, some people throw in a few raisins or sautéed pine nuts, walnuts or almonds.

Stuffed vegetables are versatile enough to play the role of first course, side dish or main course, depending on the filling. Most home cooks prepare a generous amount to serve hot one day and cold the next. These vegetables can also be reheated, since they taste best when very tender.

CAULIFLOWER KUGEL WITH MUSHROOMS

Vegetables for kugel can be grated, as in Sweet Carrot Kugel (page 257) or Potato and Vegetable Kugel (page 37). Or they can be cooked and puréed, as in this savoury cauliflower version, which bears a certain resemblance to a French vegetable timbale mixture but does not contain cream.

The flavouring mixture for this kugel, of sautéed onions and mushrooms seasoned with paprika, is a favourite in the eastern European Jewish kitchen, and is also a delicious addition to cooked rice or pasta or to chicken or meat stews.

MAKES 4 TO 6 SERVINGS

1 large cauliflower, 1 kg (2¼ lb)	2 large eggs, size 1 or 2
salt	15 ml (1 tbsp) matzo meal, or 30 ml (2 tbsp) breadcrumbs
60 ml (4 tbsp) vegetable oil	freshly ground pepper
1 medium onion, chopped	2.5 ml (½ tsp) paprika
100 g (4 oz) medium or small mushrooms, quartered	40 g (1½ oz) walnuts, coarsely chopped (optional)

Preheat oven to 190°C (375°F) mark 5. Divide cauliflower into medium florets. Cut peel from large stalk and slice stalk. Boil cauliflower in a large saucepan of boiling salted water for 8–10 minutes or until stalks are vey tender. Drain well and cool. Purée in food processor, leaving a few chunks. Transfer to a bowl.

Heat 45 ml (3 tbsp) oil in medium frying pan, add onion and sauté for 5 minutes. Add mushrooms and sauté together over medium heat for about 5 minutes or until mushrooms and onions are light brown.

Add eggs and matzo meal to cauliflower mixture. Season well with salt and pepper. Lightly stir in mushroom mixture and any oil in pan.

Oil a shallow 20-cm (8-inch) square baking dish. Add cauliflower mixture. Sprinkle 15ml (1 tbsp) oil over top and sprinkle with paprika, then with walnuts. Bake for 30 minutes or until set. To serve, cut carefully in squares and run knife around edges. Use spoon to remove portions.

POTATO KUGEL WITH ASPARAGUS AND BROCCOLI

When our good friend, Gregory Dinner, invited us to Thanksgiving dinner one year, I did not expect to eat the best potato kugel I had ever tasted. He gave me the recipe, which he received from his grandmother, Rose Miller. She was born in Denver and still lives there, but her family originally came from Poland. The kugel has become one of the Dinner family's traditional dishes; for them neither a Passover nor a Thanksgiving would be complete without it. In London, where Gregory now resides, it's not so easy to get schmaltz (rendered chicken fat) for making this kugel, and so he uses a 'vegetarian schmaltz' made from vegetable fat. Another possibility is preparing your own schmaltz; see page 344.

MAKES 6 SERVINGS

6 large boiling potatoes, about 1 kg (2¼ lb)	*105 ml (7 tbsp) schmaltz (rendered chicken fat), margarine or butter*
salt	
350 g (12 oz) asparagus, peeled and cut into 2.5–4-cm (1–1½-inch) pieces	*3 medium onions, chopped freshly ground pepper*
350 g (12 oz) broccoli, divided in fairly small florets	*1 large egg, size 1 or 2, beaten*
	2.5 ml (½ tsp) paprika

Put potatoes in a large saucepan with water to cover and a pinch of salt and bring to the boil. Cover and simmer over low heat for 35–40 minutes or until very tender. Drain and leave until cool enough to handle.

Boil asparagus in a medium saucepan of boiling salted water to cover for 3 minutes or until tender. Remove asparagus with slotted spoon, rinse with cold water and drain. Add broccoli to the boiling water and boil, uncovered, for about 4 minutes or until just tender. Rinse with cold water and drain.

In a large frying pan heat 60 ml (4 tbsp) schmaltz, add onions and sauté over medium heat until golden brown, for about 20 minutes. Remove 50 g (2 oz) sautéed onions for mixing with potatoes. To remaining onions in frying pan, add asparagus and broccoli, sprinkle with salt and pepper, and toss over low heat for 2 minutes.

Peel potatoes while still fairly hot. Mash them with a potato masher or food mill, not in a food processor. Add remaining 45 ml (3 tbsp) schmaltz and stir until melted in. Add beaten egg and reserved 50 g (2 oz) fried onion. Add salt and pepper to taste.

In a greased 1.7-litre (3-pint) casserole, layer half the potato mixture, top with all of the asparagus and broccoli mixture, then with remaining potatoes. Smooth top. (Casserole can be covered and refrigerated overnight.)

Preheat oven to 180°C (350°F) mark 4. Sprinkle casserole with paprika and bake, uncovered, for about 50 minutes or until top is firm and light golden at edges. Leave to stand for about 10 minutes.

SWEET CARROT KUGEL

Carrots symbolize prosperity because of their golden colour and are a favourite for the Rosh Hashanah table, but baked puddings like this are served on a variety of festive occasions.

MAKES 4 TO 6 SERVINGS

3 extra-large eggs, size 1, separated
75 ml (5 tbsp) sugar
4 medium carrots, about 250 g (9 oz) total, peeled and grated
25 g (1 oz) blanched ground almonds

60 ml (4 tbsp) matzo meal
45 ml (3 tbsp) plain flour
pinch of salt
20 ml (4 tsp) sweet red wine
10 ml (2 tsp) lemon juice
8.75 ml (1¾ tsp) grated lemon rind

Preheat oven to 180°C (350°F) mark 4. Oil a 1-litre (1¾–2-pint) baking dish. Beat egg yolks with 45 ml (3 tbsp) sugar in a large bowl for about 2 minutes or until thick and light. Stir in grated carrots, almonds, matzo meal, flour and salt. Add wine, lemon juice and lemon rind and mix well.

Beat egg whites until stiff but not dry. Add remaining 30 ml (2 tbsp) sugar and whip at high speed for 30 seconds or until glossy. Fold one-quarter of whites quickly into carrot mixture. Spoon this mixture over remaining whites and fold together quickly but lightly. Transfer to baking dish. Bake for 35–40 minutes or until firm and golden brown. Serve hot or warm.

STUFFED AUBERGINE WITH MEAT, PINE NUTS AND ALMONDS

In Mediterranean countries, aubergines, courgettes and peppers are the most frequently chosen vegetables for stuffing. A favourite type of stuffing among Jews of the eastern Mediterranean, from Greece to Lebanon, is this one, made with the sautéed flesh of the aubergine, rice, nuts and meat. In these countries the meat used is likely to be lamb; in Israel it will usually be beef.

MAKES 4 TO 6 SERVINGS

about 1 kg (2–2½ lb) small or 2 medium aubergines	salt

MEAT STUFFING

90 g (3½ oz) long-grain white rice, rinsed and drained	45 ml (3 tbsp) olive oil
	1 medium onion, finely chopped
750 ml (1¼ pints) boiling salted water	225 g (8 oz) lean minced beef
10 ml (2 tsp) vegetable oil	30 ml (2 tbsp) chopped fresh parsley
45 ml (3 tbsp) pine nuts	2.5 ml (½ tsp) salt
45 ml (3 tbsp) slivered almonds	2.5 ml (½ tsp) ground pepper

45 ml (3 tbsp) olive or vegetable oil	60 ml (4 tbsp) water
	4 medium garlic cloves, halved
15–30 ml (1–2 tbsp) tomato purée	

Cut stalk ends from aubergines. Halve aubergines lengthways. Peel if desired; if aubergine is fresh, there is no need to peel it. When they get older, the peel gets tough. Use a spoon to scoop out centres, leaving boat-shaped shells. Set aside centres for use in stuffing. Sprinkle aubergine shells with salt. Put them in a colander upside down and drain for 30 minutes. Preheat oven to 220°C (425°F) mark 7.

Cook rice for stuffing in a saucepan of boiling salted water for 10 minutes. Rinse with cold water and drain well. Transfer to a large bowl.

Heat vegetable oil in a medium frying pan, add pine nuts and almonds, and sauté over medium heat for about 3 minutes or until lightly browned. Remove with slotted spoon. Add 15 ml (1 tbsp) olive oil to pan and heat it. Add onion and cook over low heat until soft but not brown. Leave to cool. Mix with beef, rice, parsley, salt, pepper and sautéed nuts.

Chop flesh removed from aubergine. Heat 30 ml (2 tbsp) oil, add chopped aubergine and sprinkle with salt. Sauté over medium-low heat, stirring often, until tender, about 10 minutes. Leave to cool and mix with stuffing. Taste for seasoning.

Rinse aubergine shells, pat dry and put them in a baking dish. Fill them with stuffing. Mix tomato purée with water and spoon mixture over aubergine. Add enough water to dish to cover aubergine by one-third. Add garlic to dish. Spoon remaining 15 ml (1 tbsp) oil over aubergine, cover and bake for 15 minutes. Reduce oven temperature to 180°C (350°F) mark 4 and bake for 15 more minutes. Uncover and bake, basting occasionally, for 30 minutes or until aubergine is very tender. Serve hot or warm.

BAKED AUBERGINE WITH TOMATOES, CHEESE AND SESAME SEEDS

Kashkaval cheese, which originated in the Balkans, is a popular partner for aubergine in Israel. As this cheese is rarely available, the dish is delicious when made with Swiss or gouda cheese.

MAKES 3 MAIN-COURSE OR 4 TO 6 FIRST-COURSE OR SIDE-DISH SERVINGS

1 large aubergine, about 550 g (1¼ lb)
salt
105 ml (7 tbsp) plus 10 ml (2 tsp) mild olive oil
1 large onion, about 225 g (8 oz), halved and thinly sliced
1.25 ml (¼ tsp) dried thyme, crumbled

1.25 ml (¼ tsp) dried oregano, crumbled
freshly ground pepper
350 g (12 oz) small ripe tomatoes, peeled
15 ml (1 tbsp) sesame seeds
225 g (8 oz) Swiss or kashkaval cheese, coarsely grated

Cut peel from aubergine. Cut into 1-cm (⅜-inch) slices crossways. Sprinkle slices lightly with salt on both sides and put in a colander. Put a bowl with a weight on top and leave to drain for 1 hour, turning slices after 30 minutes. Pat dry with paper towels.

Preheat oven to 220°C (425°F) mark 8. Heat 15 ml (1 tbsp) oil in a heavy medium frying pan over low heat. Add onion, thyme, oregano and pinch of salt and pepper and cook, stirring often, until very tender and light brown, about 20 minutes.

Cut tomatoes into 0.5-cm (¼-inch) slices horizontally. Arrange slices in one layer on rack. Carefully poke out seeds, using point of sharp knife. Set rack on a foil-lined baking dish. Sprinkle tomatoes lightly with salt. Bake for 10 minutes. Reserve at room temperature. Reduce oven temperature to 200°C (400°F) mark 6.

Toast sesame seeds in a small heavy frying pan over medium-low heat, stirring, until light brown, about 2 minutes. Transfer to a small bowl.

Heat 30 ml (2 tbsp) olive oil in a large heavy frying pan over medium heat. Quickly add enough aubergine slices to make 1 layer. (If slices are added too slowly, first ones soak up all of oil.) Sauté until just tender when pierced with fork, about 2 minutes on each side, then remove to plate. Sauté remaining aubergine in 2 batches, heating 30 ml (2 tbsp) oil in frying pan before each batch. (Ingredients can be prepared up to 4 hours ahead up to this point and kept at room temperature.)

Lightly oil a 1.1-litre (2-pint) gratin dish or other shallow baking dish. Arrange a layer of half the aubergine slices in dish, cutting large ones in half so they fit, and sprinkle with pepper. Spread cooked onion evenly over aubergine. Sprinkle with 50 g (2 oz) grated cheese. Arrange remaining aubergine on top in 1 layer and sprinkle with pepper. Top with tomatoes in 1 layer. Sprinkle tomatoes with 10 ml (2 tsp) olive oil, then with remaining cheese, last with sesame seeds.

Bake until cheese melts, about 15 minutes. Grill until topping browns lightly. Leave to stand for 5 minutes before serving. Serve hot, from baking dish.

EASY CURRIED AUBERGINE

Although this aubergine stew is cooked in the same manner as ratatouille and its other Mediterranean relatives, fresh ginger, coriander and other Indian spices give it a unique flavour. It is based on a dish I tasted at the home of my relatives from India. Serve it with simple foods such as roast chicken or grilled lamb chops. It is easy to prepare and is good hot or cold.

MAKES 4 SERVINGS

1 medium aubergine, 500 g
(1 lb 2 oz)
45 ml (3 tbsp) vegetable oil
1 medium onion, chopped
15 ml (1 tbsp) finely chopped, peeled fresh ginger
5 medium garlic cloves, finely chopped
10 ml (2 tsp) ground coriander
10 ml (2 tsp) ground cumin
2.5 ml (½ tsp) turmeric

good pinch cayenne pepper
30 ml (2 tbsp) chopped fresh coriander
salt to taste
450 g (1 lb) ripe tomatoes, peeled, seeded and coarsely chopped; or 1 × 794-g (28-oz) can plum tomatoes, drained and chopped
10 ml (2 tsp) tomato purée
30 ml (2 tbsp) water

Cut aubergine into 2.5 × 2.5 × 2-cm (1 × 1 × ¾-inch) dice. In a heavy 2-litre (3½-pint) casserole, heat oil, add onion and ginger and cook over low heat for 7 minutes, or until they are soft but not brown. Add garlic, ground coriander, cumin, turmeric, cayenne and 15 ml (1 tbsp) fresh coriander. Cook mixture, stirring, for 1 minute.

Add aubergine and salt and mix well over low heat until aubergine is coated with spices. Add tomatoes and cook mixture over high heat, stirring, until juice flows from tomatoes and begins to boil. Mix tomato purée with water, add to aubergine mixture and bring to the boil, stirring. Cover and simmer over low heat, stirring often, for 40 minutes, or until aubergine is very tender and mixture is thick. Taste for seasoning. (Stew can be kept, covered, for 3 days in refrigerator.) Serve hot or cold, sprinkled with remaining 15 ml (1 tbsp) fresh coriander.

STUFFED CELERY IN QUICK TOMATO SAUCE

Celery stalks are easy to stuff and, because of their small size, are convenient for serving as either an appetizer or a main course. The sauce is popular among Sephardic Jews and is very flavourful considering how simple it is – it consists of sautéed onion, garlic, tomato purée and water. Serve hot or at room temperature.

MAKES 4 SERVINGS

AROMATIC MEAT STUFFING

1 medium onion, finely chopped	2.5 ml (½ tsp) dried thyme
2 slices white bread	2.5 ml (½ tsp) dried oregano
225 g (8 oz) lean minced beef	1.25 ml (¼ tsp) cayenne pepper
15 ml (1 tbsp) chopped celery leaves	2.5 ml (½ tsp) paprika
15 ml (1 tbsp) chopped fresh parsley	freshly ground pepper to taste
30 ml (2 tbsp) chopped fresh coriander (optional)	1 medium garlic clove, chopped
	2.5 ml (½ tsp) salt
	1 large egg, size 1 or 2

6 celery stalks	4 small garlic cloves, finely chopped
30–45 ml (2–3 tbsp) vegetable oil	20 ml (4 tsp) tomato purée
100 g (4 oz) onion, chopped	350 ml (12 fl oz) water
	salt and freshly ground pepper

Put onion in a strainer and sprinkle lightly with salt. Leave to stand for about 5 minutes. Dip each bread slice in a bowl of water to moisten. Rinse onion in strainer, then add soaked bread to onion and squeeze both dry.

Mix beef with onion, bread, celery leaves, herbs, spices, garlic and salt. Add egg. Mix very well with your hands to be sure mixture is evenly combined.

Peel celery to remove strings. Cut celery into 7.5-cm (3-inch) lengths and pat dry. Put meat mixture inside celery pieces, mounding it slightly, and press to adhere well.

Heat oil in a large deep frying pan over medium heat. Add stuffed celery, filling side down, and fry for 3 minutes. Remove with slotted spatula. Remove all but about 30 ml (2 tbsp) fat from pan. Add onion and sauté for 7 minutes or until beginning to brown. Add garlic and sauté for a few seconds. Whisk tomato purée with water and add. Add a little salt and pepper and bring to a simmer. Carefully add celery, stuffing side up. Cover and cook over low heat for 30–40 minutes, until celery is very tender; add a little water occasionally if sauce becomes too thick. Taste sauce and adjust seasoning.

COURGETTES WITH TOMATOES AND DILL

I like to serve this flavourful, easy-to-make side dish from the Sephardic kitchen for Rosh Hashanah or Succot, when courgettes and tomatoes are at their peak. It tastes good hot or at room temperature and makes a delightful partner for roast or grilled chicken.

MAKES 6 SERVINGS

45 ml (3 tbsp) olive or vegetable oil

2 medium onions, finely chopped

700 g (1½ lb) ripe tomatoes, peeled, seeded and chopped

2.5 ml (½ tsp) sugar

salt and freshly ground pepper

7.5 ml (1½ tsp) paprika

scant 15 g (½ oz) fresh parsley, chopped

scant 15 g (½ oz) fresh dill, chopped, or 15 ml (1 tbsp) dried

900 g (2 lb) medium courgettes, sliced about 3.75 cm (¾ inch) thick

Heat oil in a deep frying pan or casserole. Add onions and sauté over medium-low heat for about 7 minutes or until just beginning to turn golden. Add tomatoes, sugar, salt, pepper and 5 ml (1 tsp) paprika. Reserve 15 ml (1 tbsp) parsley and 15 ml (1 tbsp) fresh dill for sprinkling, and add rest of herbs to tomato sauce. Cook, stirring often, over medium-high heat for 7 minutes or until thick.

Add courgettes to tomato sauce and sprinkle with salt and remaining paprika. Cover and cook over low heat, stirring occasionally, for 30 minutes or until very tender. If pan becomes dry, add a few spoonfuls water during cooking. Sprinkle with reserved herbs.

NOTE: For bright-coloured courgettes, cook for only 10 minutes.

SPICY MEAT-STUFFED PEPPERS

Peppers are the easiest vegetable to stuff because they have a natural cavity for stuffing. Choose peppers that are straight and can stand up easily, since these are baked upright. Although the stuffing uses a familiar base of meat and rice, this Yemenite-style version has a distinctive taste because it is flavoured with fresh chilli, cumin and turmeric.

MAKES 5 OR 6 SERVINGS

SPICY MEAT STUFFING

90 g (3½ oz) long-grain white rice, rinsed and drained

750 ml (1¼ pints) boiling salted water

30 ml (2 tbsp) olive or vegetable oil

1 medium onion, finely chopped

225 g (8 oz) lean minced beef

1–2 jalapeño chillies, seeds removed, finely chopped

1 medium garlic clove, finely chopped

30 ml (2 tbsp) chopped fresh coriander or parsley

2.5 ml (½ tsp) ground cumin

2.5 ml (½ tsp) turmeric

2.5 ml (½ tsp) salt

1.25 ml (¼ tsp) ground pepper

5–6 medium red or green peppers

15 ml (1 tbsp) tomato purée

60 ml (4 tbsp) water

30 ml (2 tbsp) olive or vegetable oil

Cook rice in a saucepan of boiling salted water for 10 minutes. Rinse with cold water and drain well.

Heat oil in a frying pan, add onion and cook over low heat until soft but not brown, about 7 minutes. Leave to cool. Mix with remaining stuffing ingredients and taste for seasoning.

Preheat oven to 180°C (350°F) mark 4. Cut a slice off stalk end of peppers. Reserve slice; remove stalk, core and seeds. Spoon stuffing into whole peppers and cover with reserved slices. Stand them in a baking dish in which they just fit. Mix tomato purée with water and spoon mixture over peppers. Sprinkle with oil and bake, uncovered, for about 1 hour or until very tender.

TWO-WAY SWEET AND SOUR CABBAGE

Cabbage is an important ingredient in the Jewish kitchen. I feel that this versatile vegetable has been somewhat overlooked in recent years, and since I like it, I chose it as the subject for my first article for Gourmet magazine.

Either red or green cabbage can be used in this dish, a favourite of Russian and central European Jews. Although the cabbage is braised until tender, it cooks for less time than in traditional recipes and therefore is in keeping with modern taste. Serve the cabbage with any meats or with roast poultry.

MAKES 3 OR 4 SERVINGS

½ large red or green cabbage, about 550 g (1¼ lb), cored and rinsed
5 ml (1 tsp) salt
30 ml (2 tbsp) vegetable oil
½ large or 1 small onion, chopped

40 g (1½ oz) raisins
5 ml (1 tsp) sugar
120 ml (4 fl oz) water
10–15 ml (2–3 tsp) lemon juice
freshly ground pepper

Slice cabbage and cut it into strips. In a large bowl, sprinkle cabbage evenly with salt and toss. Leave to stand for 45 minutes. Squeeze cabbage hard by handfuls to remove excess liquid.

Heat oil in a large casserole, add onion and cook over low heat, stirring occasionally, for 5 minutes, or until soft and lightly browned. Add cabbage and cook, stirring for 1 minute. Add raisins, sugar and water. If using red cabbage, add 15 ml (3 tsp) lemon juice now. Bring to a simmer, stirring. Cover and cook over low heat, stirring occasionally, for 20 minutes for green cabbage or 30 minutes for red cabbage, or until very tender.

Uncover and cook cabbage over medium heat, stirring, until liquid evaporates. If using green cabbage, stir in 10 ml (2 tsp) lemon juice now or to taste. Add a pinch of pepper and taste for seasoning. Serve hot or cold.

GARLIC-SCENTED ROAST POTATOES

This is my aunt's recipe for the perfect accompaniment for brisket, but these tasty crisp-crusted potatoes are wonderful with any roast meat or poultry.

MAKES 6 SERVINGS

90 ml (6 tbsp) vegetable oil	3 medium garlic cloves, finely
900 g (2 lb) baking potatoes,	chopped
peeled and quartered	paprika
3.75 ml (¾ tsp) salt	30 ml (2 tbsp) chopped fresh
	parsley (optional)

Preheat oven to 160°C (325°F) mark 3. Pour oil in a baking dish that can hold potatoes in 1 layer. Add potatoes and toss to coat them with oil. Sprinkle evenly with salt and garlic and toss again. Lightly sprinkle with paprika.

Bake potatoes, uncovered, turning them over from time to time, for 1¼–1½ hours or until they are tender and have a light golden crust. Add oil if dish appears to be getting dry. Sprinkle potatoes with parsley just before serving.

POTATO AND WALNUT FRITTERS

In keeping with the tradition of serving foods fried in oil for Hanukkah, these mashed potato fritters make good appetizers for Hanukkah parties, or crunchy accompaniments for roast or grilled chicken or meat. They can also be served like falafel, with a variety of salads.

MAKES ABOUT 4 SERVINGS

2 boiling potatoes, about	50 g (2 oz) walnuts, chopped
250 g (9 oz) total	freshly ground pepper
salt	1.1–1.4 litres (2–2½ pints)
2 large eggs, size 1 or 2	vegetable oil, for deep frying

Put potatoes in a saucepan, cover with water and add salt. Bring to the boil, cover and simmer for about 25 minutes or until tender. Drain, peel and mash. Mix with eggs and walnuts and season.

Heat oil for deep frying to 185°C (360°F); if a deep-fat thermometer is not available, test by adding a small piece of potato mixture to oil – it should bubble energetically.

Take a rounded teaspoon potato mixture. Dip another teaspoon into hot oil and use it to push mixture off other spoon into oil. Do not push it from high up or oil will splash. Continue to make more fritters from remaining mixture but do not crowd them in oil. Fry for 2–3 minutes or until golden brown on all sides. Transfer to a tray lined with paper towels. Keep warm by placing in a 150°C (300°F) mark 2 oven with door ajar while frying rest. Serve hot.

OKRA WITH TOMATOES AND CORIANDER

This is a typical way of cooking okra in Israel among Jews from Middle Eastern countries, and is my favourite recipe for the vegetable. If you leave the okra pods whole and do not overcook them, they will not be sticky.

MAKES 4 SERVINGS

900 g (2 lb) okra	15 g (½ oz) fresh coriander,
75 ml (5 tbsp) olive oil,	chopped
preferably extra-virgin	900 g (2 lb) ripe tomatoes,
1 large onion, chopped	diced
5 medium garlic cloves, finely	salt and pepper
chopped	cayenne pepper to taste

Cut off okra stalks. In a large, deep frying pan or sauté pan, heat 45 ml (3 tbsp) oil over medium heat and add onion, garlic and half the coriander. Sauté, stirring often, until onion begins to turn golden. Add okra and sauté, stirring, for 2 minutes.

Add tomatoes, salt and pepper. Bring to the boil. Cook over medium-low heat for 20–30 minutes or until tender. Stir in remaining 30 ml (2 tbsp) oil and remaining coriander and remove from heat. Add cayenne pepper if desired. Taste and adjust seasoning. Serve hot, lukewarm or cold.

LEEK FRITTERS

In the Sephardic kitchen, leeks play a major role in a variety of dishes. They are used to flavour soups and frittatas, and are made into fritters, in which the vegetable's taste is intensified from the frying. More substantial fritters are also made in this manner with a combination of leeks and minced beef.

MAKES 8 SERVINGS

1.8 kg (4 lb) leeks, cleaned	freshly ground pepper
salt	freshly grated nutmeg to taste
2 large eggs, size 1 or 2	about 1 litre (2 pints)
25 g (1 oz) matzo meal, or	vegetable oil, for frying
more as needed	lemon wedges, for serving
2.5 ml (½ tsp) dried leaf	
thyme, crumbled	

Cut leeks into about 10-cm (4-inch) pieces. Cook in a large pan of boiling salted water for about 10 minutes or until tender. Drain well. Finely chop with a knife. Drain again in a strainer and squeeze firmly by handfuls to remove excess liquid. Transfer to a bowl. Add eggs, matzo meal, thyme and salt, pepper and nutmeg to taste.

Shape mixture into flat cakes, using about 30 ml (2 tbsp) mixture for each; if mixture won't hold together in cakes, stir in a little more matzo meal, 5 ml (1 tsp) at a time. Put cakes on a plate.

Heat oil in a deep-fat fryer or heavy medium saucepan to 180–185°C (350–360°F) on a deep-fat thermometer, or until oil sizzles vigorously when a small piece of leek mixture is added. Fry leek patties in batches until light golden brown, about 1–1½ minutes. Drain on paper towels. Keep fritters warm in a 150°C (300°F) mark 2 oven while frying remaining ones and until ready to serve. Serve with lemon wedges.

EASY CAULIFLOWER LATKES

These are good as an appetizer topped with soured cream or Yemenite Tomato Dip (page 163). I also like them plain as an accompaniment for roast chicken.

MAKES 6 SERVINGS

1 large cauliflower, about 900 g (2 lb)	90 ml (6 tbsp) unseasoned breadcrumbs
salt	2 large eggs, size 1 or 2
90–105 ml (6–7 tbsp) vegetable oil	freshly ground pepper
1 medium onion, finely chopped	

Cook cauliflower in a large pan of boiling salted water, uncovered, over high heat for about 12 minutes or until very tender. Meanwhile, heat 30 ml (2 tbsp) oil in a large heavy frying pan, add onion and cook over medium-low heat for about 10 minutes or until soft and golden brown.

Drain cauliflower thoroughly and mash with a fork or chop in a food processor. There should still be pieces but not large ones. Add breadcrumbs, eggs, fried onion and salt and pepper to taste and mix well with a wooden spoon.

Wipe pan used to fry onion, add 60 ml (4 tbsp) oil and heat it. Take generous 15 ml (1 tbsp) cauliflower mixture in your hand and press to make it compact. Flatten it to a cake about 1 cm (½ inch) thick and add to pan. Make 4 or 5 more cakes and add them. Fry over medium heat for about 3 minutes on each side or until brown. Turn carefully using a wide fish slice or spatula. Drain on paper towels. Keep warm by placing in a 150°C (300°F) mark 2 oven with door ajar while frying rest. Add more oil to pan if it becomes dry. Serve plain or with soured cream.

SPINACH PANCAKES

These are pretty topped with a dollop of soured cream or yogurt and sprinkled with diced tomato or chives. They can also be served with yogurt-mint topping (see Courgette Pancakes with Garlic, page 130), or, for a spicy note, with Chilli-Garlic Chutney (page 154).

MAKES 22 TO 24 SMALL PANCAKES; 4 TO 6 SERVINGS

1 kg (2¼ lb) fresh spinach, stalks removed, leaves rinsed well, or 2 × 275-g (10-oz) packets frozen, thawed	salt and pepper freshly grated nutmeg to taste 50 g (2 oz) plain flour 2 large eggs, size 1 or 2 1.25 ml (¼ tsp) salt
25 g (1 oz) butter or margarine	60 ml (4 tbsp) vegetable oil, for frying

Cook fresh spinach in a large pan of boiling salted water for 3 minutes or until tender. Rinse with cold water. Squeeze fresh or thawed frozen spinach to remove excess liquid. Chop finely.

Melt butter in a medium frying pan over medium heat. Add spinach and cook for about 2 minutes, stirring. Season with a pinch of salt, pepper and nutmeg. Transfer to a large bowl.

In a medium bowl mix flour, eggs, 1.25 ml (¼ tsp) salt and a pinch of pepper and nutmeg to a very thick batter. Add batter to spinach and mix very well. Taste for seasoning.

Heat oil in a heavy frying pan over medium heat. Fry spinach mixture by tablespoons, flattening each after adding it, for about 2 minutes or until golden brown on each side. Transfer to paper towels to drain. Serve hot.

NOODLES, RICE AND OTHER GRAINS

A golden kugel, or casserole, of baked noodles was the dish I looked forward to most every Friday night ever since I was a child. As an accompaniment for the Sabbath roast chicken, my mother's recipe calls for egg noodles of medium width mixed with either sautéed mushrooms and onions for a savoury kugel, or with sliced apples and cinnamon for a slightly sweet version. For dairy meals she makes kugel by a similar method, but generally stirs in soured cream and occasionally cottage cheese.

Noodle kugels are very easy to prepare, since the pasta is simply mixed with eggs, seasonings, and other ingredients and then baked. They can be made with cooked broccoli, peppers or mixed vegetables; or for the sweet version, with a variety of fresh or dried fruits, such as pears, apricots and raisins.

In the Jewish kitchen, pasta is also prepared in other ways besides kugel. It is served with sauce, as in Pasta Shells with Tunisian Artichoke Meat Sauce, or as an accompaniment for stews like Hungarian goulash. Egg barley, sometimes called farfel, is a very small type of pasta that is usually tossed with fried onions and served as a side dish with roast chicken or stewed meats.

Couscous is the 'pasta' of Jews from Morocco, Algeria and Tunisia and is often the focus of the Friday night family dinner. Although couscous comes in tiny particles and looks like a grain, it is made of semolina and water, like pasta. Ninette Bachar from Tunisia, who is the next-door neighbour of my in-laws in the Tel Aviv suburb of Givatayim, taught me how to steam it the traditional way. She showed me how to moisten the couscous, then to steam it several times above a simmering lamb stew in the top part of a special small-holed steamer called a *couscoussier*. After each steaming she removed the couscous and rubbed it between her fingers to ensure that the grains remained separate.

When prepared this way, the light golden couscous is the centre for a grand dinner, also called a 'couscous' in which the grain is accompanied by lamb stew, by Aromatic Meat Patties (page 246), or by a lavish assortment of stuffed vegetables. When served like this, couscous is truly a feast, but it can be enjoyed for casual meals as well, because it is widely available in quick-cooking versions.

Rice is at least as important in the Jewish diet as pasta, especially among Sephardim. A stroll in the central Jerusalem market of Mahane Yehuda reveals the grain's importance for the Israeli menu. There are enormous sacks of various types of rice from different parts of the world – basmati rice from India and Persian rice from Isfahan, for example.

As a simple accompaniment, rice is most often cooked in Israel in one of three basic ways; white rice, yellow rice and red rice. All three are usually versions of pilaf, for which the rice is lightly sautéed before the liquid is added. Yellow rice is flavoured with cumin and turmeric (or occasionally saffron), and the red version contains tomato. For special occasions, rice might be garnished with nuts and raisins. Rice accompanies chicken, meats and fish, whether these are grilled, roasted or stewed. Even vegetables are served with rice for a vegetarian meal, especially if these are 'saucy' vegetables such as Sautéed Aubergine in Spicy Tomato Sauce (page 93).

Bulgar wheat, also called cracked wheat, is another popular grain among Middle Eastern Jews. Like rice, it is cooked as pilaf to accompany meats, but also is the basis for other specialities like the meat-filled pastry known as Kubeh (page 172) and the tangy salad called Tabbouleh (page 189).

Buckwheat, or kasha, is a favourite among Russian and Polish Jews as an accompaniment for meat and as a filling for pastries, especially knishes. Barley is used most often in soups, and whole wheat berries are a frequent addition to the slowly simmered stew known as Hamin (page 156).

NOODLES WITH SAUTEED CABBAGE AND ONIONS (CABBAGE PLETZLACH)

I n this Hungarian-Jewish recipe, the cabbage takes on a slightly sweet taste from slow cooking with fried onions. A combination of oil and margarine is a frequent choice for sautéing today, both for reasons of nutrition and so the dish can be served with either dairy foods or meat. Occasionally chicken or goose fat is used, when the noodles will be served with meats or poultry. Butter is preferred by some cooks when they are serving the dish with fish or in a dairy meal.

MAKES 4 SIDE-DISH SERVINGS

½ large green cabbage, 700 g (1½ lb), cored and rinsed	½ large onion, finely chopped
5 ml (1 tsp) salt	2.5 ml (½ tsp) sugar
60 ml (4 tbsp) vegetable oil and 25 g (1 oz) margarine; or 75 g (3 oz) butter or chicken fat	freshly ground pepper
	150 g (5 oz) broad egg noodles

Shred cabbage with a knife. In a large bowl, sprinkle cabbage evenly with salt and toss. Leave to stand for 45 minutes. Squeeze cabbage by handfuls to remove excess liquid.

Heat 60 ml (4 tbsp) oil in a large frying pan, add onion and sauté over medium heat for 5 minutes, or until beginning to soften. Add cabbage, sugar and pepper to taste and mix well. Cover and cook over low heat, stirring often, for 30 minutes or until very tender. Uncover and cook over medium-high heat, stirring, until lightly browned.

In a large pan of boiling salted water, cook noodles for 7 minutes or until just tender. Drain thoroughly and add to cabbage. Add 25 g (1 oz) margarine. Toss over low heat just until mixed. Taste for seasoning. Transfer to a heated serving dish.

273

PASTA SHELLS WITH TUNISIAN ARTICHOKE MEAT SAUCE

Jews from North Africa often make use of artichokes. They might be baked with a meat stuffing, added to a stew like Msouki (page 63) or simmered in a sauce for pasta like this one. Here artichoke hearts are combined with mushrooms, capers and a generous amount of garlic, to give this 'spaghetti sauce' its Mediterranean character. Shells are a wonderful pasta shape for serving with minced meat sauces because the meat lodges inside them.

MAKES 6 MAIN-COURSE SERVINGS

75 ml (5 tbsp) olive oil
12 medium garlic cloves, finely chopped
450 g (1 lb) lean minced beef
700 g (1½ lb) ripe tomatoes, peeled, seeded and chopped; or 1 × 794-g (28-oz) can and 1 × 397-g (14-oz) can plum tomatoes, drained
1 bay leaf
salt and freshly ground pepper
60 ml (4 tbsp) tomato purée

60 ml (4 tbsp) water
225 g (8 oz) small button mushrooms, quartered
75 ml (5 tbsp) capers, lightly rinsed
4 fresh artichokes or 16 frozen artichoke heart pieces
1 lemon
450 g (1 lb) medium pasta shells
30 ml (2 tbsp) chopped fresh parsley

Heat 45 ml (3 tbsp) oil in a heavy casserole over low heat. Add 15 ml (1 tbsp) garlic and cook over low heat for ½ minute, stirring. Add beef and sauté over medium heat, crumbling with a wooden spoon, until it changes colour. Add tomatoes, bay leaf, salt and pepper and bring to the boil, stirring (and crushing canned tomatoes, if using). Add tomato purée and water, stir and bring to the boil. Simmer, uncovered, over low heat, stirring occasionally, for 30 minutes. Add mushrooms and 45 ml (3 tbsp) capers. Cover and simmer for about 15 minutes or until mushrooms are tender and sauce is thick.

If using fresh artichokes, squeeze juice of ½ lemon into a medium bowl of cold water. Prepare artichoke hearts, cook them and remove chokes (see page 344). If using frozen artichokes, cook them in a medium saucepan of boiling salted water with 5 ml (1 tsp) lemon juice for about 7 minutes. Cut each fresh artichoke into 8 pieces. If frozen artichoke pieces are large, cut them in half.

Discard bay leaf from beef sauce. Add remaining garlic and cook over low heat for 2 minutes. Add artichokes and reheat. Taste and adjust seasoning; sauce should be quite highly seasoned to balance sharpness of capers. (Sauce can be kept, covered, for up to 2 days in refrigerator. Reheat it over low heat, covered.)

Cook pasta, uncovered, in a large pan of boiling water over high heat, stirring occasionally, for 5–8 minutes or until tender but firm to the bite. Drain well and transfer to a large heated bowl. Toss with remaining 30 ml (2 tbsp) oil. Add sauce and 15 ml (1 tbsp) capers and toss. Season. Sprinkle with parsley and remaining capers.

EGG NOODLES FOR SOUP

Clear chicken soup (page 345) with homemade noodles is a treasured speciality. In some eastern European Jewish communities, a young woman's ability to roll noodle dough very thinly was a sign that she was fit to be a good wife. Thanks to pasta machines, today it's easy for everyone to roll the dough and so people have to use new standards of suitability for marriage!

MAKES ABOUT 250–275 G (9–10 OZ) FRESH NOODLES

175 g (6 oz) plain flour	5–25 ml (1–5 tsp) water, if
2 large eggs, size 1 or 2	needed
1.25 ml (¼ tsp) salt	a little flour, if needed

Combine flour, eggs and salt in food processor. Process until ingredients are well blended and dough holds together in sticky crumbs that can be easily pressed together, about 10 seconds. If crumbs are dry, sprinkle with water, about 5 ml (1 tsp) at a time, processing for about 5 seconds after each addition, adding enough to obtain moist crumbs. Press dough together to a ball. Transfer to a work surface and knead for a few seconds, flouring lightly if dough sticks to surface, until it is fairly smooth.

Wrap dough in cling film or set it on a plate and cover with an inverted bowl. Leave to stand for 30 minutes. (Dough can be kept for up to 4 hours in refrigerator; leave to stand for about 30 minutes to come back to room temperature before using.)

Generously flour 2 or 3 baking sheets. Turn smooth rollers of a pasta machine to widest setting.

Cut dough into 4 pieces; leave 3 pieces wrapped or covered. Flatten 1 piece of dough in a 10-cm (4-inch) square and lightly flour it. Run it through rollers of machine at widest setting. Fold in thirds so ends meet in centre, press seams together and flatten slightly. Run dough through rollers again. Repeat folding and rolling, lightly flouring only when necessary to prevent sticking, until dough is smooth, about 7 more times. Turn dial of machine 1 notch to next setting. Without folding piece of dough, run it through machine. Continue to feed dough through rollers without folding, turning dial 1 notch lower each time; dust with flour as necessary and cut dough in half crossways if it gets too long to handle. Stop when dough is 1.5 mm (¹⁄₁₆ inch) thick (generally next to narrowest setting.)

Hang dough sheet to dry on a pasta rack or on back of a tea towel-lined chair. Repeat with remaining dough. Dry dough sheets for about 10 minutes or until firmer and have a leathery texture.

To cut noodles, move the adjustment of pasta machine to narrow noodle setting. Put each sheet of pasta through machine, holding it with 1 hand and catching pasta with other hand. If strands stick together while being cut, dough is too wet; dry remaining dough sheets a little bit longer before cutting them. Separate the strands.

Leave noodles to dry on a pasta rack or on a floured baking sheet for at least 10 minutes, if using immediately, or up to several hours. Gently toss the noodles that are on baking sheets occasionally to prevent sticking. (Noodles can be refrigerated, covered loosely, on tray; or can be gently put in plastic bags. They will keep for up to 5 days in refrigerator; they can also be frozen.)

For serving in a clear soup, the noodles are usually cooked in boiling salted water, then are drained and added to the soup. They can also be tossed with olive oil, butter and sautéed onions.

NOTE: To make dough by hand instead of in a food processor, mound flour on work surface or in a large bowl. Make a well in centre. Add eggs and salt to well and blend with fork. Gradually draw flour from inner edge of well into centre, first with fork, then with your fingers, until all the flour is incorporated. Add water by teaspoons if flour cannot be incorporated; dough will be very stiff and dry but will soften during kneading. Knead dough on a clean work surface, flouring only if dough is sticky, for about 5 minutes or until fairly smooth and pliable. Stand for 1 hour before using.

NOODLE KUGEL WITH ONIONS AND MUSHROOMS

Our family has always loved noodle kugels with mushrooms, and so my mother prepares them in several versions. This rich kugel, which is flavoured with cottage cheese and soured cream, is best as a main course for a vegetarian or dairy supper. For serving with poultry or meat, simply omit the dairy products and use oil or margarine for sautéing the onions and mushrooms.

MAKES 4 OR 5 MAIN-COURSE OR 6 TO 8 SIDE-DISH SERVINGS

200–225 g (7–8 oz) medium egg noodles
65 g (2½ oz) butter, margarine or vegetable oil
1 large onion, chopped
450 g (1 lb) small button mushrooms, quartered
salt and freshly ground pepper to taste
2 medium garlic cloves, finely chopped

7.5 ml (1½ tsp) paprika
2 large eggs, size 1 or 2, beaten
250 ml (8 fl oz) cream-style cottage cheese
120 ml (4 fl oz) soured cream
scant 15 g (½ oz) snipped fresh dill or 15 ml (1 tbsp) dried
1.25 ml (¼ tsp) cayenne pepper, or to taste

Preheat oven to 180°C (350°F) mark 4. Cook noodles, uncovered, in a large pan of boiling salted water over high heat for about 4 minutes or until nearly tender but firmer than usual. Drain, rinse with cold water and drain again. Transfer to a large bowl.

Heat 50 g (2 oz) butter or oil in a large frying pan over medium-low heat. Add onion and sauté for about 12 minutes or until very tender. Add mushrooms, salt, pepper, garlic and 5 ml (1 tsp) paprika and sauté for about 12 minutes or until mushrooms are tender and onion is browned. If liquid remains in pan, cook over high heat, stirring, for a few minutes until it evaporates. Cool slightly.

Add eggs, cottage cheese, soured cream, dill and cayenne to noodles and mix well. Stir in mushroom mixture. Taste and adjust seasoning; mixture should be seasoned generously. Butter or oil a 1.7-litre (3-pint) baking dish and add noodle mixture. Sprinkle with remaining 15 ml (1 tbsp) oil or dot with butter, then dust with remaining paprika. Bake, uncovered, for 1 hour or until set.

SPAETZLE

Whether served in soup or tossed with sautéed onions as a side dish, spaetzle, a cross between a dumpling and a noodle, are a favourite dish among Jews from Alsace, Germany and Hungary. If you like, instead of adding these to a pan of melted butter or margarine, add them to a sautéed mushroom mixture, as in Noodle Kugel with Onions and Mushrooms (page 277).

MAKES 4 SIDE-DISH SERVINGS

175 g (6 oz) plain flour
2.5 ml (½ tsp) salt
2 large eggs, size 1 or 2
60 ml (4 tbsp) water
60 ml (4 tbsp) milk or
   additional water

50 g (2 oz) butter or
   margarine, melted
freshly ground white pepper
   (optional)

Mix flour and salt in a large bowl and make a well in centre. Add eggs, water and milk to well and whisk to combine. Draw in flour with a wooden spoon and beat just until smooth; batter will be quite thick. Leave to rest for 15 minutes. Put melted butter in an oven-proof serving dish.

Bring a medium saucepan of salted water to a simmer. Use a colander or flat grater to make spaetzle; if using grater, set it on pan so it is easier to handle. Using a spatula, push 30–45 ml (2–3 tbsp) dough through holes of colander or large holes of grater so that dough falls in small pieces into water; move spatula backwards and forwards to push dough through holes. Move colander or grater so all of dough does not fall in same place. Continue to make spaetzle until about one-quarter of the dough is used.

After spaetzle float to top of pan, cook them over medium heat for about 2 minutes or until no longer doughy; taste to check. Remove with slotted spoon, drain well and transfer to dish of melted butter. Keep warm in lowest setting oven while cooking remaining spaetzle, in batches. If desired, sprinkle spaetzle lightly with salt and white pepper before serving. (Spaetzle can be refrigerated after being tossed with butter. Reheat, covered, at 180°C (350°F) mark 4; gently stir 2 or 3 times.)

SAVOURY LENTILS
WITH RICE
(MAJADRAH)

L entils have been served in the Middle East ever since Esau sold his birthright to Jacob for a bowl of lentil stew. Majadrah, or lentil and rice stew, used to be considered part of poor people's cuisine among the Jews of Lebanon, said Suzanne Elmaleh of Jerusalem, who taught me how to prepare it. Today in Israel the dish has become very fashionable, not only because it tastes good but also for nutritional considerations, since it makes a healthy vegetarian dish. Its flavour depends on thoroughly sautéed, deeply browned onions. Some cooks add 5 ml (1 tsp) cumin to the onions.

The classic way to prepare the stew is to use twice as much rice as lentils and to garnish it with crisp, deep-fried chopped onions, but today many people prefer to use equal portions of lentils and rice, as here. The favourite partner to accompany the hot lentil stew is a refreshing Cucumber Salad with Yogurt and Mint (see page 188).

MAKES 2 OR 3 MAIN-COURSE OR
4 OR 5 SIDE-DISH SERVINGS

---

225 g (8 oz) lentils
450 ml (¾ pint) water
75 ml (5 tbsp) vegetable oil
2 large onions, chopped

200 g (7 oz) long-grain white
*   rice*
salt and freshly ground pepper

Combine lentils and water in a medium saucepan. Bring to the boil, cover and cook over medium heat for about 20 minutes or until lentils are just tender. Drain liquid into a measuring jug and add enough water to make 450 ml (¾ pint); reserve.

In a heavy frying pan heat oil over medium heat. Add onions and sauté, stirring occasionally, until they are well browned, about 15 minutes. Add onions and their oil to pan of lentils. Add measured liquid and bring to the boil. Add salt and rice and return to the boil. Cover, reduce heat to low and cook, without stirring, until rice is tender, about 20 minutes. Taste and adjust seasoning. Serve hot.

NOTE: If you wish to double the rice, as in the classic version, add enough water to lentil cooking liquid to make scant 1 litre (1¾ pints).

AROMATIC YELLOW RICE

Turmeric and cumin give this rice dish its bright colour and zesty flavour. It is frequently prepared in Israel by Jews of Kurdish, Yemenite and other Middle Eastern origins and by Jews from India, and is a perfect accompaniment for grilled fish, meat or poultry.

MAKES 3 OR 4 SIDE-DISH SERVINGS

15 ml (1 tbsp) vegetable oil	200 g (7 oz) long-grain white
1 medium onion, thinly sliced	rice
5 ml (1 tsp) ground cumin	450 ml (¾ pint) hot water
2.5 ml (½ tsp) turmeric	salt and freshly ground pepper

Heat oil in a medium saucepan. Add onion and cook over low heat, stirring occasionally, until soft but not brown. Stir in cumin and turmeric and cook for another minute, stirring. Add rice and sauté for 2 minutes, stirring.

Add water, salt and pepper and bring to the boil. Stir once with a fork and cover. Cook over low heat, without stirring, for 18–20 minutes or until rice is tender and liquid is absorbed. Remove from heat and leave to stand, covered, for 10 minutes. Taste and adjust seasoning. (Rice will keep hot for about 45 minutes. It can be prepared 2 days ahead and kept, covered, in refrigerator. To reheat, heat 15 ml (1 tbsp) oil in a large frying pan, add rice and heat over low heat, stirring gently with a fork.) Fluff it with a fork just before serving. Serve hot.

SPICY COUSCOUS
WITH GARLIC

Among Jews from Tunisia, this dish is sometimes called 'Sunday couscous' because it is the way families make good use of leftover steamed couscous from *Shabbat*. The recipe is a terrific way to turn instant couscous into a zesty side dish in just a few minutes. The Tunisians use ground caraway seeds, but I have substituted whole ones since they are much easier to find. This dish is good with either ordinary or whole wheat couscous.

MAKES 2 OR 3 SIDE-DISH SERVINGS

30 ml (2 tbsp) Chilli-Garlic Chutney (page 154) or 7.5 ml (1½ tsp) Tabasco sauce, or to taste	3–4 medium cloves garlic, very finely chopped
45–60 ml (3–4 tbsp) olive oil, preferably extra-virgin	5 ml (1 tsp) paprika
2.5 ml (½ tsp) caraway seeds	salt and freshly ground pepper
	30 ml (2 tbsp) water
	200 g (7 oz) precooked couscous

In a bowl, whisk together chutney, 45 ml (3 tbsp) olive oil, caraway seeds, garlic, paprika, salt and pepper and water.

Cook couscous according to packet directions. Add sauce to couscous and mix gently. Adjust seasoning and add remaining oil if desired.

COLOURFUL VEGETABLE COUSCOUS

For this North African Jewish dish, which can be a side dish or a vegetarian main course, the vegetables can be varied according to the seasons. Use as many or as few varieties as you like.

MAKES 4 MAIN-COURSE OR 6 SIDE-COURSE SERVINGS

150 g (5 oz) dried chick peas or 1 × 439-g (15½-oz) can	freshly ground pepper
1.1 litres (2 pints) water (for dried chick peas)	2 medium carrots, peeled and sliced
salt	2 small tomatoes, cored and quartered
45 ml (3 tbsp) olive oil	225 g (8 oz) courgettes, cut into thick slices
2 large onions, sliced	5–10 ml (1–2 tsp) tomato purée
5 ml (1 tsp) ground cumin	
2 garlic cloves, chopped	

QUICK COUSCOUS

350 ml (12 fl oz) stock from vegetables	2.5 ml (½ tsp) salt
75 ml (5 tbsp) olive oil or butter	pinch of pepper
400 g (14 oz) precooked couscous	pinch of nutmeg
	pinch of ground cloves
	hot pepper sauce, for serving

281

To prepare dried chick peas, sort through them, discarding any pebbles or other foreign material; rinse thoroughly. Put them in a
saucepan with 450 ml (¾ pint) water and bring to the boil. Boil for
2 minutes; cover and leave to stand for 1 hour. Drain thoroughly.
Return to saucepan. Add 750 ml (1¼ pints) cold water and bring to
the boil. Cover and simmer for about 1½ hours, adding hot water
occasionally to keep them covered with water. Add a pinch of salt
and continue simmering for 30–45 minutes or until tender. If using
canned chick peas, discard liquid, rinse chick peas and drain.

Heat oil in a very large frying pan over low heat. Add onions and
cook, stirring, until soft but not browned. Add cumin and garlic and
sauté for ½ minute. Add chick pea liquid or water, salt and pepper
and bring to the boil. Cover and simmer for 15 minutes. Add carrots
and simmer for 15 minutes. Add tomatoes, courgettes and chick
peas. Cover and simmer for 15 minutes. Uncover and simmer for
5 minutes more.

Remove vegetables with a slotted spoon and reserve. Reserve
350 ml (12 fl oz) vegetable stock for cooking couscous and keep it
warm. Boil remaining vegetable stock, stirring often, for about
5 minutes to concentrate its flavour. Whisk in tomato purée and taste
for seasoning.

In a medium saucepan combine reserved vegetable stock and
30 ml (2 tbsp) olive oil or butter. Bring to the boil. Stir in couscous,
salt, pepper, nutmeg and cloves. Cover pan immediately and leave to
stand, off heat, for 5 minutes. Pour remaining olive oil over couscous
or cut remaining butter in small pieces and scatter over couscous.
Cover and leave to stand for 1 minute.

Fluff couscous with a fork to break up any lumps, tossing it until
oil or butter is absorbed. Taste and adjust seasoning. Cover to keep it
warm.

To serve, pile couscous in a cone shape on a large serving plate.
Spoon some of the vegetables around sides and serve remaining vegetables and stock from a bowl or tureen. Serve in shallow bowls, so
that each person can moisten his or her couscous with stock to taste.
Accompany with hot pepper sauce.

COUSCOUS WITH RAISINS AND DATES

This buttery version of couscous is a great dairy dish for the holiday of Shavuot. After I tasted this speciality at a couscous restaurant in Paris, I kept coming back and ordering it. It makes a delicious brunch treat, and is also good for breakfast or dessert.

The method given in the recipe is for raw couscous. If you are using packaged precooked couscous, cook the couscous according to the packet instructions, adding the dates after the water.

MAKES 4 OR 5 MAIN-COURSE SERVINGS

450 g (1 lb) couscous	*175 g (6 oz) raisins*
120 ml (4 fl oz) water	*150 g (5 oz) butter, at room*
2.5 ml (½ tsp) salt	*temperature, cut into pieces*
250 g (9 oz) dates	*450 ml (¾ pint) hot milk*

Fill a couscous pan or base of a steamer about two-thirds full of water and bring to the boil. Meanwhile, rinse couscous in a bowl and drain in a fine strainer. Transfer to a shallow bowl and rub grains to be sure they are separate. Leave to dry for about 10 minutes.

Put couscous in steamer part of couscous pan. Tie a damp tea towel around base of steamer part so steam won't escape from sides. Steam couscous uncovered above boiling water for 30 minutes.

Remove couscous, put it in a large bowl, and leave to cool. Mix water and salt. Sprinkle couscous lightly with salted water, rubbing and tossing it between your fingers to prevent grains from sticking together.

Return couscous to steamer and set it again above boiling water. Steam uncovered for about 15 minutes. Put dates on top and steam for 5 minutes longer or until steam comes through couscous.

Meanwhile, in a separate pan simmer raisins in hot water to cover for about 10 minutes or until tender. Drain thoroughly.

Put dates on a plate. Transfer couscous to a large bowl and add butter. Mix lightly with a fork or with your fingers. To serve, mound couscous on a serving plate and arrange dates and raisins on top. Serve in bowls. Serve hot milk separately in a jug, for pouring over couscous.

BULGAR WHEAT PILAF WITH MUSHROOMS, PEAS AND PINE NUTS

At the Israel Museum, I attended an exhibition of the customs of the Kurdish Jews and was glad to see that cuisine was highlighted as a prominent element. There was a dinner of typical dishes, and one of these was a delicious peppery bulgar wheat pilaf, which served as a bed for an aromatic meat stew.

Bulgar wheat, sometimes known as cracked wheat, is a staple of Jews from Middle Eastern countries. It is a wonderful ingredient with great flexibility. It can be simply marinated without being cooked to make Tabbouleh (page 189) or it can be made into a dough for a meat-filled appetizer known as Kubeh (page 172).

MAKES 4 SIDE-DISH SERVINGS

---

60 ml (4 tbsp) vegetable or olive oil, or butter
½ medium onion, finely chopped
2 medium garlic cloves, finely chopped
115 g (4½ oz) medium bulgar wheat
350 ml (12 fl oz) water
salt and freshly ground pepper

100 g (4 oz) button mushrooms, halved and thinly sliced
175 g (6 oz) cooked peas
30 ml (2 tbsp) chopped fresh Italian parsley or curly parsley
30 ml (2 tbsp) toasted pine nuts

Heat 30 ml (2 tbsp) oil in a heavy medium saucepan over medium heat. Add onion and cook, stirring often, for about 5 minutes or until softened. Add garlic and cook for 1 minute. Add bulgar and sauté, stirring, for 2 minutes. Add water, salt and pepper and bring to the boil. Reduce heat, cover and cook for 15 minutes until water is absorbed. (Pilaf can be kept warm, covered, for 15 minutes.)

Heat the remaining 30 ml (2 tbsp) oil in a large frying pan over medium heat. Add mushrooms, salt and pepper. Sauté for about 4 minutes or until golden brown. Add peas and heat gently.

Gently stir mushroom mixture into bulgar pilaf using a fork. Stir in parsley, taste and adjust seasoning. Transfer to a serving dish, sprinkle with pine nuts and serve immediately.

BREADS

I grew up in America eating delicious bread, without even realizing that much of the bread in the country was characterless and cotton textured. The reason for my good fortune was that all the bread in my parents' home came from Jewish bakeries. I still like to buy Jewish rye bread with caraway seeds, pumpernickel, bialys and onion pletzlach. I also purchase challah and bagels, but I make these at home whenever I can. I also bake pita, or pocket bread, which I often enjoyed in Israel with falafel and other treats. Fresh, good-quality pita and challah are often hard to find and so the best solution is to bake your own.

CHALLAH

Challah (sometimes spelled *hallah*), a rich loaf with a deep brown crust and soft white crumb, is America's most popular egg bread. A festive bread traditionally prepared for the Sabbath and other Jewish holidays, it is usually a plaited free-form loaf but it can also be shaped in spirals or wreaths or baked in a loaf tin.

The tantalizing aroma of challah baking always brings back memories from nearly twenty years ago, of a small bakery in a Tel Aviv suburb. Just before midnight every Thursday, when the streets were quiet and everyone was asleep, the bakers started preparing challahs for the Friday morning shoppers. My husband and I would walk to the neighbourhood bakery and would buy one of the beautiful, hot, just-out-of-the-oven, golden-crusted challahs for a midnight snack. By the time we arrived home not much of the loaf was left for eating with butter.

Challah combines the advantages of the richest of egg breads, French brioche and of homemade white bread. While white bread uses water or milk as its moistening liquid and brioche uses mainly

285

egg, challah uses some of each and achieves some of the lightness of white bread and some of the richness of brioche. Unlike brioche, which contains a generous amount of butter, challah is usually enriched with oil and the dough is much easier to handle.

Like most yeast-leavened doughs, challah dough is kneaded in order to distribute the yeast evenly and ensure that the bread has a uniform texture. Although kneading the dough by hand takes only a few minutes and is a pleasant task, it can also be done in a mixer or in a food processor and then is effortless. Rising times can be flexible, and it is therefore possible to fit breadmaking into busy schedules. (See the first tip, page 288.)

To impart a tender, somewhat cakelike texture to the bread rather than a dense, chewy one, the dough should be soft. Because the absorption power of flour varies with humidity and the flour itself varies from place to place and with the seasons, adding just the right amount of flour to make the dough perfect requires a little experience. The best texture and flavour result when the minimum amount of flour to prevent sticking is added. If a little too much flour is added during kneading, however, the bread will still taste good.

Challah has a delicate flavour, which makes it a good accompaniment for a meal. For a different twist, a variety of sweet or savoury flavourings, such as dried fruits, nuts, herbs, cheeses, and even vegetables, can be added to the dough.

Bread is a joy to make. In contrast to many pastries and other baked goods, with bread there is no need to hurry and little to worry about. The dough is easy to prepare and fun to work with. The result is delicious, aromatic bread that turns snacks into special treats and helps transform meals into feasts.

BAGELS

Fresh hot bagels with butter, or with the traditional accompaniments of lox and cream cheese, are one of the attractions of a Bar Mitzvah celebration. In New York and Los Angeles there are twenty-four-hour bagel bakeries, with hot bagels ready at any hour of the day or night.

Yet there is no need to wait for special occasions or to travel far in order to enjoy these delicious ring-shaped rolls. Indeed, homemade bagels may taste even better. They fill the kitchen with a wonderful aroma, and are one of the quickest breads to make.

A special technique gives bagels their unique texture, and enables us to 'cheat' a little on the rising time: bagels are boiled before they are baked. Boiling gives them a quick push so they puff in the water, complete their rising, and begin to cook. A little sugar added to the water helps give the bagels a crisp crust. Before they are baked, the drained bagels are brushed with beaten egg for a shiny glaze.

One of two methods can be used to make the hole: the dough can be shaped in balls and the centre pushed out with your finger; or it can be formed into thin ropes, and the ends pressed together. The ball technique is more practical, because bagels formed by the rope method may open in the water. Both methods use up all the dough.

Although basic bagels came to us with the Jews from eastern Europe, flavoured bagels appear to be distinctly American. Like other breads, bagels can be varied by the addition of cheese, herbs, garlic or nuts, or with sweet ingredients like honey and raisins.

Bagels are simple to make, though some recipes are quite strange. In a Jewish story about Chelm, the legendary town of fools, the baker of a neighbouring town agreed to give Chelm's representatives his bagel recipe – start with holes, put dough around them, cook them in boiling water, then bake them in the oven. It has been reported that there are no bagels in Chelm to this very day.

KNEADING EGG BREAD DOUGH BY HAND

Egg bread dough can be kneaded by either of the following methods:
Slapping method: For soft dough, this kneading technique is preferable. Using fingertips of both hands, lightly scoop up dough and slap it vigorously onto work surface. Grasp dough again, at about a 90-degree angle from first time (which has the effect of turning the dough), and repeat. Continue slapping dough, adding flour 15 ml (1 tbsp) at a time if necessary to prevent excessive sticking, until it is smooth and elastic and holds together in 1 piece; it may still be slightly sticky but will be much less sticky than it was before kneading. The trick in this method is to touch dough lightly and quickly so it does not have a chance to stick much to fingers.
Conventional method: If you prefer, knead the dough by this method, but it will require a little more flour. Push the dough away from you against the work surface with the palm of your hand. Turn it, fold the top third down towards you, and repeat. Continue kneading dough, adding flour 15 ml (1 tbsp) at a time if necessary to prevent excessive sticking, until it is smooth and elastic.

TIPS ON BREADMAKING

● To easily fit bread making into a busy schedule, you can refrigerate the dough. The best time to do this is before its second rise, so that this rise takes place in the refrigerator. If this is not convenient, the dough can be refrigerated after it has just begun its first rise or after shaping. Cover it tightly so it does not dry and try not to keep it longer than twelve hours. In the refrigerator the dough continues to expand slowly and stops once it is thoroughly chilled. Before baking, it should be brought to room temperature and left to finish rising.

● Use dry yeast before the expiry date; after that date, the yeast loses some of its leavening power. 25 g (1 oz) fresh yeast is equivalent to 25 ml (5 tsp) dried yeast – 15 g (½ oz).

● Plaited loaves keep their shape best when made of a stiff dough but are somewhat dry when baked if the dough is too stiff. Add just enough flour to the dough so it can be rolled into ropes for plaiting without sticking to the surface. If too much flour is added or if the surface is floured too much during plaiting, the ropes become flat instead of round.

● Letting the dough rise twice in the bowl helps ensure a bread with an even texture.

● If you let dough rise by setting it on top of stove, be sure to take it off when preheating the oven.

● If it is difficult to judge whether a batch of dough (but not a shaped bread) has risen enough, a common test is to quickly poke it with 2 fingers. If the finger imprints remain, the rising has been sufficient.

● When brushing a loaf with glaze, avoid letting glaze drip onto the tin, especially when using a loaf tin, because it can make bread stick. Wipe excess glaze off the brush against the side of the bowl before brushing glaze on a loaf. To glaze a plaited loaf, brush each section separately.

● Liquid ingredients such as honey are added to the dough from the beginning and provide part of the liquid content. Nuts or large amounts of cheese are generally added to the dough after it has risen so that they will not slow down the rising process.

● If not eating the loaf within a day, a convenient way to store it is to slice, wrap and freeze it; warm before serving.

CHALLAH
(EGG BREAD)

The well-known Jewish egg bread originated in eastern Europe but now is enjoyed by Jews of all origins. Making it at home is most satisfying and those who have never baked bread before will find it surprisingly easy. It can be made with very little sugar, or with a fairly generous amount for a more cakelike loaf. For an article on challah that I wrote for *Bon Appétit* magazine, I explored various techniques for making and shaping the dough, and these are presented here.

MAKES 1 MEDIUM LOAF

120 ml (4 fl oz) plus 30 ml (2 tbsp) warm water, 40–46°C (105–115°F)	2 large eggs, size 1 or 2, at room temperature
12.5 ml (2½ tsp) dried yeast	7.5 ml (1½ tsp) salt
22.5 ml (1½ tbsp) sugar	1 large egg, size 1 or 2, beaten with a pinch of salt, for glaze
about 300–350 g (11–12 oz) unbleached plain flour	
90 ml (6 tbsp) vegetable oil	10–20 ml (2–4 tsp) sesame seeds or 5–15 ml (1–3 tsp) poppy seeds (optional)

Pour 60 ml (4 tbsp) of the warm water into small bowl. Sprinkle yeast over water, then sprinkle 5 ml (1 tsp) of sugar over yeast. Leave to stand until foamy, about 10 minutes. Stir if not smooth. Oil or grease large bowl. Follow instructions for making dough either by hand, in mixer or in food processor.

To make dough by hand: Sift 300 g (11 oz) flour into a large bowl. Make large deep well in centre and add yeast mixture, remaining sugar, oil, eggs, remaining water and salt. Mix ingredients in well with wooden spoon until blended. Mix in flour, first with a spoon, then by hand, until ingredients come together to a dough. Dough should be soft and sticky. Knead dough vigorously on work surface until very smooth and elastic, about 7 minutes; during kneading, add more flour 15 ml (1 tbsp) at a time if dough sticks, adding just enough to make dough manageable. (For hints on kneading, see page 287).

EVERY DAY JEWISH DISHES

To make dough in mixer with dough hook: Sift 300 g (11 oz) of flour into bowl of mixer fitted with dough hook. Make large deep well in centre and add yeast mixture, remaining sugar, oil, eggs, remaining water and salt. Mix at medium-low speed, pushing flour in often at first and scraping dough down occasionally from bowl and hook, until ingredients come together to a dough that just begins to cling to hook, about 7 minutes. Dough should be soft and sticky. Knead by mixing at medium speed, scraping down twice, until dough is smooth, partly clings to hook and almost cleans sides of bowl, about 5 minutes. Pinch dough quickly; if it sticks to your fingers, beat in more flour 15 ml (1 tbsp) at a time until dough is no longer very sticky. If you have added flour, knead dough at medium speed about 2 minutes until soft, smooth and elastic.

To make dough in food processor: Combine 300 g (11 oz) of flour, remaining sugar and salt in food processor fitted with dough blade and process briefly to mix them. Add yeast mixture, oil and eggs. With blades of processor turning, pour in remaining water. Process until ingredients come together to a soft dough. It will not form a ball. Process for about 30 seconds to knead dough. Pinch dough quickly; if it sticks to your fingers, add more flour 15 ml (1 tbsp) at a time until dough is no longer very sticky. Knead again by processing for about 30 seconds or until smooth. Remove dough and shape in rough ball in your hands.

Put dough in oiled bowl and turn dough over to oil all surfaces. Cover with warm, slightly damp towel or cling film and leave to rise in warm draught-free area until doubled in volume, about 1¼ hours.

Remove dough to work surface. Knead dough lightly again to knock out air. Clean bowl if necessary. Return dough to bowl, cover and leave to rise again until doubled, about 1 hour.

Knead dough lightly on work surface, flouring lightly only if dough sticks. Shape as desired (see shapes, opposite).

Cover shaped loaf with warm, slightly damp tea towel and leave to rise until nearly doubled in size, about 1 hour. Meanwhile, position shelf in centre of oven and preheat to 190°C (375°F) mark 5.

Brush risen loaf gently with beaten egg and sprinkle with seeds. Bake until top and bottom of bread are firm and bread sounds hollow when tapped on bottom; for baking times, see shape.

Cool on wire rack. Bread is best on day it is made. (Bread can be kept, wrapped, for 1 day at room temperature; or freeze.)

Challah Shapes

Simple loaf: Oil or grease 20 × 10-cm (8 × 4-inch) loaf tin (for tall loaf) or 23 × 13-cm (9 × 5-inch) tin (for shorter loaf). Pat dough to rough rectangle about 20 × 10 cm (8 × 4 inches) (for smaller tin) or 25 × 13 cm (10 × 5 inches) (for larger). Roll up from longer side, Swiss roll fashion, to obtain cylinder, pressing firmly. Pinch ends and seam tightly. Then roll cylinder again on work surface to press seam further. Place in tin seam side down and bake as follows: 50 minutes for 20 × 10-cm (8 × 4-inch) tin, 40 minutes for 23 × 13-cm (9 × 5-inch). Run thin-bladed knife around bread to unmould only if it sticks.

Free-form plait: Lightly oil baking sheet. Shape dough in rough cylinder and cut dough into 3 equal parts. Knead one part briefly and shape in cylinder. Roll backwards and forwards firmly on working surface, pressing with your hands held flat and elongating cylinder from centre to edges as you roll, to form smooth rope about 51 cm (20 inches) long and about 2 cm (¾ inch) wide and, if desired, tapered slightly at ends. Repeat with other two parts.

To plait dough, put ropes side by side with one end of each closer to you. Join ends far from you, covering end of rope on your right side with end of centre rope, then end of left rope. Press to join. Bring left rope over centre one. Continue bringing outer ropes alternately over centre one, plaiting tightly. Pinch each end and tuck them underneath. Set plaited bread carefully on prepared baking sheet and bake for approximately 40 minutes.

Plaited crown or wreath: Prepare plait as for free-form plaited loaf, but make each rope about 63 cm (25 inches) long and about 1.5 cm (⅝ inch) wide and tapered slightly at ends. Set plaited dough carefully on oiled baking sheet. Bring ends of plait together, curving plait into wreath and pinch ends tightly together. Bake for approximately 35 minutes.

Plait in loaf tin: This technique gives a rectangular loaf with a slight plaited pattern on top. Oil or grease 20 × 10-cm (8 × 4-inch) loaf tin. Prepare plait as for free-form plaited loaf, but make each rope about 25 cm (10 inches) long. Plait tightly, pinch ends and tuck them under. Slip loaf into prepared tin. Bake for approximately 50 minutes. Run thin-bladed knife around bread to unmould it if it sticks.

Spiral loaf: This loaf rises to a dome shape. Lightly oil a baking sheet. Shape dough in a rough cylinder. Roll dough backwards and forwards firmly on work surface, pressing with your hands held flat and elongating the cylinder from centre to edges as you roll, to form smooth rope about 71 cm (28 inches) long and 3.5 cm (1¼ inches) wide. Flour very lightly only if necessary, so dough won't stick. Wind dough around one end in spiral; tuck other end underneath and pinch to attach it to dough. Set bread carefully on prepared baking sheet and bake for approximately 40 minutes.

Flavouring variations

Light challah: Decrease oil quantity to 30 ml (2 tbsp). Increase the water by 30–45 ml (2–3 tbsp).

Rich challah: For a richer bread for dairy meals, substitute 90 ml (6 tbsp) cooled melted butter for oil and warm milk for water.

Sweet challah: Increase sugar to 45–60 ml (3–4 tbsp). The dough will require a few tablespoons more flour. It will take longer to rise than basic challah dough and will rise less, especially if largest quantity of sugar is added. Leave to rise and shape as desired; if using loaf tin, use 20 × 10-cm (8 × 4-inch) size. Bake loaf at 190°C (375°F) mark 5 for 15 minutes. Reduce oven temperature to 180°C (350°F) mark 4 and continue baking according to shape chosen, adding 2–3 minutes to baking time. (If loaf browns too quickly, cover loosely with brown paper or foil.)

Large challah: For a fairly large challah, use these proportions: 450 g (1 lb) flour, 250 ml (8 fl oz) water, 25 ml (5 tsp) yeast, 30 ml (2 tbsp) sugar, 120 ml (4 fl oz) vegetable oil, 2 large eggs, size 1 or 2, and 10 ml (2 tsp) salt. After leaving to rise, shape as a free-form plait. Bake at 180°C (350°F) mark 4 for 1 hour.

SHABBAT BREAKFAST BREAD (KUBANEH)

This unique Yemenite bread, which is baked all night in a tightly covered dish, is prepared for Sabbath breakfast or brunch. It defies all the usual rules for bread baking – it bakes at a very low temperature rather than at high heat, and it is baked covered, so it steams, rather than uncovered. And it is absolutely delicious. When I prepared this for a cooking class on Jewish breads in California, the students were wild about it. Before baking, you can put a few eggs (in their shells) in the baking dish; they come out brown and are a good accompaniment for the bread. In some families, this bread is served with sugar for sprinkling; in others, it is accompanied by Yemenite Tomato Dip (page 163) and Chilli-Garlic Chutney (page 154).

MAKES 8 SERVINGS

12.5 ml (2¼ tsp) dried yeast	65 g (2½ oz) margarine or
75 ml (5 tbsp) lukewarm	butter, cut into pieces
water	175 ml (6 fl oz) boiling water
90 ml (6 tbsp) plus 5 ml	350 g (12 oz) plain flour
(1 tsp) sugar	100 g (4 oz) very soft
7.5 ml (1½ tsp) salt	margarine or butter, for
	spreading on dough

Sprinkle yeast over lukewarm water and add 5 ml (1 tsp) sugar. Leave for 10 minutes until yeast is foamy.

In a mixing bowl, combine remaining sugar, salt, 65 g (2½ oz) margarine and boiling water. Stir until sugar and margarine are completely dissolved. Stir in yeast mixture. Add flour and mix with a wooden spoon until dough becomes difficult to stir. Knead in remaining flour.

Knead dough vigorously on a lightly floured work surface, adding flour by the tablespoon if necessary, until dough is very smooth but still soft, about 10 minutes. Put dough in a clean, oiled bowl, cover with a damp cloth and leave to rise in a warm place for 1 hour or until nearly doubled in volume.

Knock back dough, knead it briefly in bowl, cover and leave to rise again in a warm place for about 1 hour; or refrigerate for 3–4 hours.

Generously rub a deep 1.7-litre (3-pint) baking dish with margarine or butter. Divide dough into 8 pieces. With a lightly oiled rolling pin, roll out one piece on a lightly oiled surface to a rectangle about 0.3-cm (⅛-inch) thick. Spread with about 10 ml (2 tsp) butter or margarine. Roll up like a Swiss roll. Flatten resulting roll by tapping it with your knuckles and spread it with about 5 ml (1 tsp) butter, then roll up in a spiral and place it in baking dish so that spiral design faces up. Continue with remaining pieces of dough, placing them one next to the other and touching each other in dish. If any margarine or butter remains, put it in small pieces on top. Cover with greased paper or foil placed on surface of dough and with a tight lid.

Preheat oven to 110°C (225°F) mark ¼. Bake for 3 hours or until golden brown. Turn out onto a plate, then reverse onto another plate and put back into baking dish, so it is now upside down. Cover and bake for another hour; or reduce oven temperature to lowest setting and bake overnight. (Bread can be baked ahead and reheated in its covered baking dish for about 45 minutes in a 110°C (225°F) mark ¼ oven.) Serve warm.

ONION-PARMESAN PLAIT

Although challah rarely contains dairy products so that it will be a suitable accompaniment for all types of foods, this delicious version, with cheese in the dough and sautéed onions enclosed in each plait, is perfect for a vegetarian or dairy dinner or party. Kosher parmesan cheese, which does not contain rennet, is made in both the United States and Israel.

MAKES 1 MEDIUM LOAF

Challah dough (page 289), made with 5 ml (1 tsp) sugar, 60 ml (4 tbsp) oil, 6.25 ml (1¼ tsp) salt, and remaining ingredient quantities as in challah recipe
65 g (2½ oz) freshly grated parmesan cheese
1 large onion, finely chopped

40 g (1½ oz) unsalted butter
10 ml (2 tsp) dried leaf oregano, crumbled
1 large egg, size 1 or 2, beaten with pinch of salt, for glaze

NOTE: When making dough, sprinkle 5 ml (1 tsp) sugar over yeast mixture. Make dough by any method, adding cheese when ingredients are just mixed. Leave dough to rise twice.

While dough is rising, prepare onion mixture. Pat finely chopped onion dry with several changes of paper towels. Melt butter in a large heavy frying pan over medium-low heat. Add onion and oregano and cook, stirring often, until soft but not brown, about 10 minutes. Reduce heat to low and cook, stirring occasionally, until dry, about 20 minutes. Transfer mixture to bowl and cool.

After dough has risen a second time, lightly oil a baking sheet. Knead dough lightly on work surface, adding flour 15 ml (1 tbsp) at a time only if necessary so that dough can be rolled out; it should still be soft and slightly sticky so that it can be easily pinched around onions.

Roll dough into a 33 × 23-cm (13 × 9-inch) rectangle. Cut dough into three 33 × 7.5-cm (13 × 3-inch) strips. Spoon onion mixture evenly down centre of each strip. Spread mixture over strip, leaving a 1-cm (½-inch) border of dough free of onion on each side. Join long sides of strips by pinching together borders of dough, to form a rope enclosing the onions. Pinch ends and edges to seal very well. Turn over so that seams face down. Roll lightly on surface to smooth seams.

To plait dough, put ropes side by side, with one end of each closer to you. Join ends far from you, covering end of rope on your right side with end of centre rope, then end of left rope. Press to join. Bring left rope over centre one. Continue bringing outer ropes alternately over centre one, plaiting tightly. Pinch each end and tuck them underneath. Set plaited bread carefully on prepared baking sheet.

Cover with warm, slightly damp cloth and leave to rise until nearly doubled in size, about 1 hour. Meanwhile, position shelf in centre of oven and preheat to 190°C (375°F) mark 5.

Brush risen loaf gently with beaten egg. Bake until top and bottom of bread are firm and bread sounds hollow when tapped on bottom, about 40 minutes. Cool on wire rack.

PITA (POCKET BREAD)

Pita, also known as pocket bread, has become popular in recent years. Good pita should be slightly chewy but tender. Pita can be found in most supermarkets. New varieties, such as small pita puffs and wholewheat pita, have been developed.

In Israel freshly baked pita is available everywhere but many people like to bake it at home. One of my in-laws has an authentic Yemenite round clay pita oven, resembling an Indian tandoori oven, that she built with her own hands. To bake the pita, she sticks the dough to the searing-hot sides of the oven, as Indian cooks do when baking *naan*. Other cooks in Israel either use a special electric pita pan, which bakes the pita from above and below, or simply bake pita in a very hot oven.

My mother-in-law adds about 15 ml (1 tbsp) aromatic black caraway seeds (also known simply as 'black seeds') to the dough and they add a wonderful flavour. Sesame pita is made by rolling each ball of dough in sesame seeds before flattening it.

Pita tastes best fresh, but if it gets stale, it can be cut into quarters to make triangles and toasted.

MAKES 8 TO 10 PITAS

25 ml (5 tsp) dried yeast	*450 g (1 lb) strong bread flour*
325 ml (11 fl oz) lukewarm water	*10 ml (2 tsp) salt*

To make dough in a food processor: Sprinkle yeast over 120 ml (4 fl oz) lukewarm water in a bowl and leave for 10 minutes. Stir to dissolve yeast. In a food processor, process flour and salt briefly to mix them. Add remaining water to yeast mixture. With blades of processor turning, gradually pour in yeast-liquid mixture. If dough is too dry to come together, add 15 ml (1 tbsp) water and process again. Process for 1 minute to knead dough.

To make dough by hand: Sift flour into a bowl and make a well in centre. Sprinkle yeast into well. Pour 120 ml (4 fl oz) water over yeast and leave for 10 minutes. Stir to dissolve yeast. Add remaining water and salt and mix with ingredients in middle of well. Stir in flour and mix well, to obtain a fairly soft dough. When dough becomes difficult to mix with a wooden spoon, mix in remaining flour by hand. If dough is dry, add 15 ml (1 tbsp) water. Knead dough by slapping it vigorously on a lightly floured working surface until dough is very smooth and elastic. If it is very sticky, flour it occasionally while kneading.

Transfer dough to an oiled bowl and turn dough over to oil its entire surface. Cover with a damp tea towel and leave to rise in a warm place for 1–1½ hours or until doubled in volume.

Knead dough again briefly on a floured surface until smooth. Roll it to a thick log. With a floured knife, cut dough in 8 or 10 equal pieces and, with cupped palms, roll each to a smooth ball on an unfloured surface; flour only if dough begins to stick. Put on a floured board or other surface. Cover and leave to rise for about 30 minutes or until doubled in volume. Preheat oven to highest setting.

Lightly flour 2 baking sheets. Using a floured rolling pin, roll 4 balls of dough on a lightly floured surface to 15-cm (6-inch) circles, about 0.5 cm (¼ inch) thick. Try to keep them round, but do not worry if they are a little uneven. Transfer 2 rounds to each baking sheet.

Bake for about 3 minutes until beginning to brown. Turn over and continue baking for 2–3 minutes until firm. Repeat with remaining dough. If not serving pitas immediately, leave to cool on wire racks and keep them wrapped tightly in cling film or plastic bags; freeze those that will not be used within 2 days.

NOTE: Sometimes one or two pitas don't puff enough to form a pocket, but they are still good to eat.

VARIATION
Sesame Pita

Roll each ball of dough in 5 ml (1 tsp) sesame seeds before rolling it out.

BASIC BAGELS

The word *bagel* entered the English language from Yiddish, and bagels are the best-known of Jewish rolls. Many a bar mitzvah or other Jewish party features bagels with cream cheese and lox or smoked white fish, accompanied by thin slices of red onion and tomato. In many families this combination is also a treat for a relaxed breakfast. The bagels are served warm or at room temperature. They are also popular lightly toasted and buttered, and make great sandwiches.

The cooking procedure for bagels is unusual because they are boiled before they are baked. The dough is firmer than for challah or other breads, so the bagels will hold together during the boiling. There are two main types of bagels; egg bagels, as in this recipe, and water bagels, which are represented by our recipe for Garlic Bagels (page 301).

MAKES 12 BAGELS

450 g (1 lb) strong bread flour	*10 ml (2 tsp) sugar*
175 ml (6 fl oz) lukewarm water	*60 ml (4 tbsp) vegetable oil*
12.5 ml (2½ tsp) dried yeast	*2 large eggs, size 1 or 2*
	8.75 ml (1¾ tsp) salt

FOR BOILING AND FOR GLAZE
1.7 litres (3 pints) water	*1 large egg, size 1 or 2,*
22.5 ml (1½ tbsp) sugar	*beaten with a pinch of salt*

Sift flour into a large bowl. Make a well in centre. Pour in 60 ml (4 tbsp) lukewarm water. Sprinkle yeast on top and add 5 ml (1 tsp) sugar. Leave for 10 minutes until yeast is foamy. Add remaining sugar, oil, eggs, remaining water and salt. Mix with a wooden spoon until ingredients begin to come together to a dough. When mixing with a spoon becomes difficult mix in remaining flour by hand.

Knead dough vigorously on a work surface until very smooth and no longer sticky, about 10 minutes. Put dough in a clean oiled bowl, cover with a damp cloth and leave to rise in a warm place for about 1 hour or until light but not doubled in volume. (Dough can be made 1 day ahead; it should be left to rise 30 minutes, then should be knocked back and refrigerated overnight. Be sure it is covered with a

298

damp cloth so it doesn't dry out; let it come to room temperature before continuing.)

To shape bagels, knead dough again lightly. Roll it to a thick log and cut it into 12 pieces with a floured knife. Roll each piece of dough to a very smooth ball by holding it under your cupped palm on an unfloured surface, and rolling it over and over on surface, pressing firmly. The more the dough is rolled, the more even in shape the final bagel will be. Flatten ball slightly. Make a hole by flouring your index finger and pushing it through centre of round of dough. Twirl round of dough around your finger to stretch hole, then insert 2 fingers and continue twirling. Gently pull edges to even out shape of bagel. Cover and leave to rise on floured board for 15 minutes.

Preheat oven to 200°C (400°F) mark 6. Bring water and sugar to the boil in a wide pan. Add 3 or 4 bagels and boil for 1 minute. Turn them over and boil for 1 minute. If holes begin to close, force them open with handle of a wooden spoon. With a slotted spoon, transfer bagels to a cloth or to paper towels. Repeat with remaining bagels.

Put bagels on 2 lightly floured or greased baking sheets. Brush with egg glaze. Bake for about 20 minutes or until browned; if both baking sheets don't fit on centre oven shelf, bake them one above other and switch their positions after 10 minutes. If not serving them right away, cool them on a wire rack and wrap them. They keep for 2 days at room temperature. They can also be frozen and reheated before serving.

TIPS ON MAKING BAGELS

- Bagels should be chewy and therefore are best when made with bread flour. Plain flour can be substituted, but the bagels will be a little softer.
- Homemade bagels have a good, fresh flavour but are not as evenly shaped as commercial ones.
- In the recipes here, the instructions given are for mixing and kneading the dough by hand or for using a food processor. Either technique can be used for any of the bagel recipes. If you prefer to make the dough in a mixer with a dough hook, follow the instructions for mixing by hand; once the dough is mixed, let the machine run until the dough is very smooth.

299

CHEESE AND HERB BAGELS

Most bagels are firm textured, but those made with cheese are more delicate and should be simmered instead of being boiled. I like these with cream cheese and tomato.

MAKES 12 BAGELS

12.5 ml (2½ tsp) dried yeast	7.5 ml (1½ tsp) dried leaf
175 ml (6 fl oz) lukewarm	oregano
water	2.5 ml (½ tsp) dried leaf
10 ml (2 tsp) sugar	thyme
450 g (1 lb) strong bread	8.75 ml (1¾ tsp) salt
flour	75 g (3 oz) unsalted butter,
175 g (6 oz) Swiss cheese,	melted and cooled
grated	2 large eggs, size 1 or 2

FOR BOILING AND FOR GLAZE

1.7 litres (3 pints) water	1 large egg, size 1 or 2,
22.5 ml (1½ tbsp) sugar	beaten with a pinch of salt

To make dough in a food processor, sprinkle yeast over 60 ml (4 tbsp) lukewarm water in a bowl, add 5 ml (1 tsp) sugar and leave for 10 minutes until yeast is foamy. In a food processor, process flour, remaining sugar, cheese, oregano, thyme and remaining salt briefly to mix them. Add butter and eggs and process with a few on/off turns to mix. Add remaining water to yeast mixture. With blades of processor turning, gradually pour in yeast liquid mixture. If dough is too dry to come together, add 15 ml (1 tbsp) water and process again. Process for 1 minute to knead dough.

Put dough in a clean oiled bowl, cover with a damp cloth and leave to rise in a warm place for about 1 hour or until light but not doubled in volume. (Dough can be made 1 day ahead; it should be left to rise for 30 minutes, then should be knocked back and refrigerated overnight. Be sure it is covered with a damp cloth so it doesn't dry out; let it come to room temperature before continuing.)

Shape dough in bagels as in previous recipe. Cover and leave to rise on floured board for 15 minutes.

Preheat oven to 200°C (400°F) mark 6. To simmer bagels, bring water and sugar to the boil. Add 3 or 4 bagels and simmer them over medium heat for 1 minute. Turn them over and simmer for

1 minute. If holes begin to close, force them open with handle of a wooden spoon. With a slotted spoon, transfer them to a cloth or to paper towels. Repeat with remaining bagels.

Put bagels on 2 lightly floured or greased baking sheets. Brush with egg and bake for about 20 minutes or until browned.

GARLIC BAGELS

These are water bagels and are more chewy than those containing egg. Serve them buttered, with scrambled eggs or with cheese.

MAKES 12 BAGELS

450 g (1 lb) strong bread flour	5 ml (1 tsp) sugar
250 ml (8 fl oz) plus 30 ml (2 tbsp) lukewarm water	75 g (3 oz) unsalted butter
12.5 ml (2½ tsp) dried yeast	4 garlic cloves, finely chopped
	8.75 ml (1¾ tsp) salt

FOR BOILING AND FOR GLAZE

1.7 litres (3 pints) water	1 large egg, size 1 or 2,
22.5 ml (1½ tbsp) sugar	beaten with a pinch of salt

Sift flour into a large bowl. Make a well in centre. Pour in 60 ml (4 tbsp) lukewarm water. Sprinkle yeast on top and add sugar. Leave for 10 minutes until yeast is foamy.

Melt butter in a medium saucepan, add garlic and cook over low heat, stirring, for about 1 minute or until softened but not brown. Leave to cool slightly.

To well in flour, add garlic and butter in which it was cooked, remaining water and salt. Mix with a wooden spoon until ingredients begin to come together to a dough. When mixing with a spoon becomes difficult, mix in remaining flour by hand.

Knead dough vigorously on a work surface until very smooth and no longer sticky, about 10 minutes. Put dough in a clean oiled bowl, cover with a damp cloth and leave to rise in a warm place for about 1 hour or until light but not doubled in volume. (Dough can be made 1 day ahead; it should be left to rise for 30 minutes, then should be knocked back, covered with a damp cloth, and refrigerated overnight. Let it come to room temperature before continuing.)

Shape, boil and bake bagels as in Basic Bagels (page 298).

WHOLEWHEAT BAGELS

Honey gives these bagels a touch of sweetness. They are good with smoked turkey or chicken, or for breakfast with cream cheese or butter.

MAKES 12 BAGELS

225 g (8 oz) strong bread flour	*12.5 ml (2½ tsp) dried yeast*
225 g (8 oz) wholewheat flour	*60 ml (4 tbsp) honey*
175 ml (6 fl oz) lukewarm water	*60 ml (4 tbsp) oil*
	2 large eggs, size 1 or 2
	8.75 ml (1¾ tsp) salt

FOR BOILING AND FOR GLAZE

1.7 litres (3 pints) water	*1 large egg, size 1 or 2, beaten*
22.5 ml (1½ tbsp) sugar	*with a pinch of salt*

Sift both types flour into a large bowl. Make a well in the centre. Pour in 60 ml (4 tbsp) lukewarm water. Sprinkle yeast on top and add 10 ml (2 tsp) honey. Leave for 10 minutes until yeast is foamy. Add remaining honey, oil, eggs, remaining water and salt. Mix with a wooden spoon until ingredients begin to come together to a dough. When mixing with a spoon becomes difficult, mix in remaining flour by hand.

Knead dough vigorously on a work surface until very smooth and no longer sticky, about 10 minutes. Put dough in a clean oiled bowl, cover with a damp cloth and leave to rise in a warm place for about 1½ hours or until light but not doubled in volume. (Dough can be made 1 day ahead; it should be left to rise for 45 minutes, then should be knocked back, covered with a damp cloth and refrigerated overnight. Let it come to room temperature before continuing.)

Shape, boil and bake bagels as in Basic Bagels (page 298).

VARIATION
Walnut and Raisin Bagels

Add 7.5 ml (1½ tsp) ground cinnamon to dough with the honey. Add 75 g (3 oz) coarsely chopped raisins and 25 g (1 oz) chopped walnuts to finished dough before letting it rise. Knead to distribute raisins and walnuts evenly. Bake these bagels at 190°C (375°F) mark 5 for 20–25 minutes or until browned.

SHABBAT PASTRY ROLLS (JIHNUN)

This rich Yemenite pastry is made of very thin, tender layers of dough rolled up in cigar shapes. In many Yemenite homes it is baked overnight for *Shabbat* and served for breakfast or brunch, with sugar for sprinkling or with Yemenite Tomato Dip (page 163) and Browned Eggs (page 216).

Most often the dough for Jihnun is enriched with margarine, but it can be flavoured instead with *samneh*, the aromatic Yemenite-style clarified butter that resembles Indian ghee.

MAKES 6 GENEROUS SERVINGS

425 g (15 oz) plain flour	*1 large egg, size 1 or 2*
30 ml (2 tbsp) sugar	*300 ml (½ pint) water*
5 ml (1 tsp) baking powder	*175 g (6 oz) margarine, cut*
7.5 ml (1½ tsp) salt	*into 6 pieces*

Combine flour, sugar, baking powder and salt in a food processor and process to blend. Add egg and 250 ml (8 fl oz) water and process with on/off turns to mix. With motor running, gradually add remaining water, about 60 ml (4 tbsp), adding enough so mixture comes together to a smooth, fairly stiff dough. It will be sticky.

Remove from processor. Knead dough well by slapping dough vigorously on the work surface. Divide into 6 pieces and knead each one with a slapping motion until smooth. Roll each in your palm to a ball. Put on an oiled plate or tray, cover with cling film and refrigerate for at least 4 hours or overnight.

Oil your working surface and rolling pin. Leave margarine to stand at room temperature until very soft. Roll out 1 ball of dough on oiled surface to very thin 30-cm (12-inch) square. To help stretch dough, pull it gently from time to time by hand, until very thin. If dough tears, simply press it together. Spread with a piece of soft margarine. Fold in half, then in half again to make a long strip. Roll up strip from a short side in a tight cylinder. Repeat with 5 remaining pieces of dough. Put in greased, shallow 20-cm (8-inch) square baking dish. Cover with foil and a lid and refrigerate for at least 2 or up to 8 hours.

Preheat oven to lowest setting. Bake pastries for 13–14 hours or until golden brown. Serve hot.

CAKES, BISCUITS AND DESSERTS

 When I lived in Israel, my relatives, friends and neighbours always had a pastry on hand during the weekends. 'Come over for coffee and cake' was a frequent invitation. This practice enabled us to get together easily and at a moment's notice and to enjoy tasting each other's homemade desserts. French Jews liked to bake fruit tarts, Jews from the Middle East specialized in nut-filled filo pastries and American Jews often served chiffon cakes.

Most of all, I notice an Austro-Hungarian influence on Jewish Israeli baking. Thus, the most popular desserts are light nut cakes and tortes, and all sorts of Viennese pastries. Jews of every extraction also love Israeli-style Bavarian cream, which is prepared in a different way from the classic dessert but still is light, smooth and creamy.

Since Jewish bakeries and delicatessens are found in many American cities, they helped make several European pastries and desserts well known in the United States and these became associated with Jewish cooking. Strudel, rugelach, blintzes and cheesecake, for example, originated in eastern Europe and were adopted by Jews, who continued to prepare them after they emigrated to the New World.

For serving after meals that feature a meat or poultry main course, Jewish cooks have developed a variety of desserts that do not contain dairy products. Many are based on fruit, and therefore are light, refreshing and relatively low in calories. Cakes and pastries are often made in two versions, depending on how they will be served: with non-dairy margarine so they will be pareve and thus suitable for all meals, or with butter for dairy-meals and for tea time.

Since cakes and other desserts are most often prepared for festive occasions, many of them appear in the holiday chapters of this book.

SOURED CREAM COFFEE CAKE WITH WALNUTS

When I was growing up, a slice of this tender cake with a ripple of cinnamon-nut filling running through it was a *Shabbat* morning treat that my brother and I looked forward to. This is the type of simple, honey cake that nobody can resist, whether it is served with a cup of coffee or a glass of milk.

MAKES 10 TO 12 SERVINGS

100 g (4 oz) walnuts, chopped
7.5 ml (1½ tsp) ground cinnamon
265 g (9½ oz) sugar
200 g (7 oz) plain flour
7.5 ml (1½ tsp) baking powder

2.5 ml (½ tsp) bicarbonate of soda
5 ml (1 tsp) vanilla essence
350 ml (12 fl oz) soured cream
100 g (4 oz) unsalted butter
3 large eggs, size 1 or 2

Position shelf in centre of oven and preheat to 180°C (350°F) mark 4. Generously butter a 24-cm (9½-inch) Bundt tin, kugelhopf mould, or fluted ring tin, taking care to butter ring and each fluted section. Mix walnuts, cinnamon and 45 ml (3 tbsp) sugar. Sift flour, baking powder and bicarbonate of soda into a bowl. Stir vanilla into soured cream.

Cream butter in a large bowl until light. Add 225 g (8 oz) sugar and beat until smooth and fluffy. Beat in eggs, one by one. At low speed, stir in flour mixture alternately with soured cream mixture, each in 2 portions.

Pour slightly less than half the mixture into prepared tin. Sprinkle with half the cinnamon-walnut mixture. Gently spoon dollops of cake mix over mixture, using just enough to cover it. Sprinkle with remaining walnut mixture. Gently drop remaining cake mix in dollops over it. Spread gently to cover nut mixture. Bake for about 55 minutes or until fine skewer inserted in cake comes out clean.

Cool cake in tin for 10 minutes. Run a thin-bladed flexible knife around ring but not around sides of tin. Invert cake onto a wire rack and cool completely. Transfer cake to a serving plate. (Cake can be kept, wrapped, for up to 2 days at room temperature or 3 days in refrigerator.) Serve at room temperature.

CHOCOLATE-ORANGE MARBLE CAKE

A lmost every Ashkenazic Jewish mother has her favourite recipe for marble cake, made with chocolate and white mixtures. This is a particularly rich version that makes use of a generous amount of chocolate for the dark mixture and freshly grated orange rind to flavour the white mixture.

MAKES 10 TO 12 SERVINGS

---

100 g (4 oz) plain chocolate, chopped
225 g (8 oz) unsalted butter or non-dairy margarine, at room temperature
275 g (10 oz) sugar

4 large eggs, size 1 or 2, at room temperature
200 g (7 oz) cake flour, sifted
5 ml (1 tsp) vanilla essence
30 ml (2 tbsp) finely grated orange rind

Preheat oven to 180°C (350°F) mark 4. Butter and flour a 23-cm (9-inch) spring clip tin with 6-cm (2½-inch) side, tapping tin to remove excess flour.

Melt chocolate in medium bowl set above hot water over low heat. Stir until smooth. Remove from above water and leave to cool.

Cream butter in a large bowl, if possible using paddle beater of mixer, until butter is soft, smooth and most of it clings to side of bowl. Gradually beat in sugar. Beat mixture at medium speed until it is very pale, smooth and fluffy, about 4 minutes. Beat in 3 eggs, one by one, beating thoroughly after each and scraping mixture down occasionally. Beat fourth egg in small bowl. Add it to mixture, 15 ml (1 tbsp) at a time, beating thoroughly after each addition. With last few additions, mixture will look like it is beginning to separate but it will come together when flour is added.

Sprinkle about one quarter of flour over mixture and stir it in, using spatula. Stir in vanilla. Stir in remaining flour in 3 batches. Mix well; be sure there are no lumps.

Transfer 2 cupfuls mixture to a bowl and stir in grated orange rind. Stir cool melted chocolate into remaining mixture.

Spoon about half the chocolate mixture into prepared tin without spreading. Spoon about half the orange mixture over chocolate mixture. Spoon remaining chocolate mixture on top. Spoon remaining orange mixture over chocolate mixture. Tap tin several times on work surface to level mixture. Draw knife through mixture several times with swirling motion to marble them slightly; chocolate mixture should show only slightly at top. Tap tin again several times on work surface to level.

Bake until fine skewer inserted in centre of cake comes out completely clean, about 50 minutes. Cool in tin on wire rack 10 minutes. Release spring and remove sides of tin. Cool cake to lukewarm. Turn over onto another rack. Carefully remove base of tin with aid of palette knife. (Cake can be kept, wrapped in cling film or foil, for up to 3 days at cool room temperature or up to 1 week in refrigerator; or it can be frozen.) Serve cake at room temperature.

VANILLA POUND CAKE

These cakes are popular items at Jewish bakeries and also are favourites for making at home, since many people prefer a freshly baked, simple un-iced cake of this type for enjoying with a cup of tea or coffee.

MAKES 10 TO 12 SERVINGS

165 g (5½ oz) plain flour	3 large eggs, size 1 or 2, at
6.25 ml (1¼ tsp) baking	room temperature
powder	10 ml (2 tsp) vanilla essence
175 g (6 oz) unsalted butter	75 ml (5 tbsp) double cream,
or margarine, at room	single cream, milk or water
temperature	icing sugar, for dusting
250 g (9 oz) sugar	(optional)

Preheat oven to 180°C (350°F) mark 4. Butter and flour a non-stick 23 × 12-cm (9 × 5-inch) loaf tin, tapping tin to remove excess flour. Sift flour with baking powder.

Cream butter in a large bowl, if possible using paddle beater of mixer, at medium speed until butter is soft, smooth and most of it clings to side of bowl. Gradually beat in sugar. Beat mixture at medium speed until it is very pale, smooth and fluffy, about 4 minutes. Beat in 2 eggs, one by one, at medium speed, beating thoroughly after each. Beat third egg in small bowl. Add it to mixture gradually, beating thoroughly after each addition. Mixture may

307

look like it is beginning to separate but it will come together when flour is added.

With mixer at low speed, add about one quarter of flour mixture to mixture. Blend in vanilla and about 15 ml (1 tbsp) cream. Blend in remaining flour in 3 batches, alternating with remaining cream. Stir at low speed just until blended.

Spoon mixture carefully into tin. Smooth top with spatula. Tap tin a few times on work surface to level mixture. Set tin in oven with a short side of loaf tin facing back of oven. Bake until fine skewer inserted in centre of cake comes out completely clean, about 50 minutes.

Cool cake in tin on wire rack for 10 minutes. Run thin-bladed flexible knife around edges of cake and turn cake out onto wire rack. Carefully turn cake back over and cool it completely. (Cake can be kept, wrapped in cling film or foil, up to 3 days at cool room temperature or up to 1 week in refrigerator; or it can be frozen for about 2 months.)

Serve cake at room temperature. Sift icing sugar over it if desired. Cut cake into 1–2-cm (½–¾-inch) slices with a serrated knife.

RASPBERRY ALMOND TART

Fresh fruit tarts are a beloved dessert among French Jews, because they are beautiful, enticing and rich but do not require dairy products.

MAKES 6 TO 8 SERVINGS

French Sweet Pastry (recipe follows), chilled until firm

ALMOND FILLING

90 g (3½ oz) blanched almonds	*1 large egg, size 1 or 2*
100 g (4 oz) sugar	*1 large egg yolk, size 1 or 2*
75 g (3 oz) unsalted margarine, at room temperature	*15 ml (1 tbsp) raspberry brandy or kirsch*
	30 ml (2 tbsp) plain flour

150 g (5 oz) redcurrant jelly	*275 g (10 oz) fresh raspberries*

Butter a 25-cm (10-inch) round flan tin with removable bottom. Leave pastry dough to soften for 1 minute before rolling it. Roll out dough on a cold, lightly floured surface to a round about 0.5 cm (¼ inch) thick. Roll up dough loosely around rolling pin and unroll it over tin. Gently ease dough into tin. Using your thumb, gently push dough down slightly at top edge of tin, so top edge is thicker than remaining dough. Roll rolling pin across tin to cut off dough. With your finger and thumb, push up top edge of dough all around tin so it is about 0.5 cm (¼ inch) higher than rim. Prick dough all over with a fork. Refrigerate for 1 hour or cover with cling film and refrigerate overnight or freeze for up to 2 weeks.

Position a shelf in lower third of oven and preheat to 220°C (425°F) mark 7. Heat a baking sheet on shelf in oven.

Grind almonds with 30 ml (2 tbsp) sugar to a fine powder. Beat margarine until soft. Add remaining sugar and beat until mixture is smooth. In a small bowl, beat egg with yolk. Gradually add beaten eggs to margarine mixture. Add brandy. Stir in almond mixture and flour.

Spread almond filling in lined flan tin. (It will seem like a small amount but it puffs.) Bake tart on hot baking sheet for 10 minutes. Reduce temperature to 180°C (350°F) mark 4 and bake for another 30 minutes or until filling sets and is golden brown. Transfer to a wire rack to cool.

Melt jelly over low heat, stirring often. Brush about three-quarters of the jelly on tart. Arrange berries on top. If desired, dab berries very lightly with jelly. Serve tart at room temperature.

FRENCH SWEET PASTRY

This biscuit-like dough makes a delicious base for fruit tarts, such as Raspberry Almond Tart on page 308.

MAKES ENOUGH FOR A 25-CM (10-INCH) ROUND FLAN

---

150 g (5 oz) plain
  flour
25 g (1 oz) cake flour
75 g (3 oz) sugar
1.25 ml (¼ tsp) salt

100 g (4 oz) unsalted
  margarine or butter, very
  cold, cut into pieces
1 large egg, size 1 or 2,
  lightly beaten

To make pastry in a food processor: Combine both types of flour, sugar and salt in a food processor. Process briefly to blend. Scatter margarine pieces over mixture. Mix using on/off turns until mixture resembles coarse breadcrumbs. Pour egg evenly over mixture in processor. Process with on/off turns, scraping down occasionally, until dough forms sticky crumbs that can easily be pressed together but does not come together in a ball. If dough is too sticky, sprinkle with 15 ml (1 tbsp) flour and process again. Transfer dough to a work surface.

To make pastry by hand: Sift both types flour onto a work surface and make a well in centre. Add egg, sugar and salt and mix using your fingertips. Pound margarine to soften it and cut it in pieces. Add it to well and quickly mix with other ingredients in well until partly mixed. Gradually draw in flour to make coarse crumbs. Toss mixture, rubbing it between your fingers, until crumbs begin to stick together.

Blend dough further by pushing about one quarter of it away from you and smearing it with heel of your hand against work surface. Repeat with remaining dough in 3 batches. Repeat with each batch if dough is not yet well blended.

Using a spatula, transfer dough to a sheet of cling film, wrap it and push it together. Shape dough in a flat round. Refrigerate for 4 hours. (Dough can be kept for 2 days in refrigerator.)

MERINGUE-TOPPED CHEESECAKE

A meringue topping adds to the impression of lightness of this cheesecake made in the eastern European style. The lemon-scented filling, made of cottage cheese and cream cheese, is also lighter than that of many cheesecakes. Perfect for Savuot, it also makes a lovely summer dessert when accompanied by a mixture of strawberries and raspberries.

MAKES 8 TO 10 SERVINGS

SWEET PASTRY

2 large egg yolks, size 1 or 2	150 g (5 oz) sugar
30 ml (2 tbsp) soured cream	pinch of salt
165 g (5½ oz) plain flour	90 g (3½ oz) unsalted butter
5 ml (1 tsp) baking powder	or margarine

LEMON-CHEESE FILLING

450 g (1 lb) creamed cottage cheese	4 large eggs, size 1 or 2, separated
450 g (1 lb) cream cheese, softened	1 large egg yolk, size 1 or 2 grated rind of 1 lemon,
200 g (7 oz) sugar	7.5 ml (1½ tsp)
	10 ml (2 tsp) vanilla essence

MERINGUE TOPPING

3 large egg whites, size 1 or 2	75 g (3 oz) sugar
1.25 ml (¼ tsp) cream of tartar	

For the sweet pastry, beat egg yolks with soured cream and set aside. Combine flour, baking powder, sugar and salt in a food processor. Process briefly to blend. Scatter butter pieces over mixture. Mix using on/off turns until mixture resembles coarse breadcrumbs. Pour soured cream mixture evenly over mixture in processor. Process with on/off turns, scraping down occasionally, until dough forms sticky crumbs that can easily be pressed together and just begins to come together in a ball. If mixture is dry, add 2.5 ml (½ tsp) water and process briefly again.

Pat pastry into a lightly buttered 23–25-cm (9–10-inch) spring clip

311

tin to line it 5 cm (2 inches) up side. Prick base and sides lightly. Freeze for 20 minutes. Preheat oven to 190°C (375°F) mark 5. Bake pastry case for 15 minutes, until very light golden. Remove from oven. Reduce oven temperature to 180°C (350°F) mark 4. Leave to cool while making filling.

Force cottage cheese through a strainer, pushing with back of a spoon. Beat cream cheese with 175 g (6 oz) sugar in mixer until smooth. Beat in 5 egg yolks, one by one. Stir in cottage cheese, lemon rind and vanilla. Whisk 4 egg whites until soft peaks form. Beat in remaining 30 ml (2 tbsp) sugar and whip until stiff but not dry. Fold into cheese mixture. Transfer to pastry case. Bake for 50–60 minutes or until top is light brown, set and beginning to crack. Remove from oven, set tin on wire rack and leave to cool for 30 minutes. Leave oven at 180°C (350°F) mark 4.

For the topping, combine egg whites, cream of tartar and sugar in bowl of mixer. Set bowl in a pan of hot water over very low heat and stir whites with whisk for about 3 minutes or until mixture is slightly warm and sugar dissolves. Remove from pan of water and whip at high speed of mixer until whites are stiff. Spread over filling, using palette knife to decorate it in a ridged design if desired. Return cake to oven and bake for about 8–10 minutes or until meringue is light beige.

Cool cake to room temperature. Stick 5 wooden cocktail sticks at edges of cake and 1 in centre and cover cake loosely with paper towel; this keeps paper towel from sticking to meringue. Refrigerate cake for 2 hours before serving. (Cake can be kept for 2 days in refrigerator.) Cut cake and serve cold.

CINNAMON-NUT-RAISIN CRESCENTS (RUGELACH)

Crescent shaped rugelach, of eastern European origin, may be the best-known Jewish biscuits in America – and for good reason. When made with a rich, flaky dough like this one, they are absolutely irresistible. Jewish bakeries like Canter's in Los Angeles present these in a variety of fillings, shapes and colours: cinnamon-walnut, chocolate, cheese, apricot and raspberry.

With this easy-to-handle cream cheese and soured cream dough, rugelach are a delight to prepare at home.

MAKES 48 SMALL BISCUITS

CREAM CHEESE DOUGH

175 g (6 oz) cream cheese
225 g (8 oz) cold unsalted
  butter
225 g (8 oz) plain flour

1.25 ml (¼ tsp) salt
75 ml (5 tbsp) soured cream
5 ml (1 tsp) water, if needed

WALNUT-RAISIN-CINNAMON FILLING

100 g (4 oz) sugar
15 ml (1 tbsp) ground
  cinnamon

100 g (4 oz) walnuts, finely
  chopped
75 g (3 oz) raisins, chopped

Cut cream cheese into 15 ml (1 tbsp) pieces and leave to soften at room temperature. Cut butter into small pieces of about 7.5 ml (½ tbsp) and keep cold until ready to use.

In a food processor combine flour, salt and butter and process with on/off turns until mixture resembles coarse breadcrumbs. Add cream cheese and soured cream, distributing them fairly evenly over mixture. Process with on/off turns until dough just holds together. Add 5 ml (1 tsp) water if necessary. Wrap dough, press together to a ball and flatten to a round. Refrigerate for 4 hours or up to 2 days.

Lightly butter 2 or 3 baking sheets. Mix sugar and cinnamon for filling. Divide dough into 4 pieces. Press one quarter of dough to a round, then flatten it. Roll it to a 23-cm (9-inch) circle about 0.25 cm (⅛ inch) thick. Sprinkle one quarter of sugar-cinnamon mixture (about 30 ml (2 tbsp)) all over circle, then sprinkle one quarter of nuts and raisins near outer edge of circle. Press with rolling pin so they adhere to dough. Using a heavy knife, cut circle in 12 wedges, making each cut with a sharp movement of heel of knife. Roll up tightly from wide end to point; be sure filling is enclosed, since raisins can burn if exposed. Put biscuits on baking sheets, with points of triangles facing down, spacing them about 2.5 cm (1 inch) apart. Curve each to a crescent, if desired. Refrigerate while shaping more biscuits. Refrigerate all for at least 20 minutes before baking. (Unbaked biscuits can be frozen.)

Preheat oven to 180°C (350°F) mark 4. Bake biscuits for 22–25 minutes or until light golden. Cool on wire racks. (Biscuits can be kept for 4 days in airtight containers.)

CRISP ALMOND SLICES (MANDELBROT)

*M*andelbrot is a Yiddish word meaning 'almond bread', and indeed, the almond-studded dough is first shaped in a loaf and baked. It is then cut in slices and these are baked again, to make toasted biscuits. The double baking dries the biscuits so they keep well, and they therefore are best enjoyed with a drink.

MAKES ABOUT 36 BISCUITS

3 large eggs, size 1 or 2	*7.5 ml (1½ tsp) baking*
275 g (10 oz) sugar	*powder*
250 ml (8 fl oz) vegetable oil	*1.25 ml (¼ tsp) salt*
10 ml (2 tsp) grated lemon	*100 g (4 oz) slivered almonds,*
rind	*chopped*
5 ml (1 tsp) vanilla essence	*15 ml (1 tbsp) sugar mixed*
450 g (1 lb) plain flour	*with 5 ml (1 tsp) ground*
	cinnamon, for sprinkling

Grease a baking sheet. In a mixer bowl, beat eggs, sugar and oil until blended. Beat in lemon rind and vanilla. Sift flour with baking powder and salt. Add to egg mixture. Stir on low speed of mixer just until blended. Stir in almonds on low speed.

Shape dough into 4 rolls each about 5 cm (2 inches) in diameter; their shape will not be very even, as dough is sticky. Place on baking sheet. Refrigerate for 30 minutes. Preheat oven to 180°C (350°F) mark 4. Use spatula to smooth dough and to push again into log shape, since it will have relaxed and spread a little. Sprinkle top with sugar and cinnamon and pat to make it adhere to sides as well.

Bake for 30 minutes or until lightly browned and set. Transfer carefully to a board and leave to stand until cool enough to handle. With a sharp knife, carefully cut in diagonal slices about 1 cm (½ inch) thick; dough will be slightly soft inside. Return slices to cleaned baking sheets in one layer; you will need 2 or 3 baking sheets.

Bake for about 7 minutes per side or until lightly toasted so they are beige and dotted in places with golden brown; side of biscuit touching baking sheet will brown first. Watch carefully so biscuits don't brown throughout. Cool on a wire rack. Keep in airtight containers. (They keep for about 2 weeks.)

CHOCOLATE-FILLED WALNUT RINGS

I learned to prepare filled biscuits of this type in Israel, where they are sometimes called 'naughty children' for obvious reasons! They are made of a round base spread with filling and topped with a ring-shaped biscuit, so that the filling peeks out. Instead of the chocolate filling, sometimes date filling or red jam is used.

MAKES 16 LARGE BISCUITS

WALNUT COOKIES

260 g (9¼ oz) walnuts	20 ml (4 tsp) grated lemon
175 g (6 oz) sugar	rind
65 g (2½ oz) plain flour	75 g (3 oz) unsalted butter or
6 large egg whites, size 1 or	margarine, melted and
2, at room temperature	cooled

CHOCOLATE-WALNUT FILLING

100 g (4 oz) plain or bitter	50 g (2 oz) icing sugar, sifted
chocolate, chopped	50 g (2 oz) unsalted butter or
about 100 g (4 oz) walnuts	margarine, softened

Preheat oven to 180°C (350°F) mark 4. Butter and flour 2 baking sheets. Mark 16 circles, using a 6-cm (2½-inch) cutter and spacing them about 4 cm (1½ inches) apart.

Grind nuts with 90 ml (6 tbsp) sugar in a food processor until as fine as possible, scraping inwards occasionally; they should remain light and not pasty. Transfer to a large bowl. Sift flour onto nuts and stir until blended.

Whip egg whites in a large bowl until soft peaks form. Gradually beat in remaining 90 ml (6 tbsp) sugar and whip at high speed until whites are stiff and shiny but not dry.

Gently fold lemon rind and walnut mixture into egg whites. When mixture is nearly blended, gradually pour in cool melted butter while folding. Fold lightly but quickly just until mixture is blended.

Using a piping bag and medium star tube, pipe rings of mixture in 8 of the marked circles: one ring at border of each circle and a second ring inside first and touching it. Pipe remaining mixture in complete rounds in remaining marked circles by beginning at centre and piping in a spiral motion from centre to fill circle.

Bake biscuits for about 15 minutes or until light brown. Do not over-bake or they will be bitter. Transfer them immediately to a wire rack.

Melt chocolate in a small bowl above hot water over low heat. Stir until smooth, then leave to cool. Grind nuts with 30 ml (2 tbsp) icing sugar in a food processor until as fine as possible.

Cream butter in a small bowl, add remaining 90 ml (6 tbsp) icing sugar, and beat until smooth and fluffy. Stir in chocolate, then nuts.

When biscuits are cool, spread filling on full rounds, using about 15 ml (1 tbsp) filling per biscuit. Set rings on top. Refrigerate for 30 minutes. (Biscuits can be kept, covered, for 3 days in refrigerator.)

HONEY-GLAZED BISCUITS WITH WALNUTS (TAYGLACH)

Tayglach are a sweet and sticky confection of pastry and nuts in a honey-flavoured syrup, best served with coffee or tea. They are a speciality for the Jewish New Year, and many Jewish bakeries prepare them only for this holiday. Actually, there are three types of tayglach; those served in a thin syrup, those drained of their syrup, or as in this version, those left in thick syrup until firm.

MAKES ABOUT 30 PIECES

165 g (5½ oz) plain flour	pinch of salt
1.25 ml (¼ tsp) baking powder	2 large eggs, size 1 or 2
	3 large egg yolks, size 1 or 2
1.25 ml (¼ tsp) ground ginger	30 ml (2 tbsp) vegetable oil

HONEY SYRUP

350 g (12 oz) honey	5 ml (1 tsp) ground ginger
225 g (8 oz) sugar	

100 g (4 oz) walnuts, coarsely chopped	about 75 g (3 oz) desiccated coconut, for rolling

Preheat oven to 180°C (350°F) mark 4. Oil 2 large baking sheets.

Sift flour with baking powder, ginger and salt into a medium bowl. Make a well in centre and add eggs, yolks and oil. Stir until combined. Knead on a lightly floured surface to a soft, smooth dough. If dough is very sticky, knead in about 15 ml (1 tbsp) more flour.

Cut dough into 8 pieces with floured knife. Using both hands, roll a piece of dough on a lightly floured surface into a thin rope about 1 cm (½ inch) in diameter. Cut rope into 1-cm (½-inch) lengths, using the heel of a floured heavy knife. Repeat with remaining pieces of dough. Place dough pieces on baking sheets without letting them touch each other. Bake for about 10 minutes or until light brown underneath. Remove from oven.

Combine honey, sugar and ginger in large heavy saucepan. Cook over low heat, stirring occasionally, to dissolve sugar. Bring to the boil over moderate heat, taking care that mixture does not boil over. Cook over low heat for about 5 minutes, or until syrup reaches 130°C (260°F) on sugar thermometer (hard-ball stage).

Carefully add baked tayglach and chopped nuts to syrup and simmer over medium-low heat, stirring occasionally, for about 10 minutes or until tayglach are golden brown. Meanwhile, line a large baking sheet with foil and oil the foil.

Stir tayglach mixture to distribute nuts evenly and spoon mixture onto lined baking sheet. Flatten so that tayglach form one layer and leave to cool completely.

Turn tayglach over onto a board and carefully peel off foil. Cut into 2.5-cm (1-inch) squares or diamonds. Roll in grated coconut. Store in shallow airtight containers at room temperature until ready to serve. Serve in sweet papers.

NOTE: If tayglach stick together while being stored, cut them into pieces again; or, if making them to keep for some time, keep them in large blocks and cut them as needed. Alternatively, keep them in a large enough container so they do not touch one another.

CHOCOLATE COCONUT RUM BALLS

These chocolate balls are fun to make because they taste different every time, depending on what type of cake or biscuits you use to make them. They are a frequently made confection in Jewish homes. Although originally this was a way to use up leftover cake or biscuits, now people even buy biscuits in order to make these sweets. My mother prefers to use chocolate cake so the flavour is most intense, but almost any cake or biscuits will give good results.

Rum balls don't necessarily contain rum. The main thing is they contain chocolate, cake or biscuit crumbs, and a variety of other goodies – raisins, nuts, coconut or all three. They can be rolled in coconut, chopped almonds or chocolate vermicelli.

MAKES ABOUT 30 BALLS

40 g (1½ oz) raisins (optional)	120 ml (4 fl oz) sweet wine or orange juice
30 ml (2 tbsp) rum or brandy, or chocolate, orange or chocolate-orange liqueur (optional)	75 g (3 oz) unsalted butter or margarine, at room temperature, cut into pieces
100 g (4 oz) bitter or plain chocolate, chopped	100 g (4 oz) plain biscuits
30 ml (2 tbsp) cocoa powder	25 g (1 oz) chopped pecans or walnuts
30 ml (2 tbsp) sugar	about 115 g (4½ oz) desiccated coconut

Combine raisins and rum in a jar and cover. Leave to stand for about 1 hour for raisins to absorb flavour.

Heat chocolate, cocoa, sugar and wine or juice in a heavy, small saucepan over low heat, stirring often, until chocolate melts. Remove from heat and add butter. Stir until melted. Crush biscuits to fairly coarse crumbs, then stir crumbs into chocolate mixture. Add nuts and raisins with their rum. Mix well. Cover and refrigerate until firm enough to shape in balls, about 1½–2 hours.

Shape mixture into balls, using about 10 ml (2 tsp) for each. Put on plates and refrigerate for 5 minutes to firm slightly. Put coconut in a shallow bowl or tray and roll balls in it. Set balls on plates. Refrigerate for 1 hour before serving. (Can be kept in an airtight container for up to 1 week in refrigerator.) Serve in sweet papers.

ASHKENAZIC POPPY SEED BISCUITS

A favourite among Jews from central Europe and Alsace, these poppy seed-topped biscuits are made from rich One, Two, Three Dough.

MAKES ABOUT 48 BISCUITS

| One, Two, Three Biscuit Dough (page 137) | 30–60 ml (2–4 tbsp) poppy seeds |

Prepare dough and refrigerate. Use one quarter of dough at a time, rolling it out on a lightly floured surface until slightly less than 0.5 cm (¼ inch) thick. Using a 7.5-cm (3-inch) biscuit cutter, cut in circles. Sprinkle each with about 1.25 ml (⅛–¼ teaspoon) poppy seeds, according to your taste. Press to make them adhere to dough. Put biscuits on greased baking sheet, spacing them about 2.5 cm (1 inch) apart and refrigerate. Refrigerate scraps.

Roll remaining dough and scraps and shape more biscuits. Refrigerate biscuits for at least 30 minutes before baking to firm dough. (They can be kept, covered, overnight in refrigerator.)

Preheat oven to 190°C (375°F) mark 5. Bake biscuits for 8–9 minutes or until they are very light brown at edges.

STRAWBERRY PECAN SQUARES

This delicious Austrian-style bar biscuit is popular in Israel. It uses a single biscuit dough that serves both as a base and as a crumbly streusel topping.

MAKES ABOUT 28 SMALL BARS

PECAN BISCUIT DOUGH

95 g (3¾ oz) pecans	10 ml (2 tsp) grated lemon
3 large egg yolks, size 1 or 2	rind
100 g (4 oz) sugar	225 g (8 oz) unsalted butter
1.25 ml (¼ tsp) salt	or margarine, cut in 16
10 ml (2 tsp) vanilla	cubes, cold
essence	200 g (7 oz) plain flour

TOPPING

150 g (5 oz) strawberry	25 g (1 oz) plain flour
jam	25 g (1 oz) pecans, coarsely
30 ml (2 tbsp) sugar	chopped

Chop nuts fairly fine in food processor, then transfer to a bowl. Combine egg yolks, sugar, salt, vanilla, lemon rind and butter in processor. Mix using 10 on/off turns, then process continuously for 5 seconds until nearly blended. Add flour and pecans and process for about 2 seconds. Scrape down and process for about 3 seconds or until dough begins to form sticky crumbs. Wrap dough, press together and shape in a rectangle. Refrigerate for 1 hour.

Preheat oven to 180°C (350°F) mark 4. Cut off one quarter of dough and reserve in refrigerator. Pat out remaining dough in an unbuttered 33 × 23-cm (13 × 9-inch) baking tin.

Stir jam. Using a spatula, spread gently over dough, leaving a 1-cm (½-inch) border. Cut reserved dough into 10 pieces. Return to cleaned food processor and add sugar and flour. Process with a few on/off turns until sugar and flour are blended in but dough is still very crumbly. Crumble dough quickly between your fingers and sprinkle crumbs evenly over jam. Sprinkle with chopped pecans.

Bake for about 33 minutes or until crumbs are firm and light brown. Cool in tin on a wire rack until lukewarm. Cut in 4 × 5-cm (1½ × 2-inch) bars in tin.

MOIST COCONUT MACAROONS

A familiar Passover sweet, coconut macaroons are served as a snack or a treat with coffee or tea. I find fresh, home-baked macaroons clearly superior to those that come in packets. And they are very easy to make.

MAKES ABOUT 30 MACAROONS

2 large egg whites, size 1 or 2	grated rind of ½ lemon
165 g (5½ oz) sugar	115 g (4½ oz) desiccated
10 ml (2 tsp) lemon juice	coconut

Preheat oven to 150°C (300°F) mark 2. Line a baking sheet with foil or greaseproof paper and lightly grease paper.

Beat egg whites until soft peaks form. Gradually beat in sugar. Continue beating for ½ minute or until very stiff. Gradually beat in lemon juice. Add lemon rind and one-third of the coconut and fold in lightly. Sprinkle in remaining coconut in 2 more portions, folding lightly after each.

Using a piping bag fitted with a large tube, or 2 spoons, form mounds of mixture 4 cm (1½ inches) in diameter on lined baking sheet, spacing them about 2.5 cm (1 inch) apart. Bake for 18 minutes or until macaroons are light beige. Leave in oven, with door wedged slightly open, for 20 minutes.

Remove from oven and cool for a few minutes on baking sheet. Carefully remove macaroons from paper and cool on a wire rack. (Macaroons can be kept for several days in airtight container at room temperature.)

NUT AND CHOCOLATE-STUDDED MERINGUES

Both Ashkenazic and Sephardic Jews love to serve meringues for Passover. These light, crunchy meringues can be made with pecans, walnuts, hazelnuts or a mixture of nuts.

MAKES ABOUT 24 MERINGUES

matzo cake meal, for flouring
4 large egg whites, size 1 or 2,
  at room temperature
1.25 ml (¼ tsp) cream of
  tartar (optional)
250 g (9 oz) sugar

75 g (3 oz) pecans, coarsely
  chopped
100 g (4 oz) bitter or plain
  chocolate, cut into tiny
  cubes
75 g (3 oz) pecan halves

Preheat oven to 140°C (275°F) mark 1. Lightly grease corners of 2 baking sheets with margarine and line them with foil. Grease and lightly flour foil with matzo cake meal, tapping baking sheet to remove excess.

Whip egg whites with cream of tartar in a large bowl until stiff. Gradually beat in 100 g (4 oz) sugar at high speed and whip until whites are very shiny.

Gently fold in remaining 150 g (5 oz) sugar in 2 batches, as quickly as possible. Quickly fold in chopped pecans and chocolate pieces. Spoon mixture in irregular mounds onto prepared baking sheets, using generous 15 ml (1 heaped tbsp) for each and spacing them about 4 cm (1½ inches) apart. Set a pecan half on each meringue.

Bake for 30 minutes, then reduce oven temperature to 120°C (250°F) mark ½. Bake for 30 minutes more or until meringues are firm to touch, dry at bases and can be easily removed from foil. They will be light beige.

Transfer meringues to a wire rack and cool. Put them in airtight container as soon as they are cool. (Meringues can be kept in airtight containers at room temperature for up to 1 week in dry weather. If they become sticky from humidity, they can be baked in a very low oven for about 30 minutes to recrisp.)

DRIED FRUIT COMPOTE WITH WINE

Jews from all over Europe prepare this simple but tasty dessert. Some cooks use water and lemon juice as the cooking liquid, others use tea, but I like to use wine, either red or white, because the wine and the fruit exchange flavours beautifully. I find that prunes are the best fruit for preparing this way, but a packet of mixed dried fruit gives the dessert an interesting mix of colours and textures.

This dessert keeps very well. Since it uses no dairy products, it can be served after a meal containing meat. It also makes a good accompaniment for vanilla ice cream or for plain cakes.

MAKES 6 TO 8 SERVINGS

450 g (1 lb) prunes (with stones) or mixed dried fruit (prunes, pears, apricots)	*120–250 ml (4–8 fl oz) water*
	1 cinnamon stick
	100 g (4 oz) sugar
1 bottle dry red or white wine	

Put fruit and wine in a glass bowl. Cover with a plate to help keep fruit submerged. Leave to soak overnight at room temperature.

Gently put fruit and its wine in a saucepan and add enough water to barely cover fruit. Immerse cinnamon stick in liquid and sprinkle mixture with sugar. Very gently stir over low heat to dissolve sugar. Cover and cook over low heat for 30 minutes or until tender. Transfer to bowl and leave to cool, spooning wine over fruit from time to time. Serve cold, as dessert. (Fruit can be kept, covered, for 2 weeks in refrigerator.)

ISRAELI-STYLE BAVARIAN CREAM WITH CHOCOLATE SAUCE AND PECANS

Judging by the number of restaurant menus on which it appears, Bavarian cream is the most popular dessert in Israel. But it is a special version of the dessert – a vanilla Bavarian cream topped with dark chocolate sauce or chocolate syrup and sprinkled with chopped nuts. Unlike the classic European Bavarian, based on a custard sauce enriched with egg yolks, the Israeli version usually includes the whipped egg whites too, and is therefore lighter. It is served straight from the dish instead of being unmoulded.

MAKES 8 OR 9 SERVINGS

---

350 ml (12 fl oz) milk
1 vanilla pod, split
 lengthways; or 10 ml
 (2 tsp) vanilla essence
15 ml (1 tbsp) powdered
 gelatine
60 ml (4 tbsp) water
5 large egg yolks, size 1 or 2,
 at room temperature

105 ml (7 tbsp) sugar
250 ml (8 fl oz) double
 cream, well chilled
3 large egg whites, size 1 or 2
Chocolate Sauce (recipe
 follows)
50 g (2 oz) pecans, diced,
 chopped or whole

Bring milk and vanilla pod (but not essence) to the boil in a heavy medium saucepan. Remove from heat, cover and leave to stand for 15 minutes. Sprinkle gelatine over water in a small cup and leave to stand while preparing custard.

Whisk egg yolks lightly in a large heatproof bowl. Add sugar and whisk until thick and smooth. Reheat milk mixture to the boil, then remove vanilla pod. Gradually whisk hot milk into yolk mixture. Return mixture to saucepan, whisking. Cook over medium-low heat, stirring mixture and scraping bottom of pan constantly with a wooden spoon, until mixture thickens slightly and reaches 73–76°C (165–170°F) on a thermometer; begin checking after 5 minutes. (To check without a thermometer, remove custard from heat, dip a metal spoon in custard, and draw your finger across back of spoon – your finger should leave a clear trail in mixture that clings to spoon.) Do not overcook custard or it will curdle.

Remove custard from heat and immediately add softened gelatine, whisking until it dissolves completely. Pour into a large bowl and stir for about ½ minute to cool. Cool to room temperature, stirring occasionally. Add vanilla essence.

Refrigerate mixture for about 20 minutes, stirring often, or set bowl of mixture in a larger bowl of iced water for about 10 minutes, stirring very often. Chill until mixture is cold and beginning to thicken but is not set.

Prepare eight 150-ml (¼-pint) ramekins or other individual serving dishes or a 23-cm (9-inch) square serving dish.

Whip cream in a chilled bowl until nearly stiff. Set aside. In another bowl, whip egg whites until stiff. Gently fold cream into custard, followed by egg whites. Pour mixture into prepared dishes and smooth top. Cover and refrigerate for at least 3 hours or until set. (Dessert can be kept for up to 2 days in refrigerator.)

Serve dish in ramekins; or cut in 8 or 9 squares and use wide spatula to transfer to plates. Spoon a little cool Chocolate Sauce over each serving and decorate with nuts.

CHOCOLATE SAUCE

Serve this with Israeli-Style Bavarian cream, or with Pear Strudel (page 105) and vanilla ice cream, or use it to make 'Passover Profiteroles' using Passover 'Rolls' (page 50).

MAKES 350 ML (12 FL OZ)

225 g (8 oz) bitter or plain chocolate, chopped	120 ml (4 fl oz) water
50 g (2 oz) unsalted butter or margarine, cut into 8 pieces	5 ml (1 tsp) vanilla essence

Melt chocolate with butter and water in a medium bowl set above hot water over low heat. Stir until smooth. Remove from pan of water and cool for 10 minutes. Gradually stir in vanilla. (Sauce can be kept, covered, for up to 1 week in refrigerator.)

If preparing sauce ahead, even for serving cool, reheat it above hot water. If desired, cool it to room temperature. (If sauce is removed from refrigerator and brought to room temperature without reheating, it is too thick.)

SPICED APPLE BLINTZES

Apple blintzes, originally from eastern Europe, are one of the most prized of Jewish desserts. Although many recipes call for grated or sliced raw apples, I prefer to sauté the fruit first, so it is meltingly tender. These blintzes sprinkled with cinnamon and sugar are a lovely finale to a holiday dinner.

MAKES 6 SERVINGS

APPLE FILLING

900 g (2 lb) Golden Delicious apples	2.5 ml (½ tsp) ground cinnamon
50 g (2 oz) unsalted margarine or butter	75–100 g (3–4 oz) sugar, according to sweetness of apples

Basic Blintzes (page 207) cooked in a 20-cm (8-inch) pan	5 ml (1 tsp) ground cinnamon mixed with 15 ml (1 tbsp) sugar, for sprinkling
40–50 g (1½–2 oz) margarine or butter, for frying or baking	

Peel and halve the apples. Core them and cut into thin slices. Melt margarine in 2 large frying pans or sauté pans. Add apples, sprinkle with cinnamon and sauté over medium-high heat, turning pieces over from time to time, for 2 minutes. Cover and cook over low heat for 10 minutes or until apples are just tender. Raise heat to high and add 45 ml (3 tbsp) sugar to each pan, turning apple wedges over so both sides are coated with sugar. Leave pan over high heat just until sugar dissolves.

Combine apples in one pan and heat briefly. Remove from heat. Taste and add more sugar or cinnamon if necessary; heat, tossing apples gently, just until sugar dissolves. (Filling can be kept for 1 day in refrigerator.)

Spoon 30–37.5 ml (2–2½ tbsp) filling onto brown side of each blintze along one edge. Fold over edges of blintze to right and left of filling so that each covers about half the filling; roll up, beginning at edge with filling. (Blintzes can be filled 1 day ahead and refrigerated, covered.)

Blintzes can be baked or fried. To bake them, preheat oven to 220°C (425°F) mark 7. Arrange blintzes in one layer in a greased shallow baking dish. Dot each blintze with small pieces of margarine. Bake for about 15 minutes, or until heated through and lightly browned.

To fry blintzes, heat margarine in a frying pan, add blintzes open end down and fry over low heat for 3–5 minutes on each side; be careful not to let them burn.

Sprinkle blintzes with cinnamon and sugar. Serve hot.

POLISH STRAWBERRY SOUP

Polish Jews brought their taste for creamy berry soups to Israel, where they are now enjoyed by people of many origins. Some cooks turn this easy-to-make soup into an appetizer by adding less sugar, but I like it best as a refreshing spring or summer dessert.

MAKES 4 SERVINGS

700 g (1½ lb) strawberries	15 ml (1 tbsp) potato flour or
450 ml (¾ pint) water	cornflour, dissolved in
150 g (5 oz) sugar	30 ml (2 tbsp) cold water
	250 ml (8 fl oz) soured cream

FOR DECORATION
about 120 ml (4 fl oz) soured   4 strawberry slices
  cream

Put half the berries in a saucepan with the water and bring to a simmer. Cover and simmer for about 8 minutes or until berries are soft and liquid is red. Meanwhile, purée remaining berries in a food processor or blender until smooth and pour into a bowl. Remove cooked berries from saucepan with a slotted spoon and purée them in a food processor or blender. Add to purée of raw strawberries.

Add sugar and dissolved potato flour to liquid in pan and bring to a simmer, stirring. Remove from heat. Whisk soured cream until smooth in a bowl. Gradually whisk liquid into soured cream. Stir in strawberry purée. Chill thoroughly.

To serve, decorate each serving with a dollop of soured cream topped with a strawberry slice.

SABRA SORBET

A Sabra is a person who was born in Israel, and also is the name of a famous Israeli chocolate-orange liqueur. Here, the liqueur is combined with orange juice as a refreshing sorbet, an ideal light dessert after a *fleishig*, or meat, dinner. If you like, serve it with slices of prickly pears, a fruit known in Israel as *sabras*. Israelis say this fruit is like them – tough and prickly on the outside but sweet on the inside!

MAKES ABOUT 6 SERVINGS

175 g (6 oz) sugar
120 ml (4 fl oz) water
rind of 1 medium orange,
    pared in thin strips with
    vegetable peeler
500 ml (18 fl oz) strained
    fresh orange juice

60 ml (4 tbsp) Sabra
    chocolate-orange liqueur
15 ml (1 tbsp) strained fresh
    lemon juice, or to taste
    (optional)

Combine sugar, water and orange rind strips in small heavy saucepan. Heat over low heat, stirring gently, until sugar dissolves completely. Stop stirring. Bring to full boil over medium-high heat, then boil for 30 seconds. Pour into heatproof bowl and cool completely. Cover and refrigerate for at least 1 hour. (Syrup can be kept for 1 week in refrigerator.)

Remove strips of rind from syrup with slotted spoon. In a large bowl, add syrup to orange juice and mix thoroughly. Stir in liqueur. Taste and add lemon juice if desired. Mixture should taste quite sweet; sweetness of sorbet will be less apparent when it is frozen.

Chill a medium metal bowl and airtight container in freezer. Transfer sorbet mixture to ice cream machine and process until mixture has consistency of soft ice cream; it should not be runny but will not become very firm. Transfer sorbet as quickly as possible to chilled bowl; it melts very quickly. Cover tightly and freeze until ready to serve. If keeping sorbet longer than 3 hours, transfer when firm to airtight container and cover tightly. (Sorbet is best served within 3 hours but can be kept up to 4 days.)

Soften slightly before serving. Serve in thoroughly chilled dessert dishes or wine glasses.

APPLE CINNAMON
ICE CREAM

Although I rarely use non-dairy cream or milk substitutes, when it comes to ice cream I find it sometimes worthwhile to make an exception! This pareve ice cream gains a lovely flavour from cinnamon and apple juice. It is lighter than most ice creams because of its high proportion of fruit juice. Serve it on its own or with Apple Compote (page 129) or Strawberry Sauce (page 73).

MAKES ABOUT 8 SERVINGS

450 ml (¾ pint) apple juice	*5 ml (1 tsp) ground cinnamon*
6 large egg yolks, size 1 or 2	*250 ml (8 fl oz) non-dairy*
75 g (3 oz) sugar	*creamer or single cream*

Bring apple juice to the boil in a small heavy saucepan. Remove from heat.

Whisk egg yolks lightly in a medium bowl. Add sugar and cinnamon and whisk until smooth. Gradually whisk in hot apple juice. Return mixture to saucepan. Cook over medium-low heat, stirring and scraping bottom of pan constantly with a wooden spoon, until mixture thickens slightly and reaches 73–76°C (165–170°F) on a thermometer; begin checking after 4 minutes. (To check without thermometer, remove pan from heat, dip a metal spoon in sauce and draw your finger across back of spoon – your finger should leave a clear path in mixture that clings to spoon.) If necessary, cook for another ½ minute and check again. Do not overcook mixture or it will curdle. Pour immediately into a bowl and stir for about ½ minute to cool.

Stir non-dairy creamer into mixture. Cool completely, stirring occasionally. Pour into ice cream machine and process until frozen. Meanwhile, chill bowl in freezer. Transfer ice cream quickly to chilled bowl, cover tightly and keep in freezer until ready to serve. (Can be kept for 1 week in freezer.) Soften slightly before serving.

CREAMY NOODLE KUGEL WITH ALMONDS

Cooking fine noodles in milk gives this kugel a wonderfully rich taste. It is a good dessert for winter or for Shavuot. Since this is a holiday for honouring the first fruits of the season, a fitting accompaniment for the dessert is slices of fresh summer fruit, such as peaches, nectarines or apricots.

MAKES 6 SERVINGS

600 ml (1 pint) milk
100 g (4 oz) very fine noodles
pinch of salt
grated rind of 1 lemon
75 g (3 oz) sugar
25 g (1 oz) butter or
  margarine

25 g (1 oz) almonds, coarsely
  chopped
2 large eggs, size 1 or 2,
  separated

Bring milk to the boil in a heavy, medium saucepan. Add noodles and salt and cook over low heat, stirring occasionally, for 20–30 minutes or until noodles are tender and absorb most of milk. Do not drain.

Meanwhile, preheat oven to 180°C (350°F) mark 4. Butter a 1-litre (1¾–2-pint) baking dish and sprinkle a little sugar in sides of dish. Set this dish inside a larger baking dish.

Stir lemon rind and 45 ml (3 tbsp) sugar into hot noodle mixture. Cool for several minutes. Stir in butter, almonds and egg yolks.

Beat egg whites until soft peaks form. Beat in remaining 45 ml (3 tbsp) sugar at high speed and whip until whites are stiff. Fold whites, in 2 portions, into noodle mixture. Transfer to baking dish. Add hot water to larger baking dish to come halfway up sides of dish containing noodle mixture. Bake for 40–45 minutes or until a small knife inserted into noodle mixture comes out dry. (Kugel can be kept, covered, for 2 days in refrigerator. Reheat in a medium oven.) Serve hot.

EASY CHOCOLATE-SPONGE FINGER PUDDING

Chocolate is a favourite flavour in Israel and among Jews in general. In my research for my book on chocolate desserts, *Chocolate Sensations*, I learned that chocolate was brought from the New World to Spain but I was not aware of the major role played by the Jews in introducing chocolate to the rest of Europe. Parisian chef Alain Dutournier told me recently that in his home region in southwestern France, near the border with Spain, many of the master chocolatiers were of Jewish origin. Bayonne, a major city in the region, was the first city in France where chocolate was made, and remains a chocolate centre to this day. And chocolate making in Bayonne was started by Jews who had settled in southwest France after being chased out of Spain during the Inquisition. The new product rapidly gained favour in the area and spread throughout France.

This is a delicious, very simple chocolate dessert, with a base of cognac-dipped sponge fingers, a centre of super-rich chocolate pudding and a generous topping of whipped cream. (If you are concerned about the safety of using raw eggs in a recipe, you may wish to choose another dessert.)

MAKES 6 TO 8 SERVINGS

60 ml (4 tbsp) cognac or brandy	225 g (8 oz) plain chocolate, chopped
60 ml (4 tbsp) water	175 g (6 oz) unsalted butter
175 g (6 oz) sponge fingers	2 large egg yolks, size 1 or 2

TOPPING AND DECORATION

250 ml (8 fl oz) double cream	5 ml (1 tsp) cognac or brandy
10 ml (2 tsp) sugar	15 g (½ oz) plain chocolate

Mix cognac and water in a shallow bowl. Quickly dip each sponge finger in mixture and set it in a 23–25-cm (9–10-inch) spring clip tin; do not leave them in mixture too long or they will become soggy.

Melt chocolate and butter in a large bowl set above hot water over low heat. Stir until smooth, then remove from pan of water and leave to cool for 2 minutes. Beat yolks in a small bowl. Gradually beat 45 ml (3 tbsp) chocolate mixture into yolks. Return this mixture to pan of chocolate and mix quickly and thoroughly. Pour mixture over sponge fingers and refrigerate for about 1 hour or freeze for 30 minutes or until firm.

Whip cream in a chilled bowl until it begins to thicken. Add sugar and brandy and continue whipping until stiff. Spread whipped cream over chocolate mixture. Grate a little chocolate on top for decoration. Refrigerate for at least 2 hours before serving. (Dessert can be made 1 day ahead and kept in refrigerator.)

To unmould, slide a thin-bladed knife carefully around dessert. Release spring and remove sides of tin.

VARIATION
Chocolate-Sponge Finger No-Bake Pie

Instead of preparing this dessert in a spring clip tin, make and serve it in a 23–25-cm (9–10-inch) pie dish.

SUMMER FRUIT SALAD WITH RASPBERRY SAUCE

Fruit salad is the natural choice to end a meal in many kosher homes and is especially popular today because it is a healthy dessert.

Strawberry Sauce (page 73) can be substituted for the Raspberry Sauce, if you like. For a simpler dessert, instead of using a berry sauce you can sprinkle the cut fruit with an additional 15–30 ml (1–2 tbsp) sugar, 10 ml (2 tsp) lemon juice and 30 ml (2 tbsp) of your favourite fruit liqueur. Or for a fancier finale, you can top this with ice cream, sorbet or whipped cream.

MAKES 4 TO 6 SERVINGS

3 peaches or nectarines	1 kiwi fruit (optional)
3 apricots (optional)	30 ml (2 tbsp) sugar
275 g (10 oz) strawberries, lightly rinsed and hulled	Raspberry Sauce (recipe follows)
275 g (10 oz) blackberries or raspberries	

Slice peaches or nectarines in wedges. Slice apricots. Put slices in a bowl. Quarter strawberries lengthways and add to bowl. Add black-berries. Peel kiwi, halve lengthways and cut into half slices.

Sprinkle fruit with sugar. Using a spatula, mix ingredients as gently as possible. If desired, cover and chill for about 30 minutes.

To serve, add about half the Raspberry Sauce to fruit salad and mix gently. Divide salad among 4 to 6 dessert dishes or stemmed glasses. Serve remaining sauce separately.

RASPBERRY SAUCE

This sauce is wonderful with cheesecake, blintzes, vanilla ice cream or fruit salad.

MAKES ABOUT 250 ML (8 FL OZ)

350 g (12 oz) fresh raspberries; or 1 × 275–350-g (10–12-oz) packet frozen unsweetened or lightly sweetened raspberries, thawed	*75 g (3 oz) icing sugar, sifted 5–10 ml (1–2 tsp) fresh lemon juice (optional)*

Purée berries in food processor or blender. Add icing sugar and pro-cess until very smooth. Taste and add another 15 ml (1 tbsp) sugar if desired. Strain into a bowl, pressing on pulp in strainer; use spatula to scrape mixture from underside of strainer.

Cover and refrigerate for 30 minutes. (Sauce can be kept, covered, for 1 day in refrigerator.) Stir before serving and add lemon juice to taste. Serve cold.

MENUS FOR CELEBRATIONS

Jewish cooking is much more than holiday food. Here are some kosher menus for festive occasions, and menus that turn everyday meals into celebrations.

Please note that in each menu the number of people each dish will serve varies according to the number of dishes you wish to prepare. In many menus there is a choice of preparing one or a selection of first courses, desserts and sometimes even main courses. You can multiply the ingredient quantities in the recipes according to the number of dishes as well as the number of people you are serving.

A SPRINGTIME POLISH LUNCHEON MENU

Feasting on salmon, asparagus and strawberries is a lovely way to welcome spring, and they are featured in this menu. You can serve it for a light lunch, with the salmon as a main course, or add a roast chicken and serve it with the kugel to make a more substantial menu. To make the cooking easy, the salmon, salad and dessert are prepared ahead.

Beetroot Salad with Apples (page 100)

Sweet and Sour Salmon (page 218)

Potato Kugel with Asparagus and Broccoli (page 256)

**Strawberry Pecan Squares (page 320),
served with fresh strawberries**

A SUMMER VEGETARIAN MENU

Kosher pareve and dairy meals fit in with the rules of many vegetarians. Therefore, many Jews who keep kosher, whether they are vegetarians or not, often eat vegetarian menus. In Israel this style of dining is especially popular in the summer, when there are so many wonderful Mediterranean vegetables and fruits. Sephardic dishes, such as the aubergine dishes and the okra in this menu, lend themselves especially well to vegetarian meals.

Spicy Potato Salad (page 63)

Avocado and Egg Salad (page 167)

Easy Curried Aubergine (page 261)

Pita (page 296)

Okra with Tomatoes and Coriander (page 267)

Easy Rice Pilaf (page 157)

Raspberry Almond Tart (page 308)

**Sabra Sorbet (page 328);
or fresh fruit**

A MENU FOR A KIDDUSH

Kiddush is literally a blessing over wine, but also refers to the food that is sometimes served at the synagogue for this occasion. On Sabbath, after services, if someone is having a bar mitzvah, bat mitzvah, wedding or other cause for celebration, the individual's parents or the individual might give a kiddush and invite the congregation to the party. It consists mainly of appetizers and desserts. In Jerusalem, it nearly always features Jerusalem Noodle Kugel. When I was growing up in Washington, D.C., the kiddush always featured bagels, lox and cream cheese.

Creamy Aubergine Salad (page 184)

Hummus (Chick Pea Dip) (page 175)

Tahini Sauce (Sesame Dip) (page 177)

Bright Red Cabbage Salad (page 133)

Challah (page 289), rolls and crackers

Gefilte Fish (page 24)

Pickles, olives and marinated herring

Jerusalem Noodle Kugel (page 150)

Chocolate-Orange Marble Cake (306)

Ashkenazic Poppy Seed Biscuits (page 319)

Chocolate Coconut Rum Balls (page 318)

AN EASY POT LUCK APPETIZER PARTY

This casual menu is popular for parties in Israel. Most of the appetizers will be salads and spreads, some of which can be brought by friends or purchased. One or more homemade pastries is usually served, and is generally the item that disappears the fastest. A platter of cold meats is often available for heartier appetites.

Creamy Potato Salad with Gherkins (page 179)

Bulgarian Aubergine Salad with Grilled Peppers (page 183)

Bright Red Cabbage Salad (page 133)

Bulgar Wheat and Parsley Salad with Mint and Tomatoes (Tabbouleh) (page 189)

Mushroom Turnovers (page 170)

Sliced smoked turkey, turkey pastrami, salami and other cold meats

Cocktail rye bread, pumpernickel and Pita (page 296)

Chocolate-Orange Marble Cake (page 306)

Apple Cake with Pecans and Cinnamon (page 123)

A DESSERT PARTY

Having friends over for cake and coffee is a friendly and easy way to entertain instead of preparing a full dinner. This is also a convenient and welcome way to serve at a meeting of a club or organisation. Dessert parties are best for late in the evening or in the afternoon. It's a good idea to offer some appetizer-type food as well, such as an aubergine salad with pita or perhaps some bagels with lox and cream cheese, in case someone is hungry for some 'real food' before the sweets.

Roasted Aubergine Salad with Olive Oil and Garlic (page 33)

Pita (page 296)

Creamy Cheesecake (page 74)

Pear Strudel (page 105)

Chocolate-Almond Cake with Chocolate-Honey Frosting (page 94)

Cinnamon-Nut-Raisin Crescents (Rugelach) (page 312)

A FALAFEL PARTY

Falafel and salads are fun to serve any time of the year, but especially in autumn or winter. It's best to have a friend who will share in the work of frying the falafel. You can either serve the falafel in pita bread, or put it on serving dishes together with several spreads such as hummus, tahini sauce and aubergine salad.

Marinated Aubergine Slices (page 174)

Chilli-Garlic Chutney (Zehug) (page 154)

Israeli Vegetable Salad (page 34)

Tahini Sauce (Sesame Dip) (page 177)

Aubergine Salad with Tahini (page 182)

Falafel (Chick Pea Croquettes) (page 165)

Pita (page 296)

Pickles and olives

**Israeli-Style Bavarian Cream with Chocolate Sauce
and Pecans (page 324)**

A BAR MITZVAH BRUNCH

A bar mitvah or bat mitzvah is a special occasion and calls for a big party, to which relative and friends are invited. If this will be a brunch party, dairy foods are the favourites, especially blintzes, luscious pastries and noodle kugels. For the following menu, the filo pastries are Sephardic, and the piroshki, blintzes and kugel are Ashkenazic specialities. The cake should be the favourite of the bar mitzvah boy or the bat mitzvah girl.

Creamy Aubergine Salad (page 184)

Potato and Lox Salad (page 180)

Grilled Pepper and Tomato Salad (page 186)

Challah (page 289), rolls and Pita (page 296)

Cheese Filo Turnovers (Cheese Bourekas) (page 70)

**Sephardic Spinach-Stuffed Filo Turnovers
(Spinach Bourekas) (page 162)**

Browned Eggs (Huevos Haminados) (page 216)

**Chive Blintzes with Cabbage and Soured Cream
(page 209),
or
Piroshki with Salmon and Cabbage (page 168)**

**Classic Cheese Blintzes with Strawberry Sauce
(page 72)**

Cinnamon-Scented Apple Noodle Kugel (page 151)

Chocolate-Nut Chiffon Cake (page 152)

A WEDDING PARTY, BUFFET STYLE

For weddings, the food should be lavish, be elegant, and make use of the best ingredients. It is a good idea to stick to familiar dishes – this is not the time to experiment with unusual combinations! Of course, the selection of dishes should be colourful and varied. In this menu, which features both Ashkenazic and Sephardic recipes, the food can be presented buffet style, which makes serving easy. There is a choice of three main courses, but the selection of dishes will still be ample if you choose to prepare only two of them. In the case of the roast chicken, the stuffing should be baked separately to facilitate serving.

Potato Salad with Smoked Turkey (page 181)

Grilled Pepper and Tomato Salad (page 186)

Chopped Liver and Aubergine Pâté (page 118)

Large Plaited Challah (page 291), rolls and Pita (page 296)

Selection of olives, pickled vegetables and cooked chick peas

Baked Lamb with Orzo (page 252)

Crisp Turkey Schnitzel (page 242)

Roast Chicken with Pecan and Herb Stuffing (page 148)

Courgettes with Tomatoes and Dill (page 263)

Savoury Mushrooms with Thyme and Olive Oil (page 47)

Easy Rice Pilaf (page 157)

Chocolate-Almond Cake with Chocolate-Honey Frosting (page 94)

Summer Fruit Salad with Raspberry Sauce (page 332)

COOKING
TECHNIQUES

Preparing Artichoke Hearts

Squeeze juice of ½ lemon into a medium bowl of cold water. Break off stalk of an artichoke and largest leaves at bottom. Put artichoke on its side on board. Holding a very sharp knife or small serrated knife against side of artichoke (parallel to leaves), cut lower circle of leaves off, up to edge of artichoke heart; turn artichoke slightly after each cut. Rub cut edges of artichoke heart with cut lemon. Cut off central cone of leaves just above artichoke heart. Cut off leaves under base. Trim base, removing all dark green areas. Rub again with lemon. Put artichoke in bowl of lemon water. Repeat with remaining artichokes. Keep artichokes in lemon water until ready to cook them.

To cook artichoke hearts, squeeze any juice remaining in lemon into a medium saucepan of boiling salted water. Add artichoke hearts, cover and simmer over low heat until tender when pierced with knife, 15–20 minutes. Cool to lukewarm in liquid. Using a teaspoon, scoop out hairlike 'choke' from centre of each fresh artichoke heart.

Preparing Rendered Chicken Fat (Schmaltz)

Chicken fat is firm and must be 'rendered' or cooked, so it can be used in recipes. Rendered chicken fat can be purchased in jars but it's more economical to prepare your own, and then it has no preservatives. Save the fat from chickens (found near the tail) and fatty portions of skin in the freezer until you have fat from at least four chickens. The fat is rendered with a chopped onion, which gives it a delicate onion flavour. The chicken skin cooks to crisp bits that make tasty snacks and are sometimes added to chopped liver, noodles or kasha.

Rinse the skin and fat, cut them in pieces and sprinkle with salt. Heat a heavy frying pan over low heat, add the skin and fat, and cook until the fat melts. Add one or two chopped onions and sauté until golden. Continue to sauté until skin and onions are crunchy. Strain fat, reserving onions and skins if desired. Pour the fat into jars and keep in the refrigerator.

MAKING CHICKEN SOUP OR STOCK

Follow the recipe for Ashkenazic Chicken Soup with Fresh Dill and Light Matzo Balls (page 99) or use your own recipe for any delicately flavoured chicken soup or stock. When you don't have homemade soup, use packaged soup or stock, preferably unsalted or lightly salted.

BASIC TOMATO SAUCE

This sauce is a favourite accompaniment for stuffed vegetables, sautéed vegetables, fish, pasta and white rice.

MAKES ABOUT 450 ML (¾ PINT)

30 ml (2 tbsp) olive or
  vegetable oil
½ medium onion, chopped
2 large garlic cloves, finely
  chopped
900 g (2 lb) ripe tomatoes,
  peeled, seeded and chopped;
  or 2 × 794-g (28-oz) cans
  plum tomatoes, drained and
  chopped

15 ml (1 tbsp) tomato purée
1 bay leaf
2.5 ml (½ tsp) dried thyme,
  oregano or basil (optional)
salt and freshly ground pepper

Heat oil in a large saucepan or deep frying pan over medium heat. Add onion and sauté, stirring occasionally, for about 5 minutes or until beginning to brown. Add garlic, tomatoes, tomato purée, bay leaf, thyme, salt and pepper. Cook over medium heat, stirring often, for about 15–20 minutes or until tomatoes are soft and mixture is thick and smooth. Discard bay leaf. Taste and adjust seasoning. (Sauce can be kept, covered, for 2 days in refrigerator or it can be frozen.) For a smoother sauce, purée in food processor or blender.

A BRIEF GUIDE
TO KEEPING
KOSHER

All the recipes in this book are kosher. But keeping kosher is a way of life that involves many rules regarding choice of foods, menu planning, and use of dishes and kitchen utensils.

Kosher foods are those that are permitted by the Jewish religion. Kashrut, the body of laws of keeping kosher, is extensive and involved. Following is a brief introduction, but anyone who would like to begin to keep a kosher kitchen can find many books dedicated to the subject.

The essentials of keeping kosher can be divided into three aspects; which foods can be eaten, how foods can be combined in a menu, and how certain foods should be 'koshered', or prepared to make them kosher.

In the Torah, or Jewish bible, kosher animals are defined as those that chew their cud and have split hooves. Therefore, beef, veal and lamb are kosher, and pork is not. Poultry is also kosher.

Fish must have scales and fins. This includes most fish, but of course excludes all shellfish.

The Torah prohibits cooking a kid in its mother's milk. From this have been derived the regulations against combining dairy products and meat or poultry in the same meal. In fact, dairy foods and meat foods are kept completely separate and require two sets of dishes. Different pots, pans, plates and silverware are used for cooking, serving and eating meals that include meat, called *fleishig* meals in Yiddish or *bsari* in Hebrew, and those that contain dairy products, which are called *milchig* in Yiddish or *halavi* in Hebrew.

Besides the two categories of dairy and meat foods, there is a third, known as pareve. Pareve, or neutral, foods go with everything. They can be eaten in a meal with either dairy or meat products. Included are fish, eggs, vegetables, fruits, breads and grains, as well as vegetable oils and some margarines. Margarine sometimes contains dairy products, but if it is labelled pareve, it is suitable for all three types of meals.

For meat and poultry to be kosher, there are other special conditions that must be met. First, animals must be slaughtered in a certain manner; therefore, game birds that have been shot are not kosher. Kosher meats can be purchased from a kosher butcher, or packaged at some supermarkets.

In addition, meat and poultry must be koshered to rid it of as much blood as possible, since blood is not kosher. This can be done at home or by the butcher. The process involves salting the meat, and because the meat absorbs a certain amount of salt, not much salt is needed when cooking it.

To kosher meat or poultry, rinse it well, then soak it in water for 30 minutes. Rinse the meat again, then put it on a board set at an incline so the juices can drip into the sink. Next sprinkle the meat with coarse salt, also known as kosher salt, and leave it to stand for 1 hour. Then thoroughly rinse the meat again.

Livers are koshered in a different way. They are rinsed and grilled, which also cooks them completely. To do this, rinse the livers just before grilling them, then sprinkle them with salt and grill, turning them a few times, so all sides become grilled. For grilling, put the livers on foil so they do not come in contact with the grill pan.

Keeping dairy and meat separate also leads to avoiding certain products, such as cheeses that are made with an animal product called rennet, or yogurt made with animal-based gelatine. Kosher gelatine is vegetable based.

Kosher products are labelled with symbols to make them easy to recognize. The best-known one is Ⓤ, the seal of approval of the Union of Orthodox Jewish Congregations. Some products are labelled with K for Kosher. There are other kosher symbols for products in certain cities; a local rabbi can be consulted for a list of these.

INDEX

349